Knowledge, Desire and Power in Global Politics

IN MEMORY OF
MY MOTHER AND FATHER:
SUN DERONG (1928–2006)
PAN ZHIJIA (1921–2004)

Knowledge, Desire and Power in Global Politics

Western Representations of China's Rise

Chengxin Pan

Senior Lecturer in International Relations,
Deakin University, Australia

Edward Elgar
PUBLISHING

Cheltenham, UK • Northampton, MA, USA

Published by
Edward Elgar Publishing Limited
The Lypiatts
15 Lansdown Road
Cheltenham
Glos GL50 2JA
UK

Edward Elgar Publishing, Inc.
William Pratt House
9 Dewey Court
Northampton
Massachusetts 01060
USA

Paperback edition 2015

A catalogue record for this book
is available from the British Library

Library of Congress Control Number: 2012946658

This book is available electronically in the **Elgar**online
Social and Political Science subject collection
DOI 10.4337/9781782544241

ISBN 978 1 84542 915 7 (cased)
     978 1 78536 087 9 (paperback)

Typeset by Servis Filmsetting Ltd, Stockport, Cheshire
Printed and bound in Great Britain by the CPI Group (UK) Ltd

Contents

Preface

Among the most reported stories in the first decade of the twenty-first century, topping the list was not the global financial crisis, the long-running Iraq War, or even the 'September 11' terrorist attacks—it was the rise of China.[1] These findings, announced by Global Language Monitor in 2011, were based on a study of global media reporting trends among 75000 print and electronic media sources. Were there a similar survey on the issues concerning the international scholarly community, China's rise would almost certainly rank among the most closely scrutinised as well. Long gone, it seems, are the days when an American publishing company did not publish a single book on China for fifteen years.[2] With such extensive coverage on China's ascendancy today, there seems hardly a need for yet another study on this subject. Existing commentaries, books, and articles must have already covered a sufficiently wide range of perspectives.

Despite or precisely because of the vast amount of literature on this issue, I feel compelled to join the chorus. However, in doing so this book does not, as do many other books, seek to examine whether China is rising or not, or what its rise means. This is not because I believe such questions are unimportant or have already been settled; I do not. Rather, I believe what China's rise means cannot be independently assessed in isolation from what we already *mean* by China's rise. Though tautological it might sound, the latter question draws attention to the meaning-giving subject of China watchers. It turns the spotlight on our thoughts and representations of China's rise, which constitutes the main focus of this book.

Though it may appear that way in the eyes of some, going along this path is not a cunning attempt of finding a literary niche in an increasingly crowded field to score some cheap points all the while dodging the heavy lifting of tackling complex 'real-world' issues surrounding China. Nor is it to deliberately court controversy or strike an affected pose of malaise about an otherwise vibrant field of study. To me, this book is a necessary move justified on both theoretical and practical grounds. Theoretically, the book rejects the prevalent assumption about the dichotomy between reality and representation. *Contra* positivism, we cannot bypass thoughts and representations to come into direct contact with China as it is. What we see as 'China' cannot be detached from various discourses and representations of it. Works that purport to study China's rise, as if it were a transparent and empirically observable phenomenon out there, are always already inextricably enmeshed in representations. In all likelihood, those works will then become themselves part of such representations, through which still later studies will gaze at 'China'. In this sense, my focus on representation is less an expedient choice than ontological and epistemological necessity.

On practical grounds, given the inescapable immanence of representation and discourse in the social realm, a proper study of discursive representation is not a retreat from the real world but a genuine engagement with it in the full sense of the words. Perhaps with the exception of sleepwalking or unconscious twitching, no human action (let alone social action) can do without thought and representation. Constructivists are right in saying that words have consequences. But we may add that all social domains and human relationships are mediated through and constituted by thought and representation. China's relationship with the West is certainly no exception. With regional stability, prosperity and even world peace at stake, there is now an urgent, practical need to understand how the various strains of representation and discourse pervade and condition this critical and complex relationship.

For these reasons, this book turns to Western representations of China's rise. In particular, it focuses on two influential paradigms: the 'China threat' and the 'China opportunity'. Commonly held by their respective exponents as objective truth about the implications of China's rise, both paradigms, despite their seemingly contrasting views, are reflections of a certain Western self-imagination and its quest for certainty and identity in an inherently dynamic, volatile and uncertain world. While understandable, such a desire often proves elusive in the social world. With no lasting law-like certainty in sight, the desire for certainty then often comes full circle to two subsets of desire: namely, fears and fantasies. For these forms of desire can provide some emotional substitutes for the holy grail of certainty and truth. In this book, I will argue that the two China paradigms are, respectively, discursive embodiments of these two popular types of emotional substitutes. As such, they are not objective China knowledge, but are closely linked to habitual Western self-imagination and power practice. By probing into the interrelationship between knowledge, desire and power, the book aims to deconstruct contemporary Western representations of China's rise. Although it will tentatively point to some methodological openings for what one might call 'critical China watching', due to its scope and ontological stance as well as limits of space, it promises no ready-made alternative toolkit through which to better understand China as it is. Alas, the 'China as it is' simply does not exist except in our ingrained desire and conventional imagination.

Conceiving and writing this book has been a long, challenging, but ultimately stimulating and rewarding journey. Along the way, it has been made possible and enjoyable by a large number of people, to whom I have accumulated enormous intellectual and personal debts. Regrettably it would not be possible to mention all the names here, hence my apologies to anyone I may have inadvertently omitted.

Although the book does not bear resemblance to my PhD thesis completed at the Australian National University (ANU), some of its initial seeds of ideas were sown during my time in Canberra. I therefore would like to thank Jim George, a model scholar, inspiring teacher and generous friend, for his tireless guidance, numerous thought-provoking conversations and incisive critique. This book owes a profound and lasting intellectual debt to him and his uncompromising stance on quality in scholarship.

My thanks are also due to Simon Dalby, Tessa Morris-Suzuki, Stephen Rosow, Ian Wilson, and Yin Qian, whose insightful and constructive feedback and comments were indispensable to an earlier phase of this project. I have the good fortune to have known Roland Bleiker, Shaun Breslin and Linda Chelan Li, and to have worked closely with Baogang He, Geoffrey Stokes and David Walker. They all are exemplary scholars, outstanding mentors and generous colleagues, and are often my first ports of call for advice and guidance. To them I extend my deep gratitude. Similarly, I was very fortunate to have had many a great teacher and scholar at my alma mater, Peking University, notably Yuan Ming, Jia Qingguo, Wang Jisi, the late Liu Suchao, Xu Zhenzhou and Zhu Feng, among many others. Their examples and encouragement led me eventually to a pursuit in academia. Also at Beida, I learned a great deal from colleagues and friends such as Zhao Xuewen, Zhao Weimin, Yang Kangshan, Zhang Liming and Sun Zhanlong.

For their insight, advice, conversation, encouragement and generosity at various junctures of my academic journey, I also thank Nick Bisley, Jean-Marc Blanchard, Morgan Brigg, Anthony Burke, Priya Chacko, Gerald Chan, Stephen Chan, Gordon Cheung, Matthew Clarke, David Fouquet, Baogang Guo, John Hart, Kanishka Jayasuriya, Damien Kingsbury, David Lowe, Michael McKinley, Fethi Mansouri, Michael Shapiro, Gary Smith, Roland Vogt, Rob Walker, Yao Souchou, You Ji, Yu Bin, Yongjin Zhang, and David Zweig. Together with my numerous colleagues at Deakin University across several campuses, they have contributed to my thinking in a number of valuable ways and well beyond this book, but needless to say I alone bear responsibility for the book's shortcomings.

Malak Ansour, Heidi and Michael Hutchison, Kim Huynh, David Kennedy, Kong Tao, Katrina Lee-Koo, Weijian Lu, Anne McNevin, Jeremy Moses, Xiaolong Ni, Ben Wellings and Guangyu Zhang were among an amazing group of fellow travellers at the ANU. They remind me of my 'old' classmates and friends at Beida as well: Fan Shiming, He Zhaotian, Shao Yanjun, Wang Lian, Yu Tiejun, Zhou Youguang, among many others. While many of them have moved on to new and exciting places, their generosity, sense of humour, and friendship remain unsurpassed to this day.

For several research grants that greatly assisted the completion of the book, I thank the Faculty of Arts and Education, School of Humanities and Social Sciences (formerly School of International and Political Studies), Centre for Citizenship and Globalisation and Alfred Deakin Research Institute at my

University. On different occasions, the University of Melbourne and the Hong Kong University of Science and Technology (HKUST) hosted me as a visiting fellow, and my research benefited from the hospitality and resources of both fine institutions. In particular, I would like to thank Derek McDougall (Melbourne) and Barry Sautman (HKUST) for their support as well as many fruitful conversations. Liu Mingsheng, Li Shuo and Jiang Bin made my one-year stay in Melbourne immensely enjoyable and for that I am grateful.

My publisher Edward Elgar has shown unwavering confidence in me since he first saw my book proposal in Melbourne. My editors Alexandra O'Connell, Jennifer Wilcox and Chloe Mitchell have been incredibly patient and helpful at every stage of preparation and production of the book. Andrew M. Watts's help was instrumental to the Index. An anonymous reviewer of the proposal, two anonymous referees of the manuscript and a copyeditor made a number of helpful suggestions. My thanks go to them all.

Xuemei deserves my special thanks for her love, understanding, and sacrifice. As do my two beautiful daughters, Amy and Lily. The love and joy they bring to me each day has been an endless source of pride and inspiration. As I watch them grow, I learn along with them and become, as a result, a fuller person. Also, I would like to thank my sister and brothers in China; they know how much they mean to me.

Above all, I dedicate the book to the memory of my parents. At this moment of reflection, my overwhelming feeling is a profound and ever-aching sense of loss and regret: although I had known all along that nothing I could do would ever adequately repay their nurture and love, at least the book, I had hoped, could be such a gesture; but even this small gesture has arrived far too late. In the end, they had not quite understood what their youngest child was doing over so many years, and so far away from home. Yet, through two remarkable lives, they had taught me by example the most valuable knowledge of all: how to become a human. This knowledge I could never dream of fully grasping, but it is a privilege to know that it is always there for me to return to for guidance, inspiration, comfort and precious memory.

1. Introduction: knowledge, desire and power in Western representations of China's rise

> ... there is no knowledge—political or otherwise—outside representation.
>
> Homi Bhabha[1]

> ... the real issue is whether indeed there can be a true representation of anything, or whether any and all representations, because they are representations, are embedded first in the language and then in the culture, institutions, and political ambience of the representer.
>
> Edward W. Said[2]

> ... the facts of history never come to us "pure", since they do not and cannot exist in a pure form: they are always refracted through the mind of the recorder. It follows that when we take up a work of history, our first concern should be not with the facts which it contains but with the historian who wrote it.
>
> E. H. Carr[3]

THE RISE OF THE 'CHINA'S RISE' LITERATURE

For centuries, China has been a fixture in the Western imagination, variously described as the 'land of milk and honey', a 'sleeping giant', the 'sick man of Asia', the 'Yellow Peril' and the 'Red Menace'. Now fast emerging as a global powerhouse, this once 'sleeping giant' has once again come to preoccupy the Western consciousness. With its profound yet uncertain impact on regional and global power balance, a new growth field of watching China's international relations (IR) has gathered pace, characterised in particular by an explosion of literature on China's rise.[4] Indeed, not a day goes by without one being reminded of the 'awakening', 'rise', 'rising', 'ascent', or 'domi-

1

nance' of China. This expanding literature has been fittingly called the 'China's rise literature'.[5]

That much has been said and written on China's rise is no surprise. Yet, what is puzzling is that little seems to have been explicitly said and written about this particular genre of China literature, which itself is nothing short of a phenomenon. Whilst many in the China watching community are taken up with the 'empirical' issues of what China is and what its rise means, few seem to have seriously contemplated what this growth field is all about. This book, in turning a critical gaze on this discursive phenomenon, aims to address this neglected but critical issue along with some attendant questions. What, for instance, is the study of China's international relations? Where does it come from? What is it exactly that we are doing when we purport to merely observe China's rise? Why does China watching in IR rarely deviate from certain enduring modes of representation, such as 'threat' and 'opportunity'? And what roles do those modes of representation play in both our understanding of, and our interaction with, China?

CHINA WATCHING RARELY WATCHES ITSELF

These questions may strike many scholars as trivial and superfluous, if not odd. To others they may immediately smack of empty epistemological speculations—surely China watching is about uncovering and accumulating knowledge on China, with its core business centred on understanding key empirical issues that really matter in China's relations with the world, issues ranging from power, capabilities, interests, intentions and identity to foreign policy, grand strategy and behaviour patterns. Thus, where periodically there have been welcome attempts to reflect on the 'state of the art' in China watching,[6] the main objectives of those reflections have been to help 'build cumulative knowledge' and to explore some 'potential avenue for new research'.[7] Predictably, such stocktaking has been largely positive and self-congratulatory in tone. At the 'Trends in China Watching' conference held at George Washington University in 1999, participants seemed genuinely impressed by 'the diversity of approaches and perspectives' in the field, which they regarded as 'the most valuable asset China watchers have today'.[8] Two prominent experts on Chinese foreign policy, Robert Ross and Alastair Iain Johnston, would concur. In their edited book on new directions in this China field, they claim that China scholars are now in a better position to meet the growing demand for sophisticated analysis on China's foreign policy.[9] For still others, 'the field is doing a good job of keeping up with and interpreting fast-changing developments in China, and... the international "state of the field" can be judged to be healthy and growing'.[10]

Growing this field may be, but healthy it seems not. According to Roland Barthes, a 'healthy' sign should be honest about its own arbitrariness. Rather than pretending to be 'natural' or 'objective', it admits 'its own relative, artificial status'.[11] Judging by this requirement, the IR branch of China watching appears far from healthy. As just noted, amidst an ongoing celebration of its scientific contribution to China knowledge, this field has thus far shown little critical self-reflection required of a healthy sign. True, some China watchers are aware of the limits of their own work and even the problematic status of China watching as objective knowledge. G. John Ikenberry and Michael Mastanduno lament that 'the rich comparative and foreign policy scholarship on China' is 'under-theorized', and they call for its better engagement with the 'theoretical insights of international relations'.[12] David Shambaugh notes that while 'rich in monographic literature on different periods and bilateral interactions', the field 'lacks studies with aggregate and reflective perspectives'.[13] In a semi-autobiographical reflection on China watching, Richard Baum admits that objectivity in China studies is 'an elusive grail' and that our understanding is often coloured by 'personal sentiments and emotions'.[14] Such reflections, however, often limited in scope and made in passing, remain a rare commodity.

Such a problem is not unique to IR China watchers. Anthropologists are said to be skilled at 'probing other cultures' but often fall short of reflecting on their own.[15] Likewise, political scientists, always ready to expose the political and ideological baggage of practitioners, seldom subject their research to similar scrutiny.[16] All this, it seems, reveals a common pitfall in human understanding itself: 'The Understanding, like the Eye, whilst it makes us see, and perceive all other Things, takes no notice of it self: And it requires Art and Pains to set it at a distance, and make it its own Object', thus wrote John Locke.[17] If human understanding needs to better understand itself, China watching as a particular subset of human understanding should also make itself its own object and allow for self-watching.

In research, watching the self may come in different forms. Autoethnography, for one, calls for the explicit use of the self as a methodological resource in the production of knowledge.[18] In this book, by 'self' I mean not literally the personal experience of China watchers (though that is no doubt fascinating in itself), but rather their collective knowledge products, the broader intellectual, socio-political context of their knowledge production, and their underlying ideas and imaginations of themselves as the knowing subject. Thus defined, self-watching in China studies requires not only a methodological shift, but also an ontological and epistemological rethinking (if we suppose that the former can ever be separated from the latter).

A key suspect for the conspicuous absence of healthy self-reflection in China watching has to be the ever-appealing positivism, an epistemological

glue which helps hold an otherwise 'argumentative China watching community' together.[19] As an extremely influential theory of knowledge, positivism
presupposes the existence of an objective reality 'out there', independent of
our thought but ultimately amenable to scientific analysis.[20] Crucially,
claiming to have reached 'the end of the theory of knowledge', positivism
performs 'the prohibitive function of protecting scientific inquiry from
epistemological self-reflection'.[21] In this way, the epistemological question
of how we know what we know seems no longer necessary. Insisting on a
clear distinction between 'observable facts and often unsustainable "speculations about them"', David Martin Jones is irritated by the postcolonial effort
of 'exposing representation in literary "texts" or in film and music rather than
addressing the empirical realm of social facts'.[22]

Rallying around the positivist tradition, most China watchers in the IR
field treat China as something made up of such observable facts. However
complex those facts may be, and however difficult for China watchers to
completely detach themselves from personal biases, it is believed that there is
an ultimately knowable Chinese reality. The main task of China watching, by
definition, should be about watching China. If China knowledge is indeed
objective, scientifically testable, and professionally cumulative, then it would
seem meaningless, if not self-indulgent, to dwell on questions such as what
China knowledge is, who is producing it, how and for what purposes.[23]
Consequently, it is no surprise that few in the China-studies community have
shown interest in such philosophical reflections and still fewer are keen on
epistemological debates on China watching;[24] such debates, standing apparently in the way of accumulating further knowledge on China, would appear
not only unhelpful but needlessly polemic and divisive.

A CASE FOR WATCHING CHINA WATCHING

Critical epistemological reflection on the field of China's international
relations is anything but trivial. At one level, some measure of self-
reflectivity is not only necessary but also unavoidable. It pervades all literary
works, as literature is always implicitly a reflection on literature itself.[25] All
forms of knowledge contain within themselves some conscious or unconscious, direct or indirect, autobiographical accounts of the knowing/writing
self at either individual or certain collective levels. As evidenced in the self-
image of positivist knowledge in general, the very absence of critical self-
reflection in China watching already denotes a particular way of speaking
about itself, namely, as a cumulative body of empirical knowledge on China.
The problem is that this scientistic self-understanding is largely uncritical and
unconsciously so. If Pierre Macherey is right that what a work does not say is
as important as what it does say,[26] then this curious silence and unconscious-

ness in the writing of China's rise needs to be interrupted and made more conscious, a process which Jürgen Habermas calls reflection.[27]

Besides, it seems impossible for China watching to watch only China. Aihwa Ong notes that 'When a book about China is only about China, it is suspect'.[28] We may add that it is also self-delusional. China as an object of study does not simply exist in an objectivist or empiricist fashion, like a free-floating, self-contained entity waiting to be directly contacted, observed and analysed. This is not to say that China is unreal, unknowable or is only a ghostly illusion constructed entirely out of literary representation. Of course China does exist: the Great Wall, the Communist Party, and more than one billion people living there are all too real. And yet, to say something is real does not mean that its existence corresponds with a single, independent and fixed meaning for all to see. None of those aforementioned 'real' things and people beam out their meaning at us directly, let alone offer an unadulterated, panoramic view of 'China' as a whole. China's existence, while real, is better understood, to use Martin Heidegger's term, as a type of 'being-in-the-world'.[29] The 'in-the-world-ness' is intrinsically characteristic of China's being, which always needs to be understood in conjunction with its world, a world which necessarily includes China-bound discourse and representation.

R. G. Collingwood once said that 'all history is the history of thought', meaning that no historian can speak directly of hard historical facts without reference to various thoughts about those facts.[30] Likewise, insofar as China cannot exist meaningfully outside of language and discursive construction of it, no study of it is ever possible, let alone complete, without studying our thoughts about it. For this reason, echoing George Marcus and Michael Fisher's call for ethnography to 'turn on itself' and 'to create an equally probing, ethnographic knowledge of its social and cultural foundations',[31] this book takes the representation of China (rather than 'China' itself) as its main object of study. It calls for a critical autoethnographic turn in China watching.

Certainly, there has been no shortage of study on Western representations of China. Alongside Western intellectual interest in this country is a long-standing tradition of documenting this interest, as evidenced in an extensive and diverse body of literature on Western images of China.[32] If we also count the works on Western perceptions of Asia, the size of that literature is even more impressive.[33] But this makes it all the more conspicuous that to date precious little has been said or written about contemporary China watching in global politics.

For instance, a large portion of the existing study is fixated either on past perceptions of China or perceptions of China's past. Historical investigation, valuable as it is, cannot substitute for an up-to-date account of contemporary Western knowledge on China. Meanwhile, most literature tends to limit its purview to 'non-scholarly' sources, such as government documents, official speeches, mass media, public opinion, travel writings, novels, documentaries and films. As a result, by design or by accident, scholarly literature is often able to escape attention.

Furthermore, even as some academic writings in historiographical, socio-logical, philosophical, cultural, and linguistic contexts have begun to be critically scrutinised, [34] with few exceptions Western IR scholarship on China's rise continues to be overlooked. [35] This is especially curious given that since the US consolidated its global dominance after World War II (WWII), IR discourses have become a main frame of reference for main-stream Western worldviews. [36] Is this because discipline-based scholarship such as IR is better able to minimise the prejudice of Orientalism? Edward Said once claimed that 'interesting work is most likely to be produced by scholars whose allegiance is to a discipline defined intellectually and not to a "field" like Orientalism defined either canonically, imperially, or geographi-cally'. [37] However, it would be naïve, as Said himself would probably agree, to give the disciplines of IR and Political Science such benefit of the doubt. Though apparently defined intellectually rather than geographically, neither field is politically innocent or neutral. In fact, both remain largely an Ameri-can/Western social science, whose implicit or unintended loyalty to the United States (US) is probably not dissimilar to that of Orientalism to Europe. [38] Indeed, precisely because these disciplines have now gained a false reputation of being value-free or scientifically objective, their contribution to Western construction of other societies could be all the more significant and lasting, thus deserving closer investigation. Failing that, it would be difficult for us to grasp the dynamics and complexities of contemporary Western representations of China in global politics.

No doubt, critical scholarship in the fields of IR and postcolonial studies has begun to problematise mainstream IR knowledge. Several important works in IR and cultural studies have examined at length the social construc-tion of self/Other and the politics of representation in relation to the South, the East ('Near East'), and Asia. [39] However, none of their focus is primarily on Western representations of China. Said's seminal work *Orientalism*, despite its sweeping subtitle 'Western Conceptions of the Orient', is con-cerned mainly with the Middle East. [40] When sometimes Said is invoked in China analysis, it is often, perhaps justifiably, to probe China's own 'Orien-talist' legacy (or in Xiaomei Chen's term, Occidentalism). [41]

Finally, where there exists useful criticism of Western IR discourses on China's rise, the criticism is often confined to empirical debate or concerned with factual or narrowly-conceived methodological matters related to specific works, claims, or issues. [42] Most participants in such debates agree that there is a real China out there, and that the main problem with Western representation lies in its misrepresentation, bias, or tainted perceptions: once such distortion is rectified, objective knowledge of China will be within reach. For example, having insightfully noted that 'Our uncertainties about China are as much a product of uncertainties about ourselves as they are about China', Brantly Womack then goes on to suggest that we should strive for an 'accurate understanding of China' through looking at the 'real' China and 'its internal dynamic'.[43] To many, Womack's approach makes perfect sense: How could it be otherwise? And yet, appeals to 'reality' through more empirical research are ultimately of limited value. As Eric Hayot et al. put it, 'noting the discrepancy between reality and representation, as it applies to particular objects of discourse, no longer works as critique... critique has to acknowledge imagination as something *more* than a distorter of fact'.[44]

Understanding representation as 'something more' than an empirical matter is crucial, though this does not mean that empirical analysis has become irrelevant; it has not and will not. But if our critique of Western representations stays at an empirical level, it will be ultimately ineffective, if not misleading itself. For one thing, there is no compelling reason to suggest that our newer empirical data can serve as a more reliable base on which to build China knowledge. Moreover, as will be made clear in the book, the overall function of Western representations is self-imagination. For all their claims to scientific objectivity, they have not been primarily about presenting an empirically accurate picture of China in the first instance. As such, no amount of 'accurate' empirical facts or logical reasoning contrary to Western assumptions of China is likely to succeed in challenging those assumptions.

Consequently, in spite of the vast body of works that focus on Western images and representations of China, there is a glaring lack of critical analysis of contemporary Western thought on China's rise in the field of IR (broadly defined), a gap which this book aims to fill. The book is not interested in asking whether or to what extent various forms of China knowledge accurately reflect 'Chinese reality'. Nor will it offer my own 'authentic' or 'objective' picture of that reality—so long as it is 'my own', it can be neither authentic nor objective. Instead, it will examine how various representations of 'Chinese reality', created under the guises of objective knowledge, are discursively and socially constructed, and how such constructions function in international relations theory and practice. Different from a conventional study of national image in foreign policy making, the main concern of the book is with a sociology of knowledge and politics of representation in relation to China watching.

To this end, the book draws attention to two dominant and recurring themes and assumptions on China's rise: the 'China threat' and 'China opportunity'. These themes may be variously termed as 'regimes of truth', 'metanarratives', or a certain 'style of thought',[45] but here they are referred to as 'paradigms', a term made academically popular by Thomas Kuhn.[46] More on the definition of the term will be said in a moment and in the next chapter. For now, like colonial discourse, a paradigm is 'a signifying system without an author'.[47] In this sense, to illustrate my misgivings with the two China paradigms is not to pick on any individual scholars/authors or their specific works, even though in order to critically engage with those paradigms we have no choice but to rely on examples found in specific publications.

Also, these paradigms are not to be confused with any specific arguments or theoretical frameworks. A paradigm is a type of basic conceptual lens through which what can and cannot be known about a certain object of study is delineated, and from which certain specific arguments and theoretical frameworks can flow. Though the paradigms of 'China threat' and 'China opportunity' may be found more readily in the IR field of China watching, they are not the exclusive patents of IR scholars. To better illustrate these two paradigms, it is necessary to select the relevant literature on an eclectic basis. Coming within the purview of my analysis are, consequently, not just academic writings on China's foreign policy and international relations, but also other pieces in the 'China representation' puzzle such as media reports, commentaries, and official discourses.

As well as cutting across genre lines, the 'China threat' and 'China opportunity' paradigms are not confined within any particular geographical boundaries. True, the US has played a leading role in setting the agenda for Western perceptions of China's rise and much attention of the book will therefore be paid to the American discourse, but these paradigms are by no means distinctively American. This is why I use the designation 'Western' to cast a wider geopolitical net (and at the same time to leave out 'non-Western' sources to avoid making my enterprise too unwieldy). Of course, by 'Western' here I do not really mean 'Western' per se, whatever that term might mean. My source materials, in most cases, are drawn from English literature published in a few selected Western countries, notably the US, Britain, and Australia. Discourses from other Western countries, such as France and Germany, will not be examined, for the simple reason that their inclusion is beyond the scope and capacity of this single volume. Furthermore, even as I focus almost exclusively on English literature, I do not claim to do full justice to the inherently heterogeneous quality of China writings in those 'Anglophone' locales. My understanding is that no matter how hard we try to narrow down our scope of investigation, we are bound to encounter still subtler spatial differences, contextual nuances, and temporal variations, which could well exist in the writings of the same author. Consequently, this study, its subtitle notwithstanding, does not claim to capture the full complexities or 'totality' of Western IR representations of China's rise, let alone China watching in general.

We always need to maintain a vigilant suspicion of all forms of generalisation, but that suspicion should not turn into a paranoia about generalisation altogether. Without a certain degree of generalisation no analysis would be possible. Given its finite vocabulary, language is necessarily reductionist in its representation of an infinite world. It is in this context, as well as for stylistic reasons, that I have to employ such generalised, inherently problematic terms as 'China watching' and 'Western representations', even though I cannot emphasise enough that their specific usage here should never be misconstrued as an indictment to *all* China watchers or *all* Western representations of China.

KNOWLEDGE, DESIRE AND POWER: A DECONSTRUCTIVE/CONSTRUCTIVIST FRAMEWORK FOR ANALYSIS

This book draws on deconstructive and constructivist approaches. Since it is not a book *about* either approach or about ontology/epistemology per se, it will not systematically engage with those theoretical issues except for the following outline of their relevance to this study. The deconstructive approach is employed to question the underlying dichotomy of reality/knowledge in Western study of China's international relations. My contention is that the paradigms of 'China threat' and 'China opportunity' are not 'true' (or 'false') representations of Chinese reality, but rather discursive strategies of Othering predicated on certain presuppositions and fore-understandings in Western tradition, desire, and self-imagination. From a constructivist standpoint, I then argue that these paradigms are not mere word games or fanciful imaginations that have nothing to do with China. To the extent that they condition the way we give meaning to that country, they are socially constitutive of it, not least by shaping the way we deal with it in practice. Accordingly, my deconstructive analysis is not a mere textual exercise; it is concerned with the complex connections between these paradigms and Sino-Western interactions. These arguments will be fleshed out in the main chapters, but for now some explication of the theoretical and methodological underpinnings of this book is in order.

Deconstructing Reality/Knowledge: Knowledge as Situated Interpretation

As a complex and controversial strategy in philosophical and literary criticism, deconstruction defies clear definition and explanation. At the risk of oversimplifying this slippery yet important term, I define the primary function of deconstruction as serving to expose the artificial and arbitrary nature of oppositions, dichotomies, and hierarchies that have been taken for granted in a certain discourse. In this way, deconstruction helps reveal the discursive and social practices of exclusion and marginalisation which are chiefly responsible for maintaining and reproducing the 'naturalness' of those binary oppositions and hierarchies.[48] In mainstream IR discourses on China, one fundamental binary opposition is the dichotomy of reality and knowledge. According to this dualism, Chinese reality exists prior to and independent of China knowledge, with the latter derived from the former mainly through scientific research. Yet, this binary assumption about Chinese reality and China knowledge is deeply flawed and will be subject to deconstruction.

I submit that reality, or at least social reality, has no a priori or independent meaning outside of knowledge and discourse. If there appears to be an objective fact out there, that is because people who believe so already share a common discourse about that 'fact'. Thus, thought and reality are not two discrete, mutually exclusive categories as they appear.[49] They are inherently interconnected. Indeed, 'interconnectedness' is not strong enough a word to depict their almost inseparable ontological existence, for it is only through knowledge and discourse that social reality comes into being and makes sense, just as it is only through light that things can become visible to our eyes. In the words of Maja Zehfuss, 'what we conceptualise as real is itself an effect of representations'.[50] The world appears observable and meaningful to us never directly through itself, but only 'indirectly' through the 'light of interpretation' cast by texts, discourses, and language. If we merely stare at things without processing them through thought and language, our gaze will be like a blank look, unable to capture much meaning despite their clear presence in front of our eyes. As soon as we begin to describe what we have seen, that description must already be captive to language and prior knowledge. 'The world exists independently of language', notes David Campbell, 'but we can never *know* that (beyond the fact of its assertion), because the existence of the world is literally inconceivable outside of language and our traditions of interpretation'.[51]

For instance, China as the world's most populous nation seems to be a self-evident fact both beyond doubt and beyond interpretation. Yet, such apparently objective, non-interpreted facts are not the primary concern of China watchers. No scholar is likely to make a career out of collecting and writing on such 'trivia' alone, just as no anthropologist would find it either stimulating or worthwhile to 'go round the world to count the cats in Zanzibar'.[52] For us, often what matters is not 'pure' reality, but interpreted and contested reality. At issue here is not just whether China *is* the world's most populous nation, but also the 'so what?' questions: What that means (or often, *will* mean) for China and the world and what to do about it. As soon as meaning is at issue, commonly-agreed 'brute-facts' will be hard to come by. In the eyes of nineteenth-century missionaries, a populous China represented a promised land for religious conversion. During WWII, the US saw China's massive manpower as a great asset in fighting the Japanese. For business people whose worldview is inevitably defined by market and profit, China's vast population takes on a quality of enormous commercial opportunities. By contrast, for racists or racially sensitive observers, 1.3 billion Chinese may symbolise 'Yellow Peril' and amount to a 'China threat'. Clearly, none of these claims are stand-alone facts; as 'facts', they are always already a product of particular interpretation. Indeed, even the 'bare-bone' fact that China is the most populous nation is not entirely independent of language and interpretation, given that concepts such as *nation* and *population* are modern inventions and constructs rather than naturally existing categories. Consequently, *social* reality, which is what I mean by 'reality' or 'fact' throughout this book, is inherently discursive and interpretive, and interpretation cannot be disconnected from thought, knowledge, and language. To quote philosopher and linguist Wilhelm von Humboldt,

> Man lives with his objects chiefly—in fact, since his feeling and acting depends on his perceptions, one may say exclusively—as language presents them to him. By the same process whereby he spins language out of his own being, he ensnares himself in it; and each language draws a magic circle round the people to which it belongs, a circle from which there is no escape save by stepping out of it into another.[53]

Of course, to say that social reality is bound up with language and interpretation is not to argue that reality can be freely arranged into any number of discursive permutations or that one interpretation is as valid as another. We cannot access reality except through language, but this is not the same as saying that we cannot know anything beyond language per se, or that all knowing makes equal sense to everyone—were that the case, we in the academia might as well go home and find another line of work.

While reality is knowable only through interpretation, its knowing is not subject to the 'limitlessness of interpretation'. Like 'texts', reality imposes restraints upon its interpretation.[54] To return to the earlier example, while China's population means different things to different observers under shifting circumstances, one cannot reasonably claim that there are now more people living in Australia than in China. While it is true that 'a person reading a text is himself part of the meaning he apprehends',[55] the reader as a being-in-the-world does not and cannot interpret a given text or reality at will. All interpretation relies on language, but language is above all a social commodity, a carrier of the perceptions, attitudes, and goals of its society.[56] Thus interpretation is by necessity always grounded in and constrained by certain 'preunderstandings' which in turn are conditioned on their culture, tradition, language, and a particular readership/audience that the relevant language entails.[57] The 'life span' of an interpretation (or how far it can 'travel') depends on its communicability and social reception within its situated language and culture. While there are no pre-discursive or non-interpreted social facts and no formal limit on the range of interpretive possibility, in practice interpretation is rarely linguistically or textually random or anarchical, something we make up as we go along; rather, it is always *inter*textually situated in the sense that texts are dependent on and connected to other texts. In this sense, we need not fear the much-maligned relativist spectre of 'anything goes'; those who follow that path would soon realise that they cannot go very far. 'The historian', wrote E. H. Carr, 'is of his own age, and is bound to it by the conditions of human existence. The very words which he uses—words like democracy, empire, war, revolution—have current connotations from which he cannot divorce them'.[58] Like reading a text, our interpretation of reality is neither objective knowledge nor purely subjective speculation. Rather, it is a *social* text which necessarily speaks to other social texts. Such an undeniable and irreducible intertextual-ity constitutes what Said calls the materiality and worldliness of texts, so that those texts may effectively 'solicit[ing] the world's attention'.[59]

In this way, while China knowledge (as in the form of the recurring themes of 'threat' and 'opportunity') is derived from interpretation, it is a particular form of worldly, intertextually situated interpretation that has thus far proved effective in soliciting the West's attention and capturing its self-imagination. It is often on this basis that China knowledge appears to be objective truth. However, that truth status should best be understood as an effect of its already shared and unquestioned interpretiveness. The intertex-tual contexts from which it arises have become so widely accepted that we tend to forget its 'original' status *qua* historically specific interpretations.

For this reason, Western representations of China's rise are not only inter-pretive, but also collectively and autobiographically so: they tell us less about China 'itself' (as a text) than about China watchers (as readers), their audi-ence, and social, cultural and historical milieu. At least from Marco Polo onwards, the production of China knowledge has been subject to the logic and political economy of such situated intertextuality and worldliness. In *The Chan's Great Continent*, Jonathan Spence quotes an intriguing conversation between the fabled Venetian traveller and his Chinese host, the Kublai: 'When you return to the West', Kublai asks Marco Polo, 'will you repeat to your people the same tales you tell me?' Marco Polo gives no direct response. 'I speak and speak', he tells Kublai, '…but the listener retains only the words he is expecting…. It is not the voice that commands the story: it is the ear'.[60]

Indeed, it is the ear of the audience, or the intertextual and worldly con-straint, to which a China watcher needs to respond or endear oneself, whether consciously or not. To be sure, the intertextual context within which China knowledge is produced is not fixed, nor is it always a 'Western' context. Chinese voices, discourses and interpretations can, should, and have often been part of that interpretive process. In *China Watcher*, Baum tells a revealing story in the 1960s about a peculiar way in which China watchers, with Communist China off limits, often gazed at it from afar by interviewing mainland refugees in Hong Kong. He writes that:

Two particularly well-informed illegal aliens from Guangdong [known as Xiao Yang and Lao Yang] became more or less permanent fixtures at the Universities Service Centre in the late '60s. They were interviewed so frequently and so intensively by center-based scholars that it became a standing joke among us—told only half in jest—that the vast majority of scholarly books, articles, and Ph.D. dissertations written about China during the Cultural Revolution decade, 1966-76, were based on information provided by these two individuals. My own 1975 book on the *Four Cleanups, Prelude to Revolution*, is no exception.[61]

This episode shows that a significant part of Western understanding of Chinese politics and society at that time might have come from two Chinese informants. It is safe to assume that what those informants told their Western interlocutors was not China per se either, but their *situated interpretations* of China or, more precisely, their interpretations of some specific vignettes of their own localised experience in China. In turn, those interpretations, if not already intentionally or unintentionally prompted or skewed to suit the needs of their Western interviewers, would certainly be subject to re-interpretation by the latter, in line with their worldliness and interpretive conventions. One source of such conventions, as American sociologist Richard Madsen notes, has been the writings of early Protestant missionaries to China, whose 'framework of assumptions about how to understand and what to do about China' in part laid the groundwork for today's secular China studies.[62] Therefore, what can be and has been known about China is always already to some extent shaped by the intertextual situatedness of China watchers (including those who are Chinese). No one visits or studies China 'as entirely a stranger: we already know or think we know what is to be expected'.[63] Veteran American journalist James Mann pithily described a similar process through which Western media coverage of China operates:

The biggest problem is that the media coverage of China tends merely to reinforce whatever is the reigning stereotype or image, or "frame," of China in any particular decade or era. In the 1950s, the coverage in the United States was of Chinese as disciplined automatons. In the 1980s, it was "China goes capitalist." In the early 1990s, it was "crackdown in China." Now, it's "China rising" (and "China gets rich"). Once an impression gels, then the extended press coverage—by which I mean, TV specials, newsmagazine covers, newspaper features—all either repeat the impression or at least play off it in some way or another.[64]

Explaining the problem, Mann believes that it is mainly those 'back in the home offices' such as producers, editors, and the like who help shape the China coverage according to the governing images of the day.[65] He probably could have added Western audience to that mix. Without the audience, or the ear, 'Rigorous research into specific aspects of contemporary China which does not capitalise on existing presumptions—the usual human rights, repressive regime, rampant capitalism etc frames—does not get past the niche market of China specialists, if it is published at all'.[66] In that case, many authors probably would never bother to begin with. Consequently, certain popular images will persist while alternative views struggle for attention. Some decades ago, the Australian journalist Peter Hastings hoped to write more reports on Asia but his boss, Sir Frank Packer (the father of the late Australian media tycoon Kerry Packer), frowned upon the idea: 'Nothing in it... *Who* wants to read about those places?'[67] Of course, in reality there was always much in it; it just happened that nothing there seemed to interest 'us'. Thus, like Asia, China's existence as an object of media curiosity or social inquiry from the outset owes a lot to this 'who'—the consumers in the marketplace of knowledge—and their expectations, presuppositions, fore-understandings, and established self-imaginations.

The Nexus of Knowledge/Desire: China Paradigms as Western Self-imagination

Upon another look, Packer's question 'Who *wants* to read about those places' not only says much about the importance of readership and audience in the making of news, but also unwittingly reveals the central role of desire in the production and dissemination of knowledge. By *desire* I do not mean simply the 'desire to know' (*epistemophilia*), but also the myriad of human desires behind the desire to know. The received wisdom is that knowledge is an objective reflection of reality through reason, but as David Hume argues, 'Reason is, and ought only to be the slave of the passions and can never pretend to any other office than to serve and obey them'.[68] At the root of knowledge is not just reason, but also desire. Desire fuels the need to acquire and produce knowledge, which in turn serves to rationalise and help fulfil desire. Hans Furth calls them the 'two sides of the same coin'.[69] Noting a similar 'interplay of knowledge and pleasure', Foucault argues that knowledge always needs to speak to desire, and desire must express itself in the form of knowledge.[70] Desire is not just an attribute of the object of social study, but it also suffuses the process and end product of the study itself. It not just 'complicates an analyst's task' in knowledge accumulation;[71] it is the precondition of such knowledge's social production and public consumption.

To connect knowledge with desire is not to suggest that knowledge is reducible to any individual whim. Like language, knowledge is first and foremost a social property, whose reception *qua* knowledge must depend on its intersubjective appeal to collective emotion and social desire. Writings are driven by the desire to write, which in turn is conditioned on the desire to read/know in the wider emotionally imagined community, a process governed throughout by the 'erotics of knowledge'.[72] If it is through knowledge that reality is made meaningful, it is social desire that makes certain knowledge desirable and its production possible and profitable. To be sure, the role of desire in such a process is often invisible, silent, unconscious, and largely unacknowledged. That is because while ultimately knowledge is both a product of and for desire and emotion, in order to be worthy of the name, knowledge has to conceal its emotive trace. Or so it is believed.

Even with the concealment, modern science cannot deny its roots in the modern desire for certainty and identity. It is neither coincident nor ironic that Descartes, whose anxious desire for certainty finds expression in the 'Cartesian Anxiety' of an Either/Or (either there is a secure foundation upon which our knowledge can be based, or we will be engulfed in uncertainty and darkness),[73] is credited with laying the foundation for modern science. It is not despite but because of the Cartesian Anxiety that Descartes 'discovered' human reason (*cogito ergo sum*, or 'I think, therefore I am') as the secure, indubitable foundation for certainty. From this emerges also the certain identity of modern man as the rational knowing subject, an identity which promises the ability to obtain objective knowledge about the world.

Yet objective certainty, however desirable or precisely because it is *desirable*, is an illusory effect of desire. The desire for certainty may be satisfied only within desire and through the certainty of desire. When certainty is not within reach, the modern knowing subject, unable or unwilling to give up its quest, turns to the illusive certainty and comfort of what John Dewey called 'emotional substitute': 'in the absence of actual certainty... men cultivated all sorts of things that would give them the *feeling* of certainty'.[74] Trust is one such feeling, which is not based on objective certainty, but cultivated through a process of 'emotional inoculation'.[75] Fears and fantasies are two other forms of emotional substitute, especially useful for making sense of strangers. By fantasising about an uncertain other's assimilability and eventual transformation into the self, one can gain a sense of certainty. Alternatively, one may arrive at a sense of predictability by reducing that other to an already known prototype of menace. Either way, these emotional substitutes provide the much-desired antidote of certainty to the Cartesian Anxiety: either the other can be converted, or it must pose a threat. In this way, the initial uncertainty of the other translates into the certainty of an emotive either/or.

As emotional substitutes for certainty, fears and fantasies have figured prominently in what Robert Young calls 'colonial desire', which regulates colonialists' encounters with and their knowledge of various unfamiliar Others. These emotions together make up an 'ambivalent double gesture of repulsion and attraction' towards the colonised.[76] On the one hand, colonial desire finds people of other races and colours 'disgusting' and 'repulsive', hence an object of fear and paranoia. At the same time, colonial desire projects onto those (same) people some degree of 'beauty, attractiveness or desirability',[77] thus making them an exotic source of fantasy and wonder. According to Homi Bhabha, underlying such ambivalent structures of feeling is precisely the modern desire for certainty, identity and 'a pure origin'.[78] Thanks to this ever-present modern desire, the aforementioned ambivalent colonial stereotype is able to acquire 'its currency' and 'ensure[s] its repeatability in changing historical and discursive conjunctures'. In this sense, Orientalism is best seen as 'the site of dreams, images, fantasies, myths, obsessions and requirements'.[79] What this latent form of Orientalist knowledge reveals is not something concrete or objective about the Orient, but something about the Orientalists themselves, their recurring, latent desire of fears and fantasies about the Orient. Indeed, only when imbued with such unconscious but persistent desire can Orientalism get 'passed on silently, without comment, from one text to another'.[80]

Western knowledge of China's rise is precisely such a text that has been caught up in the silent emotive current. For example, the 'China threat' paradigm bears the stamp of fears, whereas the 'China opportunity' paradigm can be best seen as manifestations of modern fantasies. These emotions about China's rise are certainly not identical to the Orientalist colonial desire in the nineteenth century. For instance, the overtly sexual/racial connotation that once was a hallmark of old-style colonial desire is no longer prevalent in contemporary writings on China. What used to be some of the main obsessions in European colonial fears and fantasies, such as miscegenation and racial hybridity, have now been repackaged as issues of multiculturalism, norm diffusion, socialisation, and so forth. Still, a similar structure of colonial desire lives on; even the racial facet has not disappeared completely in contemporary China watching.[81] Thus, to better understand the twin China paradigms, we need to put them in the context of (neo)colonial desire, and ask how they have more to do with the West's latent quest for certainty and identity than with the manifest search for empirical truth about 'Chinese reality'. If all social knowledge is yoked to some intertextuality and worldliness, much of the worldliness of the 'threat' and 'opportunity' discourses of China is then made up of the (renewed) fears and fantasies accompanying the Western modern desire and self-imagination.

Knowledge as Power, Theory as Practice, and Mutual Responsiveness

All knowledge, insofar as it is a manifestation of desire, implies a power relationship with its desired object. 'Where there is desire, the power relation is already present'.[82] Thus, knowledge loses its ostensible innocence and reveals its ties with power. As Foucault argues, 'there is no power relation without the correlative constitution of a field of knowledge', nor is there 'any knowledge that does not presuppose and constitute at the same time power relations'. Taken together, power and the production of knowledge 'directly imply one another' and are mutually dependent and reinforcing.[83]

The power/knowledge nexus has a constructivist import. Social knowledge cannot be an objective reflection of reality, but it is not merely a text disconnected from reality either. It is able to inform practice and help construct the reality it purports only to describe. If reality is subject to wordly interpretation, then the interpreting word is ultimately worldly with 'real-world' consequences.[84] Jim George notes that 'the process of discursive representation is never a neutral, detached one but is always imbued with the power and authority of the namers and makers of reality—it is always knowledge *as* power'.[85] In a similar vein, Nicholas Onuf suggests that 'saying is doing: talking is undoubtedly the most important way that we go about making the world what it is'.[86] With his 'Axis of Evil' utterance, for example, George W. Bush effectively told Americans that 'We can't go back to sleep again'.[87] In other words, something would have to be done (and indeed has been done).

In assuming knowledge as power and theory as practice, we should refrain from taking some self-serving short-cuts. As we are most closely attached to our own desire and most acutely aware of our knowledge, we might assume that the knowledge in the power/knowledge nexus is largely 'our' knowledge and the power mostly 'our' power. Such an assumption is evident, for example, in much of the mainstream IR literature on 'norm diffusion' and 'socialisation', which often implicitly privileges Western knowledge and power. But this ethnocentric reading of power/knowledge is problematic. Reality is subject to interpretation and construction by knowledge, ideas and norms, but it is almost always a result of *co*-interpretation and *co*-construction by a myriad of sources of knowledge as power. Western knowledge is no doubt a dominant source (let's assume for a moment that Western knowledge is singular); nevertheless, it is only one among many contenders in an increasingly democratic world of representation. Consequently, to argue for theory as practice is not to say that the world is mainly of *our* making. As Fredric Jameson reminds us, all history is contemporary history, but that 'does not mean that all history is *our* contemporary history'.[88]

At this point, the notion of knowledge as power needs to be tempered and complemented by an awareness of what I call 'mutual responsiveness' in the social world. Mutual responsiveness, as I have noted elsewhere, is a fundamental ontological condition of the world where various actors and 'objects' are intersubjectively connected.[89] If in the end I cannot help making a foundational truth claim somewhere, this is it. Being part of this mutually responsive world, social research is not immune to this condition, a phenomenon identified by Anthony Giddens as the 'double hermeneutic'.[90] That is, unlike in the natural sciences where the object of study does not seem to directly answer back, social knowledge has to live with the subjectivity and agency of its 'objects'. Indeed, that knowledge is always subject to interpretation, appropriation, disruption, alteration, and rejection by its 'objects'. Not only is our knowledge capable of constituting social reality, but the 'objects' of our knowledge, through their knowledge of their world, including their interpretations of both our knowledge and practice, are also capable of taking part in the co-construction of that reality. Thus the 'wholeness' of any social reality cannot be reduced to the unilateral constitutive effect of any *particular* discourse or knowledge, however powerful or universal it may appear. In this context, China is always more than the effect of Western representations of it. Its own subjectivities play various roles in the ongoing co-construction of itself and its international relations. Without taking this factor into account, our knowledge of China is at best partial knowledge. China knowledge, in the proper sense of the words, should after all be a kind of moral, intersubjective knowledge (or *phronesis*),[91] a knowledge which so far remains underdeveloped and little-appreciated in the 'China's rise' literature.

AN OVERVIEW AND BRIEF SELF-REFLECTION

Informed by the deconstructive-cum-constructivist framework and mutual responsiveness perspective, this book will critically engage with the 'China threat' and 'China opportunity' paradigms. Chapter 2 illustrates how this dual mode of representation characterises Western perceptions of China's rise. In Chapter 3, I bring the deconstructive strategy to bear on this ambivalent bifocal lens in China watching. Its ambivalence towards China's rise says more about Western desire in general and Western fears and hopes in particular, and these China images are both predicated on and constitutive of Western self-imagination in terms of who 'we' are and who 'we' are not.

In Chapters 4 and 5, I probe into the nexus between knowledge, desire, and power in the 'China threat' paradigm and argue that the production of this particular body of knowledge has been linked to the political economy of fear. With a specific focus on the US, I will examine both how the 'China threat' paradigm is integral to the functioning of the military-industrial complex and military Keynesianism, and how military Keynesianism in turn contributes to the vibrancy of the 'China threat' knowledge industry. In short, this knowledge is both in the service of power and underpinned by it. Furthermore, often taken as objective truth, this paradigm informs a confrontational policy on China. By helping provoke nationalistic and realpolitik responses from China, such a policy makes the 'China threat' more likely in reality. In this way, as will be outlined in Chapter 5, the 'China threat' paradigm can become a self-fulfilling prophecy.

Chapters 6 and 7 then turn to the 'China opportunity' paradigm. In Chapter 6, I argue that although the 'China opportunity' imagery often justifies a policy of engagement, its built-in normative objective of converting China is ultimately a false promise, which sets itself up for eventual disillusionment. In Chapter 7, I will examine how this 'China opportunity'-induced disillusionment is partly complicit in the recent hardline turn in Western policy on China. Chapter 8 concludes with a discussion on what China knowledge (and IR knowledge in general) means and entails epistemologically and methodologically. On the one hand, it urges China watchers to critically reflect on both the Western self-imagination upon which their China knowledge is predicated and the political economies of their knowledge production and application. On the other hand, it stresses the need to engage with Chinese subjectivities and discourses through ongoing dialogue. Together, it gestures towards a more self-conscious, ethically responsible way of knowing China as a being-in-the-world. Though the book does not prescribe any concrete advice to policy makers on how to make better China policy, some broad policy implications of this study should become clearer as one reads through.

Although or precisely because the book seeks to fill a gap in the existing literature on Western representations of China, it is itself intertextually connected to that literature and would not have been written without it. Its various perceived inadequacies provide the rationale for this study. Meanwhile, as shown through the references, the book also draws from other scholars a number of insights, such as the bifocal, emotive, autobiographical and political nature of Western representations of the Other. Together they become part of the intertextual background of this book. As a contingent, intertextually situated interpretation of a complex, fluid body of discourse, the book is not an 'objective' description of what China knowledge really is, for it cannot, nor can any other study, confront China knowledge 'in all its freshness as a thing-in-itself'.[92] Given my particular focus and the limitation of space, I can only briefly reflect on my own interpretation. But it is worth noting that such self-reflection is crucial if my critique is to retain a level of intellectual healthiness, whose absence in mainstream Western literature on China's rise has prompted this study. Bearing this caveat in mind, we now turn to the substantive chapters.

2. Threat and opportunity: a bifocal lens

The West's ultimate potential enemy is a state: a second great military-authoritarian-capitalist rogue regime, with an army partially independent of civilian authority, a navy aimed at knocking the United States off its perch, the world's second-largest economy, a racist-nationalist mythology that legitimates world domination, and disputes with all its neighbors.

MacGregor Knox[1]

China's embrace of democracy will be one of the defining moments of modern political history, no less significant than the Russian Revolution of 1917 or the fall of the Berlin Wall in 1989.

Bruce Gilley[2]

In assessing the opportunities as well as the uncertainties, more than ever, China needs to be viewed through bifocal lenses.

Claude Smadja[3]

INTERPRETIVE PARADIGMS IN WESTERN UNDERSTANDING OF CHINA'S RISE

If there are a thousand readers, there will be a thousand Hamlets. The same can be said of the many Chinas in the eyes of China watchers. Shangri-la, the Promised Land, the Good Earth, Emperor Mao's blue ants, Dr Fu Manchu, and Charlie Chan are just some of the enduring imageries associated with the Middle Kingdom. Today, with China looming large in almost every aspect of global life, the colours of its biblical coat appear even more varied and baffling. Though still labelled a Communist dictatorship by some, China is seen by others as a dynamic society on the way to greater openness and even democracy. While some pundits liken it to a twenty-first-century Wilhelmine Germany (the so-called 'Germany analogy'), others conceive it as a largely status quo power, if not yet a fully responsible stakeholder. To some, China resembles a cuddly panda, but others view it more as a hungry, fire-breathing dragon, while still others point to a fragile power under the constant danger of collapse. Concurrent with all this, China has been variably referred to as a modern-day El Dorado, a lucrative market of 1.3 billion customers, the world's workshop, the biggest polluter on the planet, one of the world's worst human rights offenders, patron of African misgovernment and leader of an axis of autocracies.

As noted earlier, no study of China can bypass such prior images and representations. Therefore, the aim of this book is to consciously engage with them. That said, the book will not join the usual fray of debating 'Which China is for real?' or empirically verifying which imagery or imageries best correspond with 'Chinese reality'. Needless to say, I myself do not have privileged access to such 'reality'. Rather, to lay the foundation for a deconstructive reading of Western representations of China's rise, this chapter will focus on how those apparently disparate, kaleidoscopic accounts of China, with some exceptions,[4] exhibit 'a few basic recurring themes'.[5] From those themes I single out two dominant modes of representations or paradigms: China as a threat and as an opportunity. Disparate as they may appear, these two paradigms often go hand in hand, creating a powerful bifocal lens through which to gaze at China. This 'bifocal quality' of Western representation of China's rise will be examined towards the end of this chapter and throughout the rest of the book.[6] For now, given that 'paradigm' provides an operating conceptual lens for my reading of the China discourses, a brief note on this term is called for.

WHAT IS A PARADIGM?

The term *paradigm* was brought into wider academic use by Thomas Kuhn's path-breaking book *The Structure of Scientific Revolutions*. According to Kuhn, paradigms are 'universally recognized scientific achievements that for a time provide model problems and solutions to a community of practitioners'.[7] Kuhn first used the term mainly to describe a particular developmental stage of natural sciences. But it is in the social science realm that it seems to have become more widely circulated, though from the outset there has been much doubt over whether there exist paradigms in social sciences and whether social sciences can ever arrive at a paradigmatic stage. For some, 'there is not going to be an age of paradigm in the social sciences',[8] while others simply claim that 'the idea of paradigm has no relevance to social science except as its own form of mimicry [of natural sciences]'.[9]

Despite such scepticism, many fields in the social sciences have routinely defined their different historical stages in terms of paradigms. At least in the eyes of their exponents, some powerful interpretive lenses in social science research, such as modernisation, globalisation, democratisation, and Orientalism, seem to have achieved nothing short of a paradigmatic status.[10] In this context, I argue that Western representations of China's rise are also influenced by certain paradigms, notably the 'China threat' and 'China opportunity'. By referring to them as 'paradigms' I do not mean that these representations are 'objective' or 'scientific'; rather, they are understood here as two fundamental images. As a fundamental image, a paradigm

> ... serves to define what should be studied, what questions should be asked, how they should be asked, and what rules should be followed in interpreting the answers obtained. The paradigm is the broadest unit of consensus within a science and serves to differentiate one scientific community (or subcommunity) from another.[11]

Thus, as paradigms, the 'China threat' and 'China opportunity' are not merely about *what* has been commonly said of China, but also about *how* China is to be understood. Here lies the proper meaning of the two China discourses as paradigms: first, both are particular, widely (albeit not universally) shared normative concerns and cognitive habits, which determine certain acceptable ways of making sense of China and facilitate the production of knowledge along those lines. The images of China as a threat per se, for example, do not automatically add up to a 'China threat' paradigm; as a paradigm, they must also consist in a shared normative understanding of what counts as objective knowledge about China. In other words, paradigms contain not only specific common understandings, but also particular cognitive frames that consciously or subconsciously regulate the routine production of those understandings as knowledge. This is what Kuhn means by referring to a paradigm as a 'preformed and relatively inflexible box': phenomena that 'will not fit the box are often not seen at all'.[12] Through such an epistemological function in regulating the manufacturing of knowledge, paradigms ensure their continued self-reproduction as paradigms.

In this sense, paradigm is not the same as theory. Although it is often loosely used and even becomes interchangeable with such terms as 'model', 'analytical framework', 'approach', and 'theory', 'not all theories are paradigm theories'.[13] Equally, while theory is often part of a paradigm, a paradigm is much more than any specific theory, for it 'stands for the entire constellation of beliefs, values, techniques, and so on shared by members of a given community'.[14] Thus defined, paradigm is more all-encompassing and enduring than particular theoretical perspectives. Whereas a theory is often 'accessible' only to a small number of scholars, the two China paradigms are able to reverberate across a much broader and more diverse audience. Precisely because of its wider appeal than some obscure theoretical formulations, a paradigm can obtain and prolong its seemingly paradigmatic status.

Of course, the discursive dominance of the two paradigms over the cultural and knowledge practice of representing China is far from total or complete, let alone unchallengeable. Nor can the vagaries of Western representations of China's rise be reduced to one paradigm or the other or both. Alternative ways of understanding China do exist outside of this paradigmatic duopoly. The recurring 'China collapse' thesis is one example, and the occasional reference to China as a model for the West may be another. [15] That said, the 'threat' and 'opportunity' paradigms remain two of the most powerful modes of representation in the 'China's rise' literature.

THE 'CHINA THREAT' PARADIGM

The 'China threat' is a fundamental image that casts China's rise and its international implications primarily in a negative, alarming, and threatening light. It is more than a particular argument, or a singular 'China threat theory', as many of its Chinese critics often call it. Rather, it represents a paradigm that, as a lasting normative concern and cognitive habit, both informs and lends coherence to otherwise divergent ways of looking at China in scholarly analysis, government documents, popular culture and mass media.

A good starting place to look for manifestations of the 'China threat' paradigm is mass media, which is often where shared intersubjectivity and normative concern—the foundation of a paradigm—are forged and converge, and where the cognitive habit is nurtured and put on regular display. As a columnist for *The Ottawa Sun* puts it: 'Watch the evening news or pick up a newspaper and you're almost certain to see something about China's many sins—economic and moral'. [16] One media fascination with China is particularly illustrative here. In March each year, when China's National People's Congress approves its annual budget, there is an all too predictable round of media coverage on China's military spending, with a spate of reports invariably sounding alarms on its double-digit expenditure increase and the lack of transparency. This particular discursive ritual is both a sign of the 'China threat' paradigm at work and a regular contribution to that paradigm. Thanks to this fundamental image, it is the Chinese military budget, not the much larger US military spending, that has been routinely perceived as an issue of international security concern.

This paradigm does not confine itself to military matters. As China's economic juggernaut continues to power ahead, the issues of Chinese trade practices, currency, and the safety standards of the 'Made in China' brand have all come under the purview of the 'China threat' discourse. The result is the representation of a manufacturing superpower that threatens not only Western jobs but also its sense of security and pride. This preoccupation with the China threat is immediately palpable through such sensational headlines as: 'Job Losses: Made in China', 'Inflation Made in China', 'Another Danger Made in China', 'Tracing a Poison's Global Path Back to China', 'Is China Trying to Poison Americans and Their Pets?', and 'China's Milestone, Our Millstone'. To a US Senator, the words 'Made in China' have become 'a warning label', all but reminiscent of Theodore Roosevelt's use of the word 'Chinese' as a derisive adjective in his political vocabulary.[17]

Looked through the 'China threat' paradigm, any societal disturbance or environmental problems in China may also take on a menacing quality. At the height of the SARS crisis, the front cover of the 5 May 2003 issue of *Time* Magazine (Asia) boasted literally the bold headline: 'SARS NATION', a not so subtle suggestion promptly reinforced by an adjacent picture of the Chinese national flag superimposed with an X-ray of lungs with pneumonia. Five years later, the 3 May 2008 issue of *The Economist*'s cover story ran the title 'Angry China', accompanied by a close-up illustration of a fierce, glaring-eyed dragon in a confronting colour of red. That story, in response to angry Chinese reactions to the violent protests against the international legs of the Beijing Olympics torch relay, sought to remind the China threat from the angle of Chinese nationalism. In both cases, a strong normative concern with the *China* threat came first, and the empirical concern with the actual threat of pandemic diseases or nationalism per se came second. Otherwise, it begs the question of why the 2009 outbreak of swine flu in the US did not generate a similarly alarming headline, or why the Beijing Olympics, even well before it was held, were compared almost exclusively with the 1936 Berlin Olympics, not with other Olympic Games.

Western public opinion provides another avenue to appreciate the 'China threat' paradigm in operation. The theme of China as a (potential) threat has been a regular fixture in China-related questionnaires. In a late 2007 survey entitled 'Hope and Fear: American and Chinese Attitudes Towards Each Other', about two-thirds of US respondents believed that China's emergence as a global economic power represented either a 'serious' or 'potential' threat to the US. On the military front, the proportion of the same views on China jumped to 75 per cent.[18] In early 2008, a Gallup poll of Americans revealed that China replaced North Korea as one of the top three US enemies. At the same time, the Harris survey for the London-based *Financial Times* showed that in the eyes of many Europeans, China was the biggest threat to global stability.[19]

For all their contribution to the 'China threat' paradigm, mass media and public opinion are only its most visible outlets. One cannot really appreciate the full depth of this paradigm without looking at the more analytical and intellectual domain of China watching in IR. It is no exaggeration to say that there is now a cottage industry devoted to the 'empirical' and theoretical analysis of China as a threat.[20] This more or less scholarly section of the 'China threat' paradigm can be categorised into two sub-paradigms: capability-based threat discourses and intention-based threat discourses.

Capability-based China Threat Discourses

One of the perennial questions in the 'China's rise' literature has been about Chinese power or capabilities. A 2008 Pentagon initiative termed Minerva called upon university academics to understand and deal with security threats to the US in the twenty-first century. Among those named issues, the Chinese military was listed as the number one concern, ahead of other threat candidates such as Iraq, terrorism, and Islamic fundamentalism. [21] As evidenced in numerous analyses of Chinese power and a vast body of literature on power transition in the context of China's rise, [22] structural realism is principally behind this focus on capabilities. From this theoretical vintage point, the distribution of power among states is the most important factor in understanding state behaviour, and the more powerful a state, the more likely it will pose a threat to the survival of other states.[23]

For some analysts, at the core of the China threat is its military power. China's double-digit increase in military expenditure, for example, forms the basis of Bernstein and Munro's argument in their influential book *The Coming Conflict with China*. Brushing aside the 'conservative' estimates of the US General Accounting Office, which put China's actual defence spending at two or three times the official figure, they believed

> that the multiple is much higher—indeed, that it is between ten and twenty times the official figure.... The International Institute of Strategic Studies in London in 1995 concluded that China's actual defense spending is at least four times greater than the official figure. If the People's Armed Police is added in, the IISS estimate would go up to a multiple of five. With a conservative calculation for purchasing power parity, we would double that again, arriving at a multiple of ten.[24]

In light of China's rapid rise and its alleged lack of transparency in Chinese military strategy, it may seem only natural for other countries to be concerned with the trajectory of Beijing's military build-up and for analysts to speculate on its military spending. Nevertheless, the very habit of multiplying Chinese official military budget figures by a factor of two, three, or even ten, is not so much a result of empirical research on Chinese military power as it is a footnote to the normative concern with China as a looming threat. This concern, for example, motivated US Congress to mandate the

Pentagon to publish annual reports on Chinese military power. First issued in 1997, those reports have almost invariably painted a picture of a growing military threat from Beijing. This American fixation on an individual country's military strength was not unprecedented, but the only precedent was in the heyday of the Cold War, when the Pentagon produced similar annual reports on the Soviet Union, its then archenemy.

Derived from a paradigmatic concern with the potential threat of China, the representation of its military power in turn reinforces the 'China threat' paradigm. Issued shortly after 'September 11', the Pentagon's 2001 *Quadrennial Defense Review Report* warned the emergence of 'a military competitor with a formidable resource base' in Asia. It did not specifically name China, but there is no mystery as to which country the Pentagon had in mind. By 2006, another *Quadrennial Defense Review Report* no longer bothered to avoid name-calling, clearly stating that 'Of the major and emerging powers, China has the greatest potential to compete militarily with the United States'.[25] In October 2008, a draft report prepared by the Defense Secretary's International Security Advisory Board (ISAB) Task Force— *China's Strategic Modernization*—insisted that 'Chinese military modernization is proceeding at a rate to be of concern even with the most benign interpretation of China's motivation'.[26]

A paradigm *qua* paradigm needs to be able to account for anomalies. An obvious anomaly for the capability-based 'China threat' paradigm is that if military capabilities are the sole criterion for threat assessment, the US would be more of a threat to China than the other way round. By many American military officials' own admission, China's military power remains modest when compared to the US. But under the 'China threat' paradigm, this 'anomaly' is either ignored, or easily circumvented by a focus on China's so-called 'asymmetric warfare capabilities', such as its so-called anti-access, area-denial (A2/AD) and cyber-espionage threats.[27]

Even if the China threat argument looks hollow in a military sense, it is able to renew its credibility in an economic context. For a start, China's economic rise seems to pose a threat in that it could have potentially disastrous resource, environmental and ecological consequences. As early as 1994, American environmentalist Lester Brown, in his famous article 'Who Will Feed China?', predicted that China's surging demand for food would dramatically increase the price of food worldwide.[28] Other observers note that as it industrialises, China will require a dramatically larger share of world resources, and place a huge strain on global energy supplies. It will then contribute significantly to pollution and global warming, and lead to the intensification of regional conflict over resources and energy, especially in places like Africa and Latin America.[29]

To many, the so-called 'China price' strategy of using cheap labour and products is at the core of the economic challenge posed by China. The China price, dubbed 'the three scariest words' in some quarters of the US industry,[30] is said to have, among other things, aggressively undercut competitors, caused massive job losses as well as increased US trade deficit and foreign debt. In February 2004, a bipartisan group of US senators argued that China's undervalued currency renminbi (RMB) has contributed to the loss of 2.6 million US manufacturing jobs.[31] Pennsylvania's Democratic senator, Arlen Specter, complained to 'Fox News Sunday' that 'We have a real problem with the Chinese.... They are very shrewd, and customarily they outmaneuver us. They take our jobs. They take our money, and then they lend it back to us and own a big part of America'.[32]

While some fall back on the old memories of the 'Yellow Peril' of Chinese coolies in nineteenth-century America to describe the new China threat,[33] University of California business professor Peter Navarro has coined a new-age terminology: 'weapons of mass production'. Writing amidst increasing disquiet about US trade deficit with China, Navarro cast almost every aspect of US-China economic relations as a military confrontation. A quick look at the contents of his book *The Coming China Wars* reveals such sensational phrases as 'Killing Us (and Them) Softly With Their Coal', 'The "Blood for Oil" Wars', 'The "New Imperialist" Wars and Weapons of Mass Construction', 'Of "Bloodheads," Gray Dragons, and Other "Ticking Time Bombs"', and 'How to Fight—And Win!—the Coming China Wars'.[34] Many Americans share Navarro's line of thinking. A Chinese company's bid to buy the American oil company Unocal in 2005, for example, was widely seen as a Manichaean struggle between China and the US. Republican congressman Dana Rohrabacher labelled the Unocal bid 'part of [China's] long-term strategy for domination', which he regarded as a far greater threat to America's freedom and prosperity than radical Islam.[35] American economist and commentator Paul Krugman, by no means a conservative hawk, compared this failed Chinese bid with Japan's buying spree in the US in the 1990s, except that he considered the Chinese challenge 'a lot more serious' than the Japanese one.

Notwithstanding China's still very low per capita GDP, its overtaking of Japan as the world's second largest economy has refuelled the speculation that China is tipped to surpass the US as the world's biggest economy (in purchasing-power-parity terms) as early as 2016.[36] Indeed, in a 2011 Pew survey, almost half (47 per cent) of Americans said that China was already the world's leading economic power, while just 31 per cent named the US.[37] The wide currency this inaccurate perception enjoys is telling. Through the omnipresent China threat lens, 'empirical facts' matter less than how the cognitive habit fears what China might turn out to be.

For still others, it is the military implications of China's economic rise that are most worrying. John Mearsheimer, a political scientist from the University of Chicago, argues that China 'would almost certainly use its wealth to build a mighty military machine' and 'would surely pursue regional hegemony'. Whether China becomes a democracy or remains an autocracy would not make much difference. And adding its vast population to the equation, Mearsheimer considers China to be the most powerful and dangerous threat the US has confronted to date.[38] Stefan Halper, a senior fellow at the Centre of International Studies at Cambridge University who served in the Nixon, Ford, and Reagan administrations, labelled China 'a gathering multi-dimensional threat' whose economic might will increasingly translate into formidable military power as its rise continues.[39]

Intention-focused China Threat Discourses

China's rapid rise in recent decades has given much credence to the capability-based approach. Still, it remains less than convincing so long as China has a long way to catch up with the US both militarily and economically. In this context, another approach turns attention to China's strategic intention. While capability-focused analysts such as Mearsheimer argue that intention does not matter much, this intention-based approach argues that how China decides to use its power, as well as the size of that power, is equally relevant.

One important variable in understanding China's strategic intention is regime type or political system. According to former US Secretary of State Condoleezza Rice, 'How a country treats its own people is a strong indication of how it will behave toward its neighbors'.[40] Here, Rice was clearly paraphrasing the gist of democratic peace theory, a theory which maintains that democratically organised political systems are more prone to peace and less inclined to go to war with other democracies.[41] By implication, non-democracies are more likely to use their power in an aggressive manner. 'Without democratization within, there is no basis for expecting more pacific behavior without', thus argues Denny Roy.[42] It is on this basis that Bernstein and Munro cast doubt on China's strategic intent and paint a picture of Chinese military adventurism:

> if the history of the last two hundred years is any guide, the more democratic countries become, the less likely they are to fight wars against each other. The more dictatorial they are, the more war prone they become. Indeed, if the current Beijing regime continues to engage in military adventurism—as it did in the Taiwan Strait in 1996—there will be a real chance of at least limited naval or air clashes with the United States.[43]

Widely regarded as a direct brainchild of the Chinese regime, Chinese nationalism is seen as another intention-related variable. The popular line of argument is that with communism roundly discredited after the Cold War, the Chinese Communist Party had to resort to nationalism as a common glue to hold the nation together and keep itself in power.[44] This state-sponsored nationalism, believed to be more virulent than civic nationalism in the West,[45] could make Chinese foreign and security policy more belligerent and less compromising.

Furthermore, Chinese authoritarianism itself seems to pose moral and ideological challenges abroad. For example, with its no-strings-attached aid policy, China is seen to have undone longstanding efforts of Western countries to promote democracy and good governance in places like Africa.[46] By acting 'as a model for dictators, juntas, and other undemocratic governments throughout the world—and, in all likelihood, a leading supporter of these regimes', China poses 'considerable problems for democratic values'.[47] So much so that Robert Kagan warns of the emergence of an alliance of autocracies and the return of the 'old competition between liberalism and autocracy'.[48]

Still another way of understanding Beijing's strategic intention is through culture. Although a cultural approach to Chinese foreign policy is not new, the late Samuel Huntington's 'Clash of Civilizations' thesis brought it to a new height. Treating China as one monolithic civilisational sphere of Confucianism, he asserted that

> U.S. conflicts with China covered a much broader range of issues than those with Japan, including economic questions, human rights, Tibet, Taiwan, the South China Sea, and weapons proliferation. On almost no major policy issue did the United States and China share common objectives. The differences go across the board.[49]

In the face of such a profound cultural cleavage, Huntington argued that China's rise would inevitably pose a challenge to the US. Nothing, not even its eventual democratisation, would be able to hold it back. First of all, given its cultural tradition, a democratic China was seen as rather unlikely. In fact, he saw 'Confucian democracy' as an oxymoron or 'a contradiction in terms'.[50] Even if China did become a democracy, he feared the paradoxical effect of democratisation, arguing that democratisation in non-Western societies may actually strengthen nativist and anti-Western political forces.[51] In brief, the cultural difference between Confucian China and the Christian West almost predetermines China's ill intention towards the West.

Martin Jacques, author of *When China Rules the World*, provides an updated version of this Huntingtonian thesis. A keen British China observer and commentator, Jacques believes that the main sources of the China threat are not political or military, but cultural. In order to decipher Chinese foreign behaviour, he argues that it is necessary to 'make sense of what has made China what it is today, how it has evolved, where the Chinese come from, and how they see themselves'.[52] From this perspective, Jacques traces Chinese nationalism back to its Middle Kingdom mentality. He believes that this imperial Sinocentrism, together with China's racial, demographic and historical uniqueness as well as its newfound power, makes it the next hegemon seeking to impose its own values and priorities onto the world.[53]

Also from a cultural standpoint, Harvard professor Alastair Iain Johnston's book *Cultural Realism* focuses on Chinese strategic culture as a set of ideational factors in the understanding of China's foreign intention. To Johnston, although China has a Confucian-Mencian tradition of accommodation in its dealing with other cultures, the essence of its strategic culture is what is known in the West as the *parabellum* (prepare for war) paradigm. This strategic paradigm believes that warfare is a relatively constant feature in international relations, that stakes in conflicts with an adversary are zero-sum in nature, and that the use of force is the most efficacious means of dealing with threat. To the extent that China's strategic culture is defined largely by these beliefs, China's rise does not inspire confidence for peace.[54]

These different approaches to China's strategic intentions notwithstanding, their conclusions are remarkably similar, that is, the repercussions of China's rise are uncertain at best and menacing at worst. Such widespread anxiety over China's intentions is not only palpable in the intellectual community, but also shared by officials in a succession of US administrations. Former Deputy Secretary of State Robert Zoellick summarised it well when he referred to 'a cauldron of anxiety about China': 'Many countries hope China will pursue a "Peaceful Rise," but none will bet their future on it'.[55] The Obama administration's *Quadrennial Defense Review Report* and *Nuclear Posture Review Report* do not directly name China as a threat or strategic competitor. But in suggesting that the lack of transparency and the nature of China's military development and decision-making processes 'raise legitimate questions about its future conduct and intentions within Asia and beyond',[56] both reports cast a wary eye on China.

Among China observers, there has been a debate on whether capabilities or intentions are the primary determinants in Chinese foreign policy-making. Overall, however, both approaches help reinforce the 'China threat' paradigm. From the outset, this paradigm has set certain normative parameters for China watching. These two strands of the threat discourse, underpinned by various analytical frameworks and empirical analysis, have rarely deviated from this fundamental China image. Their scholarly-sanctioned representations feed into media and popular imaginings of China, which together help sustain the far-reaching influence of the 'China threat' paradigm.

THE 'CHINA OPPORTUNITY' PARADIGM

The book *China's Democratic Future*, authored by the journalist turned academic Bruce Gilley, opens with a detailed account of a vivid scene of historic significance at the Gate of Heavenly Peace (Tiananmen), the symbolic heart of Chinese politics. In a bright autumn morning, right below the rostrum of Tiananmen where Mao Zedong stood and announced the founding of the People's Republic in 1949, the huge portrait of this founding leader is in the process of being taken off; the Chinese Communist Party has just lost power and Mao's portrait now becomes a symbol of a by-gone era.[57] This of course is not yet a reality; it is an exercise of the author's creative imagination. Nevertheless, perhaps inspired by the fall of both the Berlin Wall and the statue of Saddam Hussein, Gilley seems to have little doubt that what he conjures up is no pure fantasy. As if he had just witnessed history-in-the-making first-hand, he claims with reassuring authority that after nearly a century of trials and tribulations in China's modern political history, 'the prospects for the creation and maintenance of a democracy in China are now better than ever. We can already envision how it will happen and where it will lead'.[58] Not dissimilar to the missionary conviction that the 'heathen' Chinese were ripe for Christian conversion in the nineteenth century, the central message of Gilley's book is that China presents a great opportunity for democratic transformation in the twenty-first century.

Gilley is not alone in this optimism. Inside the gate of Tiananmen, president and CEO of the Washington-based Center for Strategic and International Studies, John Hamre, while on holiday in China, found himself standing in the middle of the Forbidden City, drinking a Starbucks green tea frappuccino and talking on his cell phone to his father in South Dakota. This, he wrote, 'was not the China of my imagination' but 'an exciting China, full of energy, promise, and opportunity'.[59] Both Gilley's and Hamre's visions of China, I suggest, are emblematic of another powerful paradigmatic tradition: China as an opportunity. Like the 'threat' paradigm, the 'China opportunity' theme permeates a large array of the 'China's rise' literature. Shared by different sectors of the China watching community, this paradigm can be divided into three often-interrelated sub-paradigms: the economic opportunity (trade), the political opportunity (democratisation), and the international opportunity (integration). First let us turn to the notion of China as an economic opportunity.

'One Billion Customers': The Economic Opportunity

One of the most enduring images of the China opportunity is the fabled China market. Ever since Marco Polo's eye-opening travels to the East in the thirteenth century, China, where gold was allegedly discovered in abundance,[60] has never failed to enthuse intellectuals, missionaries, explorers, as well as merchants. In the wake of Western industrial expansion in the nineteenth century, the country was perceived as a giant market 'holding out greater possibilities for trade than any other part of the world'.[61] 'How much of our tobacco might be there chewed, in place of opium!' exclaimed one excited American congressman, alluding to the then lucrative opium trade in China enjoyed by the British.[62] This long-running China market dream, never quite coming true before,[63] now finds a new lease of life amidst China's unrelenting economic growth. As the pace of its urbanisation accelerates and its living standards continue to improve, China seems to be, at long last, showing its great market potential. From food to luxury goods, and from software to motor vehicles, China has become synonymous with 'one billion customers'.[64]

Perhaps no other country in the West understands this economic opportunity better than Australia. Thanks to a China-led resource boom, Australia has enjoyed its best terms of trade since the middle of the twentieth century.[65] Relishing at her country's unique position to reap the phenomenal benefits offered by a new China, Australian Prime Minister Julia Gillard was eager to declare that 'Australia hasn't been here before'.[66]

Similarly upbeat assessments of the China market are continuously churned out by numerous multinational corporations such as Microsoft, Coca Cola, McDonalds, and KFC. David Novak, chief executive of Yum! which owns KFC, said he envisaged eventually having more than 20,000 restaurants in China. 'We're in the first inning of a nine-inning ball game in China', a beaming Novak told investors at a conference.[67] On a different aspect of the China market, the equally excited and 'pleased' Kodak Company Chairman George Fisher claimed that 'There was (and is) no base so large, no market so promising, for picture taking.... China is poised to become the largest photo market in the world'.[68]

Back in the nineteenth century, British industrialists calculated that if every Chinese man added just one inch to his shirttail, the mills of Lancashire could be kept busy for a generation. Nearly two centuries later, during US Commerce Secretary Ron Brown's trip in August 1994, Joe Gorman, the chairman of TRW Inc. (America's biggest manufacturer of auto parts) similarly calculated that 'If China were by the year 2010 or 2020 to have as many autos as the current per capita auto population of Germany today, there would be 500 million autos'.[69] Such an optimistic mindset seems irresistibly infectious. Ted Fishman, the author of the best-seller *China Inc.*, postulates that if mainland China increased its per capita consumption of food made from soy to just half the amount in Taiwan, which consumes ten times as much, it would need to import an amount equal to 60 per cent of the soybeans produced on American farms.[70] Never mind that some of the calculations are exaggerated or unrealistic, many observers believe that this modern-day El Dorado, whichever way we look at it, still easily dwarfs any other markets. Gorman again: 'Even if I am only half right or a quarter right, China is a huge market'.[71] To Fishman, 'Not all, or most, or even a third or fifth, of its population needs to reach the middle class for the world to chase its markets—a mere 50 million families is enough'.[72]

Besides its enormous consumer markets, China's growing reputation as the world's workshop adds another dimension to the China economic bonanza. With its low wages, first-rate infrastructure, and the benefits of cheap transportation costs and modern telecommunication, China promises to be an ideal production base, investment destination, and export platform in the global supply chains. In explaining this opportunity, British commentator Will Hutton argues that China's world factory status makes it an excellent destination for outsourcing, a practice which not only precludes the rise of a Chinese competitor, but also offers an advantage over a company's existing Western rivals.[73] Also, offshoring to China enables Western businesses to free up talent, machinery, and capital to higher-value industries and cutting-edge R&D, thus allowing them to capture even greater profit margins.[74] All the while, as if the China opportunity were something for everyone, it is seen as offering Western consumers a bonanza in low-cost 'Made in China' products sold in such discount chains as Wal-Mart and Bunnings, helping create what many call 'a shoppers' paradise' in many parts of the world.[75] 'On balance', thus claim the authors of *China: The Balance Sheet*, 'China's economic rise creates an opportunity for the United States and the global economy more broadly'.[76]

Democracy for China: A Political and Moral Opportunity

For many observers, the China opportunity means more than just profits and market shares, but also its potential for political liberalisation and democratisation. Indeed, these two opportunities are believed to be inextricably linked: economic development and political change go hand in hand.[77] Whilst China threat advocates tend to emphasise the economy-military nexus, some 'opportunity' proponents, such as Henry Rowen, see instead a 'wealth-democracy connection': 'the wealthier a country, the more (Western style) freedoms its people enjoy'. Rowen reassures us that this connection is not just a European artefact, but applies to China as well.[78]

This connection seems obvious on at least two fronts. At the official level, The government's economic reform and opening up policy, in an attempt to stimulate economic growth, may inadvertently open the gate for political change.[79] Perceiving a process of 'creeping democratisation' in China,

Minxin Pei once argued that China's political system was gradually moving towards a form of 'soft authoritarianism'.[80] Throughout much of the 1980s, many Western observers believed that they were witnessing an unprecedented shift in China's political landscape following its economic reform. Conservative commentator William Safire wrote in the *New York Times* that the 'big event of 1984' was the 'rejection of Marxism and embrace of capitalism by the Government of a billion Chinese'.[81] In an article titled 'China's Quiet Revolution', Donald S. Zagoria suggested that China was undergoing sweeping changes in economic, legal, political, ideological, cultural, and foreign policy areas. What followed, he argued, was a virtual dismantling of many Maoist institutions and practices and the beginning of a movement towards a more open society.[82] Until the shock of the Tiananmen tragedy in June 1989, it had been widely held that China was leading the way in rapid political liberalisation, in contrast to the then stagnant Soviet and Eastern European Communist bloc.[83] Even Ronald Reagan once famously referred to China as the 'so-called Communist China'.[84]

The faith in the potential of the Chinese leadership to move in a more liberal direction did not die with its Tiananmen crackdown. After meeting and dining with Chinese President Jiang Zemin on an official visit to China in 1998, US President Bill Clinton wrote in his memoir *My Life* that 'The more time I spent with Jiang, the more I liked him.... Even though I didn't always agree with him, I became convinced that he believed he was changing China as far as he could, and in the right direction'.[85] For some, an unmistakable sign of the Chinese regime's growing openness is the fact that the ruling Communist Party amended its constitution for the first time to allow private business people to join.[86] The significance of this change seems self-evident. In the words of Francis Fukuyama, 'A totalitarian state that permits an extensive private sector is by definition no longer totalitarian'.[87]

Another aspect of this wealth-democracy linkage is the emergence of a Chinese middle class and civil society associated with economic development. An increasingly powerful middle class, as the argument goes, would be the most reliable agent for political change. Hutton argues that 'the more China grows, the more likely it is to develop its middle class and an appetite for institutional changes'.[88] En route to his 2005 visit to China, George W. Bush made a similar point in his speech in the Japanese city of Kyoto. Citing Taiwan as a successful example of this time-honoured wealth-democracy nexus, Bush was convinced that the richer the Chinese become, the more likely they would agitate for political reform.[89] Echoing her boss on this point, Condoleezza Rice once remarked that 'The Chinese Communists are living on borrowed time; economic liberalization is going to create pressure for political freedom'.[90]

Despite the 1989 Tiananmen setbacks, the development of the middle class has continued to be cited as the best hope for a democratic China. For Fukuyama, the driving force behind the Tiananmen protests in 1989 was none other than the children of this middle class, who were no longer content with economic freedom without political liberty.[91] After Tiananmen, Californian Democratic Representative Nancy Pelosi introduced a bill to make it easier for Chinese students in the US to extend their stay and work. President George Bush Snr. agreed with Pelosi, for he in effect implemented the same protections afforded to those students as would have been mandated in the Pelosi bill. Nevertheless he vetoed the bill.[92] In their co-authored memoir *A World Transformed*, George Bush and Brent Scowcroft explain that decision this way: 'The [ongoing] exposure of Chinese students to American values was one of the great hopes for future internal change in China'. Had the Pelosi bill been approved, they feared that Beijing would retaliate by cutting off all student exchanges, thus closing this valuable window of opportunity for change.[93]

While continued exposure to Western culture helps transform China's younger generations, Chinese culture itself is seen as no essential barrier to democracy. Refuting those who see China as either unprepared for or culturally unsuited to democracy, Andrew Nathan maintains that history gives Chinese democrats ample reasons for courage and hope. As he explains:

> In the past few Chinese really wanted democracy. Today many of them do. In earlier years, authoritarianism seemed more likely to solve China's pressing problems—weakness and division. Today, democracy seems more likely to solve the pressing problems—dictatorship and political stagnation. In the past, political institutions lacked authority and administrative capability. Today the Chinese bureaucracy is large and strong. The regime's legitimacy is compromised, but many of its institutional procedures seem well-accepted. The situation, then, is different, and more favorable to democracy.[94]

For Nathan, economic development may not automatically usher in political change, but 'there are forces in the intelligentsia, professions, and the administrative bureaucracy working for human rights and a Chinese form of democracy'.[95] Thus, given time, it is believed that China's process of democratisation 'would promptly accelerate'.[96] Larry Diamond of the Hoover Institution went so far as to predict that 'If China can negotiate these treacherous steps of political liberalization in the next decade, it will be poised for a peaceful transition to democracy a decade or two later'.[97] Encouraged by China's quick response to the Sichuan earthquakes in 2008, *New York Times* columnist Nicholas Kristof, while acknowledging China's uneven record in political liberalisation, remains optimistic that China is slowly moving away from authoritarianism.[98]

A Responsible Stakeholder: The Opportunity for Global Integration

In addition to the wealth-democracy linkage, some observers believe that those opportunities in turn set the stage for integrating China into the international system. As China becomes more open economically and politically, it holds the promise of becoming a 'responsible stakeholder', a term coined by Zoellick. In his remarks to the National Committee on US-China Relations in September 2005, Zoellick noted that as a responsible stakeholder, China would share with the US a common interest in sustaining an open international economic system that had proven crucial to the prosperity of both countries and the world at large.[99]

While the Chinese initially struggled to find a Chinese equivalent to the English word 'stakeholder', this 'responsible stakeholder' rendition of the China opportunity instantly strikes a responsive chord in Western foreign policy circles. For many observers, a more responsible China bodes well for the prospect of 'locking China into an American-dominated international order'.[100] Three interrelated factors seem to underpin this optimistic assessment: China's deepening economic interdependence, its transition to democracy, and its cognitive learning of international norms and rules through a process of socialisation and norm diffusion.

First, China's economic development, as well as generating commercial opportunities, helps bolster its integration with the global economy, thus providing a strong incentive for it to behave more responsibly on the world stage. Drawing implicitly on nineteenth-century liberals' faith in the peaceful effect of commerce, many pundits are confident that Beijing's focus on economic development and trade signals a convergence of Sino-American commercial and national interests.[101] For instance, as the Chinese become as dependent on the flow of Persian Gulf oil as Americans and Europeans have, it is argued that a common interest in open sea lanes may arise, thereby brightening the prospect for cooperation.[102] In this context, Susan Shirk, former Deputy Assistant Secretary of State responsible for US relations with China, predicts that Beijing cannot but behave 'like a cautious, responsible power... intent on avoiding conflicts that would disrupt economic growth and social stability'.[103] In his characteristically playful style, *New York Times* columnist Thomas Friedman calls this whole phenomenon the 'Dell theory of conflict prevention'. The gist of his theory is this: the economic interdependence between China and its East Asian neighbours through the global supply chain will help overcome the historical and geopolitical rivalry between China and Taiwan as well as that between China and Japan. As he approvingly quoted from a senior official at Dell, contrary to some received wisdom, this supply chain makes the amiable co-existence of a strong Japan and a strong China possible.[104]

Second, with Chinese democratisation, there appears to be a better chance for China's emergence as a peaceful player in international relations. In the words of Diamond, 'a China governed by the more comprehensive architecture of democracy... would be a more responsible regional neighbor and global actor'.[105] For Gilley, a China pursuing a 'democratic foreign policy' would be 'a salutary new force for global justice, peace, and development'.[106] Almost claiming that a democratic China would offer a panacea for regional stability, Gilley then goes on to list a whole range of thorny international problems which would easily go away, such as its testy relations with the US, the Taiwan impasse, territorial claims in the South China Sea, border disputes with India and Russia, and the ethnic tensions in Tibet and Xinjiang.

Meanwhile, according to a particular cottage industry in the field of Chinese foreign policy, the country's socialisation into multilateral international institutions, norms, and regimes further enhances its 'global commitments and responsibility'.[107] In a popular attempt to gauge the level of Beijing's 'acceptance of the legitimacy of the current international economic and political system',[108] scholars have surveyed almost every aspect of China's engagement with international institutions, ranging from its relations with the United Nations to its participation in the regimes of international trade and investment, security and arms control, environmental protection, energy, telecommunications, as well as human rights.[109] And typically most of their findings are encouraging. For example, Economy and Oksenberg maintain that overall 'China has become less distinctive. Its foreign policy calculus increasingly resembles that of other major powers'. Hence their verdict that it 'has rejoined the world'.[110]

As China emerges as a responsible stakeholder on the world stage, it is believed that it will provide further economic and political opportunities. For example, Beijing's legal and commercial reforms in accordance with World Trade Organization (WTO) requirements would make China an ideal place for Americans to 'contemplate doing business or expand existing business', once claimed Robert A. Kapp, who served as president of the US-China Business Council during the period of China's entry into the WTO.[111] A number of US officials echoed Kapp's optimism. Arguing for the case of granting China's accession to this global multilateral trade regime, then Secretary of State Madeleine Albright insisted that China's WTO membership 'would give the United States more access to China's market, boost our exports, reduce our trade deficit, and create new, well-paying jobs'.[112] Similarly, Clinton's national security adviser Samuel Berger saw a positive feedback loop between China's global integration and domestic political change. As he put it, 'Just as NAFTA [the North American Free Trade Agreement] membership eroded the economic base of one-party rule in Mexico, WTO membership... can help do the same in China'.[113]

This confidence in China's transformation into a responsible stakeholder has been supported by two influential perspectives: neoliberal institutionalism and constructivism. Both approaches assume that growing interdependence and integration enables states to learn international norms and redefine their national interests and identities. For many, China represents an exemplar case of such cognitive learning. For example, by looking at its institutional integration process, Thomas Robinson provides an interesting analysis of the evolution of Chinese attitudes towards the notion of interdependence. He notes that throughout much of the 1990s, Chinese statements became increasingly favourable to this notion, thereby raising hope that, given time, China could be eventually converted to 'full interdependence' and 'end up with the same domestic structure (market economy) and foreign policy (peace and internationalism) as other developed nations'.[114] In the security realm, a systematic study of China's socialisation by Alastair Iain Johnston notes a similar trend. Between 1980 and 2000, 'Chinese leaders adopted more cooperative and potentially self-constraining commitments to security institutions'. This development, according to Johnston, testifies to both the constitutive influence of international institutions and the cognitive learning capacity of China's foreign policy makers.[115] Coupled with his study on the attitudes of a liberalising Chinese middle class towards world affairs, Johnston has provided a largely optimistic assessment on the prospect of China becoming a responsible stakeholder.[116]

'WE ARE ALL PANDA HEDGERS': THE AMBIVALENCE OF THE BIFOCAL LENS

This chapter has briefly surveyed the main arguments and theoretical underpinnings of the 'China threat' and 'China opportunity' paradigms. By way of conclusion, I should stress three points. First, to reiterate the obvious, this is not a comprehensive survey of China studies in the West. At most, it is only a snapshot of some recent Western writings on China's rise in the field of international relations. To equate the latter with Western understanding of China as a whole would be misleading, and certainly that is not this author's intention.

Second, by singling out these two paradigms, I do not seek to pigeonhole China observers into two pre-existing ideological or scholarly camps. Some analysts, motivated by the belief in either moral clarity or the supposedly timeless wisdom of power politics, do subscribe to some sharp images of the China threat. Likewise, some starry-eyed business leaders may often see China as little more than an economic opportunity. But overall these paradigms do not correspond neatly with two clearly-defined, discrete groups of observers or two homogeneous bodies of quintessential literature. The

'China threat' discourse often transcends the political divides between the conservative right and progressive left, and resonates with defence industrialists and human rights activists alike. Similarly, the 'China opportunity' paradigm is not held exclusively by any particular category of people, but is shared by a diverse group of observers of various political persuasions.

Third, to the extent that these fundamental images represent two different cognitive frameworks within which to understand China's rise, they may be treated as rival paradigms, which 'see different things when they look from the same point in the same direction'.[117] But even so, they are not mutually exclusive, incompatible, or incommensurable. As Richard J. Bernstein argues, 'There is always some overlap between rival paradigms—overlap of observations, concepts, standards, and problems. If there were no such overlap, rational debate and argumentation between proponents of rival paradigms would not be possible'.[118] In fact, a bifocal lens that encompasses both paradigms has been characteristic of mainstream Western literature on China's rise.

Often dreading and marvelling at China's economic rise at the same time, the business world is clearly prone to this bifocal framework, as trade magazines and newsletters are saturated with endless analyses of the China 'threat' and 'opportunity'. William Callahan has documented how the bifocal lens is deployed by business analysts and security experts to understand the phenomenon of 'Greater China' as both a danger of China's imperial expansion and an opportunity of the newest version of capitalist utopia.[119] Sometimes even the same observer subscribes to both imageries. The CNN commentator and anchor Lou Dobbs is a case in point. A staunch defender of American jobs and author of bestseller *Exporting America*, Dobbs lashed out at those US companies who moved their production to China, a country which, in his view, was a source of threat to the American economy and job security. But on the other hand, as an investment adviser, Dobbs had no qualms about recommending his clients to buy shares of the very companies that have established a presence in China (and India). Consequently, Dobbs's China was both an economic threat and opportunity.[120]

In the scholarly community, the bifocal lens is equally palpable. As mentioned above, on the one hand, Johnston perceives a China threat through an analysis of Chinese strategic culture, but on the other hand, he seems to believe in the malleability of Chinese interests and identity through socialisation. Drawing on a constructivist approach, he in fact sees no contradiction between these two arguments. Nor do William Kristol and Robert Kagan find it incompatible to believe at once in the China threat and in its opportunity for regime change. In a way, just as the missionaries' enthusiasm for the salvation of the Chinese heathens was often prompted by the very belief in the Chinese as great sinners, Kristol and Kagan's hope for China's political transformation is made more imperative not despite, but precisely because of their fear of China as a political and military threat.[121] Indeed, it is now difficult to find a work which does not treat China as both a challenge and an opportunity, even though most would lean towards one or the other end of the spectrum.[122]

Even policy-makers who normally favour clear-cut, unambiguous images seem to have largely avoided an either/or assessment. For instance, distancing himself from the 'strategic competitor' rhetoric of his early days in office, George W. Bush later called relations with China 'complex', in the sense that China was not just a potential threat, but also presented opportunities for cooperation, such as in the 'War on Terror'. Zoellick, best known for his preference for engaging China, was similarly ambivalent, as his 'responsible stakeholder' speech can attest. Even as analysts and policy-makers continue to effortlessly invoke such seemingly dichotomous terms as 'engagement' and 'containment' or binary questions of whether China will emerge as a partner or strategic rival, their conclusions are rarely one way or the other.[123] In this sense, the China-watching community seems to have come a long way since Harry Harding lamented more than two decades ago that 'We appear unable to see China as a complex society, in which some features are worthy of approval and others demand criticism'.[124]

Such apparent sophistication in China watching may prompt one to wonder whether it is still plausible to speak of the two China paradigms in the first place. Could they just be this author's analytical straw men? They are not. The various combinations of threat and opportunity in Western imaginings of China's rise testify to the very power of these two paradigms as the outer limits of China representation. As just noted, together they form a bifocal lens and provide an enduring ambivalent framework for China literacy. In a classic study of American attitudes towards China first published in 1958, Harold Isaacs noted the simultaneous presence of two powerful scratches on Americans' minds: a despicable China and an admirable China. As he put it astutely, 'In the long history of our associations with China, these two sets of images rise and fall, move in and out of the center of people's minds over time, never wholly displacing each other, always coexisting...'.[125] Today, one could easily substitute these scratches with the two China paradigms, and understand how, now as then, China is viewed with profound ambivalence. Speaking of this contemporary China ambivalence, what Ian Bremmer calls the 'panda hedgers' comes to mind.[126] 'Panda huggers' and 'dragon slayers' continue to exist, of course. But more often than not, these two groups are not as mutually exclusive as their stark appellations seem to suggest. In any case, both paradigms have been integral to contemporary Western understanding of China's rise. At a given time or in a single piece of writing on China, a particular imagery may be more pronounced. But as a whole, Western representations of China's rise have been characterised by this enduring ambivalence, a topic to which the next chapter will turn.

3. Of fears and fantasies: neocolonial desire in Western self/Other imagination

> *We do not see things as they are; we see things as we are.*
>
> The Talmud

> *A safe life requires safe truths. The strange and the alien remain unexamined, the unknown becomes identified as evil, and evil provokes hostility—recycling the desire for security.*
>
> James Der Derian[1]

> *A wide variety of Americans looked toward China through the lenses of their major institutions and saw not China but, as in a magic mirror, a flattering vision of themselves.*
>
> Richard Madsen[2]

CHINA WATCHING AS A MODERN WESTERN SELF-IMAGINATION

The rise of China is often understood in the West through a bifocal, threat-cum-opportunity lens. In this chapter, I want to engage with these two China paradigms, not on their own theoretical or empirical terms, but rather by asking why this bifocal lens persists in China watching and what it can tell us. At first glance, the two paradigms seem to have told us a great deal about China: inter alia, its economic rise, its various challenges, and its potentials for trade, political change, and global convergence. For many, not only does this sophisticated conceptual framework capture the complexity and uncertainty of China as a rising great power, but it also lays the foundation for a sound hedging strategy in dealing with it. Predicated on both the threat and opportunity paradigms, hedging has now replaced engagement and containment as the default China policy in many Western capitals.[3]

Certainly, the 'threat' and 'opportunity' paradigms are not total misconceptions or bias. They do reflect certain elements of truth in what can be loosely called 'Chinese reality'. However, these representations tell us not just something about China's rise, but also something about the West. In fact, they reveal more about the latter than about the country they set out to describe. When these paradigms do say something about China, in the main it has been about China's Otherness, which again is useful mostly for asserting a particular Western self. As a consequence, just as the Flowers of Wonderland rely on a 'flower/weed' framework to make sense of Alice, the ambivalent bifocal lens of threat/opportunity about China is highly autobiographical. Its dominance in China watching has less to do with 'what China is' than with China watchers' own situatedness in certain Western self-imagination.

The claim of scholarly work as autobiographical writing has been a familiar one. In a searching critique of anthropological discourse, Johannes Fabian notes that 'The object's present is founded in the writer's past. In that sense, facticity itself, that cornerstone of scientific thought, is autobiographic'. As he explains:

> When it is said that primitives are *stolid* this translates as "I never got close enough to see them excited, enthusiastic, or perturbed." When we say that "they are born with rhythm" we mean "we never saw them grow, practice, learn." And so on and so forth. All statements about others are paired with the observer's experience. [4]

Thus, in the apparently innocent writing about the other, there is more often than not some unspoken statement(s) about the writing self. Edward Said, Ashis Nandy, James Clifford, and Clifford Geertz, among others, have all exposed the autobiographical nature of writing, art collection, or studies of other societies. Geertz argues that 'All ethnography is part philosophy, and a good deal of the rest is confession'. Once you know what an anthropologist 'thinks he himself is', says Geertz, then 'you know in general what sort of thing he is going to say about whatever tribe he happens to be studying'.[5] And the reverse seems true also. 'Tell me what you are afraid of', writes Dominique Moïse, 'and I will tell you who you are'.[6]

To the extent that we are now quite familiar with what sort of thing the West has often said about China (thanks to the 'China's rise' literature), we should be able to infer from such China observations how the West thinks of itself. Western studies of China's rise, for all their alleged objectivity, are essentially about self-fashioning. Back in the 1950s, Isaacs stated that 'By examining the images we hold, say, of the Chinese and Indians, we can learn a great deal about Chinese and Indians, *but mostly we learn about ourselves...*'.[7] More recently, Jeffrey N. Wasserstrom suggested that the various positive and negative fantasies projected onto China 'reveal more about our own hopes and anxieties than they do about people living across the Pacific'.[8] If so, then the ensuing (but little-asked) questions should be: How, and what, do the 'China threat' and 'China opportunity' paradigms tell us about the Western self? What exactly are those 'hopes and anxieties'? And do they matter in Sino-Western interaction?

Simply put, these paradigms reveal what Bhabha and Young have called the 'colonial desire' of the West. The 'China threat' paradigm bears the stamp of Western fears whereas the 'opportunity' paradigm represents a specific case of Western fantasies. Together, their bifocal representation of China today is a specific mirror image of the longstanding fears and fantasies of Western (neo)colonial desire in the West's ongoing encounters with its Others (formally colonised or not). In this sense, the ambivalent China imageries—in terms of both threat and opportunity—are not especially China-specific and reveal relatively little about their 'object' per se.

To be sure, the autobiographical function of these China paradigms, as shall be illustrated shortly, is largely indirect and unconscious. Their implicit autobiographical messages are conveyed mainly through their more explicit constructions of a Chinese Other. Against such an Other, what the West is or is not can be assumed, even though the West is rarely in direct view.

IN FEAR OF CHINA: THE 'CHINA THREAT' PARADIGM IN WESTERN/AMERICAN COLONIAL DESIRE

The West has been imagining itself in various ways for centuries, if not longer, a complex subject which no doubt warrants a separate study.[9] But here I argue that the West as a modern project is modelled ultimately on an image of the modern knowing subject, who is defined by a desire for certainty and a will to truth. With this fundamental self-understanding, the West could not only feel certain about itself, but also exercise its reason and authority over an objective and knowable world 'out there'. As Charles William Maynes notes, the US, since the times of Theodore Roosevelt and Woodrow Wilson, has been convinced 'that we know the way—politically and economically—and that therefore we have an obligation, if not also a right, to lead others to a better future'.[10] In this sense, the will to truth and certainty has been central to the West's search for identity and power. The inevitable existence of uncertainty and inscrutability in nature and the outside world then becomes a standing threat to the identity and security of this modern self. At one level, the knowing subject may find refuge in fear as an emotional substitute for certainty. In other words, 'What we do not know we fear'.[11] Through fear, the unknown world becomes at least a known unknown (to borrow former US Defense Secretary Donald Rumsfeld's parlance), or a negative form of certainty in terms of Otherness, danger, and threat. Thus understood, threat is not an object out there, but a necessary corollary of the Western desire for absolute certainty and security. Even Kristol and Kagan readily admit that their much-feared 'present danger' 'has no name. It is not to be found in any single strategic adversary.... It is a danger, to be sure, of our own devising'.[12]

The China Threat as a Reflection of the Western Self-imagination

The self-imagination as the modern knowing subject affords the West a sense of scientific and moral authority. At the same time, it also justifies its need for imperial expansion and strategic dominance. Both the European Union's (EU) self-identity as a 'Normative Power Europe' and the US's God-given right to military supremacy and global leadership can be understood in this context. Indeed, for neoconservatives, the US, a quintessential Western society, is entitled to both moral clarity and military hegemony. However, as soon as the US stakes its self-identity on 'universal dominion' and absolute security worldwide,[13] its 'encounters' with numerous threats becomes a logical necessity.

The China threat is a product of precisely such encounters and self-imagination. Taking global hegemony in general and dominance in Asia in particular as part and parcel of American self-identity, one would 'naturally' treat China's regional influence as a threat; it can hardly be otherwise. But this is a challenge above all to the latter's expansionist strategic self-imagination and the certainty and continuity it entails.[14] As Huntington reasoned, 'Chinese hegemony will reduce American and Western influence [there] and compel the United States to accept what it has historically attempted to prevent: domination of a key region of the world by another power'.[15] Thanks to this longstanding American self-imagery, it is fair to say that much of the China threat is imagined as well. The much-feared Chinese 'string of pearls' strategy is a case in point. Describing China's alleged ambition of establishing a series of naval bases along various strategic choke points from Southeast Asia to eastern Africa, the term is nowhere to be seen in China's military playbook. Rather, it is mostly the work of US strategic imagination, first used in an internal report titled *Energy Futures in Asia* commissioned by the US Department of Defense.[16]

In Europe where collective self-identity is constructed less on the basis of military strength, the China threat does not figure as prominently as it does in the eyes of American strategic planners. Indeed, in 2009, Kagan expressed his displeasure at what he saw as Europe's indifference to the proliferation of military threats. Though not explicitly acknowledging the central role of self-identity in the construction of threat, he nevertheless correctly attributed their divergent threat perceptions to the different ways in which the US and Europe identify themselves. As he wrote:

> If Europe's strategic culture today places less value on hard power and military strength and more value on such soft-power tools as economics and trade, isn't it partly because Europe is militarily weak and economically strong? Americans are quicker to acknowledge the existence of threats, even to perceive them where others may not see any, because they can conceive of doing something to meet those threats.[17]

No longer primarily identifying itself in military terms, contemporary Europe now prides itself on being a normative or civic power, home to such universal values as human rights, democracy and good governance. As a result, it sees the China difference both as an opportunity for political change and an ideological challenge to the teleological certainty of the European self. Of course, moral clarity is not unique to Europe, but is integral to the US self-imagination as well. As such, in addition to the fear of China's strategic ambition, Washington is similarly ambivalent about the opportunity and threat of the Chinese Other. Through the same prisms of democracy and modernisation, Americans constantly 'found China lacking' or even threatening. Nancy Bernkopf Tucker rightly argues that 'Unless the United States changes [the moral parameters of its political self-imagination], that conclusion will not change'.[18] In other words, its fear of China has less to do with China's difference per se than with the particular way in which the Western self is constructed. If there *is* a China threat, its menace lies primarily in its perceived psychological 'disruption' of the lingering Western/American colonial desire about how the world should be run and about how history should progress.[19]

No doubt, some would protest that the 'China threat' conclusion stands on the firm ground of realism, and has nothing to do with the way the West identifies itself. For example, according to Mearsheimer, in a world of anarchy, 'states can never be certain about the intentions of other states',[20] and therefore have to treat each other as a potential threat. Yet, I would argue that such an insatiable demand for transparency from others is itself a telltale sign of the Western quest for certainty, security, and identity as the modern knowing subject. Similarly, the realist first-image of human nature, which is often implicitly invoked in the explanation of the China threat, has less to do with human nature per se than with the Western quest for scientific truth about human society. The Hobbesian 'discovery' of the first man and human nature, as C. B. Macpherson argues, was not the objective knowledge of man per se, but rather a conscious or unconscious autobiographical reflection of Western modern man and his living condition in a 'bourgeois market society'.[21] Insofar as the 'China threat' paradigm has been informed partly by the Hobbesian fear of every man against every man, this China threat representation is best seen as a mirror image of some historically specific and selective self-experience of the West.

Two specific arguments in the 'China threat' discourse are illustrative of this point. The first is the widely-invoked Germany analogy. Former US Deputy Secretary of Defense Paul Wolfowitz, who was instrumental in the formation of Washington's official view of China as a 'strategic competitor', [22] was convinced by the 'obvious and disturbing analogy' between Wilhelmine Germany and today's China. Though briefly acknowledging the differences between the two powers, he insisted on their many 'similarities'. For him, just as Germany's transition from the statesmanship of Bismarck to the incompetence of his successors contributed to the tragedy of World War I, so too China, which is in the process of a similar transition 'from two decades of extremely skilful management of its international relationships to a new leadership of *uncertain* quality', poses a serious threat to the international order. [23] In an influential piece published in *The National Interest*, Richard Betts and Thomas Christensen similarly argue that

> Like Germany a century ago, China is a late-blooming great power emerging into a world already ordered strategically by earlier arrivals; a continental power surrounded by other powers who are collectively stronger but individually weaker (with the exception of the United States and, perhaps, Japan); a bustling country with great expectations, dissatisfied with its place in the international pecking order, if only with regard to international prestige and respect. The quest for a rightful "place in the sun" will... inevitably foster growing friction with Japan, Russia, India or the United States. [24]

What this Germany analogy can tell us is that the Western knowledge of the China threat is based, more than anything else, on a fear of repetition of a European nightmare scenario. Its fear of China, situated in the broader sense of paranoia that Europe's past may become Asia's future, [25] is derived less from China's rise or its uncertain intentions than from the self-righteous certainty about the universality of Western historical trajectory.

The America analogy tells a similar story. Kagan argues that 'if Americans want to understand Chinese power and ambition today, they could start by looking in the mirror'. [26] This is exactly what Mearsheimer has done. After extrapolating American history in the nineteenth and twentieth centuries to a status of the unchangeable 'tragedy' of great power politics in general, Mearsheimer insists that China will have to, almost slavishly, follow the same path:

> for sound strategic reasons, [China] would surely pursue regional hegemony, just as the United States did in the Western Hemisphere during the nineteenth century.

So we would expect China to attempt to dominate Japan and Korea, as well as other regional actors, by building military forces that are so powerful that those other states would not dare challenge it. We would also expect China to develop its own version of the Monroe Doctrine, directed at the United States. Just as the United States made it clear to distant great powers that they were not allowed to meddle in the Western Hemisphere, China will make it clear that American interference in Asia is unacceptable.[27]

Clearly, Mearsheimer's 'China threat' assessment is based not so much on what China does in the present as it is on what the US itself did in the past.[28] His repeated anxious 'expectations' of China testify to a paranoia of both China's Otherness and its emerging sameness. His fear reflects, in the final analysis, the lingering ambivalence of colonial desire towards the mimicry of the American self-experience by an Oriental Other. The autobiographical nature of the 'China threat' discourse is so obvious that many references to the 'China menace' (such as the 'Beijing Consensus' and 'Chinese Lake') are directly modelled on the Western/American self. Little wonder that Mel Gurtov, while reading a 2005 US Defense Department report on China's military threat, found the report's comments on China ironically more fitting to describe US power and intention than China's.[29]

The US is certainly not unique in the projection of self-experience onto the understanding of others. As scholars of literary criticism and Australian colonial history have pointed out, Australia's fixation with the fiction of an Asian invasion has been bound up with its self-consciousness as a settler country, which itself was born of invasion. Australia's anxiety about its northern neighbours, in which China often looms large, has been sustained by the fear that a nation created by European invasion could subsequently be taken over by an Asian/Chinese invasion.[30] Thus, the anxiety and fear of China felt by the West does not stem primarily from what China is or what it does, but from an anxious Western self, or more precisely, from its own historical role in the production of anxiety and fear suffered by others. Perhaps unwittingly, the 'China threat' paradigm exhibits an unspoken fear of the logic of mutual responsiveness in international relations: with China's rise, there is a danger that China might begin to imitate what 'we' have done to others, this time at 'our' expense.

Constructing the Western Self in the 'China Threat' Paradigm

The 'China threat' paradigm is a discursive construct closely linked with Western/American colonial desire and historical experience. It reflects the inability or at least unwillingness of the Western/American self to make sense of China beyond their own fear and realpolitik trajectories. In doing so, its ethnocentric representation of China provides the West with a measure of strategic familiarity and moral certainty, thus reaffirming the self-imagination of the West.

The imagination of an external 'threat' or Other has long been instrumental to the formation and maintenance of self-identity.[31] In the logic of what Michael Hardt and Antonio Negri call 'colonialist representations', the difference of the Other, first having been pushed to the extreme, 'can be inverted in a second moment as the foundation of the Self. In other words, the evil, barbarity, and licentiousness of the colonized Other are what make possible the goodness, civility, and propriety of the European Self'. They go on to say that 'Only through opposition to the colonized does the metropolitan subject really become itself'.[32] The threatening imagery of 'wilderness' in the early periods of American nation-building served a similar purpose in that it helped maintain America's 'New World mythology'. As James Robertson notes, 'there is no New World without wilderness. If we are to be true Americans (and thus part of that New World and its destiny), there *must* be wilderness. The symbol is an imperative for our real world'.[33]

The construction of self-identity through the discourses of threat, Otherness and wilderness perhaps culminated in the poetics and politics of the Cold War, 'an important moment in the (re)production of American identity'.[34] In this process, discourses of international relations and foreign policy played a central role. They helped create and police boundaries and Otherness so that a unified self could be identified and protected. As Campbell notes, 'The constant articulation of danger through foreign policy is thus not a threat to a state's identity or existence: it is its condition of possibility. While the objects of concern change over time, the techniques and exclusions by which those objects are constituted as dangers persist'.[35] In this sense, although the Cold War was a pivotal moment in the Western/American construction of threat, such a discursive practice is not confined to the Cold War.[36] It is, as noted before, embedded in the modern quest for certainty, and the Cold War mentality is only a historically specific manifestation of that ongoing modern colonial desire.

Not surprisingly then, the Cold War's end did little to disrupt the discursive ritual of constructing Otherness. If anything, the fall of the Berlin Wall and the demise of the 'Evil Empire' demanded more threats, simply because their very absence would become a threat to the coherence and unity of the West/the US. Without clearly identifiable enemies, 'there can be no overarching ontology of security, no shared identity differentiating the national self from threatening others, no consensus on what—if anything— should be done'.[37] For this reason, Mearsheimer quite accurately predicted that 'we will soon miss the Cold War'.[38]

Mearsheimer's prediction certainly rang true within a number of US government agencies and institutions, most notably the Pentagon and the

Central Intelligence Agency (CIA), whose very identity and institutional certainty had hinged on fighting the Cold War Communist 'Other'. If the 'Communist threat' no longer existed, the Pentagon would find it a lot harder to justify its massive military spending, if not its very *raison d'être*. More importantly, if history had indeed been won and there was little left to fight for, would the moral leadership of the US 'as a force for good in the world' still be in demand?[39] In the words of Huntington: 'if there is no evil empire out there threatening those principles, what indeed does it mean to be an American, and what becomes of American national interests?'[40] Would the West, a 'highly artificial' construct, be able to survive?[41] Worse still, might the rest of the world, now no longer in need of the 'indispensable nation', break loose or even turn around and resent the latter's hegemony?

In this context, it became imperative for the West to continue invoking threat, which would also help counter the internal danger of 'declining strength, flagging will and confusion about our role in the world'.[42] Hence the persistent colonial desire for a threatening Other, which by now is not only a source of paranoia, but also one of secret fascination. Clearly mindful of this Western paradoxical affection for enemy, Georgi Arbatov, Director of a Moscow think tank, told a US audience the year before the collapse of the Berlin Wall: 'We are going to do something terrible to you—we are going to deprive you of an enemy'.[43] Arbatov was no doubt correct to imply that for the US living without an identity-defining enemy would be terrible indeed, but he only got half right. For the 'enemy' *qua* enemy to the US is often not determined by that 'enemy' itself. Rather, as noted before, it is primarily a category in the colonial desire built into the modern American self-imagination. Consequently, 'To prove that we are menaced is of course unnecessary... it is enough that we *feel* menaced'.[44] That is, it is not up to the 'enemy' to decide whether or not it can cease to be an enemy. While the USSR as a specific threat might have gone, the 'emotional substitute' of fear in the Western/American self-imagination lived on, always eager and able to find its next monster to destroy.

As a consequence, the post-Cold War period witnessed a proliferation of freshly minted threats, ranging from Robert Kaplan's famous 'Coming Anarchy' thesis through Mearsheimer's 'Back to the Future' scenario to Huntington's 'clash of civilizations' prediction.[45] Meanwhile the emergence of the Iraq threat in the waning days of the Cold War temporarily allowed George Bush Snr. to regain 'a whole plateful of clarity' about 'good and evil, right and wrong'.[46] Yet, for many anxious strategic planners, to best demonstrate why the US should remain an indispensable nation, the most indispensable enemy had to be China. The 'beauty' of this mega threat lies in its apparent ability to satisfy the colonial desire of Western/American self on both strategic and moral grounds.

Strategically, China's vast size would be the most obvious and convenient justification for the often expensive strategic programmes pursued by Washington. This was true even in the midst of the Cold War when America's main obsession was with the Soviet Union. In 1967, President Lyndon B. Johnson ordered his Secretary of Defense Robert McNamara to build an anti-ballistic-missile (ABM) system. McNamara was personally opposed to such a system, believing that it could be easily countered by a slight increase in the number of Soviet offensive missiles. But unable to challenge the President's order, McNamara gave a speech, which, after stating all the reasons why an ABM was a bad idea, concluded that the US still needed one to defend against an attack by China. Assistant Secretary of Defense Paul Warnke walked into McNamara's office later that day and asked, 'China bomb, Bob?' McNamara simply replied: 'What else am I going to blame it on?'[47]

The end of the Cold War has only further cemented China's role as the indispensable threat. Representing a most suitable strategic target for the tools at hand, China, as Bruce Cumings explains, has basically become 'a metaphor for an enormously expensive Pentagon that has lost its bearings [since the end of the Cold War] and that requires a formidable "renegade state" to define its mission (Islam is rather vague, and Iran lacks necessary weight)'.[48] Only in the aftermath of 'September 11' was China temporarily let off the hook, when terrorism in general, and the more tangible 'Axis of Evil' in particular, served an essentially similar function of reassuring American self-identity and certainty.[49]

As well as helping sustain the military-industrial complex, the China threat also has moral and political utility for the vitality of Western self-image. Beijing's continued existence as an authoritarian regime contributes both to the self-congratulatory image of 'democratic peace' in the West in general, and to the need for American leadership and moral authority in particular. Insofar as China reminds us that 'history is not close to an end',[50] the US-led West can continue to be called upon by the oppressed for moral leadership. Facing a China-led coalition of the world's despotic regimes, the enlargement of the Western self to form a league of democracies can be relatively easily justified, perhaps even with a measure of urgency.[51] In short, the moral challenge posed by China serves as a valuable discursive site where the Western/American self can continue to be coherently imagined, constructed and enacted.

The China Threat as a Construction of Otherness

With its contribution to the Western/American self-imagination, the 'China threat' paradigm is also a construction of Otherness. This is not primarily because this paradigm portrays China as a *threat*. Rather, it is because in its quest for certain knowledge about China, it has sought to deny Chinese subjectivities, to impose upon China a fixed subjectivity, or to reduce its subjectivities to a singular, homogeneous whole. These discursive tactics of denial, imposition and reduction vis-à-vis Chinese subjectivities are some of the hallmarks of Othering.

These 'Othering' strategies are easily identifiable in many common arguments of the 'China threat' paradigm. Capability-based arguments, for instance, openly bypass Chinese concerns and subjectivities by focusing squarely on its material capabilities, as if China as an international actor could be reduced to its defence spending and military hardware alone. From this perspective, China's power status becomes the sole starting point for understanding its international relations. Its power—especially military power—metonymically passes as China per se. One of the most dominant components of the China debate has been predictably the 'assessment of China's overall future military power'. [52] The following questions, for example, '[Is] China a rising power, and if so, how fast and in what direction [is it headed]?' [53] have been a standard opening gambit in numerous IR analyses on China. John Fairbank once told us that 'as we phrase questions, so we get answers'. [54] If one takes China's military capabilities as a point of departure, it is no surprise that the built-in answer is the China threat.

Capability-based representations of China are not completely oblivious to intentions, but they insist that intentions are merely epiphenomenal to capabilities. As Bernstein and Munro claim, 'China is so big and so naturally powerful that [we know] it will tend to dominate its region *even if it does not intend to do so as a matter of national policy*'. [55] Drawing on their assessment of China's military power, they confidently declare what China's 'real' goal is: 'China is an unsatisfied and ambitious power whose goal is to dominate Asia.... Its goal is to ensure that no country in its region... will act without first taking China's interests into prime consideration'. [56] When it comes to China's professed goals and objectives, they dismiss them as propaganda out of hand. As the argument goes, 'China's peace offensive was a tactical move', which does not change the fundamental nature of its hegemonic ambition. [57]

Unlike capability-based discourses, intention-based approaches to China's rise look at its civilisational characteristics and strategic culture, among other things. Huntington's *The Clash of Civilizations and the Remaking of World Order* and Johnston's *Cultural Realism*, both examined briefly in the previous chapter, readily come to mind as representatives of the latter approaches. Departing from structural realists' almost exclusive focus on military capabilities, Huntington's book engages with the history, ideas, values, and customs of the Sinic civilisation. Yet, the conclusions of his culture-informed analysis turn out to be not much different to those of the capability-based discourses. His book treats civilisations as essentially distinctive, self-contained entities, and sees cultural differences between the West and China in essentialist, absolute and mutually exclusive terms. Based on Edward Friedman's claim that 'what is authentically Chinese' is 'patriarchal, nativistic, and authoritarian', Huntington painted a stark contrast with what is 'authentically' Western, a unique combination of 'universal' values such as the rule of law, social pluralism, and individualism.[58] In this way, cultural differences between China and the US become a fixed dichotomy of particularity versus universality. To the extent that he believed that 'Civilizations are the biggest "we" within which we feel culturally at home as distinguished from all the other "thems" out there', to invoke this kind of cultural identity, as he himself acknowledged, is to define 'the state's place in world politics, its friends, its enemies'.[59] Thus, by drawing a cultural 'fault line' between self and Other, Huntington's grand theory is nothing short of a more totalising construction of Otherness than the conventional state-centric argument is usually capable of. In his 'clash of civilizations' thesis, the threatening quality of the Sinic civilisation is not only imposed on China proper, but also on the so-called 'Sinic cultural area' of East Asia as a whole (though with the convenient exclusion of Japan).

In *Cultural Realism*, Johnston similarly promises to move beyond the structuralist, capability-based explanation of China's strategic behaviour. With a close reading of 'the classic texts in Chinese strategic thought' and asking how its strategic culture may provide an insight into Chinese foreign policy,[60] his efforts are in many ways commendable, for rarely have Western scholars bothered to go to such great lengths to gauge China's intentions. What is problematic with his analysis, though, is that he is convinced in advance that there *is* a single Chinese strategic culture.[61] Even as his survey does come across two major strategic cultures, namely, the Confucian-Mencian paradigm and the *parabellum* paradigm, Johnston views the former as essentially an ideal type of strategic culture with a largely symbolic role in influencing strategic options.[62] Consequently, he suggests that there remains essentially *one* singular Chinese strategic culture, the *parabellum* paradigm, which then becomes *the* strategic culture in China.

Thus, despite Johnston's worthy attempt to understand China on its own cultural terms, the quest for certainty rooted in the Western self-imagination remains at play. Such a quest, among other things, dictates that his notion of strategic culture be 'empirically testable'. To that end, Johnston insists on positively specifying 'what the scope and content of strategic culture is and what it is not'.[63] Hence, he ends up with a conception of strategic culture defined by 'questions about the role of war in human affairs, the nature of conflict with the enemy, and the efficacy of violence in dealing with the adversary'.[64] Certainly, these questions are both relevant and important to any study of strategic culture. But they beg another question: Why should strategic culture be reduced to those questions alone? By directing one's attention to questions about *war, conflict,* and *violence* while brushing aside other kinds of questions (e.g., about peace, reconciliation, and benevolence) that are equally relevant and integral to strategic culture, one is not simply engaging in an objective study of strategic culture, but rather participating in a selective and reductionist discursive practice. In limiting his study to a narrow set of questions about war, conflict, and violence, Johnston both reduces Chinese strategic culture to the use of strategic force, and declares the 'irrelevance (to behavior)' of the Confucian-Mencian stress on benevolence, righteousness, and virtue as a basis for security and harmony.[65] Indeed, he goes to some considerable lengths to count China's use of force against Mongols raiding *within* Ming territory as evidence of Chinese realpolitik aggressiveness.[66]

As a result, for all his repeated qualification that strategic culture is historically contingent and may be (un)learned, Johnston's interpretation of the historical records in the Ming dynasty does not leave much room for contingency. The reader is left with the impression that realpolitik thinking is intrinsic to Chinese strategic culture, which is precisely an impression China specialist Warren Cohen walks away with:

> If Johnston's analysis of China's strategic culture is correct—and I believe it is—generational change will not guarantee a kinder, gentler China. Nor will the ultimate disappearance of communism in Beijing. The powerful China we have every reason to expect in the twenty-first century is likely to be as aggressive and expansionist as China has been whenever it has been the dominant power in Asia.[67]

Aided in part by Johnston's findings, Cohen was able to spend just 'a few minutes' lecturing a visitor from Singapore (who did not view Chinese foreign policy as so 'aggressive and expansionist') on the subject of 'the history of the Chinese empire' and 'thousands of years of attacks on China's neighbors'. To wrap up his lecture, he prescribed that visitor a reading: Johnston's *Cultural Realism*.[68]

Another, perhaps cruder, tactic of Othering in the 'China threat' paradigm involves neither an analysis of China's military capabilities nor its intentions. Rather, it follows a deductive logic based more explicitly on an either/or dichotomy in the Western/American quest for absolute certainty and security: *either* China guarantees absolute peace for the United States, *or* it cannot but be treated as a threat. The reasoning of Betts and Christensen's above-mentioned article serves as a good example here:

If the PLA remains second-rate, should the world breathe a sigh of relief? *Not entirely*.... Drawing China into the web of global interdependence may do more to encourage peace than war, but it *cannot guarantee* that the pursuit of heartfelt political interests will be blocked by a fear of economic consequences.... [And] U.S. efforts to create a stable balance across the Taiwan Strait might deter the use of force under certain circumstances, but *certainly not all*.[69]

Of course, they could not get, nor do they expect, affirmative answers from China to any of those relentless quests for absolute certainty. Consequently, their conclusion has to be certainty in a negative form—the China threat:

The truth is that China can pose a grave problem even if it does not become a military power on the American model, does not intend to commit aggression, integrates into a global economy, and liberalizes politically. Similarly, the United States could face a dangerous conflict over Taiwan even if it turns out that Beijing lacks the capacity to conquer the island.... This is true because of geography; because of America's reliance on alliances to project power; and because of China's capacity to harm U.S. forces, U.S. regional allies, and the American homeland, even while losing a war in the technical, military sense.[70]

At this point, neither China's capabilities nor intentions seem to really matter; the China threat has already been predetermined by the either/or logic. Because of this, some 'China threat' theorists see no irony or paradox in justifying the policy of containing China not in spite of, but on the very basis of China's current weakness. For instance, Mearsheimer wrote in 2001 that 'China is still far away from having enough latent power to make a run at regional hegemony, so it is not too late for the United States to reverse the course and do what it can to slow China's rise'.[71] Here, it is evident that the China threat is an Othering effect of Western/American colonial desire from which China cannot escape no matter what its capabilities or intentions might be. This China insight may have the much-prized virtue of analytical parsimony, but it does not occur to those theorists that such logic could be used to describe any country, including the US.

In brief, by representing China as a monolithic whole, dismissing its subjectivities, and/or imposing onto it a singular, fixed subjectivity of power politics, the 'China threat' paradigm acts as a discursive construction of an objectified Other. Cast as an Other and threatening object, China by definition lacks the kind of rationality and subjectivity that are characteristic of the Western knowing subject. Nor is it eligible to have its own security concern, which may explain why there exists a 'severe disproportion between the keen attention to China as a security concern and the intractable neglect of China's [own] security concerns in the current debate'.[72] Even when it is allowed for some security interests, it is alleged that it often has no idea what those interests are.[73] Lucian Pye once argued that China is such an erratic state that it acts 'in ways that seem perversely self-damaging in the eyes of those who believe they have that country's interests at heart'.[74] Perhaps it is at this level that the Othering effect of the 'China threat' paradigm is most devastating.

THE 'CHINA OPPORTUNITY' PARADIGM AS WESTERN/AMERICAN SELF-FANTASY

To the 'China threat' proponents, China's difference and potential sameness in strategic behaviour are essentially a source of fear. For 'China opportunity' advocates, however, China, in spite of or because of its difference, is an occasion for (neo)colonial fantasy. Together, the rise of China has been treated as both a threat and an opportunity. To fully appreciate the ambivalence of this bifocal representation, I now turn to the second China paradigm. In the pages that follow, I will trace how, like its 'China threat' counterpart, the 'China opportunity' is a particular reflection of Western self-imagination. I will also examine how as a result the 'China opportunity' imagery carries with it a similar though subtler effect of Othering.

Othering China in the 'Opportunity' Paradigm

At first sight, the 'China opportunity' paradigm sounds more positive than the 'China threat' discourse. It does not, for example, treat China as fundamentally different or threatening. Whilst some 'China opportunity' advocates remain wary about the Chinese regime and its long-term strategic ambition, most are optimistic about the Chinese people and the various opportunities the country has to offer. Indeed, for Edward Friedman, such positive representations constitute a break with 'a long-discredited Eurocentric "othering" that distinguishes the good West from all the bad rest'.[75]

True, to distinguish the good West from the bad China is probably a case of 'othering'. Yet, depicting China as an opportunity (for the West) does not necessarily mean a deviation from Eurocentrism. The construction of Otherness, as noted before, is not so much about treating others as threats per se as it is about the employment of such discursive tactics as imposition, reduction, and denial when it comes to understanding others' subjectivities. On this account, there is little improvement in the paradigmatic shift from the 'China threat' to the 'China opportunity'.

Consider, for example, the enthusiastic portrayal of China as a modern-day El Dorado made up of 'one billion customers'. Though a seemingly true and innocuous assessment, it reduces China to a huge yet impersonalised market, with a billion faceless customers and easy-to-control cheap labour. In short, China is little more than 'an outlet for American commerce and investment'. [76] The diversity and richness of Chinese geography, history, humanity and subjectivity matters little, if at all. The only hint of Western historical sensitivity over China is manifested in the updating of the customer numbers from '400 million' in the 1930s to a current round-up figure of 'one billion'. In order for China to be seen as an opportunity, this Othering (objec-tification) of China as a market is not accidental, but appears essential. Otherwise, the sheer number of the Chinese population could instead stir up fear. As one of the Cold War architects George F. Kennan explained in 1948 with regard to Asia more generally:

We have about 50% of the world's wealth but only 6.3% of its population. This disparity is particularly great... between ourselves and the peoples of Asia. In this situation, we cannot fail to be the object of envy and resentment. Our real task in the coming period is to devise a pattern for relationships which will permit us to maintain this position of disparity without positive detriment to our national secu-rity. [77]

Therefore, the imagination of China as a market is a necessary fantasy in place of an otherwise looming danger of the 'envy and resentment' from its vast population. Seen through an 'opportunity' lens, China can remain an attractive but passive Other, ready to be explored and exploited. This Other-ing tendency has, for example, enabled the West to take China's WTO entry as 'almost exclusively a matter of improving [Western] access to China's markets, not enhancing Chinese access to other markets'. [78] Just as the 'China threat' paradigm deprives the Chinese of any security concern of their own, so the emphasis on 'China as a fabled market'/'the world's workshop' is primarily about keeping China as a place to which 'our access, as a country and as individual citizens, is free and comfortable'. [79] This quote, originally expressed by a senior economist from the RAND Corporation in the 1960s, captured a longstanding sexualised colonial desire of turning the colonised society into an accessible, feminised object. Such desire was clearly evident in the remarks by a top-ranking member of the American business commu-nity on the China opportunity: 'we are talking about the future of e-commerce, the biggest business innovation of our time... in China, the biggest market in the world.... *and that gives me a hard-on! And I want it to give you a hard-on too!!*' [80]

Under this economic-cum-sexual fantasy, the Chinese may be looked upon with some fascination and fondness, but a precondition of that fondness is that the Chinese shall remain nameless consumers or machine-like labourers. The following observation on Chinese migrant workers, made by an Ameri-can manager of a US-owned plant in China, is instructive: 'They are young. They are quick. There is none of this 'I have to pick up the kids' nonsense you get in the States'. [81] This praise of young (often female) Chinese workers, like the excitement about the China economic opportunity in general, is hardly a celebration of Chinese subjectivity, but rather an expression of the latent colonial attraction to their value as an easily controllable and exploitable Other. When Robert A. Kapp, president of the US-China Business Council, disavowed that 'U.S. companies do not approach China as a land of 1.3 billion customers, waiting to be harvested like ripe peaches',[82] he was not suggesting that Western businesses should not harbour such desire at all, but rather, he was urging that they should also exercise 'due diligence' given the significant risks involved.

The 'Othering' practice is also at work in the discourse of global integration. On appearance, this discourse seems to reject the notion of China as an outright menacing Other. Recognising China as a potential part of 'us', it invites China to 'work with us to sustain the international system' as a responsible stakeholder.[83] However, an assumption of China's Otherness, who is denied coevalness with the West,[84] remains obvious. For instance, underlying Oksenberg and Economy's observation that 'China has rejoined the world' is a belief that prior to that process, China was *not* part of the world. Indeed, to them, prior to the 1970s China was such a strange Other that 'it seemed as if the then 800 million Chinese lived on another planet'.[85]

For other observers, despite its potential, today's China remains an outsider. According to a study, to join the world as a responsible state, China has to make significant shifts from authoritarian rule to a more democratic form of governance. With a new set of criteria for membership in international society centring on such new standards of civilisation as human rights and democracy, it is argued that China's shifts are 'hazardous' and challenging, if not impossible. Yet unless it makes such transformations, 'China will, in important ways, remain outside global society'.[86] Thus, the representation of China as an opportunity or 'a work in progress' for global convergence has been premised all along on the conception of China as an Other.[87] Were it not for its Otherness, it probably would not be considered a political 'opportunity' in the first place.

The same can be said of the 'opportunity' discourse of 'democracy for China'. For example, after presenting the results of the 'first scientifically valid national sample survey' on Chinese political behaviour and attitudes, two experts on Chinese politics conclude that:

> Nothing in our data supports the theory that Chinese political culture is an absolute bar to democracy. When compared to residents of some of the most stable, long-established democracies in the world, the Chinese population scored lower on the variables we looked at, but not so low as to justify the conclusion that democracy is out of reach. In general, as theory predicts, the more urban and educated sectors showed more democratic attitudes, supporting expectations derived from moderni-

zation theory that China's culture will move closer to the patterns characteristic of democratic countries as the economy grows.[88]

Though the authors put China and Chinese culture *almost* on a par with 'the most stable, long-established democracies' (presumably the West), it is not difficult to notice the implied dualistic assumption about the West and its Chinese Other. By declaring that the Chinese population as a whole 'scored lower' in a 'scientifically valid' survey than the long-established Western democracies and that China will eventually be able to move 'closer' to 'us', they leave little doubt that the Chinese, despite their future potential, remain inferior in the temporal pecking order of political development and therefore are not quite part of 'us' yet.

To be sure, this 'democracy for China' narrative seems well-intended, perhaps aimed to counter the old colonial stereotype of 'Oriental despotism' that Chinese culture is hopelessly stagnant and unchangeable. Yet, even so, it remains mired in the discursive practice of Othering, albeit in a subtler and less visible manner. To illustrate, it may be useful to draw upon Todorov's critique of Las Casas's sympathetic representation of the American Indians at the time of Conquistadors' colonisation of America. Las Casas, a sixteenth-century Spanish historian and Dominican bishop, argued passionately against the treatment of native American Indians as inferior or unequal. He defended the Indians' rights and highlighted their essential resemblance to Christians. But this egalitarian representation of the Indians, according to Todorov, is just another way of constructing the Indian 'Other'. For from Las Casas's works, 'we learn nothing of the Indians. If it is incontestable that the prejudice of superiority is an obstacle in the road to knowledge, we must also admit that the prejudice of equality is a still greater one, for it consists in identifying the other purely and simply with one's own "ego ideal" (or with oneself)'.[89] Although this is not to draw a direct parallel between Las Casas's construction of the Indians and the contemporary discourse of 'democracy for China', Todorov's criticism of the former is nevertheless pertinent here. If it is ethnocentric to view China as incapable of change or development at all, it is no less ethnocentric to see it as capable of change only towards a particular kind of subjectivity—a subjectivity of one's own. If the former represents an age-old colonial stereotype of a changeless Chinese Other that always needs external stimulus, the latter is nothing more than the other side of the same fantasy coin. Either way, the 'Eurocentric othering' is far from discredited as Friedman would have us believe.

The China Opportunity as Western Autobiographical Imagination

Both the threat and opportunity paradigms involve the construction of the Chinese Other, but their 'Othering' strategies differ. In the threat paradigm, the dichotomy of self and Other is arranged along a spatial axis. Through the opportunity lens, the Chinese Other appears in a linear temporal coordinate, usually equated with tradition, past, history, backwardness, anachronism, adolescent, or a work in progress. These temporal terms may sound fair and innocent enough; yet, they make sense only in their corresponding binary oppositions such as tradition/modernity, backwardness/progress, past/future, and 'unruly adolescents'/'mature adults'.[90] What the second halves of these binaries imply is a narcissistic imagination of the Western self. Like the 'threat' discourse, the 'China opportunity' paradigm is both deliberately performative and autobiographical.

Take, for example, the following passage found in a typical Western travelogue about China:

> Can there be any people in the world who deserve more to succeed, and to see and feel in their own lives the prosperity and freedom that we in the Western world take for granted? I do not think so.... now, in spite of all their country's imperfections, many of them are on the verge for the first time of tasting some kind of progress.[91]

By claiming that the Chinese begin to taste 'for the first time' the kind of progress and freedom 'we' in the West already 'take for granted', the author could not have made a clearer temporal dichotomy between the Western self and the Chinese Other.

Over the past few centuries, different patterns of the 'China opportunity' discourse have conveyed different messages about the Western self. One of the earliest 'China opportunity' imageries, the 'fabled China market', had little resemblance to Chinese reality at the time, when China was closed off to the outside world and showed little interest in trading with the Europeans. As attested by the often-cited story of the Lancashire mills, the China market was above all a mirror image of the Western self-imagination as a centre of progressive capitalism. It reflected the capitalist-cum-colonial desire for new markets for increasing Western industrial surplus. Similarly, eighteenth- and nineteenth-century American merchants' 'mysterious attraction' to Chinese decorative artefacts had more to do with the then-emerging popular material culture back home, a culture which believed that 'a fantasy world could be conjured up through commercial interest'. Indeed, America's then fascination with everything Chinese, as one scholar puts it, 'tells us as much about ourselves as about China'.[92]

In the early phase of Sino-Western encounters, Western self-fashioning also found its way into the religious imagining of China as the 'promised land'. In many ways, such an image was an index of the then predominantly religious self-imagination in the West in general and the US in particular. Albert J. Beveridge of Indiana, a Senator and prolific historian, saw America as God's 'chosen nation to finally lead in the regeneration of the world'.[93] For Nebraska's Republican Senator Kenneth Wherry, 'with God's help', Americans could 'lift Shanghai up and up, ever up, until it is just like Kansas City'.[94] If that was to be believed, then imagine how wonderful a place the US would be. Back then, many missionaries understood too well the value of the Chinese Otherness (in terms of heathens) as a foil for Western self-importance. The reflection of a young American missionary by the name of William Alexander Parsons Martin serves as a good example. After a long voyage, Martin arrived at the Chinese city of Canton (Guangzhou) in 1850, just eight years after the first Opium War. In a later published account of his first direct encounter with China, Martin wrote that:

> As we stepped on shore we were greeted by a hooting crowd, who shouted *Fanqui, fanqui! Shato, shato!* ('Foreign devils! cut off their heads!'). "Is this", I mused, "the boasted civilization of China? Are these the people for whom I left my home?" But, I reflected, if they were not heathen, why should I have come?[95]

For Martin, China's Otherness, in a typical fashion of colonial ambivalence, represented simultaneously a menace and an opportunity, an opportunity which could afford him a sense of self-certainty and moral purpose.

Today, religion no longer occupies such a prominent role in Western collective self-imagination, which has been increasingly defined by such secular virtues as democracy, freedom, and human rights. Not surprisingly, contemporary 'China opportunity' discourses have also shifted along those lines. In the past, it was Christ for China; now it is democracy for China. For instance, the 1989 Tiananmen demonstrations were uniformly described as a pro-democracy movement in Western media and intellectual circles. Taking place amidst the Western anticipation of the imminent 'End of History', the Tiananmen drama probably could not have been perceived otherwise. This is despite the fact that a yearning for Western liberal democracy was just one and certainly not the main factor behind those demonstrations. The *Goddess of Freedom and Democracy* erected by protestors in Tiananmen Square, often simply called the *Statue of Liberty* by American reporters, in fact 'drew largely on socialist realist antecedents and bore slight resemblance to the statue in New York harbor'.[96] Explaining the reason behind the West's fixation on democratisation and civil society in China, sociologist and China scholar Jonathan Unger suggests that 'it happens to accord with the political hopes of most of us. We *want* to perceive a society in China in the midst of gradually organizing itself and quietly undermining the strength of an oppressive state'.[97] What a powerful illustration of Western desire as China knowledge!

Similarly, the perceived promise of the Internet in transforming China has less to do with Chinese reality (witness the Google controversy in 2010) and more to do with the West's own fascination with the Internet. Predicting that China would be an unprecedented market not only for 'our products', but for 'economic freedom', Bill Clinton invited his listeners to imagine how much the Internet could change the Middle Kingdom after its accession to the WTO. The main rationale for this China optimism was again conditioned on a particular rendition of American self-experience. 'We know how much the Internet has changed America, and we are already an open society', said a buoyant Clinton. 'Now, there is no question China has been trying to crack down on the Internet—good luck. That's sort of like trying to nail Jello to the wall'.[98]

James Mann describes such 'China opportunity' and 'engagement' rhetoric as the '*China* fantasy', but one may more appropriately refer to it as an effect of Western/American *self*-fantasy. Constituted by the built-in desire to look in the experience of others for similarity and universal confirmation of the Western self, the 'China opportunity' paradigm, like its 'China threat' counterpart, denotes a similar inability of Western observers to see China beyond their own experience and desire. Setting out to know a different world that is China, the China opportunity discourse has seldom deviated from the path of Western self-understanding. If anything, one of its key functions is to reinforce that self-image.

Neither monolithic nor ontologically stable, the West as a project needs to be predicated on certain self-fantasy; it can hardly rely on any other basis. But this imagined existence is always precarious and cannot be effectively demonstrated or maintained through such self-posturing alone. Instead, it constantly requires the invocation and maintenance of an (imagined) Other. Though the Other is frequently an illusory mirror image of the Western self-imagination, at least this imaginative and discursive detour through Otherness can avoid the suspicious tautological practice of 'defining like by like'.[99] That is, the Other enables the Western 'self' to define itself through difference. For example, when Johnston suggests that US engagement with China would lead to such positive outcomes as responsibility, cooperation, transparency, sensitivity, more sophistication, maturity, and moderation, the real message is that all those desirable attributes are already characteristic of the US. But to directly say so would have been too blunt and ineffective.[100]

European images of the China opportunity perform a similar function. By actively engaging with China in the hope of converting this opportunity into reality, European countries could prove to themselves as well as to others that they are collectively a normative power not only in name, but also in practice. As Callahan notes, the main objective of the EU engagement with China is, as well as 'raising the EU's profile in China', to 'legitimize[s] the Union as a major global actor' and 'aid[s] the EU's project of crafting the image of Europe as a "civilian power"'.[101]

Consequently, the 'China opportunity' paradigm is not just about China, but is simultaneously a performative discursive device of Western self-reassurance. From the beginning, China's 'Otherness' is an opportunity *for* the West; it serves as a lively reminder of what the West has left behind. All the exciting China opportunities (such as Christianity, democracy, and international responsibility) can be seen as something 'we' have already achieved and fulfilled, and thus are in a good position to offer. In an overview of its 'Sectoral Dialogues' with China, the European Commission does not shy away from such a self-image:

> China today is experiencing challenges which Europe started to tackle a number of years ago in areas such as the environment, the internal market, and competition. The EU is demonstrating its willingness to share this experience with China. And China has shown an interest in using the best practices of the 'EU model' in these policy areas.[102]

In this way, the 'China opportunity' narrative is central to the West's ongoing spiritual journey of self-discovery. Knowing what China is helps answer the question of 'what are we for?'

Crucially, this self-discovering journey is no mere intellectual exercise. It is often intimately linked to the defence of Western strategic interests. For example, the 'what are we for?' question was first raised not by armchair intellectuals on conference floors, but by Raymond Fosdick, Dean Acheson's Far East consultant, during the Cold War. At that time, Fosdick was unhappy about the inadequacies of the US's largely negative campaign ('We are *against* communism'), since it appeared inadequate in America's military and ideological struggle against both the Soviet Union and 'the perceived attractiveness of communism'.[103] To reaffirm the Western self, the US had to, in the words of T. S. Repplier, president of the Advertising Council, 'hold up for the world a counteracting inspirational concept... a moralistic idea with the power to stir men's imagination'.[104] The result, according to Christina Klein, was the creation of the global imaginary of integration, which envisaged a world of 'open doors', 'common bonds', and enhanced 'cooperation'. This positive 'sentimental structure of feeling', as opposed to 'fear and the negative logic' of the 'global imaginary of containment', met both the 'emotional needs of Americans' and Washington's geopolitical ambition as the leading global power.[105]

Richard Nixon's visit to China in 1972 was a brilliantly executed strategic enactment of this global imaginary of integration. Thanks largely to this historic visit, the age-old China opportunity fantasy, suppressed by the 'Who lost China' debate and ensuing Cold War animosity, was instantly revived to pave the way for a sustained period of contemporary Western fascination with China's rise. Above all, Nixon's trip gave a new lease of life to the

American myth about China, a country not impervious to American values and influence after all. The renewed China myth in turn helped 'sustain [Americans'] mythical understanding of themselves'. [106] In addition to its geopolitical value in the competition against the USSR, Nixon's diplomatic breakthrough with China, as Madsen puts it, also helped arrest a worrying trend of waning US credibility and moral authority in the wake of its Vietnam debacle. As the argument went, 'At least in this part of the world, home to a fifth of the world's population, limitations were being lifted, doors were being opened'. [107] Back then, American journalist Joseph Kraft incisively commented in the *Washington Post* that 'China has been for American opinion a focus of narcissism, an occasion for striking self-adoring poses'. [108]

Such self-adoring poses are necessary ingredients of the politics of fantasy and national self-imagination. For a society to hold itself together, it certainly needs some 'common vocabularies and common hopes' to tell its members 'a story about how things might get better'. [109] Walter Lippman wrote nearly a century ago that 'No genuine politician ever treats his constituents as reasoning animals.... The successful politicians—good and bad—deal with the dynamics—with the will, the hopes, the needs and the visions of men'. [110] Through hopes and fantasies, the certainty of the Western self can continue, especially in times of trepidation and self-doubt. Not surprisingly, following the shock and horror of 'September 11', US leaders asked American citizens to go on with normal life and cling onto one of their most basic daily fantasies: consumerism and its apparent symbolism that defines both what America is for and what terrorism is against. In the absence of such fantasies, the largely imagined, contingent Western self would have to face not only its diverse pasts and multi-ethnic present, but also possibly a fragmented, Balkanised future. As Michel Oksenberg rightly put it, 'Stripped of confidence that their values transcend the cultural differences of their diverse origins, Americans would remain divided by their separate pasts'. [111]

No doubt, the West's politics of self-imagination has over the years developed a rich repertoire of fantasies, but the fantasy about China's transition in 'our' image proves more attractive and lasting than most. Compared to other fantasies, China seems to offer a value-added antidote to the predicament of Western self-imagination. As Tang Tsou observed half a century ago, 'America was deeply inspired by the vision of a huge country with an ancient civilization transforming herself into a modern, democratic, Christian nation and following the lead of the United States'. [112] The obvious rationale for this China fascination was that 'If China with its old and radically different culture can be won, where can we not prevail?' [113] Little wonder that the stake is high and the prize is still greater in the imagination of the China opportunity. Not only can China serve as 'a new source of invigoration' for 'a West seeking solutions to a "democratic malaise"', [114] but it has also become nothing short of an ultimate litmus test, as it were, of the universality, authenticity, and vitality of the West and its system.

To conclude, rather than objective descriptions of China, both China paradigms are discursive constructions of the Chinese Other and autobiographical accounts of the Western self. They reflect the modern quest of the West to carve up a secure Archimedean point of certainty for its continuous contingent being. At one level, its anxiety that such a foundational point may be uncertain and constantly under threat is often manifested in the fear of China as a threat. At another level, its confidence about the historical certainty and universality of its being has given rise to the 'China opportunity' fantasy. These fears and fantasies (or what Wasserstrom refers to as 'our own hopes and anxieties') have their origins in the ambivalence of Western colonial desire towards their colonised racial Others. Thus, the bifocal representation of China, like Western discourses of Asia more generally, tells us a great deal about the West itself, its self-imagination, its torn, anxious subjectivity, as well as its discursive effects of Othering. [115]

4. The 'China threat' and the political economy of fear

> *Narrative is not merely a neutral discursive form that may or may not be used to represent real events in their aspect as developmental processes but rather entails ontological and epistemic choices with distinct ideological and even specifically political implications.*
>
> Hayden White[1]

> *Our fashion is to have the enemy of the year. China is big, it's large on the map, it's yellow, so there is an under-the-surface racist element, and it fits very nicely an obsessive state of mind. I imagine it will last a couple of years, because China is big enough to sustain this obsession.*
>
> Zbigniew Brzezinski[2]

POWER/KNOWLEDGE AND THE POLITICS OF FEAR

The twin paradigms of China threat and China opportunity are animated by Western/American neocolonial desire. Their constructions of self and Other are not merely discursive in nature, but have political and strategic consequences. Rather than divorced from power, they are always in the service of power and at the same time (re)produced by it through the political economies of fear and fantasy. How knowledge, desire, and power interact in the cases of these China paradigms will be the focus of Chapters 4-7.

Thus far, scholarly analysis of Western representations of China has tended to treat those representations merely as knowledge, which is then empirically evaluated against so-called 'objective facts' in China. Depending on whether they are thought to match Chinese reality or not, they are labelled either 'truth', 'misrepresentations', or something in between. But this empirically-grounded approach misses a crucial point. That is, it leaves intact and unquestioned the complicity of China knowledge in power relations. What is needed, therefore, is a critical examination of the power/knowledge nexus in the two modes of China representation. How the 'China threat' paradigm relates to the political economy of fear and informs political practice is the focus of this and the following chapter. And Chapters 6 and 7 will deal with the 'China opportunity' paradigm.

To better understand the dynamics of power/knowledge/desire in the 'China threat' paradigm, we need to recognise this paradigm for what I think it is, namely, a particular form of desire—fear—disguised as certain knowledge. Fear, it may be argued, is primarily a biological instinct inherent in probably all animals that are both capable of fear and have experienced such an emotion. And yet, in the human context at least, fear is as much a socio-cultural phenomenon as it is a natural, biological reflex. This is because most forms of fear in modern society are not experienced directly through actual physical encounters, but rather are created, mediated, maintained and rein-forced through often-institutionalised knowledge resources such as images, symbols, metaphors and, above all, discourses. Sometimes referred to as 'prevailing danger codes', those knowledge resources serve as 'an extremely dense layer of mediation between what one might be advised to fear… and what one's moment-to-moment experience appears to be'.[3]

In a study of the politics of fear in the media, David Altheide argues that fear 'did not just happen or emerge' from uncertainty, the lack of community or a sense of lack of control over our lives; rather, it is largely produced and reproduced through 'the entertainment formats of mass media and popular culture'. Only through coming to grips with this culturally-mediated dimen-sion of fear, can we better understand why one's sense of fear is often not directly or proportionally linked to the object of that fear.[4] In fact, quite often the opposite is true. For instance, Altheide points to the paradox that 'there is widespread public perception [in the West] that risk and danger are every-where, that we are not safe, and that the future is bleak', even though most in Western societies 'are safer, healthier, living longer, and more secure in their environments than virtually any population in history'.[5]

How is such a strange 'surplus' of fear produced and consumed in an oth-erwise reasonably safe and wealthy society? Michael Shapiro suggests that the increased level of popular representation in the political process has not been matched by a similar increase in people's ability to represent safety and danger as they find them in their daily lives.[6] Rather, just as more and more supermarket products nowadays are no longer made locally, so too the 'commodity' of fear is increasingly outsourced from elsewhere, manufac-tured and packaged as knowledge by all sorts of security, intelligence, health and environment experts. And just as consumers part company with their money in exchange for whatever fantasies are evoked by commercial adver-tisements, consumers of fear surrender their power to scaremongering experts and political leaders, in exchange for the promised certainty and security. In return, through their knowledge of danger and threat, those experts and politicians gain trust, power, and the ability to influence others to behave in ways that meet their expectations. In this way, whatever form of knowledge that can effectively tap into fear and constantly reproduce it is, without doubt, ideally placed to serve power and enforce discipline.

Little wonder that the discursive production of fear and threat has been a fixture in modern-day politics. In Australia, no recent federal elections were complete without some forms of politics of fear at play in the political campaigns, be it about 'boat people', terrorism, workers' rights or even interest rates. Of course, fear is not always an undesirable element in politics and social life. Moïse argues that 'an element of fear is an indispensable protection against the danger of overconfidence. Fear is a force for survival in a naturally dangerous world'.[7] However, when fear is systematically deployed in politics, it is worth asking whose interests this fear politics intends to serve and how such fear is produced and for what purposes.

The 'China threat' paradigm should be understood in this broad context. This paradigm does not reflect a pre-existing sense of fear about a menace 'out there', but rather is a discursive site where such fear is first constructed and where a particular form of political economy of fear emerges. With a specific focus on the US, this chapter will examine how the China threat knowledge, which gives the popular fear of China an aura of objective credibility, serves the political and economic interests of the power elite, and is at the same time shaped by those interests.

THE CHINA THREAT AND AMERICAN POLITICAL ECONOMY OF FEAR

The political economy of fear has been a much-cherished ingredient in statecraft for millennia. 'Let them hate as long as they fear', the Roman emperor Caligula once proclaimed. '[I]t is far better to be feared than loved if you cannot be both', admonished Machiavelli in *The Prince*.[8] Thus, Robert Higgs argues that fear is a foundation of every government's power: 'Without popular fear, no government could endure for more than twenty-four hours'.[9] While the state has traditionally relied on such visible instruments of fear as the army, the police, the legal system, and the prison to maintain discipline in a society, it has also resorted to a less visible instrument: the discursive production of fear. One particularly fertile ground for such fear-related knowledge production has been the realm of international relations, where the objects of fear appear plentiful. The French political philosopher Jean Bodin observed that 'the best way of preserving a state, and guaranteeing it against sedition, rebellion, and civil war is… to find an enemy against whom they can make common cause'.[10] Similarly, Adam Smith examined in

The Wealth of Nations how a government could use the nation's anxiety for security to induce its citizens to agree to a new tax which otherwise they would probably resent.[11] Such is the political economic use of fear especially when it is disguised as scientific knowledge.

It is in this context that the fear of the China threat has been a recurring feature in American politics in general and during the presidential and congressional midterm elections in particular. During the 2010 midterm elections, for instance, *New York Times* reported that in a space of just one week, at least 29 candidates from both sides of politics unveiled advertisements accusing their opponents of being soft on China, with the undertone that China had been the chief villain for current American economic woes.[12] The bipartisan interest in using China as a whetstone to attack political rivals—alive and well during the 2012 Presidential campaign—testifies to an enduring rare consensus on the importance of the China threat to the American politics of fear among a whole spectrum of American politicians.

During the 1992 presidential campaign, candidate Bill Clinton fiercely campaigned on a foreign policy platform of confronting 'dictators from Baghdad to Beijing'. Reinforced by the appearance of two prominent Chinese student leaders of the Tiananmen protests at the 1992 Democratic National Convention in New York, the 'butchers of Beijing' image served not only as a reminder of the danger posed by Communist China, but more importantly as a powerful symbolism of partisan politics to differentiate Clinton from the incumbent candidate George H. W. Bush.[13] To boost his sagging re-election bid, Bush Snr. was not to be outdone by his Democrat challenger. He tapped into another popular danger code about China, namely, its military menace to Taiwan. Against the discursive backdrop of China as a threat to a fledgling democracy in Taiwan, Bush Snr. announced in a campaign appearance before General Dynamics workers in Fort Worth that America would sell 150 F-16 fighters to the island for an estimated US$6 billion. Selling F-16s to Taiwan to deter a China threat, as the then Assistant Secretary of Defense for International Security Affairs James Lilley frankly stated, would help counter Bush's 'coddling Communist dictators' image,[14] in the hope that a tougher stance on the 'China threat' could mean more votes at the ballot-box.

For much of the 1990s after Clinton took the White House, the use of the spectre of China for partisan politics continued unabated, though this time it was mainly conservative Republicans' turn to use the mantra of 'being soft on China' to attack Clinton and what they called 'Panda huggers' in Washington. William Triplett II, co-author of the sensational book *The Year of the Rat: How Bill Clinton Compromised U.S. Security for Chinese Cash*, serves as an instructive example here. This one-time chief Republican counsel to the Senate Foreign Relations Committee never doubted the merit of using the

China threat in Washington's power play. For him, 'to expose wrongdoing by China and to frustrate and embarrass those who were trying to improve America's ties with Beijing' are simply the two sides of the same coin.[15]

While the political economy of fear shifted its focus to terrorism in the wake of 'September 11', the 2008 US presidential campaign saw the return of attention to the China menace. In the run up to the Ohio primary in April 2008, Hillary Clinton spoke at a trade forum in Pittsburgh: 'Today, China's steel comes here and our jobs go there. We play by the rules and they manipulate their currency. We get tainted fish and lead-laced toys and poisoned pet food in return'.[16] There was little doubt that the 'us/them' dichotomy was carefully scripted in her speech to strike a responsive chord with her mainly blue-collar audience. Her political flirting with China-bashing was so blatant that one of her foreign policy advisers, Richard Baum, resigned in protest, citing that she 'has chosen to take the low road in her effort to gain our party's presidential nomination'.[17] Yet on the so-called 'low road' she was far from a lone traveller. The other Democrat contender (and later President) Barack Obama resorted to essentially the same tactic. Though his campaign was allegedly all about 'hope', he nevertheless played the politics of fear when it came to China, accusing Beijing of 'grossly undervaluing its currency', unfairly 'dumping goods into our market', and violating intellectual property rights.[18]

It is not that such accusations are entirely false. Much rather, instead of helping find sensible solutions, those accusations, usually heard loudest on campaign trails, were framed specifically in a climate of fear for self-interests and instant political advantage. In this context, the American labour movement is in the same league as those political high-fliers. Within this powerful movement are a coalition of trade officials, workers, and left intellectuals who have long used China as a lightning rod to rally against big businesses that have threatened the foundation of unionised labour by shutting down production lines and moving them offshore (often to China). Accusing business interests of kowtowing to dictators in Beijing and sacrificing human rights and moral principles for big dollar, they aimed at seizing the high moral ground in the anti-globalisation labour movement. Commenting on the American labour movement's campaign against the US granting permanent normal trade relations (PNTR) status to China, Kent Wong and Elaine Bernard rightly argue that the China debate 'emerged as a test of labour's ability to influence Congress, and established a litmus test for politicians'. Its opposition to China's WTO entry was used as 'a symbol of labor's opposition to the threat of globalization and unfair trade agreements'.[19]

On the other side of the battle line, big businesses also raise the spectre of Chinese competition to discipline their employees at home, pressure local governments to hand out more incentives, and win business deals. In 2005,

US oil giant Chevron and the Chinese National Offshore Oil Corp (CNOOC) went head to head in their competing bids for the US oil company Unocal. A full team of Chevron lobbyists worked tirelessly to scuttle CNOOC's chances, citing the inherently risky nature of a Chinese takeover, a message which, given its resonance with the China threat image, was never really a hard sell on Capitol Hill. Representing the California district where the headquarters of Chevron are located, the then House Resources Committee Chairman Richard Pombo moved quickly to demand an immediate review of the Chinese bid, while co-authoring a House resolution stating that a CNOOC takeover 'would threaten to impair the national security of the United States'.[20] Running up against not only a commercial rival but also a sophisticated, highly charged atmosphere of fear politics, CNOOC soon backed down; one week later, Unocal became part of Chevron. Even though Chevron's cash-and-stock offer was $700 million lower than the value of CNOOC's all-cash bid, the former's intimate knowledge about the operation of US politics more than made up for the difference in bid value. Over the three-year period from 2002–2005, Chevron had made over $100 000 in campaign contributions to Washington lawmakers. According to data compiled by the Center for Responsive Politics, Pombo alone received $13 500.[21]

While Chevron and Pombo exploited the fear of China as an economic menace, Congressman John Murtha of Pennsylvania, formerly Chairman of the House Appropriations Committee, viewed it as a military one. Either way, the fear of China served a similar function of advancing their political interests in their electoral district. In an effort to curry favour with local voters, Murtha had tried to boost the local economy by bringing in major defence contractors as well as numerous pet projects. With the help of defence investment, local businesses were gradually transformed from assembling circuit boards for PC monitors to becoming part of the supply chain of America's vast defence industry network, landing lucrative orders from the likes of Raytheon, Northrop Grumman and L-3 Communications. As local industry was increasingly busy assembling missile electronics, bomb-spotting robots and navigation circuits for the Bradley Fighting Vehicle and unmanned helicopter drones,[22] Murtha's political fortune also became deeply interwoven with the balance sheet of the US defence industry. One such telltale sign was revealed when on the programme of NewsHour with Jim Lehrer, he expressed dismay that 'we only bought four or five ships this year'.[23] Realising that fighting terrorist groups such as al-Qaeda and low-intensity insurgents in Afghanistan and Iraq could never sufficiently justify big-ticket defence purchases, the Democrat congressman did a famous about-face by abandoning his original support for the Iraq War and began to wonder whether China was the real threat 'down the road'. He now claimed that Iraq threatened to drain resources from 'procurement programs that ensure our military dominance' globally,[24] and instead saw the China threat as a more profitable source of fear that could allow the flow of resources to the kind of procurement programmes most beneficial to his own political fortune as well as his district.

Similarly, self-interests led Senator Joe Lieberman to cobble up the danger of 'the proliferation of new trouble spots around the world', which, of course, included China. At the Seapower Subcommittee Hearing for the Senate Committee on Armed Services in April 2006, he said that 'If we do not move to produce two submarines a year as soon as possible, we are in serious danger of falling behind China'. On the surface, his reference to the China challenge was motivated by a concern with its implications for US 'national security and economic stability' and the prestige of New London as the world's submarine capital. But upon a closer look, Lieberman's anxiety turned out to be mainly about the fate of Virginia-class submarines, which, at $2.5 billion each, were built by General Dynamics' Electric Boat Corporation in his home state, Connecticut. His worry was that if the building of new submarines did not keep pace, not only would many submarine designers and engineers be laid off, but also the welfare of his defence industry campaign contributors, not to mention his own seat, could be in trouble.[25]

US MILITARY KEYNESIANISM AND THE MILITARY-INDUSTRIAL COMPLEX'S 'CHINA SYNDROME'

By now, it appears that the US political economy of fear in relation to China has a distinct ring of militarism. Chalmers Johnson calls it the American version of 'military Keynesianism'. First used by the exiled Polish economist Michal Kalecki to describe Nazi Germany's economic recovery from the Great Depression, the term 'military Keynesianism' refers to the artificial stimulation of economic demand through government military spending.[26] By way of military Keynesianism, people can find secure jobs in the war economy, lawmakers have little trouble getting (re-)elected by content voters, and with the help of lawmakers, the military and defence contractors can continue enjoying political influence as well as reaping handsome profit. All the while, the commander-in-chief is able to muster ever-greater power and authority. As military Keynesianism takes hold, the emergence of the national security state is often not far off the horizon. Political scientist Harold Lasswell labelled this phenomenon the 'garrison state', 'a world in which the specialists on violence are the most powerful group in society'.[27]

In the American context, that most powerful group is called the military-industrial complex. Coined by President Eisenhower, the military-industrial complex consists of 'the Congressman who sees a new defense establishment in his district; the company in Los Angeles, Denver, or Baltimore that wants an order for more airplanes; the services which want them; the armies of scientists who want so terribly to test out their newest view'.[28] When Eisenhower initially canvassed this problem in his farewell address to the nation in 1961, little did he anticipate that four decades later, even the White House, whose occupants had become progressively indebted and addicted to defence contractors for their campaign contributions and job creation, would become an effective part of that powerful complex. In 2001, five of the top six donors to the House Armed Services Committee were nuclear weapons and missile defence contractors. According to the Center for Responsive Politics, in the 2004 election cycle, the arms industry contributed more than $13 million, with 62 per cent going to Republican candidates or committees.[29] Not surprisingly, by the time George W. Bush entered the White House in 2001, he had accumulated a large debt to the military-industrial complex. While there was much controversy over Bill Clinton's rewarding of his 1996 campaign donors with an overnight stay in the White House's Lincoln Bedroom, Bush easily outdid his predecessor by handing his campaign contributors—many of whom were executives of major defence contractors—powerful posts in the Pentagon. James Roche, an executive with Northrop Grumman, and Peter B. Teets, former president and chief operating officer of Lockheed Martin, were appointed respectively as secretary and undersecretary of the Air Force. Gordon England, a vice president of General Dynamics, was made secretary of the Navy.[30] Moreover, one will not forget that Vice President Dick Cheney himself came straight from the top job of the oil service and military construction firm Halliburton. Stephen Hadley, before his appointments as deputy director of the National Security Council and later the National Security Advisor, was a partner in the Washington-based law firm Shea & Gardner, which represented Lockheed Martin. In total, 32 major Bush policymakers had significant ties to the arms industry.[31]

The military-industrial complex thrives on military spending. By one (perhaps conservative) estimate, in 2002 the number of private firms in the US that profited from the military contracting systems reached 85 000.[32] But in order to maintain high-level military spending upon which the production of weapons systems is dependent, threats have to be in continuous production. For, in the words of a defence analyst from the Lexington Institute, 'The most fundamental thing about defense spending is that threats derive defense spending'.[33] To Martin Feldstein, Professor of Economics at Harvard University and one-time chief economic adviser to President Reagan, the obvious linkage between threat and defence spending is not the question. The 'real questions', as he maintains, 'are how much more [spending] is needed, what the new funds should be spent on, and how the money can be raised'.[34]

C. Wright Mills once observed that 'military threat places a premium on the military and upon their control of men, material, money, and power'.[35]

Yet, not just any type of threat will suffice for military Keynesianism to operate at full speed. The threat has to be both major and durable. The Soviet Union used to be one such source of fear. After its collapse, many military planners, who made a career out of 'containing' the Soviet threat, were in immediate danger of becoming politically irrelevant. As a journalist then put it, '"Board game" conferences to discuss choke points and sea lanes will become harder to find, and those who used to attend them will have to find another line of work'.[36] And for the defence apparatus as a whole, maintaining Cold-War-level military spending would become a tall order in a post-Soviet era. As the demand for weapons started to dwindle, many defence contractors faced the prospect of having to shut down their production line. The imperative of commercial survival would force them to look harder for new promising markets, which could explain why the oil-rich Middle East and the newly-industrialising countries in East Asia caught their attention.

But even those new markets would not last without the identification of new worthy threats. In the Middle East, thanks to the Iraqi invasion of Kuwait and the terrorist attacks of 'September 11', on both occasions the Saddam regime filled the threat vacancy. As it turned out, the 1990-1991 Gulf War, which was watched on living room televisions around the world, became a brilliant real-time advertising campaign for weapons suppliers. Within three years after the Gulf War, the US signed arms deals with Gulf countries worth billions of dollars.[37]

Although defence contractors and their CEOs made huge profits out of the Gulf War and the 'War on Terror', 'rogue states' and terrorist groups could not provide a sustained rationale for the continued production and purchase of advanced weapons systems, such as the F-35 Joint Strike Fighters, the F-22 Raptor jet fighters, Virginia-class submarines and Trident D5 submarine ballistic missiles. Neither small 'rogue states' nor the shadowy Al-Qaeda have the apparent ability to engage in submarine battles deep in the ocean, for which the Virginia-class submarine was specially designed. The F-22, dubbed 'the most unnecessary weapon system built by the Pentagon', was from the outset intended to counter some mysterious Soviet aircraft that never saw the light of day.[38] Indeed, even with the two vast battle grounds of Iraq and Afghanistan lying wide open in front of US war planners, by then Secretary of Defense Robert Gates's own admission, 'the F-22 has not performed a single mission in either theater'.[39] To his predecessor Donald Rumsfeld, Afghanistan was simply not a 'target rich' area to start with.[40]

If the spectre of terrorism alone provides limited room for the continued operation of America's colossal machine of military Keynesianism, nothing short of a 'near-peer' competitor, much like the former Soviet Union, should do. In the post-Cold War era, the only candidate is China. Only with a threat as big as China can those weapons programs grow into an optimal size and become both strategically justifiable and financially sustainable. 'When a program gets to a certain size, in the billions, it employs so many people in so many districts you can't kill it', said a congressional staffer and former Army officer.[41] For example, with its contracts in all of the 48 continental states, the B-2 Stealth Bomber, whose contract team is made up of a who's who of leading military contractors including Northrop Grumman, Boeing, Hughes Aircraft, and General Electric, has been virtually assured the widest possible support from Congress.[42] Some forty years ago, Senator J. William Fulbright remarked that 'Millions of Americans whose only interest is in making a decent living have acquired a vested interest in an economy geared to war. Those benefits, once obtained, are not easily parted with. Every new weapons system or military installation soon acquires a constituency'.[43] But even he did not foresee the magnitude of this constituency today, nor did he seem to envisage that the constituency would include the White House.

In 2001, as soon as George W. Bush came to office, the newly-elected President branded Beijing as a 'strategic competitor'. On 6 February 2006, Bush proposed a record military budget of $439.3 billion for 2007. Noticeably, on the same day he sent the budget request to Congress, the 2006 *Quadrennial Defense Review Report* was officially submitted, which contains the now well-known punch line that 'Of the major and emerging powers, China has the greatest potential to compete militarily with the United States'.[44] A sheer coincidence in timing perhaps, but such a coincidence made perfect sense given that the China threat had served explicitly as a major justification for maintaining American satellite capability, the F-22 and other new types of fighter aircraft, missile defence, new naval ships, or any other big-ticket programme.[45] For example, Robert Gates told members of the Senate Armed Services Committee in February 2008 that the F-22 fighter 'is principally for use against a near peer in a conflict, and I think we all know who that is'.[46] One person who certainly knew the answer was Bruce Carlson, commander of the Air Force Materiel Command. The Air Force had long planned to buy 380 F-22 Raptor jets, each costing around $140 million. But only 187 jets had been approved in the budget. An unhappy Carlson complained to a group of trade reporters in early 2008 that 187 was 'the wrong number', for it would leave too much room for risk to national security in future military competition or confrontation with China.[47] And for the Navy, the line of reasoning was the same. As a former naval officer put it, 'China is everyone's reason for a big Navy'.[48] Defence commentator Fred Kaplan has labelled this whole phenomenon the Pentagon's 'China Syndrome':

> Every day and night, hundreds of Air Force generals and Navy admirals must thank their lucky stars for China. Without the spectre of a rising Chinese military, there would be no rationale for such a large fleet of American nuclear submarines

and aircraft carriers, or for a new generation of stealth combat fighters—no rationale for about a quarter of the Pentagon's budget.[49]

Caught up in the 'China Syndrome' himself, Rumsfeld was 'annoyed' that 'the war in Iraq has diverted resources from his real goal of "transforming" the military into a high-tech outfit that can scare the bejeezus out of China'.[50]

THE POWER/KNOWLEDGE NEXUS IN THE AMERICAN CHINA-THREAT KNOWLEDGE COMMUNITY

The political economy of the China fear no doubt has something to do with the Cold War mentality, political self-interests, and even greed on the part of politicians and defence contractors. However, those factors alone cannot legitimately sustain military Keynesianism unless the fear is sanctioned by 'objective' knowledge. In other words, the political economy manifested in the 'China syndrome' cannot be the sole work of the military-industrial complex. Rather, demonstrating a classic case of the desire/power/knowledge nexus, it relies on the valuable service provided by the China-threat knowledge community. This epistemic community allows Sinophobia an aura of objective truth, credibility and urgency, through which public support can be easily galvanised for the power elite and their various political economic agendas under the unquestioned guise of defending national security against an existential threat. If Congressmen, the military services, and defence contractors so far have had much luck in securing the massive military budgets they have wanted, they should thank not China, but this knowledge community for its contribution of the weapon of 'truth'.

As Andrew Bacevich notes, intellectuals, through their imagination of self and Other, have played a key role in the continuation of military Keynesianism. He rightly points out that 'Militarism qualifies as our very own work, a by-product of our insistence on seeing ourselves as a people set apart, unconstrained by limits or by history'.[51] Thus, the 'China threat' paradigm as a particular scheme of self/Other construction is central to US military Keynesianism. From the beginning, the military-industrial complex has been a military-industrial-academic complex, of which the knowledge-producing community of the 'China threat' paradigm is a fully-paid-up member. Figuring prominently in this China-threat knowledge community are think tank fellows, opinion leaders, as well as university academics. By way of workshops, reports, media commentaries, opinion pieces, congressional testimonies, books, and journal articles, they contribute to the constant production of the danger code on China and a prevailing structure of feeling within which the political economy of fear in the US and the West more generally can operate without a hitch.

Some members of the China-threat knowledge community maintain the umbilical cord between knowledge and power by speaking directly to power and for power. They may be called 'embedded experts',[52] who hold public office in the national security apparatus. For example, after George W. Bush's election victory in 2000, Bush acknowledged that his administration 'borrowed' twenty of the best people from the American Enterprise Institute (AEI) for state service in America's hour of need.[53] In all, the neoconservative Center for Security Policy (CSP) supplied twenty-two former advisers or board members to the same administration.[54] It is unnecessary to add that the AEI and the CSP are both home to some of the most outspoken commentators in the China-threat knowledge community.

Other 'embedded experts' come from leading universities. Aaron L. Friedberg, well-known for his view of the China threat, is a professor of politics and international affairs from Princeton University's Woodrow Wilson School (WWS) whose graduate programmes proudly boast the rather accurate and fitting ambition of 'preparing future public service leaders'. In his other life, Friedberg served as Dick Cheney's National Security Advisor on China Affairs from 2003 to 2005 and was appointed to the Department of Defense's (DoD) Defense Policy Board in 2007. Another good example is Paul Wolfowitz, an architect of the US policy on China as a 'strategic competitor'. Before becoming Deputy Secretary of Defense from 2001–2005, Wolfowitz was the dean of the Paul H. Nitze School of Advanced International Studies (SAIS) at Johns Hopkins University, a School originally founded by Paul Nitze, a senior government official who was instrumental in shaping US defence policy on the basis of the Soviet threat during the Cold War.

During the George W. Bush presidency, the China-threat knowledge community led by some prominent neocons became immensely influential. But the knowledge/power nexus is by no means unique to the Bush administration. As exemplified by the so-called 'Blue Team', the China-threat knowledge community was politically active throughout the Clinton years in the 1990s. Named after the side that represents the US in the Pentagon's war games (the unnamed foe is called the 'Red Team'), the Blue Team was a loose community of members of Congress, top congressional staff, Republican political operatives, former intelligence officers, journalists, think-tank analysts, historians and scholars, some of whom were 'tenured professors at the country's most prestigious universities'.[55] Through this informal yet powerful network, 'China threat' experts from top universities and leading think tanks were able to collectively exert steady influence on America's national security establishment.

Manifested in the service of power by the priesthood of China-threat experts, the power/knowledge nexus is not a one-way street. In essence, it is a symbiotic relationship, for the production of such knowledge cannot be detached from the power arrangement it serves. Therefore, any understanding of this connection would be incomplete without looking at how this particular China knowledge is defined, promoted, and regulated by power. Though specific knowledge about the China threat may be the work of university academics and think tank analysts, its conceptual and financial ancestry can often be traced back to the military-industrial complex and the national security state, which, whether explicitly or implicitly, help delineate the intertextual, paradigmatic boundaries of what kind of questions can be asked, what topics are off limit, and even what counts as legitimate knowledge. Just as area studies in the US were shaped by power, ideology and geopolitics, so too is this powerful China paradigm in contemporary China watching.

Indeed, the discursive production of the China threat makes for a sizeable knowledge industry. Some of the most prominent players in this industry include both individual scholars and such media outlets as the *Weekly Standard, Commentary, Wall Street Journal, The Washington Times*, and Encounter Books, a San Francisco-based publishing house. A self-promotion material produced by the *Weekly Standard* offers a rare insight into part of the operation of this industry. 'Thanks to a unique VIP distribution system, a select list of the most powerful men and women in government, politics, and the media receive the publication via hand-delivery on Sunday morning—just in time for the nationally televised talk shows', thus boasts the neoconservative flagship magazine.[56]

Many hawkish and neoconservative think tanks such as the Project for the New American Century (PNAC) and the AEI are behind these media outlets and marketing operations. Those think tanks, pivotal in the production of the 'China threat' knowledge, in turn are staffed by retired politicians, generals, and intelligence officers from the political establishment through what some have called the 'revolving door' phenomenon. That is, former government officials, military servicemen, and defence industrialists (re)join the ranks of professors and research fellows at universities and think tanks, thereby bringing the influence of power directly to the process of knowledge production. A quick glance at the signatures on the PNAC's 1997 founding statement reveals 'a rogue's gallery of intransigent hardliners' who are mainly ex-government and ex-Pentagon officials in the Reagan era. Dick Cheney, Donald Rumsfeld, Paul Wolfowitz, William Bennett, I. Lewis Libby and Eliot Cohen are only some of the most recognisable luminaries. And there is no prize for guessing what kind of knowledge those officials-turned-national-security gurus would bring to the understanding of China. The 2000 PNAC report, entitled *Rebuilding America's Defenses: Strategy, Forces, and Resources for a New Century*, insists that China is 'the potential enemy'. The report's author, Thomas Donnelly, once worked as a professional staff member at the US House of Representatives Committee on National Security. Later, he became a Director at Lockheed Martin before his move through the revolving door again to a post at the AEI.[57]

The AEI, the CSP, and the Heritage Foundation, all key sources of the China-threat knowledge in the forms of policy briefs, research reports and opinion pieces, tell a similar story. One China specialist at the AEI, Dan Blumenthal, was previously senior director for China, Taiwan and Mongolia in the Secretary of Defense's Office of International Security Affairs. Another AEI China expert, the late James Lilley, was formerly a CIA station chief in Beijing, Director of the American Institute in Taiwan, and Ambassador to China. Harvey Feldman, Distinguished Fellow in China Policy at the Heritage Foundation, was once Director of the Office of the Republic of China Affairs and one of the architects of the 1979 Taiwan Relations Act. The ubiquitous China commentator John J. Tkacik, Jr., also at the Heritage Foundation, previously served with the US Foreign Service in Taiwan, Hong Kong, and mainland China. At the CSP, which is directed by former Pentagon official Frank Gaffney, on its Board of Directors was once Charles M. Kupperman, former vice president of Strategic Integration & Operations, Missile Defense Systems, at Boeing. Its Advisory Council, meanwhile, is regarded by some commentators as 'a virtual Star Wars hall of fame', almost entirely made up of former Star Warriors from the Reagan administration.[58]

To highlight the symbiotic link between power and knowledge in a significant section of China watching is not to suggest that practitioners cannot make a worthy contribution to the scholarly field of China studies, or that all research on the China threat is necessarily tainted by the influence of the power apparatus. Harold Isaacs, the author of the classic study *Scratches on Our Minds*, was affiliated with the CIA-assisted Center for International Studies at MIT, but his proximity to the government, as Ido Oren notes, did not stop him producing a rigorous and high-quality study of American views of China and India.[59] In some cases, close encounters with power may even make one a sharp critic of it, as in the case of Chalmers Johnson, author of *Blowback* and *The Sorrows of Empire*, who once worked as a consultant for the Office of National Estimates of the CIA.[60] However, more often than not, even with the best intention of distancing oneself from the political establishment, it is difficult for people with previous experience in the government and especially the military-industrial complex to divest themselves completely of the influence of power and its prevailing ideology, normative concerns and cognitive habits. On the China-threat front, the views of many practitioners turned scholars, closely aligned with the vested interests of their former employers, testify to this power/knowledge entanglement.

One aspect of such entanglement concerns research grants and donations. According to a 2002 report by the Association of American Universities

(AAU), the DoD is the third largest funder (after the National Institutes of Health and the National Science Foundation) of university research, which accounts for more than 60 per cent of defence basic research.[61] Similarly, a significant share of the funding received by lobbying think tanks comes from hardline foundations and defence companies. In its 1998 annual report, where the CSP acknowledged the financial support it had received since its founding, virtually every weapons-maker made it to the list, ranging from Lockheed Martin (and before their merge, Lockheed and Martin), Boeing and TRW to General Dynamics, Rockwell International and Northrop Grumman (and in its pre-merge incarnations, Northrop and Grumman). As indicated in the report's charts, about one quarter of the Center's annual incomes flowed from corporations, of which half came from defence contractors.[62]

The military-industrial-academic nexus is evident also in many university-based research projects on China. For example, after the end of the Cold War, studies on the strategic implications of China's rise have benefited from sizeable grants from the largely conservative, anti-Communist foundations such as the Smith Richardson, Bradley, Scaife, and Olin Foundations.[63] The John M. Olin Foundation, which funded the John M. Olin Institute for Strategic Studies at Harvard University (Samuel Huntington was its Founding Director), was set up by a chemical and munitions manufacturer. Some more reputable social sciences foundations, which maintain a keen interest in sponsoring China-related studies, have been revealed as once cover organisations for the CIA. Their influence on the direction of disciplines is as important as that of government funding on research during the Cold War.[64]

The DoD's Minerva Initiative provides another potential financial boon to the China-threat knowledge community. This initiative is modelled on the US National Defense Education Act introduced at the early stage of the Cold War. Initially coming with a $50 million research fund up for grabs, it calls upon university academics to offer their expertise on several Pentagon-nominated security challenges such as religious and cultural changes in the Islamic world and the development of the Chinese military and technology.[65] Co-administered by the National Science Foundation, the project states that it seeks a diverse range of views, but its aim is to 'foster a new generation of engaged scholarship in the social sciences that seeks to meet the challenges of the 21st century'.[66] It is too soon to tell how this Initiative, first launched in 2008, may come to shape the outcomes of its funded studies on China. Thus far, there is only one China-related project funded by this Initiative. However, if Project Camelot in the 1960s established by the US Army is anything to go by, it does not inspire much confidence in either its neutrality or promised intellectual diversity.[67] Consider, for example, the administrative setup of the Minerva Initiative. With the condition that Pentagon officials sit on each peer-review panel, this almost certainly guarantees that the funded proposals are as diverse as the worldview and strategic agenda of the military-industrial complex would allow, even though the Pentagon often keeps a low-profile in running those research projects.

Where foreign sources share similar political interests in the politics of fear vis-à-vis China, the production of the China threat knowledge in the US often become a transnational joint venture. As Lawrence Soley notes, many China research programmes in the US have received grants from Taiwanese foundations and business leaders, 'many of whom are also political leaders'.[68] During his time as a senior vice president at the AEI, John Bolton was paid $30 000 over three years in the mid-1990s by Taiwan's government for research papers on Taiwan's UN membership issues.[69]

It is often said that those who pay the piper call the tune. Where a research project fails to meet the funding body's expectation, not only does the prospect of securing further funding diminish dramatically, but existing funding can also be withdrawn as a 'punishment'. In June 2001, US National Intelligence Council (NIC) fired the RAND Corporation from a classified project ordered by Congress to assess China's future military capabilities. The NIC reports directly to the CIA Director, who at the time was George Tenet. Tenet's hardline view on China, as evidenced in his annual presentations on current and projected national security threats to Congress, had been well known. But RAND's findings, though depicting China as a growing military power, stopped short of calling it a clear and present danger, thereby failing to offer the kind of conclusion the NIC had desired. One analyst familiar with the project later complained that people at the NIC, themselves under pressure from Republican Hawks in Congress, 'want China to be 10 feet tall'.[70] This little episode provides an interesting glimpse into the sometimes decisive role of power in the constitution of China knowledge in the US as well as the role of desire in that power/knowledge nexus. Heavily dependent on government (especially Pentagon) funding and for fear of missing out on future contracts, RAND and other think tanks might have learned a lesson or two.

The RAND-type incident in China watching does not happen very often, but its rarity seems to be a sign of the already tacit cooperation between knowledge and power, rather than a clear indication of the independence of China knowledge from power. In any case, the broad political consensus of the military-industrial-academic complex, having circulated in the mainstream imagination for generations and obtained a degree of cultural and institutional hegemony, has rendered overt political control largely unnecessary. IR, as Peter Monaghan notes, 'is one of a number of fields that are so interwoven with the federal government, particularly with military and intelligence agencies, that they cannot avoid aping the political ideology of those agencies'.[71]

Consequently, for all the claims of the 'China threat' paradigm to be scientific knowledge and objective truth, it has its roots in power and is well-suited to the service of power. By taking note of the power/knowledge nexus in the construction and function of the China threat knowledge, I do not suggest that every single piece of work in the 'China threat' genre is written under the decree of the Pentagon in exchange for funding and/or political patronage. As noted above, the nexus often takes multiple forms, some of which are subtler, less visible and less direct than others. Indeed, it is in the interest of both knowledge and power that their liaison be kept as covert as possible. This is what Foucault means by the 'subtle mechanisms' in the production of knowledge where the exercise of power 'becomes capillary'.[72] In his account of the relationship between the state, the foundations, and international and area studies during the Cold War, Cumings used the term 'going capillary' to describe how, through small, everyday and local avenues, such as decisions on who gets tenure, who edits prestigious journals, which research project gets funded, and which textbooks are adopted, power was able to maintain its presence so that 'people do things without being told, and often without knowing the influences on their behavior'.[73] Also, once taking on a life of its own, knowledge can span an intertextual, disciplinary and institutional web within which it can self-generate, ostensibly removing itself a step further from power.

Thus far, I have critically examined the power/knowledge/desire nexus in the case of the 'China threat' paradigm. In doing so, I do not imply that the solution lies in the pursuit of pure knowledge and neutral scholarship on the part of those China watchers, who should shun government agencies, which in turn should stop funding social science research altogether. In the fields of social sciences at least, there is no such thing as pure knowledge, disconnected totally from desire and power. Indeed, as examined at the beginning of this book, pure social knowledge is neither possible nor even desirable. I am not against the power/knowledge/desire nexus per se; rather, my point is that we, as producers of knowledge, should guard against the possibility of being misused and abused by power which often serves special interests. We should be self-conscious and sensitive to the *consequences*—however unintended or even well-intended—of our knowledge as practice.

If all knowledge is linked to power in one way or another, it may beg the question of why the 'China threat' paradigm has been singled out here for criticism. The reason, I submit, is that not all knowledge/power nexuses are equal in terms of their intertextual influence or practical and moral implications. As noted above, associated with the 'China threat' knowledge has been a particular kind of political economy of fear. It not only lays the discursive foundation for military Keynesianism, but also has profound and even dangerous repercussions for Sino-Western relations in general and US-China relations in particular. When acted upon by foreign policy-makers, the 'China threat' paradigm runs the risk of turning into a self-fulfilling prophecy, an issue which will be examined in the next chapter.

5. The 'China threat': a self-fulfilling prophecy

Realpolitik, in short, is a self-fulfilling prophecy: its be-liefs generate actions that confirm those beliefs.... The point is that whether or not states really are existential threats to each other is in one sense not relevant, since once a logic of enmity gets started states will behave in ways that make them existential threats, and thus the behavior itself becomes part of the problem. This gives enemy-images a homeostatic quality that sustains the logic of Hobbesian anarchies.

Alexander Wendt[1]

Chinese nationalism cannot be comprehended in isola-tion; instead, it must be understood as constantly evolv-ing as Chinese interact with other nationalities. In particular, because of the stature of the United States and Japan, Sino-American and Sino-Japanese relations are central to the evolution of Chinese nationalism to-day.

Peter Hays Gries[2]

WHAT'S THE COST OF IMAGINING AN ENEMY?

In Charles Frazier's award-winning novel *Cold Mountain*, the male protago-nist Inman, a badly wounded soldier running away from the bloody battle-field during the American Civil War, meets a blind street vendor. Similar to his own wounds, someone must have been responsible for his blindness, Inman wonders. To Inman's surprise, however, the street vendor says he was actually born that way. Looking at his terrible wounds at the hands of known enemies, Inman somehow starts to pity that blind man. 'For how did you find someone to hate for a thing that just was? What would be the cost of not having an enemy? Who could you strike for retribution other than yourself?'[3]

As he quickly flips through these questions in his mind, suddenly Inman begins feeling lucky—at least he knows his enemy. To that blind man, knowing no enemy denies him that precious sense of certainty or a clear target for revenge.

With his known enemy, the lucky Inman is in good company. In many ways, the military-industrial complex finds itself in a similar situation, but its lucky star is the perceived certain threat of China. Without knowing this threat, the high-level military spending would be difficult to justify, and without that military spending, the political economy of fear could not function properly, nor could military Keynesianism continue to flourish. This is why Richard N. Haass, President of the Council on Foreign Relations and former Director of Policy Planning in the US State Department, observes that having survived decades of the Soviet challenge, containment might not be able to survive its own success.[4] To the military-industrial complex, the absence of a threat/enemy constitutes an ultimate threat.

While the lack of an enemy—real or imagined—appears costly indeed for the discursive identity and institutional 'survival' of the military-industrial complex, I contend that having an enemy, even an imagined one, is by no means cost-free. In fact, in the case of China, it could be very costly in that the construction and treatment of China as a threat could result in China becoming one in reality. In other words, the cost lies in the fact that the 'China threat' paradigm could become self-fulfilling in practice.

A self-fulfilling prophecy, according to American sociologist Robert Merton, means that 'a *false* definition of the situation which makes the originally false conception come true'.[5] What is 'false' in hindsight or in the eyes of a bystander is frequently defined as real by the actor in question; and 'if men define situations as real, they are real in their consequences'.[6]

In international relations, fear, often based on 'false' images, can have precisely such self-fulfilling consequences. Thucydides, the author of a realist 'great text' *History of the Peloponnesian War*, noted a self-fulfilling prophecy of fear in interstate politics. In his account for the war's outbreak, Thucydides suggested that 'What made war inevitable was the growth of Athenian power and the fear which this caused in Sparta'.[7] More than two millennia later, another realist scholar-practitioner, George Kennan ascribed the origin of the Cold War to the paranoid ideology of the Soviet Union.[8]

If so, the fear manifested in the 'China threat' paradigm could also become confirmed in reality. Two interrelated processes are at play here. First, the 'China threat' paradigm, taken as objective truth, would imply the need for containing China in practice. Second, such practice, given the logic of mutual responsiveness, is more likely than not to be mirrored back by China in either symmetric or asymmetric ways. As the latter's hardline mimicry apparently 'confirms' the initial fear of the China threat, what we are witnessing is a classic case of self-fulfilling prophecy.

THE 'CHINA THREAT' PARADIGM AND ITS SOCIAL CONSTRUCTION OF CONTAINMENT

The previous chapter examined how the knowledge of the China threat is linked to power. But its implications in power relations are not confined to the domestic sphere; they permeate also through the realms of international relations and foreign policy. In fact, the 'China threat' paradigm is instrumental to the making of the 'containment' policy towards China. Here, I use 'containment' as shorthand for a range of US policy measures directed at China in military, economic, political and moral realms. Their common aim is, with various degrees of pressure and coercion, to deter or 'dissuade' China from expanding its power beyond certain limits. Of course, this China containment strategy cannot be likened to the American Cold War containment policy towards the Soviet Union; much has changed between then and now.[9] Indeed, given its obvious Cold War connotation, 'containment' has lost its potency as a policy label among scholars or policy-makers alike; instead, people prefer to call American China policy 'hedging', 'principled engagement', 'congagement', 'balancing', 'management' or 'deterrence'. Whether or not 'containment' is the right word should not detain us here. The point is that so long as it is more or less the same 'threat' perception and institutions that continue to be behind the making of US China policy, it would be erroneous to believe that US policy has made a clear break with the past.

If containment continues to be part and parcel of US China policy, what does it have to do with the 'China threat' paradigm? It is one thing to say that there is a link between theory and ideas on the one hand and practice and foreign policy on the other, but it is quite a challenge to empirically demonstrate such a link. Gordon Craig once observed that 'To establish the relationship between ideas and foreign policy is always a difficult task, and it is no accident that it has attracted so few historians'.[10] The result, of course, has been a vicious cycle—with little scholarly interest in this matter, we end up knowing still less about the connection. Furthermore, for various reasons, both scholars and practitioners tend to play down the existence of such a connection. In the case of scholars, they often lament that their ideas are underappreciated by practitioners, whereas the latter tend to brush aside ideas coming from the ivory tower as nothing more than arm-chair commentaries. Either way, the common perception is that there has been a yawning gap between the ivory tower and the corridor of power.[11] While such a gap may well exist in certain individual circumstances or in relation to particular policy or theoretical issues, overall this does not overturn the proposition that policy necessarily operates through ideas or theories. As will be demonstrated below, without the knowledge support of the 'China threat' paradigm, containment will not be able to function as an effective policy.

First, the threat paradigm helps define (or at least renew) the purpose of containment as a policy. Bernard Schaffer tells us that policy has three dimensions of meaning: purposes; the review of information and the determination of appropriate action; and the securing and commitment of resources in its implementation.[12] We are familiar with the second and third dimensions of policy, but no policy can exist without the first, namely, a certain purpose (or purposes). In fact, functioning like a fulcrum, the articulation of a relevant purpose is often the very first—sometimes also the most difficult—step in a policy-making process. For instance, as far as US strategic planners are concerned, the main challenge lies not in implementing a policy of military build-up, but in justifying or identifying a legitimate public purpose for that policy. Likewise, for weapons manufacturers, promoting arms sales is not an overly complicated task; but in order to translate it into official policy, they require a rationale, or more specifically, a legitimate target against which their arms should be deployed. In both cases, identifying a purpose or target is crucial to policy-making.

Thanks to a China threat 'out there', a new purpose can be injected into US foreign policy. It provides a rationale for a policy that would otherwise struggle to justify its contemporary relevance. This constitutive effect on US China policy can be likened to the way in which the discourse of terrorism justified and legitimised the US-led 'War on Terror'. For a start, the terrorist threat immediately gave George W. Bush a hitherto elusive sense of certainty about his mission and policy direction. As reported in the *New York Times*, not until the 'September 11' tragedy did the President begin to feel 'sure about what he should be doing'.[13] While the rise of terrorism has enabled the US to preoccupy itself with the 'War on Terror' for more than a decade, at least for a particular section of the US foreign policy establishment, a more lasting purpose for US foreign and security policy requires the China threat.

Second, the threat paradigm contributes to policy-making by spelling out some specific policy options. From the beginning, the representation of China as a danger is not merely an intellectual question about 'what is China?'; it is always concerned with the practical question of 'what to do *about* it?' For example, in their book *The Coming Conflict with China*, Bernstein and Munro devote a whole chapter to the issue of how to manage China's rise. Among their policy recommendations are maintaining a strong US military presence in Asia, strengthening Japan, continuing arms sales to Taiwan, and restricting China's nuclear weapons arsenal.[14] Similarly, in the last pages of *The Tragedy of Great Power Politics*, Mearsheimer believes that an appropriate China policy is not what he calls the 'misguided' engagement strategy, but containment to 'slow the rise of China'.[15] Charles Krauthammer, a prominent neoconservative proponent of the China threat argument, not only advocated explicitly for containing China in his 1996 *Time* magazine article, but also detailed how this can best be done. Taking 'a rising and threatening China' as a pregiven fact, he insisted that 'any rational policy' towards the country should be predicated on various containment strategies such as strengthening regional alliances (with Japan, Vietnam, India, and Russia) to box in China, standing by Chinese dissidents, denying Beijing the right to host the Olympics, and keeping China from joining the WTO on its own terms. Speaking with a sense of urgency, he urged that this containment policy 'begin early in its career'.[16]

Feeling the same sense of urgency, Peter Navarro, in his book *The Coming China Wars*, warns consumers, corporate executives, and policy-makers of gathering storm clouds on the horizon. He then offers a range of policy prescriptions on 'How to fight—and win!—the coming China wars' (the title of his book's final chapter).[17] These require, for example, that the US 'adopt a "zero-tolerance" policy toward intellectual property theft', 'condemn China's actions in the strongest of terms, and if China's abuses of power continue, seek to strip China of its permanent veto' in the United Nations. What those policy prescriptions have in common, he adds, is that 'they require the economic and political will to stand up to China, along with the military might to back up the prescriptions'.[18]

If the military and economic threat of China entails military and economic containment, the image of China as a brutal, authoritarian state helps lay the foundation for moral and ideological sanction. Advising on how to deal with 'hostile regimes' in general, Kagan and Kristol offer a rich recipe of regime change:

> Tactics for pursuing a strategy of regime change would vary according to circumstances. In some cases, the best policy might be support for rebel groups, along the lines of the Reagan Doctrine as it was applied in Nicaragua and elsewhere. In other cases, it might mean support for dissidents by either overt and covert means, and/or economic sanctions and diplomatic isolation.... But the purpose of American foreign policy ought to be clear. When it comes to dealing with tyrannical regimes, especially those with the power to do us or our allies harm, the United States should seek not coexistence but transformation.[19]

Counting China as one of those 'tyrannical regimes', they urge that the US and the West make it harder for the Chinese regime to resolve its contradictions, thereby hastening its collapse.[20]

Of course, policy prescriptions from the China threat literature are not necessarily actual official policies, but through the influence of mainstream media and policy consultancy, the line between them is often easily crossed.

To start with, many China threat advocates, some of them prominent neocons, are high-profile media-savvy commentators. As Bacevich observes, apart from the neocon-dominated op-ed pages of the *Wall Street Journal*, each of the three leading general-interest daily newspapers in the US—the *Los Angeles Times*, the *New York Times*, and the *Washington Post*—has at least one regular neoconservative commentator: Max Boot and David Brooks respectively for the first two newspapers, and Charles Krauthammer and Robert Kagan for the third.[21] The *Weekly Standard*, a key neoconservative publication and one of the most reliable sources of the China threat analysis, boasts that its writers 'are in great demand on nationally broadcast political programs for their ideas and opinions. Frequent appearances on television testify not only to our influence in Washington but to our relevance on the national political scene'.[22] That probably is no overstatement. In July 2008, at the first sign that the Bush administration might fail to follow through a previously announced lucrative arms sales deal to Taiwan, no fewer than four China experts—Dan Blumenthal from the AEI, Aaron Friedberg from Princeton University, Randall Schriver from Armitage International, and Ashley Tellis from the Carnegie Endowment for International Peace—joined forces to persuade the administration to go ahead with that deal. In their co-authored article published in the *Wall Street Journal*, they demanded that 'Bush should keep his word on Taiwan'.[23] Less than three months later, Washington announced that more than $6 billion worth of sales in advanced weapons to Taiwan would go ahead. Although it is hard to measure and quantify the extent of their policy influence, it would be inconceivable that the opinion of those analysts, all of whom had served in Asia policy positions in the Bush administration, had made no policy impact.

In addition to media activism, many China threat analysts exert their influence through consultancy work. Michael Pillsbury, a well-known China hawk, falls into this category. Having worked at RAND and taught at several American universities, Pillsbury is regarded by the *Wall Street Journal* as 'a persistent force in shaping official American perceptions' of China, even though he appears on no public Defense Department roster.[24] Supported by his long-time mentor Andrew Marshall, head of the Pentagon's Office of Net Assessment, Pillsbury authored two books: *Chinese Views of Future Warfare* (1997) and *China Debates the Future Security Environment* (2000), which earn him a great deal of fame in China policy-making circles. As a *Washington Monthly* article notes, it was in part based on Pillsbury's work that the Pentagon's 2006 *Quadrennial Defense Review* famously identified China as the nation with 'the greatest potential to compete militarily with the United States'.[25] Moreover, some passages of the Pentagon's 2006 annual report on China's military power 'appear to be lifted directly out of Pillsbury's writings, including warnings of "asymmetric programs" in the works'.[26]

In fact, not just passages but entire policy packages are finding their way into Washington. Take, for example, China experts' frequent call for strengthening an alliance system surrounding China. On the ground, this is precisely what has been unfolding. At the centre of this alliance build-up and realignment is the beefed-up defence cooperation between the US and Japan. After Obama came to office, Japan's prime minister was his first Oval Office visitor from abroad and Japan was the destination of Mrs Clinton's first overseas trip as the Secretary of State.[27] More substantial cooperation includes their joint development of a missile defence system, the relocation of US First Army Corps command headquarters from America's west coast to Camp Zama, south of Tokyo, as well as the shift of the command operations of the Thirteenth Air Force, now in Guam, to Yokota airbase near Tokyo.[28] In this way, Japan has emerged as Washington's closest global strategic partner and its most robust partner against China.[29] In the words of Chalmers Johnson, a long-time China and Japan watcher, Japan has been turned into the 'control tower' of US-enforced security in Asia.[30]

US military relations with the Philippines have been the closest since the end of the Cold War. Military cooperation with the Indonesian military has intensified, with the 'unstated reason' being, in the words of Indonesia's Defense Minister, 'to balance the rising power of China'.[31] In Singapore, which already plays host to visiting US aircraft carriers, Fallon revealed in his March 2005 testimony that the US was actively seeking opportunities for expanded access to Singaporean facilities. And with India, Fallon noted growing US ties with the Indian Integrated Defence Staff and the Indian Armed Services.[32] In March 2006, George W. Bush made a historic visit to India, during which the two countries struck a nuclear deal, despite the fact that India was not a signatory to the Nuclear Non-Proliferation Treaty (NPT). Obama's 2010 visit to India and his call for India's permanent membership on the UN Security Council, according to commentators, both carry implications for China.[33] In late 2011, a centre-piece of Obama's visit to Australia was his announcement that Australia's northern city Darwin will host the rotational deployments of 2500 US marines, a move drawing Australia ever deeper into what defence expert Hugh White calls 'a more unified military coalition to confront China's growing maritime power'.[34]

As well as strengthening bilateral ties with Japan and Australia, the US has upgraded the trilateral strategic dialogues among Washington, Tokyo and Canberra from a bureaucratic to a ministerial level. An Australian scholar describes this new triple alliance as a 'little NATO' against China.[35] When America's steps to strengthen military ties with Thailand, Vietnam, Malaysia, Sri Lanka, and several central Asian countries are taken into account, the 'strategic net' woven by the US to 'persuade China to keep its ambitions within reason' becomes even more palpable.[36] Containing China is certainly not the only motive behind such bilateral military cooperation, but many commentators have no doubt that it is 'a central element', a view confirmed by US diplomats.[37] Commenting on those US efforts to create and strengthen alliances in the region, Samuel Berger concedes that 'continued rapprochement with India and effervescent US-Japan relations, both fully justified, now are pursued with more than a whiff of Chinese encirclement'.[38]

Certainly, 'China threat' experts cannot be given all the credit for these policy moves. For their part, many policy-makers themselves are concerned with a similar question of what to do about the China threat, an image which has now been internalised inside the Beltway. According to *Atlantic Monthly* contributing editor Robert Kaplan, this concern by practitioners often translates into the policy issue of 'how we would fight China'. Richard Bush and Michael O'Hanlon argue that what is revealed in Kaplan's 2005 *Atlantic Monthly* article is noteworthy. While dismissing the article as 'a combination of false advertising and misplaced analogies', they nonetheless point out that:

> Kaplan's article should have been taken seriously given the principal source of his information: the officers in the Pacific Command, an arm of the Department of Defense. It should be very significant that the individuals in command of America's front lines in the Pacific apparently believe there is a cold war [with China] in our future. For like their bosses in the Pentagon, *they have some power to act on their perceptions of the trajectory of Chinese military power.*[39]

Bush's and O'Hanlon's concern is well founded. In response to a perceived Chinese military threat, a series of US policy reviews, military build-up, and strategic realignment have been under way for years. For example, acting upon the assumption of Beijing's growing threat vis-à-vis Taiwan, by July 2004 Defense Secretary Rumsfeld had authorised the National Defense University, as a matter of urgency, to conduct nine war-game scenarios focusing on cross-strait relations, one of which was suggestively code-named 'Dragon's Thunder'.[40] Importantly, war games are not just that, mere games; they are often unmistakable signs of war plans in the making. According to William Arkin, an NBC News military analyst and *Washington Post* online columnist, the US has already built 'a new full fledged war plan for China'. Codenamed 'Operations Plan (OPLAN) 5077', it is the first new conventional war plan since the end of the Cold War and 'one of only three completed and full-fledged war plans of the US military... with assigned forces and more detailed annexes and appendices'.[41] The significance of such war plans, argues Arkin, is that once drafted, they will be tested through military exercises and refined through more intelligence to improve targeting and warning.[42] Such a process, initially growing out of a strategic concern, can soon take on a life of its own in the defence policy domain.[43]

The recent US military build-up in the western Pacific clearly testifies to this process. In the above-mentioned article 'How We Would Fight China', Kaplan reveals that the US has begun to triple its long-term deployment of nuclear submarines in Guam from three to ten, as well as to prepare the island to receive B-1 and B-2 long-range bombers. Indeed, at any given time, Guam's Andersen Airbase is home to some 100 000 bombs and missiles as well as 66 million gallons of jet fuel, making it the biggest strategic 'gas-and-go' airbase in the world.[44] There is little secret who the main target of this massive military build-up in Guam is. James Thomas, Deputy Assistant Defense Secretary for Plans, told the conservative *Washington Times* that 'the deployments of bomber elements to Guam on a more routine basis' are essentially the China part of a broad hedging strategy.[45] As reported in the *Atlantic Monthly*, both the bomber deployments and American nuclear upgrades have been linked to the China threat perception held by US military top brass.[46] Admiral William Fallon, formerly the US Pacific Command, once lamented that his bosses still seemed to be fighting the Cold War, as though China were the Soviet Union of old.[47]

Meanwhile, the image of China as an economic threat has led US policy-makers to assemble an impressive arsenal of economic sticks. During the 1990s, one such stick was the 'most-favoured-nation' (MFN) status (later called 'permanent normal trade relationship' or PNTR), which the US regularly threatened to withhold unless Beijing met its demands on human rights. In 2000, when that stick lost its magic, Congress promptly mandated the establishment of the US-China Economic and Security Review Commission to monitor the national security implications of China's economic rise, the only such institution in the US that targets a particular country. In July 2005, senators Charles Schumer and Lindsey Graham blamed an 'artificially undervalued' Chinese currency for the ballooning US trade deficits with China. To compel Beijing to appreciate its currency, they sponsored a bill threatening to impose an across-the-board punitive tariff of 27.5 per cent on Chinese imports. Some Congress members saw this measure as 'part of a sea change in congressional thinking that will eventually force the administration to give up its engagement strategy and begin to challenge China'.[48] In early 2006, under pressure from a US Senate legislation that urged the government to revoke its PNTR with China, Washington announced the establishment of a task force to ensure Beijing's compliance with global trade rules. This task force, also focusing on a single country, was again unprecedented in US history.[49] Indeed, Washington's uneasiness with China's economic challenge became so intense that on some days, as many as four congressional committees simultaneously had China on their agenda.[50]

Aided by the powerful perception of a rising China threat, what Robert Gates once called 'a number of programs' aimed at China now culminated in the Obama administration's 'Pivot to Asia', 'an integrated diplomatic, military, and economic strategy that stretches from the Indian subcontinent through Northeast Asia'.[51] As Walter Russell Mead summed up well after Obama's trip to Hawaii, Australia and Indonesia in November 2011:

> The cascade of statements, deployments, agreements and announcements from the United States and its regional associates in the last week has to be one of the most unpleasant shocks for China's leadership—ever. The US is moving forces to Australia, Australia is selling uranium to India, Japan is stepping up military actions and coordinating more closely with the Philippines and Vietnam in the South China Sea, Myanmar is slipping out of China's column and seeking to reintegrate itself into the region, Indonesia and the Philippines are deepening military ties with the the [sic] US: and all that in just one week. If that wasn't enough, a critical mass of the region's countries have agreed to work out a new trade group [Trans-Pacific Partnership or TPP] that does not include China, while the US, to applause, has proposed that China's territorial disputes with its neighbors be settled at a forum like the East Asia Summit—rather than in the bilateral talks with its smaller, weaker neighbors that China prefers.[52]

In isolation, each of these moves may not mean much, but the fact that they happened all at once must be more than pure coincidence. Why these coordinated moves then? Many argue that they are logical 'responses' to recent Chinese assertiveness, but this China factor alone does not provide the whole answer.[53] In any case, the 'China factor' does not exist independently of the fore-meanings provided by the 'China threat' lens. In this sense, the discourse of 'China threat' again has played a role in the contemporary US policy on China. While most social discourses carry certain policy implications,[54] what is special about the 'China threat' discourse is that its binary frameworks and unequivocal moral codes almost dictate the making of China policy. For instance, by framing US-China relations through the dichotomised lenses of security vs. threat, win vs. lose, survival vs. surrender, containment vs. appeasement, 'act now' vs. 'accept defeat forever', and so forth, this paradigm makes it not only obvious but imperative for policymakers to choose one set of options over the other. Confronting the China threat thus becomes not only a matter of military or economic security, but also a litmus test of Western/US credibility, ontological security and identity. For Ross Munro, should America fail to stand up to the China threat, it would be seen as no longer committed to security and stability in Asia. As a result, its credibility among Asian countries would suffer, which in turn could lead to a domino effect: 'Led by Japan, our friends would scurry to make concessions to China, possibly including closing their ports and airfields to U.S. armed forces. Our days as a true Asian power would be numbered'.[55]

A similar scenario was conjured up in *China's Strategic Modernization*, a draft report authored by the Defense Secretary's ISAB Task Force in October

2008. This report fears that China's growing clout could make America's allies in Asia, such as Japan and South Korea, become increasingly doubtful of US military commitment and resolve.[56] In this context, any conciliatory gesture towards China would amount to 'appeasement', showing 'signs of weakness', or even emboldening other dictators around the world.[57] Given the negative connotations of such epithets, taking a hardline stance on China becomes the only viable option.

Bill Clinton's about-face over Lee Teng-hui's US visa controversy in 1995 perfectly exemplifies the constitutive power of the 'China threat' paradigm. Initially the Clinton administration had reassured Beijing that Lee, given his official status as the president of Taiwan, would not be granted a visa to visit his alma mater Cornell University. However, looked through the 'China threat' paradigm, the whole issue soon came to be framed through the stark binaries of friend/foe and democracy/dictatorship. Consequently, not issuing Lee a visa was roundly condemned as a betrayal to a democratic friend as well as a kowtow to Beijing's authoritarian regime. Conveying precisely this clear-cut message to Clinton, Chuck Robb, a US senator and close friend of the President, went a step further by arguing that a kowtow to Beijing on this issue would 'permit China to determine the visa policy of the United States'. This line of argument immediately worked. In Robb's words, 'within minutes' of their meeting, Clinton agreed to reverse his decision and to grant the visa.[58]

During the 2005 Unocal bid controversy, Republican congressman Dana Rohrabacher passionately described the Chinese bid as evidence of China's belligerence to 'everything we stand for as a people'.[59] With the American national identity believed to be at stake, Congress almost unanimously passed a resolution condemning that bid. These examples show that the particular discursive effect of the 'China threat' paradigm not only prescribes containment, it mandates it. It is indicative of the 'tyranny of words' whereby people are 'at the mercy of labels, of expressions used as weapons'.[60]

THE CHINA THREAT AS A SOCIAL CONSTRUCT: A CASE OF MUTUAL RESPONSIVENESS

Despite the powerful effect of the 'China threat' paradigm on policy-making, we must acknowledge that the 'threat' representation is not the only contributing factor. To the extent that international relations are interactively constructed, the hardline China policy in the US is in part constituted by China's strategic behaviour. For example, the concept of 'AirSea Battle' (developed by the Washington-based Center for Strategic and Budgetary Assessments and now seriously entertained by the Pentagon as a part of a broader strategy of dealing with China) might be seen as a necessary response to Beijing's growing A2/AD capabilities,[61] rather than a pure brainchild of the 'China threat' discourse. Yet, equally, even as we turn attention to Chinese capabilities and behaviour in global politics, we must not lose sight of the constitutive role of the 'China threat' paradigm in the development of Chinese worldviews and strategic behaviour in the first instance. For example, the growth of China's A2/AD capabilities cannot possibly take place in an international vacuum; rather, they can themselves be seen as responses to still earlier Western policies on China, policies which are inevitably shaped by the 'China threat' perception. In this section, I will examine how some key indicators of the China threat, such as jingoistic Chinese nationalism, realpolitik thinking, and assertive foreign policy, can be understood not as inherent Chinese traits, but as social constructs courtesy of the 'China threat' theory as practice.

Sure, 'the degree to which China's domestic and foreign policy adjustments were influenced by US policy toward China' is very hard to empirically determine or quantify.[62] That said, it is still possible to establish their link in a qualitative manner. The link is no doubt mutual, and how China has influenced US policy has been well documented.[63] It is now time to examine the other side of the 'mutual responsiveness' coin, namely, how Chinese thinking and behaviour are constituted by Western theory and practice.

To illustrate, we first focus on two commonly known symptoms of the China threat: Chinese nationalism and China's realpolitik thinking. According to the 'China threat' paradigm, both phenomena are innate, pregiven attributes of China. Johnston argues that there was a pre-existing *parabellum* strategic culture in Chinese military classics. Meanwhile, China's new nationalism is believed to be a product of both indigenous nationalist ideas, such as culturalism, and China's rapid economic development and Chinese government manipulation.[64] As Fewsmith and Rosen put it,

> A public sense of China's 'rightful' place in the international arena has emerged alongside the country's economic development and has been cultivated by the Chinese government as part of its patriotic education campaign since 1993. Indeed, it was this consciousness of China's status in the international community that underlay much of the emergent nationalism of the 1990s.[65]

While some Chinese domestic sources are clearly at play, they alone cannot fully explain the rise of China's new nationalism since the 1990s. Take the factor of China's economic development for example. Certainly, the rapid economic growth which dates back to the 1980s does help boost Chinese national pride, and on occasions might have inflamed xenophobic extremism in some quarters of Chinese society. Yet, on balance, China's new-found prosperity has provided most Chinese with a rather benign and positive view of the outside world. If there was a correlation between nationalism and the economy, modern Chinese history shows that nationalism thrives not on healthy economic growth, but on economic stagnation and perceived national weakness. As Suisheng Zhao points out, the racially conscious term *Zhonghua minzu* (the Chinese race) did not emerge until the early Republican period when Chinese intellectuals found it necessary to invoke it to warn the country of 'the danger of annihilation under Western invasion'.[66] In line with this analysis, the most intense and virulent form of nationalism was found during the Boxer Rebellion and the Cultural Revolution, when China's economy was teetering on the verge of collapse.

To others, the rise of Chinese nationalism owes much to government propaganda and manipulation, especially its extensive patriotic education campaign. Yet, patriotic education has always existed in Chinese politics, right from the founding of the People's Republic.[67] Into the 1990s, as Kenneth Lieberthal observes, the political education, including the patriotic campaign, has in fact subsided, as most urban Chinese 'no longer participate in the political study groups that were a major feature of the system through the 1980s'.[68] Moreover, if government propaganda is the main driving force behind China's new nationalism, it is hard to explain why some of the most vocal nationalist voices come from 'the most internationally engaged sections of China'.[69] Supposedly, those sections, being further removed from government propaganda and more susceptible to Western influence, should be less, not more, nationalistic. Likewise, the factor of government propaganda does not explain why overseas Chinese, many of whom are not routinely exposed to official patriotic campaigns, are equally, if not more, nationalistic.

Furthermore, although the Chinese regime does need nationalism to boost its fragile legitimacy, the regime is keenly aware that nationalism is a double-edged sword that may also threaten its mandate of heaven.[70] Today, Beijing does not have or no longer has a monopoly over the content and direction of Chinese nationalism. In fact, it is often as wary of nationalism as it is dependent on it. As a number of studies have noted, instead of stoking up extreme nationalism, on many occasions Beijing has sought to constrain it.[71]

Nationalism and Realpolitik Thinking: Popular and Intellectual Responses to US Containment

Chinese nationalism is thus not a purely Chinese domestic phenomenon. To a large extent, its revival has been bound up with the hardening of US China policy after the end of the Cold War, although the latter is by no means the sole factor. During the Cold War, the US had, for nearly two decades, treated China as a quasi-ally and played the China card to contain their then common enemy, the Soviet Union. In 1985, the improving relationship with the West in general and the US in particular led Deng Xiaoping to famously pronounce that the international situation was marked by two major themes: peace and development. Throughout the 1980s, rather than flirting with xenophobic nationalism, China was largely in the thrall of a fever to learn from the West. In economic realms, this enthusiasm was manifested in a hunger for global linkages.[72] According to a nationwide survey in 1987, three quarters of Chinese were tolerant of the inflow of Western ideas, and 80 per cent of Chinese Communist Party members held a similar attitude.[73] In the summer of 1988, China's national soul-searching and the zeal of learning from the West reached a zenith with the repeated broadcast of a hugely popular six-part television series called *River Elegy* (*Heshang*) on the national TV network.[74] The series called upon China to reflect upon the backward 'Yellow River civilisation' and head out into the open 'azure ocean civilisation', a euphemism for Western civilisation.[75] Indeed, if there was Chinese nationalism back then, it was, according to Wang Xiaodong, 'reverse nationalism', a kind of nationalism that feels ashamed about Chinese culture.[76]

The end of the Cold War, together with the 1989 Tiananmen incident, saw a dramatic change in both Western perception and policy vis-à-vis China. As noted in earlier chapters, in the search for a new enemy, many Western, especially American, commentators and policy-makers began to find in China a new source of fear and a fresh target for containment. The emergence of China's so-called new nationalism largely coincided with this initial phase of a more confrontational US policy.

A high-water mark of the new nationalism is the publication of a highly polemic book *China Can Say No* in 1996.[77] Both the provocative title and its timing are significant in that they reveal the clearly mimicking and responsive nature of China's new nationalism. At one level, the book mirrored Shintaro Ishihara and Akio Morita's 1989 nationalist book *Japan Can Say No*,[78] which itself came after the popular Western sport of Japan-bashing during the 1980s. At the same time, within a few years after the Cold War, a widespread perception emerged in China that the US was deliberately keeping China down on a range of issues, such as attaching human rights conditions to China's MFN status, opposing Beijing's Olympics bid, orchestrating the *Yinhe* incident,[79] back-flipping on Lee Teng-hui's 1995 visit to the US, and sending two aircraft carrier battle groups to the Taiwan Strait in the Taiwan Strait missile crisis. As many Chinese participants argued at a UK conference on Chinese nationalism, the popularity of the hyper-nationalist text *China Can Say No* had more to do with its timing and context—the 1995–96 US-China standoff over Taiwan—than with a pre-existing, inherently nationalistic China.[80] Most of the aforementioned 'incidents', as we may recall, emerged amidst the pursuit of a more hardline policy on China.

If we read beyond that book's sensational sound bites and pay closer attention to its arguments, the responsive nature of Chinese nationalism becomes even more obvious. One author notes that 'I had been an internationalist, but having witnessed the various [bullying] acts of the U.S. and Britain on the issue of China's Olympics bid, I was deeply hurt and ever since have gradually become a nationalist'.[81] This transformative experience summarises well the general sentiment of the book. Another author describes how the hawkish shift in US China policy similarly changed his attitude towards America. Back in the 1970s, he felt excited to know that the Americans were on China's side against the Soviet Union. In the 1980s, his pro-American sentiment reached such a high pitch that he saw America as the model for China in almost every aspect. However, after a series of perceived hostile American actions in the early 1990s, that feeling quickly evaporated. His high hope for the US ended with a bitter disappointment.[82] Another controversial book published in the same year, *Yaomohua Zhongguo de beihou* (Behind the Demonisation of China), told a similar story of disenchantment with the US:

> If we had held some pro-American feeling before we went to the United States, this feeling which had been accumulated during our [Chinese] university and graduate school years was totally swept away once we got there and saw [firsthand] the demonisation of China and the neo-racist attack on our Chinese culture by American mainstream media.... It was Americans and their media's demonisation of China that 'instigated' our anti-American sentiment.[83]

Perhaps no other event has contributed more to the rise of contemporary Chinese nationalism than the US's 'accidental' bombing of the Chinese Embassy in Yugoslavia in May 1999. Three Chinese nationals were killed and many more wounded in that incident. Shocked by the news, many university students who cheered NBA superstar Michael Jordan and welcomed President Clinton's visit just one year before now staged demonstrations in front of the US Embassy in Beijing. On the campus of Renmin University of China, a group of Chinese students surrounded several American students, shouting 'Blood must be repaid with blood!' One student admitted that the scene looked rather ugly, but then he quickly added that 'compared to what we were responding to, it was pretty restrained'.[84] Previously popular Chinese outrage at the US had been confined to the printed media. Now for the first time, this bombing set off violent expressions of nationalist sentiments in cyberspace.[85] In response to public outcry against the NATO bombing, the online version of the *People's Daily* set up the 'Protesting against NATO Atrocities BBS Forum'. This forum later evolved into the highly nationalistic *Qiangguo luntan* (Strong Country Forum), now one of the most influential current affairs online forums in China, whose regular visitors include even Chinese President Hu Jintao.[86] For many, this incident was a significant and unforgettable formative event. Previously indifferent to international politics, many were turned nationalistic almost overnight. Even some Tiananmen demonstrators, as Chinese dissident Liu Xiaobo (who won the 2010 Nobel Peace Prize) found out, now instantly became anti-Western nationalists.[87]

Thus, this 'new nationalism' should be understood less in isolation than in terms of mutual responsiveness. Specifically, it was a 'response', as Fan Shiming puts it, to 'America's unilateralism, arrogance, hypocrisy, and hegemony in its international behaviour and foreign policy'.[88] Without the 1999 bombing, it would be hard to imagine that those anti-American demonstrations could have occurred. Similarly, had it not been for the routine flight of American spy planes along China's coast, there would not have been the 2001 spy plane incident to begin with or the subsequent outpouring of Chinese nationalism. And without the violent disruption of the international routes of the Beijing Olympics torch relay, the world probably would not have witnessed the strong nationalist backlash from mainland and overseas Chinese alike. Insofar as it often takes place in an interactive setting, the new nationalism is not just 'made in China'; it is co-constructed in the US and the West as well. Still further evidence of such reciprocity lies in a positive correlation between Western policy and Chinese behaviour: 'when the West, especially the United States, shows its respect to China, nationalistic voices decline'.[89]

If the public response to US hardline policy is characterised by nationalist fervour, then responses from Chinese intellectuals (especially IR scholars) are marked by a renewed interest in realpolitik thinking. It is true that China, in the words of Thomas Christensen, is 'the high church of realpolitik in the post-Cold War world'.[90] Many Chinese scholars are convinced that international relations still resemble what Hobbes calls 'the state of nature'.[91] Peking University professor Zhu Feng views the Western IR theory of power politics as the most important theoretical framework within which to interpret contemporary international affairs.[92] Zhang Ruizhuang, a Berkeley-trained professor at Nankai University, argues that the realist assumption of selfish human nature is a true reflection of world reality. As such, conflicts of interests among nations are inevitable: if you want peace, then prepare for war (*parabellum*).[93] From a similar vantage point, Yan Xuetong, another Berkeley graduate and director of the Institute of International Studies at Tsinghua University, argues in his book *Zhongguo guojia liyi fenxi* (An Analysis of China's National Interests) that safeguarding the national interest depends on power. In the absence of power, the former is mere wishful thinking.[94] If these ideas sound familiar, that is because to a large extent they have been appropriated from mainstream Western strategic thought.[95] Mark Leonard, the author of *What Does China Think?*, sees Yan Xuetong as almost 'the mirror image of William Kristol', a leading American neoconservative strategist. Just as Kristol is obsessed with a China threat and the danger of appeasement of Beijing, Yan Xuetong seems equally wary of the US and

strongly urges China not to show weakness. 'We think if you make concessions [to the USA, Japan and Taiwan], they will just ask for more. The
problems we are having with Japan and Taiwan are a direct result of years of
appeasement', Yan told Leonard.[96]

Of course, this 'mirror-image' argument does not mean that Chinese thinking is always a passive derivative of Western ideas. It may be argued that this
simply reflects the fact that 'realist minds think alike' when it comes to world
reality. In Yan's case, his realist thinking may also be traced back to his
personal experience of hardship as a young school-leaver sent to a construction corps in the 1960s.[97] That being so, this still does not explain why in
recent years similar perceptions of US China policy are increasingly taken up
by more liberal-minded scholars as well. During the Spy Plane incident, Chu
Shulong, a moderate liberal intellectual often cited as a contrast with his
hardline colleague Yan Xuetong, suggested that Beijing should not release
the US crew members without receiving a real apology.[98] Wang Yizhou, a
professor at Peking University, calls himself a 'realistic liberal'. But as a
scholar from a 'weak, developing country', he expresses his agony over what
he calls the 'crude reality of power politics and hegemony imposed upon the
weak in the daily practice of international politics'.[99] To both Chu and Wang,
their reluctant embrace of power politics seems to have less to do with their
theoretical persuasions and more with the perceived American containment
of China.

In saying so, I do not intend to rehash the old, Eurocentric 'impact-
response' approach, that is, China's nationalism and realpolitik thinking are
merely a product of external stimuli.[100] No doubt, the Chinese are more than
capable of fostering their own nationalist/realpolitik ideas. But even when we
rightly recognise Chinese agency here, we need to keep in mind the broader
historical context of Western construction of Chinese realism. Realism is
certainly not alien to traditional Chinese culture (such as the Legalist school),
but without European gunboat diplomacy, it is highly doubtful that it could
have flourished in a culture traditionally dominated by Confucianism.

The change of heart by the imperial commissioner Lin Zexu during the
Qing dynasty serves as a good example here. Responsible for stemming the
illicit opium trade by British merchants, Lin Zexu sought initially to persuade
Queen Victoria to cooperate through a Confucian logic of reciprocity. In his
letter to the Queen in 1839, he pleaded that 'you would not wish to give unto
others what you yourself do not want'. However, his message fell on deaf
ears. Witnessing the constant coming and going of European powers' ships
on the open sea 'as they pleased', the commissioner eventually succumbed to
the 'reality' of power politics. In 1842, he wrote to a friend that 'ships, guns,
and a water force are absolutely indispensable' for the defence of China's sea
frontiers.[101] But at that time Lin Zexu considered such an idea so

revolutionary and controversial in China that he begged his friend to keep it confidential. Lin's transformation from a Confucian scholar-official to a realist strategist is a microcosm of the lasting impact Western powers had left on Chinese strategic thinking and behaviour in modern history. Just as China's determined quest for wealth and power since the mid-nineteenth century cannot be separated from those imperial encounters, its present status as the high church of hard-nosed realism needs to be properly understood, especially, though not exclusively, in the context of contemporary Sino-American interactions.

US Containment and Chinese Foreign Policy Response

The impact of US containment goes beyond the public and intellectual realms and extends to the official domain of Chinese foreign policy-making. The relationship with the US, according to Hu Jintao, is the 'central thread in China's foreign policy strategy'.[102] That is to say, how the US acts vis-à-vis China must have been a key consideration in the making of Chinese foreign policy.

China's New Rulers: The Secret Files, published in 2002, reveals chilling views of leading Chinese Politburo Standing Committee members about US motives towards China. Alarmed by US military deployments in China's neighbouring countries, Hu Jintao believed that the Americans 'have extended outposts and placed pressure points on us from the east, south, and west. This makes a great change in our geopolitical environment'. For both Chinese Premier Wen Jiabao and then Vice President Zeng Qinghong, Washington's China strategy is to 'engage and contain'.[103] In today's terminology, it amounted to a hedging strategy.

In his study of China's new nationalism, Peter Hays Gries rightly notes the extensive influence of US China policy on Chinese worldviews. He questions the conventional wisdom in the US that treats China and Chinese nationalism in isolation from its international environment and ignores the role of China's interlocutors in shaping Chinese foreign behaviour.[104] Influenced by this wisdom, Rumsfeld famously asked at a regional security conference in June 2005: 'Since no nation threatens China, one must wonder: Why this growing [Chinese] investment [in defence]?' As the Defense Secretary of a country whose military budget was bigger than almost those of the rest of the world combined, it is remarkable that Rumsfeld managed to keep a straight face while posing that question. To Will Hutton, his remarks showed 'disingenuousness of the highest order'.[105]

The fact that Beijing's image of the US had not always been so bleak further testifies to the contingency and responsiveness, rather than the fixity and pregivenness, of Chinese official views. In China's 1998 White Paper on

National Defense, the US was mentioned ten times, almost each time in positive terms. Presumably, that reflected a secure and confident Chinese leadership after Chinese President Jiang Zemin's historic meetings with Bill Clinton in 1997 and 1998 as well as their agreement to establish a 'constructive strategic partnership'. Two years later, China's third white paper mentioned the US 13 times, and all but two of the references were negative.[106] What happened in the interval, among other things, was the US accusation of Chinese espionage and the bombing of the Chinese Embassy in Belgrade. The Chinese leadership was so shocked by the Embassy bombing that even Jiang Zemin became convinced, as Clinton recounted in his memoir *My Life*, that this incident was caused by a deliberate act of rigging the bombing target maps by those from the Pentagon or CIA who opposed Clinton's engagement with China.[107]

To many observers, US China policy is little more than hedging, rebalancing, or contingency planning, rather than sinister containment; the problem, it seems, lies with Chinese overreaction or hypersensitivity, which may have resulted from a siege mentality or distorted Chinese representations of the US.[108] There may be some elements of truth in this explanation. Yet, it is worth noting that the Chinese are not alone in showing such 'hypersensitivity'. When then *National Interest* editor Owen Harries passed through Hong Kong after the NATO bombing of the Chinese Embassy, he 'did not meet a person there—either Chinese or Western—who accepted the accident thesis'.[109] Even James Sasser, the US ambassador to China at the time of the NATO bombing, later told a Chinese journalist that he would not take the bombing as an accident 'if he were a Chinese'.[110]

Meanwhile, many Western scholars readily acknowledge that the American injunction to prevent the emergence of a new peer competitor 'can apply only to China', as no other possible adversary is able to fit the bill.[111] A 2003 RAND report on the future roles of US nuclear arsenal admits that US nuclear posture and strategy appears best suited for a pre-emptive counterforce capability against China (and Russia). Otherwise, the report says that 'the numbers and the operating procedures simply do not add up'.[112]

What is particularly troubling is that many US policy-makers seem little troubled by the Chinese reaction. In the lead up to a planned joint navy exercise between the US and South Korea in the Yellow Sea in 2010, China protested strongly against such an exercise. Shen Dingli of Fudan University asks rhetorically: 'When the US ponders the idea of deploying its nuclear aircraft carrier in the Yellow Sea, very close to China, shouldn't China have the same feeling as the US did when the Soviet Union deployed missiles in Cuba?'[113] Probably not unaware of such a Chinese concern, Pentagon spokesman Geoff Morrell remained adamant. 'Those [exercise] determinations', said Morrell, 'are made by us, and us alone. Where we exercise, when we exercise, with whom and how, using what assets and so forth are determinations that are made by the United States Navy, by the Department of Defense, by the United States Government'.[114] Evincing a tone of unilateral arrogance, his unspoken statement is that Beijing might not like it, but there was little it could do. In thinking along this line, the spokesman merely followed a well-established US tradition. Two decades ago, dismissing concerns over China's anger at the US decision to sell high-performance fighters to Taiwan, US Senator Lloyd Bentsen asked, 'What, after all, can Beijing do? Threaten to terminate its $20 billion-a-year trade surplus with us?'[115] Bentsen might have a point here. Despite or because of China's rapid rise, its economy continues to be heavily dependent on overseas, especially American, markets. And with its 'Peaceful Development' mantra, ample evidence exists of Beijing's desire to avoid confrontation with the world's hegemon.[116]

Even so, the popular assumption among some 'China threat' advocates that China has few options but to 'turn the other cheek' is not only self-contradictory, but also self-deceptive and dangerous. Granted that the US hedging strategy is mere contingency planning, it is still not immune from the dynamics of mutual responsiveness. As Robert Axelrod remarks with regard to the hedging rules in a Prisoner's Dilemma situation,

> these maximizing rules did not take into account that their *own* behavior would lead the other player to change. In deciding whether to carry an umbrella, we do not have to worry that the clouds will take our behavior into account.... Non-zero-sum games, such as the Prisoner's Dilemma, are not like this. Unlike the clouds, the other player can respond to your own choices.[117]

As noted above, Chinese responses at both public and official levels are already under way. Given a sustained US hedging, it should come as no surprise if China (especially its military) comes up with its own hedging strategy of sort.[118] For instance, Chinese military modernisation, though dubbed an 'RMA with Chinese Characteristics', has drawn much inspiration from post-Cold War revolution in military affairs (RMA) led by the US.[119] In an attempt to bring China's three military services into the age of joint operation, China's 'informationisation' effort outlined in its 2004 Defence White Paper simply 'replicates the US emphasis on satellite and airborne sensors, unmanned aerial vehicles, and information warfare'.[120] According to David Lampton, Chinese military development in recent decades has been primarily a story of reaction, not initiation.[121]

Commenting on the much-mentioned Taiwan Strait missile exercises conducted by the PLA in the summer and fall of 1995 and again in March 1996, Harries wrote that 'Ill-judged, ugly, and dangerous as was the Chinese intimidation, it was a *reaction*'.[122] That reaction came *after* America's decision to allow Taiwan president Lee Teng-hui to visit the US, where Lee delivered a triumphalist speech on the merit of the 'Taiwan Experience' and appealed for wider international recognition for the island. Later, alarmed by the US show of force through its two aircraft carrier battle groups during the 1996 missile crisis, Chinese strategic planners allegedly told Helmut Sonnenfeldt, one of Henry Kissinger's close associates, that they were rereading the early works of George Kennan, the architect of the containment policy towards the Soviet Union. Fearful that the United States was embarking on a similar course of action against China, they wanted to learn from Kennan 'how it had started and evolved'.[123]

In July 2004, the US conducted an exercise codenamed 'Operation Summer Pulse 2004', in which it unprecedentedly assembled seven aircraft carrier strike groups (CSGs) simultaneously in five regional theatres, all with a clear intention to make an impression on China that Washington was serious about defending Taiwan. That US objective certainly succeeded, but to an unexpected effect. After the US exercise, one Chinese military source quickly concluded that all this 'leaves China with no choice but to start and end the war [over Taiwan] with lightning speed'.[124] Disturbed by that unprecedented show of force, Beijing reacted, also unprecedentedly, by appointing two top anti-aircraft carrier warfare officers to head the PLA General Staff Department. Commenting on such unusual appointments, an article in the *Journal of Electronic Defense* maintains that 'Summer Pulse 04's surge of seven carrier groups must have really rattled the Chinese high command'.[125] Seven years later when China finally carried out sea-trials of its first aircraft carrier, few analysts would remember or care to draw the connection between China's determination to develop its own blue navy (and area-denial capabilities) and those earlier encounters with the US. But remembering such contexts is essential to understanding the full picture of China's recent assertiveness.

In addition to responding directly to US China strategy, Chinese foreign policy is also shaped by it in an indirect manner. This is evident in China's response to enormous domestic pressure from popular nationalists and hardline realists. Even as Beijing is aware of the danger of extreme nationalism, at the same time it has become increasingly captive and vulnerable to public opinion, especially in times of international crisis when the response from the regime is closely monitored and tied to regime legitimacy. In this context, Chinese foreign policy-making becomes increasingly a 'two-level game', argues Gries, 'with Chinese diplomats keeping one eye on domestic nationalists, even as they negotiate with their foreign counterparts'.[126] Just as the perception of a 'China threat' in the American public has profound implications for US China policy, Chinese perceptions of US containment can likewise exert considerable influence on

Beijing's foreign behaviour. During the 2001 spy plane incident, the Chinese government found its room for manoeuvre severely constrained by strong public indignation. Explaining to the Americans why Beijing could not let the US plane go without receiving an apology, an unnamed senior PLA officer pointed directly to the pressure of populist nationalism: should Beijing bow to US demand, 'the Chinese masses would immediately regard the government as being too soft, as the leaving plane could even spy on China on its return trip'.[127] A special assistant to US ambassador to China Joseph Prueher later confirmed that during the negotiation in Beijing, American diplomats 'saw a Chinese government acutely sensitive to Chinese public opinion'.[128] And as noted above, Chinese public opinion in turn has been in part shaped by US China policy.

THE 'CHINA THREAT' PARADIGM AS A SELF-FULFILLING PROPHECY

If changing Chinese public opinion and Beijing's growing assertiveness in foreign policy are better understood in the context of mutual responsiveness, then threatening as they may appear, they at least partly reflect the self-fulfilling effect of the China threat theory as practice. That is, they are to some extent socially constructed by Western representations of the China threat. At this juncture, we may return to the question raised earlier—What's the cost of having an enemy? The cost, simply put, is that perceiving China as a threat and acting upon that perception help bring that feared China threat closer to reality. Though not an *objective* description of China, the 'China threat' paradigm is no mere fantasy, as it has the constitutive power to make its prediction come true. If this China paradigm ends up bearing some resemblance to Chinese reality, it is because the reality is itself partly constituted by it. With US strategic planners continuing to operate on the basis of the China threat, this self-fulfilling process has persisted to the present day. For example, in July 2010, when China objected to the joint US-South Korean navy exercise in the Yellow Sea to no avail, it announced that its navy would conduct live fire drills in the East China Sea for the duration of the US-South Korean manoeuvres.[129] Meanwhile, a *Global Times* (a Chinese daily tabloid affiliated with the official *People's Daily*) editorial opines that 'Whatever harm the US military manoeuvre may have inflicted upon the mind of the Chinese, the United States will have to pay for it, sooner or later'.[130]

All such Chinese 'belligerence' seems to have provided fresh evidence to the 'China threat' paradigm, whose image of China has now been vindicated.[131] Without acknowledging their own role in the production of the 'China threat', 'China threat' analysts thus play a key part in a spiral model of tit-for-tat in Sino-US relations. Mindful of this danger, some cool-headed observers have warned that a US attempt to build a missile defence shield could be reciprocated by China deploying more missiles.[132] Even the highly classified US National Intelligence Estimate (NIE) report *Foreign Responses to U.S. National Missile Defense Deployment* has hinted at this possibility.[133] In early 2006, Mike Moore, contributing editor of *The Bulletin of the Atomic Scientists*, predicted that if the US continues to weaponise space by deploying a comprehensive space-control system, 'China will surely respond'.[134] And respond it did. In early 2007, it launched a ballistic missile to destroy an inoperational weather satellite in orbit. That test immediately caused a stir in the international press, even though it came after Washington's repeated refusal to negotiate with China and Russia over their proposed ban on space weapons and the use of force against satellites. A *Financial Times* article noted that 'What is surprising about the Chinese test is that anyone was surprised'.[135] In a similar vein but commenting on the broader pattern of US strategy on China over the years, Lampton notes that 'Washington cannot simply seek to strengthen ties with India, Japan, the Republic of Korea, and central Asian states as an explicit offset to rising Chinese power and then be surprised when Beijing plays the same game'.[136]

Nevertheless, such surprise is commonplace in the China watching community, reflecting an intellectual blindness to the self-fulfilling nature of one of its time-honoured paradigms. This blindness, in turn, allows the justification of more containment or hedging. In this way, the 'China threat' paradigm is not only self-fulfilling in practice, but also self-productive and self-perpetuating as a powerful mode of representation.

One might take comfort in the fact that neither Beijing nor Washington actually wants a direct military confrontation. But that is beside the point, for the lack of aggressive intention alone is no proven safe barrier to war. As in the cases of the Korean War and the Vietnam War, the outbreak of war does not necessarily require the intention to go to war.[137] Mutual suspicion, as US President Theodore Roosevelt once observed of the Kaiser and the English, is often all that is needed to set in motion a downward spiral.[138] And thanks to the 'China threat' paradigm and its mirror image and practice from China, mutual suspicion and distrust has not been in short supply.[139] A war between these two great powers is not inevitable or even probable; the door for mutual engagement and cooperation remains wide open. Nevertheless, blind to its own self-fulfilling consequences, the 'China threat' paradigm, if left unexamined and unchecked, would make cooperation more difficult and conflict more likely.

It is worth adding that my treatment of Chinese nationalism and realpolitik thinking is not to downplay their potentially dangerous consequences, much less to justify them. Quite the contrary, for all the apparent legitimacy of reciprocal counter-violence or counter-hedging, Chinese mimicry *is* dangerous, as it would feed into this tit-for-tat vicious cycle and play its part in the escalation of a security dilemma between the US and China. Thus, to emphasise Chinese responsiveness is not to deny Chinese agency or exonerate its responsibility. While the general nature of Chinese foreign policy may be responsive with regard to the US, its 'contents' are not simply passive, innocent mimicry of US thinking and behaviour, but inevitably come with some 'Chinese characteristics'. That said, those 'Chinese characteristics' notwithstanding, there is no pregiven China threat both unresponsive to and immune from any external stimulus. To argue otherwise is to deny an important dimension of Chinese agency, namely, their response-ability.

By examining the self-fulfilling tendency of the 'China threat' paradigm, we can better understand that Sino-American relations, like international relations in general, are *mutually* responsive and constitutive. Thus, both China and the US should be held accountable to the bilateral relationship of their mutual making. To the extent that this 'China threat' knowledge often denies such mutuality, and by extension, US responsibility in the rise of the China threat, it is all the more imperative to lay bare its intrinsic link with power practice.

6. The 'China opportunity': false promises (and premises)

> *The Americans were not to find their Shangri-la in China, with or without a compass.*
>
> Jonathan D. Spence[1]

> *... although we have tried hard over the years to change China after our image, we have never succeeded in doing so. In the nineteenth century, we tried to Christianize China; in the twentieth century, we tried to democratize China; currently we are eager to transform China after American economic and technological models. We are very likely to be unsuccessful once again.*
>
> John Bryan Starr[2]

CHINA OPPORTUNITY: A POSITIVE SELF-FULFILLING PROPHECY?

The preceding chapter examined the dangerous implications of the 'China threat' paradigm as a self-fulfilling prophecy. Mindful of this danger, some observers turn to the 'opportunity' paradigm which treats China as a partner or opportunity worthy of engagement. With constructive and sustained engagement from the West, China is more likely to integrate into the international system and behave responsibly, both at home and abroad. Or so it is claimed.

In his testimony before the Subcommittee on Trade of the House of Representatives in 1994, Robert Kapp, at the time the President-Designate of the US-China Business Council, was a strong advocate of this 'China opportunity' thesis. As he argued, 'The economic advancement of China, linked part and parcel to China's immense engagement with the world economy, is the best hope we have of witnessing the evolution of a more humane and tolerant Chinese domestic political environment'.[3] In laying out a scenario of China's political evolution through economic development,

Kapp was pushing for delinking China's MFN status from its human rights conditions, a policy put in place by President Bill Clinton.

It did not take long before the Clinton administration itself began buying into this optimism. Increased trade and engagement with China, Clinton now believed, would not only make it richer economically, but also more open politically and more cooperative in tackling international problems.[4] In a speech to the Council on Foreign Relations in June 1997, Clinton's top aide Berger called for the building of a new China policy consensus centred on engagement and integration. He maintained that 'to bring China into the effort as a stakeholder' was a policy choice that the US must make, so that this could 'make it more likely China makes the right choices'.[5] Despite his initial tough talk on China, President George W. Bush did not abandon that engagement policy altogether. Bush reasoned that 'Economic freedom creates habits of liberty. And habits of liberty create expectations of democracy.... Trade freely with China, and time is on our side'.[6] On the other side of the Atlantic, European leaders, such as former British Prime Minister Tony Blair, were also convinced that 'there is an unstoppable momentum' toward democracy in China, and the best way of keeping up that momentum is continued engagement.[7]

All these sanguine views seem to reflect a belief in the self-fulfilling effect of the 'China opportunity' paradigm. Some engagement advocates believe that states, through their socialisation in international institutions and interactions with other international actors, can learn new norms and rules, and in doing so, redefine their interests or even take on new identities.[8] Others make a similar point by drawing on regime theory, the English School, and path-dependency theory.[9] In short, the consensus is that through engagement, China can be shaped, socialised, or even converted.

There is no doubt that China's recent transformation would not be possible without its engagement with the outside world in general and the West in particular. As I have noted elsewhere, various transnational actors, including the US, have played a key role in some profound changes in Beijing's understanding of both its legitimacy base and responsibility, changes that are manifested in its 'Peaceful Rise' strategy.[10] Yet, despite its apparently positive effect on China, the 'China opportunity' theory as practice is not going to be a self-fulfilling prophecy. If anything, as this chapter will argue, it is essentially a false promise.

THE FALSE PREMISES OF THE 'CHINA OPPORTUNITY' PARADIGM

Underpinning the 'China opportunity' paradigm are several assumptions about the relationship between the West and China. These assumptions, I will argue, are nothing less than false premises. One key false premise is the assumed self/Other dichotomy between the West/US and China, which are seen as two separate, more or less homogeneous entities. Just as the 'China threat' discourse reduces China to a threat, the 'China opportunity' literature reifies it as an opportunity. Whether that opportunity means markets, a place ripe for democracy, or a maturing global actor, all these imageries convey a sense of homogeneity. While China's internal differences are not ignored, they are often seen as insignificant. Even as analysts write about the schism between the Communist regime and the Chinese people,[11] they often quickly describe the regime as fragile, illegitimate, or almost non-Chinese. In effect, China is again reduced to a homogeneous entity defined as a people longing for freedom and democracy, just like 'people anywhere else in the world'.[12]

Alongside the assumption of a monolithic China are some equally mono-lithic terms such as 'the West', 'the international community', or simply 'we' ('us'). For reasons of analytical convenience or stylistic neatness, we cer-tainly cannot avoid such misleadingly singular terms as 'the West', 'the United States', and 'China' altogether. But very often we are led to believe in the naturalness of the terms we have invented. 'The West' is precisely such a term in the 'China opportunity' discourse. Thomas Paine once said that 'We have it in our power to begin the world all over again'. More recently, the European Commission President José Manuel Barroso declared that 'we [the European Union] are one of the most important, if not the most important, normative power in the world'.[13] These examples testify to an enduring belief that the US and indeed the West are one, making up a unitary Western self, a transatlantic community, a civilisation, an alliance, an Enlightenment project, or a 'zone of democratic peace'. Certainly, some analysts will admit that tactically the West is not one. Robert Kagan famously wrote that 'Americans are from Mars and Europeans are from Venus'.[14] To Kagan, however, this rift is a lamentable anomaly in an otherwise unitary liberal democratic world which has lately come under a common threat.

Second, as noted in Chapter 3, the 'China opportunity' paradigm presup-poses a binary, hierarchical placement of the Western self and the Chinese Other. In this temporal hierarchy, the Western self is placed at the apex of modernity or the end of History, thus occupying an active, dominant position as the modern subject. China, on the other hand, is considered a largely passive object in need of modernisation and democratisation, for it is in an inferior stage of social and political development. Seen this way, Sino-Western relations become a more or less one-way street of Western impact and Chinese response. This, for example, is precisely how an EU official described EU-China relations: 'Officially we call it "exchange of experi-ence", but in reality we are exporting our model to China'.[15] Similar attitudes are evident in the US. For example, it is argued that by sending the right 'signals' or setting 'the terms of engagement' or 'an outer boundary' for Chinese behaviour, Washington could succeed in 'shaping the character of China's growing ambition and channeling its increasing strength in benign directions'.[16] On this basis, Johnston and Ross refer to the US as 'the subject of the study of engagement' while China is 'the object'.[17]

Related to the above-mentioned premises, another 'China opportunity' assumption concerns the broad nature of Sino-Western relations. Seeing itself as a benevolent global hegemon and a 'force for good' in the world,[18] the West considers its engagement with China a special relationship, characterised by Western altruism and generosity on the one hand and Chinese good will and gratitude felt for the West on the other. Historically, the relationship is believed to have been built on a series of good deeds by the West, who provided 'oil for the lamps of China', 'offered' China a stake in the international community, maintained regional stability whereby China could grow its economy, 'awarded' Beijing the 2008 Olympic Games—the list goes on. It was the US, once claimed Bill Clinton, that helped integrate China 'into the global economy', bring 'more prosperity to Chinese citizens', and facilitate 'the advance of personal freedom and human rights'.[19] Likewise, many US congressional members saw their approval of China's MFN status as, quite literally, a favour to the Chinese. At a workshop on Chinese foreign policy in Beijing in 2000, an American scholar, who later went on to become a senior official in the George W. Bush administration, challenged Chinese participants to think of any country that had provided as much help to China in the twentieth century as had his own country.

Given these strongly held premises, the 'China opportunity' paradigm is not a descriptive account of what China is, but from the beginning a normative prescription of what China ought to be. Its dominant imageries about China, such as 'one billion customers', 'democratisation', and 'responsible stakeholder' are all part of some longstanding goals of transforming China in Western image. To many 'opportunity' proponents, those goals are not only realistic but also measurable. Pre-empting the potential criticism that the hope for China's democratisation is utopian, Kristol and Kagan ask rhetorically:

> How utopian is it to work for the fall of the Communist Party oligarchy in China after a far more powerful and, arguably, more stable such oligarchy fell in the Soviet Union? With democratic changes sweeping the world at an unprecedented rate over these past thirty years, is it "realistic" to insist that no further victories can be won?[20]

In this context, anticipating China's transformation and democratisation has become a burgeoning cottage industry. Here, scholars routinely seek to gauge whether China's 'learning', 'compliance', or 'convergence' is 'full' or 'partial', 'genuine' or 'tactical'. Whilst Johnston and Evans come up with a typology of a continuum of the quality of Chinese cooperation, others offer a linear 'spiral model' of norms socialisation to measure Beijing's progress. Reminiscent of W. W. Rostow's famous thesis about the universal stages of economic growth and modernisation, Ann Kent divides China's compliance with the international regimes into five stages of international and domestic compliance.[21]

Certainly, the 'opportunity' paradigm is right to highlight the *social* dimension of China and its potential for change. This is a fresh contrast to the realist treatment of China as a largely asocial, ahistorical actor destined to repeat the timeless pattern of international politics handed down from the past. The problem, however, is that while paying due attention to the 'responsiveness' of China, they seem to have taken a step too far by neglecting to put such 'responsiveness' in a *mutual* and *reciprocal* context. As a result, their constructivist perspective is largely ethnocentric, conjuring up a normatively unequal relationship of social construction in which the liberal West and its norms and institutions are taken as universally pregiven, rather than historically constructed and always potentially contested. The world, it seems, is essentially of 'our' creation. As a senior adviser to George W. Bush told the journalist and best-selling author Ron Suskind: 'We're an empire now, and when we act, we create reality. And while you are studying that reality— judiciously, as you will—we'll act again creating new realities…. We're history's actors'.[22]

But that claim is part reality and part illusion. It is no doubt true that the West in general and the US in particular have profoundly shaped the landscape of international relations. Yet, given the mutual responsiveness of world politics, the Sino-Western relationship is not just of 'our' making, but also of *mutual* construction. It is an ongoing, complex social construct in a multitude of irreducibly intersubjective settings, where the rules of engagement are mutually and constantly (re)negotiated, rather than unilaterally set and exogenously determined from the civilised metropole. The 'opportunity' paradigm assumes China's convergence with 'us' which would lead to the eventual absorption of the China difference and Otherness. But it ignores the fact that difference is intrinsic and indispensable to any social relationship and even to the very being of human society itself. Universal sameness, if it is possible at all, would abolish the existence of meaningful social relations and lead to an absurd situation of total reciprocity and interchangeability, where 'the relationship with the other becomes impossible'.[23] Without doubt, state interests and identities are socially constructed by powerful discourses and shared values and norms, but if such norms are able to exert influence, that is precisely because they have been intersubjectively *shared* through a process of mutual responsiveness, rather than because of their intrinsic natural superiority across space and time. Having highlighted these false premises of the 'China opportunity' paradigm, I now turn to the question of why this paradigm is in practice false promises.

THE FALSE PROMISES OF THE 'CHINA OPPORTUNITY'

Beyond a Totalising Construction of Self and Other

All thinking and writing requires some degree of abstraction and generalisation. This is evident in the frequent use of terms such as China, the US, and Europe. Such sweeping terms are not only unavoidable but also useful in many ways. Yet, their usefulness does not alter the fact that the entities they refer to are not homogeneous actors, but artificial products of what Said calls 'imaginative geography'. It is trite but worth repeating that there does not exist one China, but rather many Chinas, which consist of multiple actors with different and changing ideas, interests, and subjectivities. Instead of a typical nation-state, it is more like a continent.[24] For every 'pro-globalisation', 'pro-Western' view found there, one can easily come across its strong detractors.[25] In the media, free-market believers constantly battle with influential scholars from the New Left, and enthusiasts of global integration often have to live alongside opponents from a more nationalistic persuasion. In *What Does China Think?*, Mark Leonard gives an indicative snapshot of significant ideational differences and clashes in China. Even among a select group of Chinese elites, endless debates take place over economic, political, strategic and cultural subjects. At a given time, it may be possible to identify a mainstream elite view in China, but it is always problematic to extrapolate it to China as a whole. Thus, the irony is that China is simply too big and too multifaceted to be regarded as a single actor called 'China'.

The West is no less heterogeneous. Former Chinese foreign minister Qian Qichen wrote in an op-ed piece that 'It is now time to give up the illusion that Europeans and Americans are living in the same world, as some Europeans would like to believe'.[26] He made the point in the context of the transatlantic rift on the controversial Iraq War. As noted earlier, Kagan, a tireless champion of a unitary West, also recognises the different strategic visions held by the US and Europe.[27] And within each constitutive component of the West, diversity continues to be the rule rather than the exception. The EU—widely seen as a model for regional integration—seems to represent the high-water mark of the unity of the West. Yet, when it comes to foreign policy, the EU is far from speaking with one voice.[28] As some have pointed out, what is remarkable about the EU is not its outcome, but its process, not its actual success in convergence towards higher standards of human rights, but 'its capacity to *manage enduring differences*'. As a consequence, 'the actual institutions of European integration always fall short of the underlying utopian vision'.[29] The European debt crisis, one might add, has only further exposed its internal diversity and division.

Similarly, Katzenstein and Keohane use the word 'polyvalence' to describe the diverse values in the US, where 'secular science and religious fundamentalism, moralism and sexual permissiveness, rigorous science and a rich popular culture' coexist. And those values 'resonate differently with the various cognitive schemas held by individuals and reinforced by groups—schemas that vary greatly cross-nationally'.[30] For instance, Huntington believed that America's national identity is 'inseparable from its commitment to liberal and democratic values'.[31] By contrast, Andrew Bacevich argues that 'who we are and what we stand for' have been signified in large part by America's 'arsenal of high-tech weaponry and the soldiers who employ that arsenal'.[32] Therefore, even American intellectuals do not have a commonly accepted definition of their national identity.

Some may argue that the unity of the West is more apparent in a cultural or ideational sense than in the realm of everyday life. Even so, despite the repeated proclamations of the end of ideology and end of History, the so-called 'vital centre' of Cold War liberalism that had defined the West in general and the US in particular is no more, if it ever existed. By Huntington's own account, the 'cultural core' of the West and the US is now under challenge, for 'We are all multiculturalists now'.[33] Some years ago, under the slogan "Hey hey, ho ho, Western culture's gotta go!" students from one of the most elite American universities (Stanford University) demonstrated against the core curriculum on Western civilisation.[34] To some extent, the West's fixation with the issue of who we are and the politics of identity is a telltale sign of its very lack of a common identity.[35] Some hold the influx of immigrants responsible for this identity 'crisis', but David Gress is perhaps closer to the point when he argues that:

> The West was never a single entity that one could define neatly as beginning in Greece, slowly growing during the Roman Empire and the Middle Ages, and reaching its fruition in the later centuries of the second millennium A.D., all the while maintaining an essential identity. Rather, throughout this history, various Wests coexisted, defined in terms of different principles, regions, beliefs, and ambitions.[36]

To be sure, at different times the West seems to have been defined collectively as Christianity, the White Man, or liberal democracy. But from the beginning such unity is best seen as a discursive construct. It cannot be maintained without a grand narrative of self-imagination that constantly invokes its imagined Others and enemies.[37] In the wake of the Soviet demise, Owen Harries predicted that the political West 'took the presence of a life-threatening, overtly hostile "East" to bring it into existence and to maintain its unity. It is extremely doubtful whether it can survive the disappearance of that enemy'.[38]

Consequently, neither China nor the West can be seen as a pre-existing homogeneous whole. Given their irreducible plurality and inherent diversity or even paradox, the 'China opportunity' promise of transforming 'China' in 'Western' image will inevitably fall flat. As Madsen points out,

> It now makes less sense to speak of 'U.S.-China relations' than to talk of how one part of the United States (for instance, Chinese Americans, southern black textile workers, or directors of multinational corporations) relates to one part of China (for instance, Beijing intellectuals, Guangdong entrepreneurs, or central government officials).[39]

True, it is possible that some parts or aspects of China may well come to resemble the typical imageries of the West; the skyscrapers and fast-food chains in China come readily to mind. But the country as a whole cannot fulfil the promise of becoming like the West. In the age of globalisation, transnational socialisation does occur, but it is not whole countries, but mostly individuals, who become socialised.[40] However tempting, the smooth scenario envisaged by Edward Friedman is unlikely to happen: 'Shenzhen [can be] Hong Kong-ized, Guangdong [can be] Shenzhen-ized, and the whole country [can be] Guangdong-ized'.[41] Furthermore, the plural nature of the West poses additional problems for the core assumption of the 'China opportunity' paradigm: there is no unitary, quintessentially Western example for China to emulate in the first place. I shall return to this point in a moment.

One-Way Conversion or Mutual Responsiveness?

Since the West and China are not homogeneous wholes, we can no longer assume a neat bilateral relationship of the Western/American knowing subject transforming a passive Chinese object. International relations, like human relations more generally, are always intersubjective. Intersubjectivity means, among other things, the existence of agency on the part of all actors, who are able to interpret, appropriate, and/or resist the influence from the other in accordance with their 'own' subjectivity.

Needless to say, China is precisely such an actor. Made up of many different and dynamic subjects, it is not 'simply passive, sponge-like, bodies floating downstream in the currents of [the international normative] environment in an unresisting or uncontested way'.[42] With an inherent capacity to respond to Western impact in its own ways, China's relationship with the West is at least a two-way street of intersubjective interaction, rather than one-way convergence. In 1993, the media mogul Rupert Murdoch, after acquiring the Hong Kong-based Star TV satellite broadcaster, declared that satellite TV was an 'unambiguous threat to totalitarian regimes everywhere'. But he forgot that one of his intended targets, the Chinese government, was also listening. Taking Murdoch's words seriously, Beijing quickly dismantled rogue satellite dishes across the country and banned Murdoch's Star TV on the mainland.[43] Within six months of the ban, Murdoch had to drop the BBC from Star TV's China signal. In 1997, he made another speech, this time saying that China 'is a distinctive market with distinctive social and moral values that western companies must learn to abide by'.[44] What a difference a few years made!

For better or worse, the existence of Chinese agency also means that the Chinese are able to modify Western influence. The much-talked phenomenon of McDonaldisation in China is illustrative here. Anthropologist Yunxiang Yan notes that the now ubiquitous restaurants have been appropriated by the Chinese 'not only as leisure centers but also as public arenas for various personal and family rituals'. In this process, McDonald's is not a passive object of Chinese appropriation either, for its management, in order to maintain success in China, self-consciously seeks to adapt to China's cultural settings.[45] Consequently, even the seemingly unstoppable McDonaldisation is never simply a matter of Western active impact and Chinese passive response. Another example is the merger deal between IBM and China's Lenovo in December 2004. A computer engineer from Lenovo summed up nicely the rationale for this deal: 'I need them and they need me'. IBM CEO Sam Palmisano agreed. Calling his company's move 'a much more subtle, more sophisticated approach', he explained that only when 'you become ingrained in their agenda and become truly local and help them advance', can 'your opportunities' be 'enlarged'.[46]

What these examples tell us is a profound dilemma of engagement. Western engagement policy works best if it seeks to accommodate the engaged; but by way of accommodation, that policy has to compromise some of its original ambition of converting China. Early missionaries understood this dilemma well when they felt the need to bend their energies and graft themselves into the living tree of China in order to make converts.[47] Western businesses in China, such as McDonalds and IBM, embody a more up-to-date version of this paradox. In fact, there is nothing paradoxical about this phenomenon. What we are witnessing here is not just Western impact and Chinese response, but *mutual* agency, *mutual* appropriation, and *mutual* responsiveness. As Madsen puts it, 'there is no such thing as a unitary American culture capable of influencing Chinese culture.... There is no unitary culture to be penetrated and no unitary culture to do the penetrating'.[48] Any agent for change, however powerful, is itself open to change in the process of its engagement with its 'object'. There is no pure agent for change or pure object of change. A subject must be at the same time an object and vice versa, and both sides will inevitably change through their interaction, even though this mutuality is rarely symmetric. What comes out of this process resembles not a straightforward, one-directional transformation of one by the other, but a level of compromise or hybridisation. While often associated with the 'effect of colonial power',[49] the production of hybridisation is in fact integral to all power and social relationship. Madsen made a similar point through his personal experience as a scholar of Chinese society and culture. On the one hand, his research and writing about China 'changed the lives of at least a few Chinese and even influenced how some of them think about their own society'. At the same time, his intellectual encounter with China—the 'object' of his study—has also made him a different person.[50] Madsen may be simply stating the obvious, but not very often do we hear such a candid reflection on Sino-Western relations at large.

Similar instances of mutual responsiveness can also be found in cyberspace. Since its inception, the Internet has been billed as one of the most revolutionary forces to change China in the direction of increasing personal freedom and political openness. No doubt, the advent of the Internet has helped empower ordinary Chinese netizens; just witness the proliferation of the Twitter equivalent of *weibo* or microblogs. Still, the reality is that the Chinese government has also managed to transform the Internet with the so-called 'great firewall of China', thanks in no small part to cooperation and technology transfer from such Western companies as Microsoft, Yahoo! and Google.[51] Lamenting this disappointing state of play in China's information age, a puzzled Ethan Gutmann wrote that

> We may have had the power, but we also had a strange unwillingness to use it.... Theoretically, China's desire to be part of the Internet should have given the capitalists who wired it considerable leverage. Instead, the leverage all seems to have remained with the [Chinese] government, as Western companies fell all over themselves bidding for its favor.[52]

For Gutmann, the problem lies mainly in 'our' lack of will to stand up to the Chinese. But a bigger 'problem', rightly or wrongly, is the imperative of mutual responsiveness in international relations. It is tempting to believe that satellite TV, the Internet, the Olympics, mobile phones and social media, given their Western origins and dominance, would one day help to transform China in Western images. But in the end those tools never operate outside the imperative of mutual responsiveness. To believe in the exclusive Western agency associated with those new media makes as much sense as arguing that eighteenth-century Chinese exports of teas and porcelain to Europe would one day make Europe more like China. True, Chinese inventions such as printing, gunpowder, and the magnet have made some profound impact on 'the whole face and state of things throughout the world',[53] but history tells us that none of the European powers who fully embraced these inventions has been Sinicised as a result.

So the key point is that China is not a blank sheet of paper on which the West can write its norms and rules at will. Mao Zedong once used the 'blank sheet of paper' metaphor to describe the newly founded People's Republic. Yet even this revolutionary figure admitted that he ended up only managing to 'change a few places in the vicinity of Beijing'.[54] That might well be Mao's false modesty, but it is clear that China is not a property for any single person or single country to simply represent, change, own, or lose. Though China has been undergoing numerous changes as a result of its contact with the West, a one-way Western transformation of the country is out of the question.

Still, the hope for a one-way conversion is commonplace. For example, in the study of China's normative learning and compliance, many analysts continue to assume that 'both norms and structures are initially external to the Chinese state'.[55] In this way, they 'bestow agency primarily to the Western and European community in promoting change within China', which leaves the latter with only two options: 'passive conformity or resistance'.[56] Translating such scholarly jargons into practical terms, a senior EU diplomat spoke for many Western observers when he maintained that the objective of engagement was to make China 'want what we want'.[57] Yet, as a senior World Bank staff member notes, 95 per cent of the changes the Work Bank helped introduce to China was in fact 'due to what Chinese officials want'.[58]

Even when it comes to the West's strong suit such as human rights norms, China has not been a completely passive actor, or merely a 'norm-taker'.[59] In August 1989, Beijing copped strong condemnations at the UN Sub-Commission on Human Rights in Geneva. Unsettled by this diplomatic loss of face, Chinese President Jiang Zemin called for research to address the issue of how 'democracy, freedom, and human rights should be looked at from a Marxist viewpoint'. Answering his call, the Central Committee of the CCP then took steps to ensure that China's viewpoint regarding human rights, democracy and freedom be heard more often on the international stage.[60] Since then, China has, with varying degrees of success, managed to put its stamp on international human rights norms. For example, thanks in part to China's efforts, the 1993 Vienna International Conference on Human Rights affirmed the right to development in the Vienna Declaration.

This illustrates that norm diffusion is not, and probably should not be, the exclusive privilege of Western powers. China, after all, is not a wishing well for the West, and never has it been. Even during the 'century of humiliation' when China was at its weakest point in its long history, Western missionaries often struggled to obtain even a modicum of success in the conversion of

Chinese 'heathens'. Meanwhile, modern Chinese reformers, in line with the doctrine of 'Chinese learning as foundation and Western learning for application' (*Zhongxue weiti, Xixue weiyong*), often managed to 'take much of only what they wanted' from their tumultuous encounters with the West.[61] In a historical account of Western advisers' attempts 'to change China', Jonathan Spence notes that on the one hand, every technique brought by Western advisers to China had eventually been assimilated, from heliocentric theories to nuclear physics. But when those techniques came with 'an ideological package' so as to force China to 'accept both together', most such efforts went nowhere.[62]

Some frustrated Westerners then routinely blame the failure on China's inscrutability, intransigence, or inertia. But the blame is often misdirected. Needless to say, China *is* capable of change; it is just that its change is neither unilinear nor uni-directional. While the West, the US, and Western-dominant international institutions have played a central role in China's modern transformation, one must not lose sight of the existence of a multitude of actors, countries, cultures, religions, multilateral institutions, and historical examples in the 'rest of the world', all capable of leaving their own mark on China. David Shambaugh observes that on the topic of improving the ruling party's political legitimacy, China 'borrowed' from a wide range of 'objects' that comprised social democratic states in Europe, collapsed communist and authoritarian party states in Central and Eastern Europe, Central Asia, East Asia, Latin America, and the former Soviet Union, as well as those few surviving communist party-states. Shambaugh calls this China's 'eclectic borrowing'.[63] In particular, the collapse of the Soviet Union served as a wake-up call for the Chinese leadership.[64]

Not long after the Soviet disintegration, political scientist Edward Friedman vowed not to repeat the failure to predict the demise of communism in the Soviet Union. He insisted that "It is important, if one is not to be surprised yet again, to open up the prospects for rupture in China today. Continuity is not the only realistic possibility."[65] He is certainly right in warning people of other possibilities about China. Nevertheless, it would be wrong to assume that a Soviet-style collapse in China was the only realistic alternative scenario. Were it so, Friedman might be in for surprise once again. Indeed, as will be mentioned in the next chapter, he would soon give up this hope and begin instead to peddle an alarming scenario of Chinese authoritarian triumphalism.

A Special Relationship?

Many 'China opportunity' observers hold that Sino-Western engagement represents a special relationship characterised by a benevolent West, with

China's best interests at heart and selflessly championing sovereign integrity, democracy, human rights, and prosperity for an otherwise troubled state. Given the special role of Western benevolence and goodwill, the least the West could expect from China would be its willingness to converge with 'us', gradually if it will.

There can be no doubt that many Westerners, past and present, have devoted their energy to the worthy cause of helping China in one form or another, thus giving this relationship a level of specialness to the people involved. That said, to claim that this represents a broader pattern in Sino-Western interaction is an exaggeration, if not a distortion. For all the Europeans' longstanding claim to have helped save and modernise China, their track record has impressed few Chinese. For much of the nineteenth and early twentieth centuries, many European countries conducted themselves in China as overbearing colonisers, whose standard strategy is otherwise known as 'gunboat diplomacy'. A trenchant description of this relationship during that time by investigative reporter Sterling Seagrave is worth quoting:

> In the south, Western traders at Canton and Macao flouted the law, smuggling in massive quantities of cheap Indian opium, driving a spike into the heartwood. *Opium became a symbol of China's sovereignty and whether foreigners could violate that sovereignty at whim....* It became a game among Westerners to provoke the Chinese at every turn and, when the Chinese struck back, to demand concessions from local mandarins. If concessions were not forthcoming, gunboats were called in; China found herself at war over issues that were trumped up and incidents that were greatly exaggerated or entirely imaginary. Many Westerners built successful careers out of bullying the Chinese.[66]

This may be fitting to characterise past European behaviour in China, but for many Americans, US China policy largely stayed away from 'the nasty imperialism and power politics of the Europeans'.[67] Its Open Door policy, for example, seemed to set the US apart from the social Darwinism of European powers. Yet, according to Hans Morgenthau, the essence of this American policy was 'what you might call freedom of competition with regard to the exploitation of China'.[68] John Fairbank, a founding father of modern China studies, told us that throughout much of the nineteenth century Americans 'were part and parcel of the general Western expansion into East Asia', and many 'basic decisions affecting American activity in China were made in London'.[69] During the 1930s, in spite of widespread US sympathy for China's suffering from Japanese invasion, not only was Washington slow to provide China with meaningful military or economic assistance, but it was also the main supplier of war materials to Japan until as late as July 1939.[70] In his book *The Making of a Special Relationship*, Michael Hunt points out that to the extent that this US-China relationship could be seen as 'special', it was not because of 'American benevolence, Chinese gratitude and mutual good will' as conventionally canvassed, but because of 'its breadth, complexity, and instability'.[71]

Overall, the main priority of both American and European policies on China during the 'century of humiliation' was to uphold 'the existing government or [support] the more conservative faction in order to promote the stability that we felt would best safeguard our own trade and investments'.[72] If Western diplomats and merchants cared more about profit than about China, missionaries did not fare much better. Some missionaries worked knowingly for British companies that engaged in opium smuggling, and had no qualms about distributing Christian tracts from the same ships that were bringing opium into the country.[73] Indeed, they seemed all too willing to seek special protection from Western consulates and take full advantage of the privilege of extraterritoriality as well as American and British gunboats, all the while without feeling the slightest bit of guilt.[74]

No wonder that many Chinese often struggled to see the various powers as anything other than one group of 'closely related barbarians'.[75] Back in 1926 even Chiang Kai-shek, upon whom the US would later place much hope for Christianising China, called the Americans a dangerously two-faced people: 'The Americans come to us with smiling faces and friendly talk, but in the end your government acts just like the Japanese'.[76] Given all this, it is not surprising that instead of converting China, the West and especially the US eventually 'lost' it.

The historical records of this special relationship of 'open door', 'Christ for China', and gunboat diplomacy in the past do not bode well for Western attempts to transform China in the present. However different contemporary Western governments have become, their engagement, rhetoric aside, has not been primarily designed to help modernise or democratise China. Of course, this is not to claim that today Western dealings with China are nothing more than a replay of the past colonial exploitation and bullying; engagement between the two sides has taken on new meanings and today China is no longer a powerless victim. Nevertheless, when replacing 'Open Door' with 'market access', 'Christ' with 'democracy', and 'gunboat' with 'alliances', one could be forgiven for feeling more than a whiff of *déjà vu*. Today, the main motivation behind Western businesses in China remains business. For the most part, they are lured to China not out of a concern for its liberal transformation per se, but in search of profit. As one Airbus official admits, 'It's the market where you have to be'.[77] GM Chairman and CEO Rick Wagoner agrees. Announcing plans to relocate GM's regional headquarters from Singapore to Shanghai, Wagoner said in June 2004 that 'Having a strong presence in this dynamic and growing market is not an option anymore, it's a necessity'.[78] Just as their nineteenth-century predecessors 'wanted to reform trade, not China', [79] contemporary Western business leaders seem to have little interest in changing China except where such change would help with their commercial operations. Otherwise, their default option is to maintain the status quo in China. Not surprisingly, when the Chinese authorities signalled their intention to censor the Internet through the so-called 'Gold Shield Project', a host of American, German and Canadian companies such as Cisco, Motorola, Siemens and Nortel were all eager to cooperate, salivating over the opportunity on offer. [80]

Likewise, the US government, despite its usual refrain of engaging China for democracy promotion, has consistently prioritised US interests. [81] Vowing not to coddle the 'butchers of Beijing', Bill Clinton, shortly after taking office, signed the Executive Order of May 1993 to link the renewal of China's MFN status with improvement in China's human rights conditions. But even before this measure celebrated its first birthday, it had drawn widespread criticisms from the American business community. William Warwick, Chairman of AT&T in China, warned that 'Either we establish a major presence in the Chinese market, or we forget about being a global player'. [82] The leaders of 800 American businesses and trade associations wrote to Clinton that his policy, if continued, would jeopardise American trade interests. Some American companies even flew their English-speaking Chinese employees to Washington to show US lawmakers how economic development in China had already transformed the country. [83] Sympathetic to the business community, the economic agencies within the Clinton administration registered similar disquiet. So did several former Secretaries of State, who berated the administration's preoccupation with advancing human rights at the expense of the all-important trade ties. A Council on Foreign Relations public event in March 1994 featured distinguished speakers from both political camps to push for 'delinking'. To secure the renewal of China's MFN status, the US Chamber of Commerce assembled a China MFN Congressional Lobbying Team specifically targeting undecided members of Congress. [84] It was not as if many would need such lobbying. With their constituencies expected to gain from expanding economic ties with China, many lawmakers were already among the most vocal supporters of renewed economic engagement with Beijing. [85]

If it is on this basis that the US lays claim to its special relationship with China, there is nothing special about it. At best, this is a normal relationship driven by mutual interests, a point which many Western practitioners quietly admit. Underneath the rhetoric, Western engagement with China is often based on pragmatic realism: China is something the West has to live with; it cannot be simply contained or wished away. However, to call a spade a spade in this context would fly in the face of the popular American self-imagery as the champion for democracy and human rights. Further, to rally the public behind the China engagement policy, that policy needs to be injected with a more positive purpose, hence the storyline of 'China opportunity'. After all, 'good' politics entails the politics of fantasy. But once politicians and business leaders begin to buy the fantasy of their own making and expect China's quick transition through economic engagement, they are on track to disappointment. Given the false premises of the 'China opportunity' paradigm, this opportunity turns out to be a false promise.

THE QUEST FOR CHINA'S CONVERSION: MISSION IMPOSSIBLE

As well as perplexed by its false premises, the notion of the 'China opportunity' itself is often vaguely defined. If it means that China will become more like 'us', that only raises more questions than answers: Who, for example, is 'us'? This popular collective 'we', as noted earlier, is inherently heterogeneous and constantly contested. As a result, there is no single Western self for China to emulate, nor is there a commonly agreed Western norm for China to follow. Despite much focus on 'bringing China into the international community', Johnston and Ross acknowledge that there has been little attempt to establish 'who constitutes this community and what are the shared global norms and rules'. To provide a remedy, they call for the creation of an ambitious 'score-card' to 'assess China's commitment to global norms, rules and institutions across time, across other states and across issue areas'.[86] And on the score-card, Johnston and Evans include a key criterion in terms of 'whether Chinese behavior complies with US interests as American political and military leaders define them'.[87] Explicit as this benchmark may sound, what remains unclear is *which* American political and military leaders actually define *what*, given that 'American leaders' are far from a homogeneous entity.

Further complicating the issue is the debate over 'genuine learning' versus 'strategic adaptation'. Some define 'genuine learning' as 'genuine (if often incremental) transformation of elite perceptions',[88] but the problem remains as to what is meant by 'genuine'. For example, does evidence of policy change qualify as genuine learning? Jack S. Levy argues that policy change is not a necessary criterion, but Iain Johnston argues that it is.[89] Granted that it is, we are still unclear whether policy change refers to 'humane governance' or 'the end of the one party system'. David Lampton believes that it should be the former. But for James Mann, 'more humane governance' is no political change at all, as it is little more than 'a new euphemism for acceptance of China's existing one-party system'.[90]

For some, though both the precise meaning and measurement of China's convergence may be messy and elusive, what really matters is that both

China and the West have begun to share a common interest in engagement and integration. For example, both seem to agree that China is an opportunity for the world. Both sides stress the importance of China becoming a responsible stakeholder. Bill Clinton observed first hand that Jiang Zemin shared his desire to integrate China into the world community.[91] But there is more to such apparent convergence than meets the eye. Despite some of the common vocabulary in use, there has been a lack of common meaning on those terms. As Lampton observes, both the US and China 'can agree about being responsible powers as a general proposition but fall out over what the content of "responsibility" may specifically be'.[92] Consequently, the two sides often talk at cross-purposes. When they do seem to agree on some common meanings, common meanings do not necessarily translate into consensus. Quite the contrary, 'a common meaning', as Charles Taylor explains, 'is very often the cause of the most bitter lack of consensus'.[93] This point has not been lost on Thomas Friedman. In a BBC documentary he made the point that 'What is most unsettling about China to Americans is not their *communism*; it is their *capitalism*'.[94]

Furthermore, granted that the West and China could settle on a common goal for the time being, that goal could turn out to be a moving target over time. Surely not all Western expectations of China are inherently elusive. Yet the problem is that as China takes one modest step forward, it often invites the expectation of another, always one step ahead of China. In this sense, the West's normative goal of changing China is not a need, but a demand. In the words of Slavoj Žižek, 'every time the subject gets the object he demanded, he undergoes the experience of "This is not *that!*" Although the subject "got what he asked for," the demand is not fully satisfied'.[95]

As an ever-changing demand, the 'China opportunity' becomes a paradox; perhaps subconsciously, its promise 'intrinsically demands an indefinite postponement of its [own] fulfillment'.[96] Similar to looking at China from a fast-moving train, the 'China opportunity' demand will not see China standing still, but actually going backward. For example, instead of seeing any progress in China over the years, many Western governments and human rights organisations have routinely issued reports charging that human rights conditions in China are getting worse by the year.[97] No wonder that a Chinese official complained at the Swiss city of Davos that 'You western countries, you decide the rules, you give the grades, you say, "You have been a bad boy"'.[98]

Of course, until China democratises, it may well deserve to be called 'a bad boy', meaning that democracy is 'our' final demand of China. But the jury is still out whether democracy *is* the final demand. There is good reason to doubt it. As an 'ultimate' ideal in the West, democracy was a fairly recent construct. In fact, as Raymond Williams notes, with only occasional exceptions, democracy, in the records that we have, was until C19 [the nineteenth century] a strongly unfavourable term, and it is only since lC19 [the late nineteenth century) and eC20 [the early twentieth century] that a majority of political parties and tendencies have united in declaring their belief in it.[99]

Before democracy came into vogue, one of the most desirable political models for Europe, ironically, had been China's enlightened despotism.[100] At least that was at the time a popular view among many European intellectuals. In any event, for the better part of the past few centuries, it was technological progress, trade, and sovereignty, rather than democracy and human rights, that had been the predominant norms of the Western-dominated international society. When European powers were eager to expand to China in the nineteenth century, the 'Middle Kingdom' was chided and punished for its technological backwardness, economic autarky, lack of national self-consciousness and ignorance of sovereign equality, rather than for its despotic political system. Less than a century later, when China has finally caught up with those standards of civilisation, little does it realise that industrialised modernity is no longer the latest hallmark of progress. If anything, in the eyes of some Western observers, it has become the opposite.[101] Nor does the Westphalian notion of sovereignty, now fully embraced by China, seem to be in fashion any more. In their place have been democracy, human rights, and humanitarian intervention which together form 'the new standards of civilisation, the new set of criteria for membership in international society'.[102] Taiwanese scholar Chih-yu Shih observes that the idea of sovereignty has played 'a joke' on China. China, after much soul-searching, finally adapted to the world of sovereign states 'only to be told 100 years later that sovereignty is no longer sufficient to win respect'.[103]

Will the norms of democratic governance and human rights be another joke for the Chinese, who finally manage to democratise, only to discover that the signposts set by the West have moved yet again? In other words, would democracy continue to occupy the pride of place in the future standards of civilisation? The answer is hard to know, of course. But one may reasonably doubt that democracy would stay on as the final normative standard; some might say it never was. Even at the heartland of democracy, there has been a general apathy towards the process and outcome, if not the ideal, of democracy among a large proportion of Western citizens. During the 'War on Terror', there has been a visible erosion of liberty in preference to national security. Huntington, who once hailed the arrival of the 'third wave of democratisation' in the late twentieth century, reminded his readers that 'Democratization conflicts with Westernization, and democracy is inherently a parochializing not a cosmopolitanizing process'.[104] In this context, it is not surprising that some leading China scholars in the US have advised Washington that 'democratization should be regarded as only one objective of American policy toward China, not as the only one'. [105] If so, then even a democratised China, contrary to Gilley's argument, may still fall short of the ever-changing demands from China opportunity advocates.

Some analysts may argue that their expectation is not so open-ended. They seem to stand ready to declare 'mission accomplished' if and when China is seen to have finally succeeded, as Hutton sees it, in ditching communism, building its Enlightenment institutions, and becoming a state that actively upholds norms of international governance. [106] Presumably such comprehensive success would at long last allow the West to tick all the boxes on its China 'score-card'. Yet, if this scenario sounds too good to be true, it probably is. How come could China become something modelled on nothing less than an idealised version of the Western self? As noted by a mission statement of the British Foreign and Commonwealth Office, these are essentially values 'which we demand for ourselves'. [107] If so, chances are that these values are yet to be fully lived up to by the US and Britain themselves. This, according to Hutton, has been 'a mistake of the first order'. [108] What this means is that China seems to be held up to higher standards and 'idealized accounts of good governance and rule of law that no country lives up to'. [109] Western countries have routinely set targets for China to meet, targets in areas ranging from human rights and democracy to non-proliferation, environmental protection and international trade. 'Were the Chinese to meet all these conditions', Warren Cohen admits, China would become one of the most liberal and responsible countries in the world, which simply would not happen. [110] Yet, that is precisely what China watchers have been expecting. What is assured, then, is that the China opportunity will be an ongoing bitter disappointment. The false promises about China are not a reflection of China's inability to change so much as a result of those promises' own elusiveness.

Added to this elusiveness is a two-pronged demand for China's conversion and Western control. In the words of the late Gerald Segal, who commanded enormous respect and influence among China watchers, the demand, specifically, is both tying China *in* and *down*. [111] This is precisely how, for example, Richard Haass interprets the function of engagement and integration in relation to China. He believes that the best way to change China is through consent, rather than coercion. American foreign policy, he argues, should aim to promote consent on international relations. 'Against such a common backdrop', he continues, 'it would be possible to integrate other countries and organizations into arrangements that could sustain a world consistent with U.S. interests and values'. [112] Although Haass immediately explains that those US interests and values 'are in no way narrowly or uniquely American', the fact that US interests and values, presumably universal, serve as the explicit benchmark for integration is revealing. Here it seems that integration is not an end in itself, but a means to the end of upholding US interests and values. Ultimately it is about making China do 'what *we* want it to do'.[113] To Bill Clinton, the main objective of engaging China was to maintain US dominance. In September 2000, in his attempt to persuade sceptics in Congress to support the PNTR deal with China, his rationale was that '*America has more influence in China* with an outstretched hand than with a clenched fist'.[114]

In his 2005 speech, Robert Zoellick similarly laid out a dual objective of conversion and control. For Zoellick, the US does not integrate China for the sake of integration. Rather, it is to serve the greater purpose of making sure that China acts responsibly in the US-dominated international system; it is in this sense that China's mere membership in this system is deemed inadequate. Commenting on Zoellick's speech, Randall Peerenboom notes that:

> Substantively, China was offered a place at the table, but on terms that decidedly served US interests: lower currency rates, more protection of intellectual property, more transparency on military spending and future military plans, and financial support for the war in Iraq, including debt reduction, even though China opposed the war . . . Zoellick also warned that until China toes the line, other countries will be forced to "hedge relations with China."[115]

Importantly, Zoellick's 'responsible stakeholder' vision for China is not a partisan idea, but a bipartisan consensus that can be traced back to the Western colonial ambivalence about the Other, namely, wanting it to become the same as 'the Western self' but not quite as powerful (lest it become out of control). Ronald Steel summarises this dual attitude as follows: 'we are not content merely to subdue others: We insist that they be like us'.[116] Thus, this is not unique to American engagement with China, but is integral to American foreign policy traditions more generally. [117] Within those traditions, moderate liberals and hawkish realists alike take comfort at US global dominance and both groups agree that this should remain so well into the future. Wolfowitz once complained that Bill Clinton's grand strategy appropriated his vision of America's sustained global superiority 'without acknowledgement'.[118] The main difference is that in order to make such dominance more legitimate and longer lasting, liberal institutionalists go a step further by demanding normative change of other countries to seal that dominance ideationally as well as militarily. As Johnston puts it, normative control is likely to 'lead to the most durable and self-reinforcing pro-social behavior'.[119]

Consequently, to many strategists, the twin smart goals of tying China in and down make perfect sense, except that the two objectives may not always be easily compatible. To hope for China's democratisation per se is certainly not delusional, but to expect a democratic *and* submissive China seems more problematic in the long run. Huntington was probably right that a more democratic China would become less pro-Western, a problem which has long baffled the coloniser. For the coloniser, the mimicry of liberty by the colonised, as Bhabha notes, brings about at once resemblance and menace.[120] In the words of Ashis Nandy, the colonised thus turn into an 'intimate enemy' of the coloniser.[121] After Japan defeated Russia in 1905, US President Theodore Roosevelt rejoiced: 'I was thoroughly pleased with the Japanese victory, for Japan is playing our game'.[122] But a few decades later, as Pearl Harbor made plainly clear, Japan's socialisation into 'our game' effectively came home to roost. In the historical context of Sino-Western relations, China also became an 'intimate enemy' of the West by appropriating Western nationalism as a weapon to fend off Western encroachment. As John Fairbank noted:

> The irony of the Westernization which occurred in the new urban centers of late-nineteenth-century China was that it brought in Western ways that eventually turned China against the West. It did this because it fostered Chinese nationalism. Foreign contact has often led to anti-foreignism, but in this case the Western example of aggressive nationalism induced more and more Chinese to respond in kind and shift from their old-style culturalism to become modern patriots.[123]

At the core of such an 'intimate enemy' phenomenon is again the logic of mutual responsiveness. So long as the Chinese are subject to the dual goal of conversion and control, there is always a possibility that they will mirror it back. In this sense, there is nothing paradoxical about the fact that a more Westernised China can be a more assertive China. Yet, from the 'China opportunity' perspective, the 'paradox' is all too abnormal. Just as containment cannot survive its success, engagement's success in converting China in Western image could end up defeating its own purpose.

To conclude, the 'China opportunity' paradigm may have informed the policy of engagement, but ultimately its dual objectives of convergence and control are false promises. While discourse is constitutive of the world, the theory and practice of the 'China opportunity' paradigm alone is not adequate in turning China into an 'opportunity' for 'us'. In a world of mutual responsiveness, the 'soothing scenario' of the 'China opportunity' can never be fully realised in the intersubjective relationship between China and the West.

7. The international politics of disillusionment

> *As these ... struggles combine and collide, the promise of a new era of international convergence fades. We have entered an age of divergence.*
>
> Robert Kagan[1]

> *False fantasies may have been revealed, but the dreams that animate them live on.*
>
> Stephen Duncombe[2]

> *Myths are essential to human life. They focus our attention on common goals and enable us to hope. But... the hope that myths inspire may be unrealistic hope. So, essential as they are, our myths occasion the danger of tragedy.*
>
> Richard Madsen[3]

International relations operate not just on the basis of hard interests and naked power; they are inherently mediated through ideas, representations and emotions.[4] In the preceding chapters, we have examined how this is reflected in the theory as practice of the two China paradigms. As ambivalent desires of fear and fantasy, these paradigms not only belong to the intellectual realm of China watching, but are also complicit in the dynamics of Sino-Western interaction. In both cases, theory is intertwined with practice.

Of course, I do not suggest a type of one-on-one correspondence between a certain theory (or emotion) and a particular type of practice or policy. Specifically, I do not claim that containment is the sole work of the 'China threat' theory, or that engagement is the only policy implication of the 'China opportunity' paradigm. As false promises, the China opportunity is an unstable, ambivalent structure of feeling that tends to oscillate between hope and disillusionment. While hope may justify engagement, what if that hope turns out to be an illusion? What if, as the argument goes, China doesn't democratise? Facing a seemingly powerful and intransigent China, will disillusionment join the emotion of fear and add fuel to the 'China threat' theory and practice? This chapter will address these questions.

'PUSHBACK': A HARDLINE TURN OF WESTERN STRATEGY TOWARDS CHINA

The first decade of the twenty-first century ended with a hardline turn in Western strategy towards China. Within a month of the first year anniversary of President Obama's inauguration, US Secretary of State Hillary Clinton openly chided China for its Internet censorship practices, whereas President Obama announced the sale of $6 billion worth of weapons to Taiwan and met with the exiled Tibetan leader the Dalai Lama in the White House. A few months later, Secretary Clinton signalled a more activist US role in the South China Sea disputes while attending an ASEAN meeting in Hanoi. All these steps, as then US Ambassador to Beijing Jon Huntsman admitted, 'trampled on' China's core national interests.[5] In his face-to-face talks with Chinese President Hu Jintao during the 2010 Toronto G-20 Summit, Obama accused China of 'willful blindness' in relation to North Korea's 'belligerent behavior'. In September 2010, with a huge bipartisan majority, the US House of Representatives passed a bill that effectively paved the way for economic sanctions against Beijing over its much-maligned currency policy, a move which came only hours after the White House brought to the WTO more cases against China.[6] Amidst these concerted US efforts of getting tough on Beijing,[7] some commentators suggest that the Obama administration has changed tack on US China policy by siding with the 'strategists' who are in favour of a more aggressive approach to managing China's rise.[8] Thomas Friedman labels the new US policy 'containment-lite'.[9] Remarkably, coming barely one year into Obama's 'new era of engagement' in world diplomacy, this new China policy, as well as the subsequent 'pivot to Asia' strategy, bears little resemblance to the so-called 'strategic reassurance' doctrine on China proclaimed by Deputy Secretary of State James Steinberg in September 2009.[10]

Across the Atlantic exists a similar story. Not only does the much-anticipated EU-China axis fail to materialise,[11] but the so-called 'honeymoon' period of the EU-China relationship proves short-lived as well.[12] Priding themselves on being members of 'Normative Power Europe', many European countries now adopt a more value-based and less accommodating stance on China than in the past. Heeding the call for 'firming up the EU approach and driving a harder bargain' in dealing with China,[13] several European political leaders, including then British Prime Minister Gordon Brown, German Chancellor Angela Merkel, the President of the European Parliament Dr Hans-Gert Poettering, and the President of the European

Commission Jose-Manuel Barroso, 'boycotted' the Beijing Olympics opening ceremony. Though then French President Nicholas Sarkozy backed away
from his initial 'boycott' threat, he went ahead with his planned meeting with
the Dalai Lama in Poland a few months later. And with the awarding of the
2010 Nobel Peace Prize to the Chinese dissident Liu Xiaobo, Europe's value-
based approach to China showed no sign of abating.

One might expect Australia to be the last country in the West to jump on
the China-hedging bandwagon. After all, the resource-rich country has been a
major beneficiary of China's economic rise. And yet, despite its frequent
disavowal, Canberra has led the way in hedging against its biggest trading
partner. Australia's 2009 Defence White Paper implicitly made China's rise a
central justification for its expansion in naval capability, the largest expansion since WWII.[14] According to a US diplomatic cable, when queried by
Secretary Clinton over 'how do you get tough on your banker?' Rudd, a self-
professed 'brutal realist', urged the need to 'deploy force' against China
should it fail to integrate into the international community. Even his seemingly innocuous 'Asia Pacific Community' initiative, as it turns out, was
designed with containing Chinese influence on the agenda.[15] With the first
batch of US marines arriving in Australia in April 2012, Canberra has left
little doubt where it stands strategically between the US and China.

Of course hardline elements have always been part of Western policy on
China. But for much of the past few decades, the dominant policy mantra in
the US, Europe and Australia has been 'constructive engagement'. Whilst
'engagement' and 'cooperation' have continued to this day, the 'competitive
dimensions' have grown 'more pronounced' in recent years.[16] So much so
that some Western analysts conclude that the US and China are now locked
in a global struggle for 'both power and belief' that will define the world
political landscape for the twenty-first century.[17] Meanwhile, nearly 55 per
cent of Chinese respondents to a *Global Times* poll in early 2010 believed
that the US and China are heading for a Cold War.[18] Even moderate Chinese
scholars such as Wang Jisi have noted that these two countries are entering a
period of strategic competition.[19]

At first glance, the West's increasing reliance on hedging is a direct response to (or 'pushback' against) a more muscular China on the world stage.
In the words of Thomas Friedman, it is triggered by 'a sudden surge' in
China's assertiveness, notably its defiant currency stance, the imprisonment
of dissidents, the continued Internet censorship, its expanding navy capability, its heavy-handed approach to the South China Sea disputes as well as a
2010 fishing boat incident near the disputed Diaoyu (Senkaku in Japan)
islands.[20]

Assertive as it is, China cannot take full responsibility for the rise of the
'pushback' strategy in the West. Part and parcel of this strategic shift have

been Western ambivalent representations of China's rise. By Western representations I do not just mean the 'China threat' paradigm or what many Chinese refer to as 'a Cold War zero-sum mindset'.[21] These factors alone cannot explain why many advocates of the recent pushback strategy are not traditional China hawks.

To fully understand this puzzle, we must now bring the 'China opportunity' paradigm into the mix. My contention is that as false promises, this paradigm inevitably gives rise to disillusionment, which in turn provides fertile ground for the seeds of fear, old and new, to germinate and grow. The ultimate paradox of this paradigm is that it undermines the very policy of engagement it seemingly promotes.

THE CHINA FANTASY AND WESTERN DISILLUSIONMENT

Accompanying the recent pushback against China is a growing sense of Western disillusionment. Without understanding this collective emotion about China, we cannot fully grasp this hardline turn. To pay attention to this emotion, one cannot go past former *Los Angeles Times* Beijing Bureau Chief James Mann's book *The China Fantasy*. Dubbed the 'bible for many of those who believe that China isn't about to change',[22] this deceptively small book begins with an account of two commonly assumed scenarios about China, the Soothing Scenario and the Upheaval Scenario. The former scenario, predicated largely on the 'China opportunity' paradigm, assumes that, with trade and economic development, China is on track to become a democracy, whereas the latter predicts that what lies ahead for China is economic collapse and political upheaval. For Mann, both scenarios, especially the soothing one, are fantasies. A third and more realistic scenario, he argues, is 'the emergence of a permanent Chinese autocracy', that is, China will neither democratise nor collapse, but may instead remain politically authoritarian and economically stable at the same time.[23]

While few have argued as eloquently as Mann, many observers are now waking up to essentially the same 'China fantasy' scenario. Ying Ma at the AEI laments that the Chinese authoritarian behemoth 'appears immune to and unmoved by U.S. wishes'.[24] Daniel Blumenthal, also at AEI, complains that 'American elite opinion has been, for the most part, dead wrong about China', for Beijing is neither democratising nor 'aligning itself with the West' to tackle international problems.[25] Ethan Gutmann, formerly an American business consultant working in Beijing, casts doubt on China's market potential. He equates the so-called economic opportunity of China with 'a sinkhole market' for Western businesses.[26] Like Mann, Gutmann argues that economic engagement with China is unlikely to bring about political freedom. If anything, the West is losing the 'new China'.

Such scepticism on the China opportunity is not new. Hardliners and neo-conservative commentators have long opposed engagement with China on the basis that its promised transformation of China is an illusion.[27] However, today Western disillusionment with China is not limited to hardliners, but has begun to infiltrate 'elite opinion' on China traditionally dominated by liberal observers and business leaders. As Shambaugh points out, 'Even those U.S. analysts who have tended to view China in a more benign fashion, and hope that a more cooperative and internationalist nation would mature on the world stage, are growing disillusioned by Beijing's recent behavior'.[28] Will Inboden, a former US National Security Council official, observes that a paradigm shift on China is under way in a cross-section of policy, academic, and commercial leaders in Europe and the US. Citing Google's threat to pull out of China as an example, he notes that while not long ago the Western business community had been upbeat about China's market potential and actively pushed for close ties between China and the West, 'now the consensus is fractured'.[29] Jeffrey Immelt, General Electric's Chief Executive, vented his dissatisfaction by telling a group of top Italian executives in Rome that 'I am not sure that in the end [the Chinese] want any of us to win, or any of us to be successful'.[30] This change of heart among American business leaders did not escape the attention of a Chinese veteran senior diplomat during his tour to the US amidst the 2010 midterm congressional elections. In an interview with a Hong Kong-based Chinese newspaper, the diplomat, Wu Jianmin, noted that during past frictions between the two countries, the American business community often stood up for China, but now for the first time it kept silent.[31]

The widespread disappointment with China is not confined to the US. 'The happy metamorphosis of the Communist chrysalis into a pluralist butterfly seems improbable in Beijing', writes the French author Guy Sorman.[32] A Brussels-based China scholar declares the European attempts to transform China 'a failure': China's performance simply has not met European expectations.[33] In Australia, after the Rio Tinto and Stern Hu affair between Australia and China in 2009, a leading scholar at the University of Sydney summarised the disillusionment this way: the 'once pervasive optimism among Western liberals that China's rise will be strategically benign and a boon to an ailing global economy is giving way to a gnawing anxiety that a strong China may not be so good for the world after all'.[34] Sharing such disillusionment, many commentators now conclude that the West has profoundly misjudged China.[35]

FROM DISILLUSIONMENT TO FEAR: PARADIGM SHIFT AND CHINA POLICY CHANGE

Over the past two centuries, China has often been a source of disappointment for the West. As China historian Jonathan Spence has skilfully demonstrated, many Western advisers in the nineteenth and early twentieth centuries who had sought to mould the Middle Kingdom in Western image quickly came to the 'dawning realization that such would not be the case'.[36] No doubt causing much Western bewilderment or angst at the time, those disillusionments could at least be offset by China's weakness or perceived insignificance for the 'family of nations': when 'the sick man of Asia' seemed unable or unfit to live up to 'our' expectations of it, it could for the most part be safely ignored.

This time around, however, that safe option is no more. China seems no longer just an 'inconsequential enemy' it once was. In the same year when Mann's *The China Fantasy* was published, a January 2007 issue of *Time* magazine featured the cover story on the rise of China, entitled 'The Chinese Century'. Richard Stengel, managing editor of the magazine whose co-founder Henry Luce wrote the famous essay 'The American Century' in the middle of the last century, noted that there now was no bigger story than China's meteoric rise and its relationship with the US in the twenty-first century.[37] Mindful of this power shift, Hugh White argues that China is 'already bigger, relative to the US, than the Soviet Union ever was during the Cold War. A Chinese challenge to American power in Asia is no longer a future possibility but a current reality'.[38] And Martin Jacques goes further. What we are witnessing, the British writer and columnist argues, is the changing of the guard from the dominant West to a rising Middle Kingdom, which will spell the end of the Western world as we know it. Four decades from now, as he predicts, 'the world will come to look like a very different place indeed'.[39]

As China has emerged from the global financial crisis apparently stronger than ever, the speculation of the arrival of 'a world without the West' led by China and other rising powers has gained further currency.[40] A stronger China, with its formula of open markets and an authoritarian political system, looks set to become an attractive model for many developing countries. Labelled by economist Joshua Cooper Ramo as the 'Beijing Consensus',[41] this new developmental model seems to threaten to undermine the now battered Washington Consensus. For example, in its report *Global Trends 2025*, the US National Intelligence Council attributes the decline of the Western model of economic liberalism, democracy, and secularism in large part to China's rising clout.[42] In late 2010, Obama had his first taste of this tectonic shift in the global balance of power at the G-20 Leaders Summit held in Seoul. Not only did Obama try unsuccessfully to rally world leaders to put pressure on China over its currency policy, but the US instead found itself a target of concerted complaints that its own Federal Reserve's 'quantitative easing' measure had artificially depreciated the US dollar.[43]

Consequently, the present Western disillusionment with China seems rather unique. Now for the first time in the last few centuries a disappointingly recalcitrant China is simultaneously a strong China, a 'strange beast' both economically and militarily powerful and politically anachronistic. For example, reluctantly coming to terms with the fact that China was not going to live up to his initial expectation, a confused Gutmann found himself

> speechless, unable to process the New China—to reconcile the rapidly modernizing state... with the peculiar combination of victim-ecstasy, belligerent racial pride, obsession with territorial claims, flashes of sadomasochistic pleasure in submitting to authority, cynical contempt for democracy and raw xenophobia that I saw on the streets. I couldn't neatly label it either: Chinese hypernationalism? Fascism with Chinese Characteristics? China was too corrupt to compare to Nazi Germany, and too inefficient to compare to Imperial Japan. Yet the movement that I was glimpsing was occurring in a country much bigger and with far more economic potential than the Axis combined.[44]

As well as resorting to the reliable 'Oriental inscrutability' script, Gutmann's confusion is clearly tinged with a sense of fear. And Gutmann is just one of many disillusioned liberal observers who now warn of China's ideological challenge to the West. Led by Mann's *The China Fantasy*, there is now a burgeoning body of literature along this line.[45] What Mann identifies as the Third Scenario of China—a permanent Chinese autocracy—now seems to represent a double affront to the Western self-imagination and identity. It is a challenge, according to the French magazine *Le Monde*, not only to the West's economic supremacy, but also to 'its right to define right and wrong, to lay down international law, and to interfere in other countries' affairs on moral or humanitarian grounds'.[46] Edward Friedman, who once bet on the collapse of the Chinese government, now goes so far as to say that a coalition of authoritarian regimes led by China 'is well on the way to defeating the global forces of democracy'.[47]

What is more, added to this 'China fantasy' fear are both a bitter resentment of betrayal and a nightmare scenario of reverse conversion at the hands of the inscrutable Chinese, a mixed feeling reminiscent of the romantic drama *M. Butterfly*. Here, the promise of the China opportunity turns into the 'devastating knowledge that, underneath it all, the object of her love was nothing more, nothing less than...a man'.[48] Such horror was similarly articulated in the 1962 Hollywood film *The Manchurian Candidate*. Set in the context of the beginning of the Cold War struggle between the capitalist free world and a menacing Red China, the story rested on a latent and perennial nightmare in Western imagination of communist brainwashing and infiltration on the one hand and Western blissful ignorance and even willing collusion on the other. The more closely one looks at the way the 'China fantasy' story is being told, the more easily one can sense its 'Manchurian Candidate' undertone: not only is the hope to change China a fantasy, but 'China itself is starting to influence its Western partners' course of development'.[49]

According to Mann, the seductive Chinese influence is now often embodied in money, Chinese money: 'the cash and allure of the China business' which has claimed its easy prey ranging from working-level civil servants and leading China scholars through top-level government officials to even US Presidents.[50] Following up on Mann's allegation, the 2009 annual report of the Congress-mandated US-China Economic and Security Review Commission devoted, for the first time, a whole section on China's external propaganda and influence operations and their impacts on the US, particularly on US academics and think tanks.[51] In Germany, many commentators were similarly dismayed and frustrated by the 'complete internalization of Beijing's line of argument' by then Chancellor Gerhard Schroeder, whereas the Mandarin-speaking Kevin Rudd during his short stint as Australian Prime Minister was repeatedly branded by political opponents and conservative columnists as the 'Manchurian candidate' and a 'roving ambassador for China'.[52] Similar jibes have been hurled at Western business representatives in China, who, according to Gutmann, behaved like 'de facto spokesmen for the Chinese leadership', 'as if they had gone native'.[53] Western Internet companies in particular have been singled out for selling Western moral conscience for profit. After repeating the familiar line that the Internet represents a most powerful agent for change in China, Leonard laments that 'it is China that has changed the Internet: forcing internet giants like Google, Microsoft and Yahoo to play by its rules'.[54] Alas, it seems that the 'China opportunity' paradigm has now been turned on its head. This anomaly even caught the attention of the US House of Representatives Human Rights Subcommittee. It called in representatives from its four high-tech corporations Yahoo!, Google, Microsoft and Cisco Systems to lecture them on the importance of social responsibility and human rights over profits.[55]

More alarmingly still, it is feared that it might not take long before China's moral challenge translates into a strategic menace. The logic sounds straightforward enough: China's threat to American moral authority would inevitably undermine the moral foundation upon which US military primacy has been justified. And so long as China remains stubbornly undemocratic, its long-term strategic intention will be uncertain and thus an eventual military challenge from China cannot be ruled out. Thus, although Mann refrains from identifying China as an impending military threat, at one point he cannot help but wonder whether Beijing is deploying a delaying tactic to give itself more time to develop a more powerful military. 'Who can say what dreams and ambitions Chinese leaders may harbor thirty years from now, once the country is richer and stronger?' he asks anxiously.[56]

Thus, behind the 'China fantasy' discourse is a powerful image of China as an emerging moral and potentially military threat which can no longer be ignored and ought to be confronted. Against this backdrop, how the disillusionment of the 'China fantasy' helps to strengthen a hardline policy towards China can be more clearly understood. By questioning the conventional image of China held by the 'China opportunity' paradigm and engagers, the 'China fantasy' discourse directly challenges the policy of engagement. Mann argues that the US policy of engaging China is sold to the American public on the basis of a fraudulent illusion, 'that is, on the false premise that trade and "engagement" with China would change China's political system'.[57] Yet, except for justifying unrestricted trade with China and diverting attention from Beijing's one-party rule and human rights abuses, engagement and integration seem to have not delivered on those promises.[58] In this sense, Aaron Friedberg rightly points out that Mann's *The China Fantasy* represents 'a scathing indictment' of the US policy of China engagement.[59]

Indeed, in light of an apparently intransigent China, engagement is seen as not only ineffective, but also close to dangerous appeasement. In effect, it would 'entail the United States backing down, as never before, on some of its democratic liberal ideals'.[60] It could also mean, among other things, that:

> America would have to abandon its residual doubts about the legitimacy of China's political system and become much more circumspect about criticising its internal affairs. That means no more lecturing China about dissidents, Tibet or religious freedom... no more lecturing China about its failure to meet US expectations on matters such as Iran, Sudan and North Korea... [and] no more lecturing China about excessive defence spending or lack of transparency about its military plans. In short, it means surrendering primacy and all that goes with it.[61]

For White, such policy adjustment, while regrettable, is necessary given the greater danger of other strategic alternatives. Yet for a country that does not accept the second place, this prospect is alarmingly unacceptable. Indeed, for some, continued engagement with China has become more dangerous than direct confrontation. Coming into office on a foreign policy platform of 'new engagement' and 'strategic reassurance' with China,[62] the Obama administration had harboured high expectations about Beijing's willingness and capacity to cooperate with the US in a number of issue-areas, including nuclear non-proliferation, climate change, and the war in Afghanistan.[63] With its high hope for Sino-US cooperation, the administration was from the beginning vulnerable to 'appeasement' accusations. For example, by not receiving the Dalai Lama during his 2009 visit to Washington, Obama 'caught flak from both the American left and right'.[64] In a scathing review of Obama's first year in office, Robert Kagan brings serious charges against Obama's China policy, which, according to Kagan, 'raises the question of whether the United States will continue to favor democracies... or whether the United States will now begin to adopt a more neutral posture in an effort to get to "yes" with the great autocratic powers'.[65] Gary Schmitt views cross-strait relations through the same 'Communist dictatorship versus democracy' prism, and labels Obama's one-China policy 'cowardice'.[66] Ellen Bork calls Obama's human rights and Tibet policy a 'timid' 'retreat', maintaining that the US 'has lost its nerve at a time when China is confidently asserting its own brand of Communist Party-led authoritarianism'.[67] According to Blumenthal, although the Obama administration seeks to avoid conflict with China, its policy actually makes such a confrontation more likely.[68]

Until recently, engagers had managed to fend off the 'appeasement' charge by pointing out that their policy, if pursued with perseverance, would deliver the promised change in the long run. They would warn of the danger of disengagement or containment: if 'we' turn our backs on China, the accomplishment in China so far would come undone and it could be pushed in the wrong direction.[69] To the 'China fantasy' analysts, despite such engagement efforts, China is already headed in the wrong direction, and worse still, its economy and military have grown much stronger thanks precisely to engagement.[70] In this debate, although some engagers continue to urge patience, they are increasingly hard-pressed to answer such challenging questions as 'What if China does not democratise?' or 'How long is the long run'?[71] As Kagan puts it, 'In the long run, rising prosperity may well produce political liberalism [in China], but how long is the long run? It may be too long to have any strategic or geopolitical relevance'.[72] Similarly, dismissing the claim that in China 'political change takes time', Mann maintains that 'yet time keeps passing by', adding that 'if the ruling Chinese Communist Party remains hostile to dissent and organized political opposition for decades or more, the American public will have been deceived'.[73]

With engagement looking increasingly indefensible as a policy option, many in the engagement camp now try to dissociate themselves from it. Richard Bredor of the US-China Business Council in Washington once conceded that 'We would never want to be in the position of defending China'.[74] As engagement becomes discredited, the only logical and responsible alternative, it seems, is to get tougher on China. As noted at the beginning of this chapter, this alternative is precisely what the new 'pushback' strategy on China is about. After President Obama apparently failed to deliver on his promise to get China's cooperation on climate change and other issues, the administration felt obliged to do something to show Americans that it was not soft on Beijing. Obama's two tough policies towards China at the beginning of 2010, one concerning the Dalai Lama visit and the other arms sales to Taiwan, appear to be a direct response to the pressure and warning from the 'China fantasy' camp. Facing the accusation that his policy had brought national humiliation, Obama could ill-afford to be seen as another Jimmy Carter (whose policy on Iran has made him a symbol of political weakness).[75]

Meanwhile, many policy-makers and officials have themselves become disillusioned with China. The US Congress, for example, has long been 'restive over a policy that appeared to deliver little but the promise of more meetings...',[76] and has led the charge of taking a tougher line. Even some practitioners of engagement in Washington, as reported by the *New York Times*, have become increasingly frustrated with the prospect of winning over the Chinese on major policy challenges, such as climate change, nuclear non-proliferation and a new, 'balanced' global economic order.[77] All this, I argue, prepared the ground for the recent assertiveness in US China policy.

Similarly, the recent EU tough stance on China reflects a parallel disillusionment. The EU Trade Commissioner Peter Mandelson, who had been a strong advocate of open EU markets for Chinese products, told his Chinese audience that China must improve its human rights record before the EU's arms embargo against China could be lifted.[78] Behind his change of heart, it seems, was his irritation at the 'lack of progress' in China, as he explained in a letter to the EU President Barroso in October 2007. He accused China, among other things, of being 'procedurally obstructive' in EU-China dialogues.[79] Mandelson reflects a broader sense of disappointment felt among many EU countries. In the 2006 European Commission communication on EU-China relations, the tone on China turned visibly more critical than previous communications. It stated that 'in Europe there is a growing perception that China's as yet incomplete implementation of WTO obligations and new barriers to market access are preventing a genuinely reciprocal trading relationship'.[80] Not surprisingly, the European frustration has been followed by the EU's more aggressive policy on China.[81]

FROM HOPE TO DISILLUSIONMENT: THE 'CHINA OPPORTUNITY' PARADIGM AS THE CHINA FANTASY

To some, if the hardline turn in Western dealings with China results largely from Western disillusionment, that disillusionment in turn is derived from China's own failure to converge with the West. As Blumenthal declares, by 'any objective measure' China simply has fallen short on a number of issues identified by the US as common security concerns.[82]

Though one's disillusionment cannot be separated from the perceived disappointing behaviour of the other, it never has a purely objective or external origin. Rather, at its core it is more often than not a psychological phenomenon conditioned on and mediated by unrealistic and unfulfilled hope on the part of the disillusioned. Thus, the 'China fantasy' is not so much a response to China's failings as it is an inevitable effect of Western hope projected onto China through the China opportunity discourse.

Hope and disillusionment often go in tandem. According to some psychology literature on disappointment, the level of disillusionment and frustration is frequently relative to that of prior hope and expectation.[83] It is because of the latter that the ground for disappointment or disillusionment is laid. One constant area of Western disappointment with China has been, for example, in its democratisation, or the lack thereof. Yet from the beginning, this disappointment is enabled by Western hope for China's democratisation, rather than by the latter's lack of political transformation per se. In the absence of such hope, an undemocratic China, like during the Cultural Revolution or during the Qing dynasty, did not give rise to this particular disappointment. Back in the nineteenth century, a strong sense of China disillusionment did exist, but much of it resulted from the initial hopes and expectations of missionaries to convert the pagan nation into Christianity.[84] In other words, it was primarily religious or commercial in nature, reflecting the predominant Western hopes at that time to 'plant the shining cross on every hill and in every valley' and to open China's door for unrestricted trade.[85] During the Cultural Revolution, China's political system was undoubtedly much more authoritarian than today. But instead of generating disillusionment, it was held up as a promising political model by left intellectuals in the West.[86] Such a misplaced hope had less to do with the actual promise found in China, but more with those intellectuals' disillusionment with their own society in the wake of the Vietnam debacle and the attendant crisis of confidence in the West. In this sense, hope and disillusionment are not just discursively interconnected with each other; they are mutually constitutive.

From this standpoint, I argue that contemporary 'China fantasy' disillusionment is largely constituted by the hope of the China opportunity. Inboden observes that 'a watershed moment [for Western disillusionment] ironically may have been the 2008 Beijing Olympics'.[87] Inboden is right on this account. But if we recognise the hope/disillusionment nexus, this coincidence is not ironic. Representing the high-water mark of Western hope for a post-Tiananmen China, the Beijing Olympics also inevitably marked the onset of Western disillusionment. The Western dream of transforming China through the Olympics (like the change in South Korea brought by the 1988 Seoul Olympics) had been building up steadily ever since Beijing won the bid in 2001. In fact, that dream could even be one key consideration when some International Olympic Committee members voted for Beijing in the first place. Former US national security adviser Zbigniew Brzezinski hoped that the Games might help accelerate the demise of Communism in China. James Lilley believed that the Games would provide incentives to the government to be more cooperative with foreign powers and more moderate with its own citizens.[88] As the Beijing Olympics drew nearer, the expectation was running so high that the *National Review* declared the Games 'a window of opportunity, not to be missed....' It reasoned that 'If...America and others press the Communists for reform, the Games may prove a help, even a boon....'[89] *Newsweek* magazine columnist Jonathan Alter went as far as to describe the Games as 'the world's last lever... to bring China further into the community of responsible nations'.[90]

Yet, despite or precisely because of such heightened hope, the Games could not but bring disappointment. Both the sense of anticipation and that of disillusionment are clearly evident in a series of *Olympics Countdown* reports prepared by Amnesty International. One report insisted that 'much of the current wave of repression is occurring not *in spite* of the Olympics but actually *because* of the Olympics'.[91] The object of hope now became the very source of frustration. With ten days to go before the opening of the Olympics, this human rights organisation promptly delivered its final verdict with a report titled *The Olympics Countdown—Broken Promises*. Such a verdict was always to be expected given the enormous amount of hope and promise preloaded onto the Olympic Games in the lead up to that sporting occasion.[92] Similarly, at the end of the Beijing Olympics, *New York Times* wasted no time in labelling the events China's 'Bad Faith Olympics',[93] meaning that Beijing had not kept its side of the bargain. But probably it would be more accurate to say that China had not lived up to Western dreams. It is also no coincidence that European countries, hitherto the most active proponents of constructive engagement with China, felt most bitter and led the way in what then Chinese ambassador to Britain Fu Ying described as the Western effort to 'demonise' China.[94]

Of course, this is not to imply that Western disillusionment stems solely from the 'China opportunity' fantasies. No doubt, it has not been helped by uncooperative and even assertive Chinese behaviour of various sorts. And yet, as noted above, Chinese behaviour in its own right does not necessarily lead to Western disillusionment, especially if it is not measured against high liberal hopes. For instance, if a realist lens of great power politics is applied, much of the Chinese behaviour would probably be considered 'normal' or 'expected' (if not desired). Thus, what China does is at most only part of the 'China fantasy' story, a story which is generated primarily through a self-serving lens of Western hope. For example, Washington's frustration with China's currency policy is not because the undervalued renminbi is actually responsible for America's ballooning trade deficit with China (while the

Chinese currency has appreciated by 30 per cent against the US dollar since July 2005, China's trade surplus with the US has kept on breaking the record over the past few years). Rather, it should be put in the broader context of the much-anticipated, oversold but not-fully-realised Chinese market potential after its entry into the WTO. Google's disappointment with China cannot be separated from the now dashed hope of the Internet as a Trojan horse to undermine the Communist regime, a hope once famously encapsulated in Bill Clinton's confident comparison of China's efforts to regulate the Internet with the futile act of 'trying to nail Jello to the wall'. Similarly, Western anger over Liu Xiaobo's incarceration had much to do with the high hope among some Western observers that Charter 08, a political reform blueprint of which Liu is an author, represented 'the most significant democratic reform movement in China in a decade'.[95] And General Electric's aforementioned complaint about China is perhaps less because the corporation had not made money there (its revenues in China equalled $5.3 billion in 2009), and more because its even higher expectation of $10 billion by 2010 was not met.[96]

Hope need not always end in disillusionment. Realistic hope, setting itself an achievable target, can result in a sense of fulfilment and satisfaction. In the business community, many pragmatists are optimistic about the economic opportunity presented by China but at the same time realistic enough about the chance of transforming China politically. For example, former Kodak Chairman George Fisher warns against going to China 'with a camouflaged agenda', for changes in China are dependent primarily on domestic needs and conditions.[97] Barry Rogstad, former president of the American Business Conference, once described the attempt to change another country 'sheer craziness'.[98] To those people, at least there was no disappointment on the political front.

However, despite this more pragmatist strain of the China opportunity discourse, most 'opportunity' advocates, either explicitly or implicitly, subscribe to a teleological normative hope of converting China at a future point. Moreover, with few exceptions, the Western hope of the 'China opportunity' is frequently paternalistic, seeing itself as well-deserved, rightful hope that should be fulfilled. It is at once self-righteous and unreflective, carrying with it a blind spot about its own false premises as identified in the previous chapter. While such hope can be met to some degree, the 'moment of consummation kindles the desire for more'.[99] Consequently, Western demand's partial fulfilment, always simultaneously gratifying and unsatisfactory, then serves to further inflate its sense of entitlement down the track, until eventually China could not keep up. Yet, even as it turns out to be a fantasy, the unreflective, paternalistic attitude in the China demand means that the object of hope, rather than the premise of the hope itself, will bear the blame for the dashed hope and postponed enjoyment (*jouissance*).[100] Such disappointment, when repeated, is fertile ground for disillusionment and resentment.

This is why the 'China opportunity' paradigm is largely responsible for the China disillusionment. It blames China for its false promises, hence the *China* fantasy (as opposed, for example, to an admission of the China opportunity fantasy). Proponents of this paradigm could readily concede that they have got China wrong,[101] but rarely do they acknowledge that they have got their very paternalistic hope wrong to begin with. Lucian Pye claimed that his political theory 'makes sense logically, but it falls apart when applied to traditional China',[102] a phenomenon which, in his view, could only be attributed to what he sees as an erratic Chinese political culture that 'thwart[s], frustrate[s], and even embarrass[es] those who try to help [China]'. He went on to say that 'For all who befriend China, the story is the same: high hopes then disappointment'. There was no doubt in his mind that China should take sole responsibility.[103] Similarly, if today a 'democratic China' envisaged by the 'China opportunity' paradigm turns out to be an illusion, China opportunity believers would argue that it is China, rather than their China expectation, that is the culprit. Bruce Gilley, for example, insists that though the democratic project in China is 'beset with difficulties in practice', it is 'faultless in appeal'.[104] While Gilley is for now an enthusiastic believer in the opportunity of China's democratisation (to recall, he argues that the prospects for a democratic China 'are now better than ever'), it is safe to predict that if such prospects remain elusive ten or twenty years from now, chances are that he would probably choose disillusionment with China over a critical reflection on his democratic project itself.

Consequently, though the 'China fantasy' discourse appears to be a critique of the 'China opportunity' paradigm (and the associated engagement strategy), in reality it has its very roots in it. By identifying China as a scapegoat for the unfulfilled China opportunity, the 'China fantasy' serves to keep the premises of this China paradigm intact. In fact, most 'China fantasy' advocates are in essence strong believers in the 'opportunity' paradigm. This may help explain why many who are disillusioned with China are not typical China-bashers or hardliners, but instead China opportunity believers who are 'mugged by reality', just as a neoconservative is often a disillusioned liberal.[105] Mann's position is again instructive here. Even as he heaps scorn on a set of illusions about the ability of commerce and economic engagement to effect political change in China, he concludes *The China Fantasy* with this telling confession: 'I have never written a book in which I hoped so fervently that I would be proved wrong. It would be heartening if China's leaders proceed along the lines that America's political leaders predict'. So it turns out that he doubts neither the desirability nor the possibility of the China opportunity project per se. His main misgiving, rather, is that Western engagers, taking that outcome for granted, are too naïve or too complacent to contemplate alternative policies to see it through.[106]

In this context, through its 'China fantasy' offshoot, the 'China opportunity' paradigm is partly responsible for the hardline turn in Western approach to China. Herein lies the danger of this China paradigm and its strategy of 'constructive engagement'. Engagement, as Jean A. Garrison points out, 'rests on the dangerous hope for regime change in China…. This "hope" raises expectations among certain constituencies that make presidents susceptible to political backlash when progress is not forthcoming'.[107] What we are witnessing today is in large degree a product of such political backlash, which, if unchecked, could launch US-China relations on a dangerous path of spiralling confrontation. In fact, such a path has been well-trodden in history. A cursory look at past Sino-Western interactions reveals that their clashes were not just due to their conflicting interests or diverging values per se, but also due to the recurring volatile dynamics of mutual hope and subsequent mutual disillusionment. Though no bilateral relationship can be free from the fluctuation of hope and disenchantment, in their dealing with China, the West in general and the US in particular have been especially prone to the pendulum cycle of paternalistic hope and 'rightful' disillusionment, with the end of each such cycle frequently marked by prolonged estrangement and open hostility.[108]

In September 1792, when Lord Macartney set out on his historic voyage to China, the United Kingdom, a rapidly industrialising nation filled with self-confidence and hope, painted the Middle Kingdom as an unlimited market open to British commerce. But as Macartney was about to return from his controversy-ridden China mission, that expectation was met with bitter disappointment. Many members of his embassy, lamenting their fractured illusions, argued that this failure warranted 'more direct methods' to prize open the China market. Macartney himself seemed cautious on the use of offensive measures against China so long as 'a ray of hope remains for succeeding by gentle ones'. Nevertheless, his thwarted mission heralded a long-lasting change in Europe's attitudes towards China from admiration to disillusionment and disdain.[109] In a way, the frustration with Chinese 'obstructiveness' to the British and European desire to conduct unrestricted trade subsequently foreshadowed nearly a century of European gunboat diplomacy in the 'Far East'.

The transformation of America's so-called 'special relationship' with China into the Cold War animosity also ran parallel with a metamorphosis from hope to disillusionment in the US.[110] As Michael Hunt observes, America's initial paternalistic vision of 'a China transformed under American guidance', at first fuelling 'a patiently paternal approach' to China, was bound to 'evolve into a policy of coercion once hope in the Chinese government was gone'.[111] Such hope, shattered by the Communist victory in China's civil war, was replaced with strong indignation with the 'ungrateful' Chinese 'who had bitten the hands that had fed and nurtured them, repaying a century of American benevolence with hatred and enmity, causing deep parental sorrow, arousing righteous anger and meriting just punishment'.[112] While the origins of their Cold War rivalry are no doubt complex and multi-faceted, Hunt is nevertheless right that 'Our own immoderate expectations of China's fitting the American mold and our surprise and overreaction to China going her own way' played a major part in 'the general instability that has characterized our bilateral relations'.[113] Perhaps it was for this reason that during the 1950s and 1960s the US seemed more resentful and fearful of China than of the Soviet Union, hence the adoption of a tougher policy of containment *and* isolation against Beijing.[114] The Soviet Union had never invoked the same level of hope and fantasy for the US as had China. History never exactly repeats itself, but the fact that China is now once again on the cusp of changing from the object of hope to that of disillusionment for the West does not bode well for Sino-Western relations.

Unrealistic as it may sound, the fantasmatic imagination of China as an opportunity for Western commercial expansion and/or democratic enlargement per se is not problematic. Social and political life cannot function without hope or even fantasy. What *is* problematic, though, is that once reified into an unreflective paradigm, such China opportunity fantasies are unable or unwilling to recognise themselves as such. At one level, given such false promises, the 'China opportunity' paradigm is too good to be true. But at another level, taking up the mantle of a regime of truth, it is considered too true to be subject to critical self-scrutiny even when it is not borne out in practice. To ease this inherent tension, the 'China opportunity' paradigm chooses to blame others, especially its very object, for its lost opportunity and delayed or 'stolen' pleasure of self-fulfilment. Through such blame shifting, the 'China opportunity' paradigm has significant, if only unintended, policy consequences, as the recent deterioration in Sino-Western relations can attest.

To be sure, the hardening of Western strategy towards China cannot be blamed on the volatility of the 'China opportunity' paradigm alone. It seems also to have coincided with a period of dented self-confidence in the U.S. and Europe in the wake of the global financial crisis and the eurozone debt crisis, with this firmness in dealing with China designed partly to dispel the perceived weakness and decline in the West. Moreover, in the chorus of getting tough on China, hardline realists have never left the centre-stage. Their unaccommodating approach to China has less to do with disillusionment and more with their longstanding fear of China's emergence as a geopolitical rival, regardless of its democratisation or not. However, attributing the hardline approach to the role of hardliners is not only tautological, but it does not adequately explain the sudden surge of aggressive posture from the West. It is in this sense that we need to understand the 'China opportunity' paradigm, not as an innocent, optimistic framework of analysis, but in terms of volatile international practice. Despite or because of its normative project of engagement with China, this paradigm has been part of the problem, rather than its solution.

8. China watching: towards reflection and dialogue

> *Without some knowledge of himself, his knowledge of other things is imperfect: for to know something without knowing that one knows it is only a half-knowing, and to know that one knows is to know oneself. Self-knowledge is desirable and important to man, not only for its own sake, but as a condition without which no other knowledge can be critically justified and securely based.*
>
> R. G. Collingwood[1]

> *Traveler, there are no roads. Roads are made by walking.*
>
> A Spanish proverb[2]

Amid the ever-growing literature on the rise of China, one paradox can hardly escape our attention. That is, evocative of the amusing saying on the Oxford postcard, the more we write and debate about China, the less we seem to know it for sure. Over the years and after so many dedicated conferences, forums and publications, we do not seem to have come any closer to settling the perplexing questions such as what China really is and what its rise means for the rest of the world. The continuing China debate testifies to this lack of consensus. The editors of a book on China watching admit that as a result of the country's growing complexity, it is increasingly difficult to 'offer assured conclusions about "China" writ large'.[3] Even William Kristol, a neoconservative authority on everything to do with international relations, once noted that 'I cannot forecast to you the action of China. It is a riddle wrapped in a mystery inside an enigma'.[4]

For some this lack of certainty is all the more reason to keep on deciphering the China puzzle, but to me it is time to reflect on the ways China knowledge has been produced. As Karl Mannheim reminded us, when people face a bewildering array of divergent conceptions of things and situations, they need to 'turn[s] from the direct observation of things to the consideration of ways of thinking'.[5] Throughout these pages, the book has sought to do just that, beginning with a deconstruction of the very dichotomies between things and thinking, reality and representation. It has explored a different set of issues that may come under the rubric of sociology of knowledge: How what we assume we already know about 'China' is not objective knowledge, but contingent representations; how those representations are themselves discursively constructed and worldly situated; and what implications they may have for Sino-Western relations in general and US-China relations in particular.

By exploring these questions, the book has turned China writing on its head. From a deconstructive-cum-constructivist perspective, it has sought to watch China watching in a way the IR field of China watching has not been systematically watched before. In particular, it has called into question the 'scientific knowledge' status of the twin China paradigms: 'threat' and 'opportunity'. What passes as 'China' through these paradigms is not an ontologically stable, unproblematic object 'out there' waiting for disinterested observation. Nor are these Western representations neutral, objective truth of that 'object'. Rather, there is something more than this: they are situated interpretations intertextually tied to the Western self-imagination, desire, and power. These paradigms tell us less about what is actually seen than about *how* it is seen and *who* might be behind this 'seeing'. They, as examined in Chapter 3, are as much about imagining the gazing self as about representing a Chinese Other.

At the core of the Western self-imagination is the modern knowing subject. Implying the existence of a certain, objectively knowable world 'out there', this self-fashioning affords the West both the confidence and duty to know and lead that world. When certain knowledge about a particular 'object', as in the case of China, is stubbornly not forthcoming, the self-professed knowing subject then resorts to certain emotional substitutes such as fear and fantasy to make up for the absence of certainty. With fear, one may restore a sense of (negative) certainty about an existential threat 'out there', a threat which seems readily accounted for by the timeless wisdom of realism (and to some extent liberalism). Alternatively, with the subliminal aid of fantasy, the West can envisage an immensely soothing scenario of opportunity, engagement and convergence that carries with it a teleological predictability about how History begins, evolves, and ends.

Thanks to those emotional substitutes, the initial 'inscrutability' of China's Otherness gives way to more comprehensible imageries: it is now either an affront to, or an opportunity for, the Western self and its will to truth and power. Either way, it becomes a reassuring object of aversion and attraction that allows for continued Western self-posturing as the modern knowing subject. Indeed, as evidenced in the two dominant sets of China discourses, the Western self and its Chinese Other are mutually constitutive.

More importantly, such mutual constructions are from the outset linked to power and political practice. At one level, they are complicit in the political economies of fear and fantasy 'at home'. At another level, they are constitutive of foreign policy which in turn helps construct the Other in reality. Consequently, the China discourses turn out to be an integral and constitutive part of their 'object of study'. For example, as illustrated in Chapters 4-5, America's 'China threat' discourse both contributes to, and is reproduced by, the US partisan politics of fear and military Keynesianism. At the same time, this threat imagery helps sustain a containment policy of sorts. By provoking similar responses from China, such a policy ends up participating in the creation of the very threat it seeks to contain.

The 'China opportunity' narrative, by contrast, tends to favour a policy of engagement. But as examined in Chapter 6, this paradigm and its associated engagement strategy are more often than not false promises. They are false in that their assumption of the West/US and China in terms of a temporal self/Other hierarchy allows their advocates to ignore or at least downplay China's inherent subjectivities and agency in this intersubjective relationship. To the extent that Sino-Western relations are intersubjective, socialisation does occur, but it takes place on a mutual basis, rather than as a one-way traffic. In this context, the promises of the 'China opportunity' become less certain and more problematic. Yet often oblivious to its own false premises, the paradigm instead blames China (and to a lesser extent, Western engagers) for its increasingly apparent 'China fantasy'. What is significant about this 'China opportunity' disillusionment is that it converges with the 'China threat' imagery and together justifies a tougher approach to a country which now not only appears unreceptive to our tutelage but also grows menacingly stronger by the day.

Consequently, for all their apparent differences, the 'threat' and 'opportunity' paradigms are the two sides of the same coin of Western knowledge, desire, and power in China watching. In essence, both are specific manifestations of a modern quest for certainty in an uncertain world. These seismic twins are not only similar in terms of their discursive functions of constructing self/Other, but they are also joined together in practice. They make up a powerful bifocal lens for China watching, a lens which can largely account for the emergence and popularity of the 'hedging' strategy towards China.

At this point, it is worth noting that my misgivings with these Western representations are not about their bias or factual inaccuracy, nor about their often critical stances on China. In any case, the alternative is not to idealise China. The preceding chapter has shed light on the volatility and danger of projecting one's hope onto the country, only to be disappointed down the track. In fact, it is no coincidence that some of China's sharpest critics today were once China opportunity enthusiasts.[6] Likewise, Western representations ought not to be condemned for their association with power and political practice per se. The main issue is not about their knowledge/desire/power nexus as such, which is probably characteristic of all social knowledge.[7] Rather, what is problematic is the particular nature of that nexus and the continued lack of critical self-reflection on the nexus (and its policy consequences) among mainstream IR China watchers. It is in this context that this book has sought to deconstruct a less than healthy field.

CHINA KNOWLEDGE AND SELF-REFLECTION

Until now, my focus seems to have been mainly on how *not* to understand China's rise. While deconstruction is all well and good, one cannot help but wonder: How *to* study China? If those paradigms are problematic or less than adequate, what are the alternative ways of knowing this important country?

These questions sound reasonable enough. Be it scholars or practitioners, when faced with an apparently unprecedented transition from a transatlantic century to a transpacific century led by the 'rise' of China (and India), one is naturally anxious to know what China is up to and how to best respond to it. Yet, however understandable this desire may be, this book has hesitated to directly volunteer answers to those questions, or at least its implicit answers would be unlikely to satisfy those demands on their own terms. There are several reasons for this. To begin with, I am sceptical of some of their underlying ontological and epistemological premises about what China is and what China knowledge should mean. For example, those questions seem to assume that this book is merely a study of China studies (or a particular section of China studies), rather than a study of China per se. Hence their insistence on knowing how we might go about studying China proper. Yet, from the beginning, this knowledge/reality dichotomy has been problematised. Since there is no China-in-itself outside knowledge, representation or discourse, what we refer to as 'China' must already be coloured by such representations. Without reference to representations we cannot for a moment speak of China or do China studies. Given that China does not exist independently of discourse and that any study becomes part of its object of study, I should say that this analysis of Western discourses of China *is* already a study of China in the proper sense of the word.

Also, underlying those questions is the belief that deconstruction is essentially destructive and thus has little constructive to contribute to China studies. However, as Derrida notes, deconstruction is 'a way of taking a position' rather than merely 'a flourish of irresponsible and irresponsible-making destruction'.[8] By way of deconstruction, this book has hoped to generate both critical and constructive reflections on the way we think about the nature of China knowledge as well as the way such knowledge can be better produced. To the extent that methodology is always implied in ontology and epistemology, my ontological and epistemological critique is not an exercise of esoteric verbal incantation, but carries important methodological messages for China watching, even though such messages could well be dismissed as hollow, mystifying or even alien by conventional standards.

One message from this study is that it is no longer adequate for us to be merely 'China' specialists who are otherwise blissfully 'ignorant of the world beyond China'.[9] China watching needs autoethnography or 'self-watching' to consciously make itself part of its own object of critical analysis whereby the necessary but often missing comparative context can help us put China in perspective. All research, to be sure, must already contain some level of reflectivity, be it about methods of inquiry, hypothesis testing, empirical evidence, data collection, or clarity of expression. And the Western representations of China's rise, predicated on some particular ways of Western self-imagination, are necessarily self-reflective in that sense. And yet, such narrow technical reflectivity or narcissistic posturing is not what I mean by 'self-watching'. In fact, the unconscious Western self-imagination as the modern knowing subject (who sets itself apart from the world and refuses to critically look at itself) is the very antithesis of self-watching.

Self-watching, I suggest, requires at once discarding this positivist self-(un)consciousness and cultivating a critically reflective, philosophising mind. 'The philosophizing mind', wrote Collingwood, 'never simply thinks about an object, it always, while thinking about any object, thinks also about its own thought about that object'.[10] This position is similar to that of 'ironists'. According to Richard Rorty, ironists are 'never quite able to take themselves seriously because always aware that the terms in which they describe themselves are subject to change, always aware of the contingency and fragility of their final vocabularies, and thus of their selves'.[11]

In the concluding chapter of his *Scratches on Our Minds*, Harold Isaacs seemed to have endorsed such 'ironist' approaches to China studies: 'we have to examine, each of us, how we register and house our observations, how we come to our judgments, how we enlarge our observations, how we describe them, and what purposes they serve for us'.[12] Back in 1972, John Fairbank put such reflection in practice by suggesting that America's Cold-War attitude towards China was based less on reason than on fear, a fear inspired not by China but by America's experience with Nazi and Stalinist totalitarian regimes.[13] These examples clearly show the possibility of reflective China watching, but alas, as noted from the beginning, such reflectivity is hardly visible in today's 'China's rise' literature. Indeed, without the trace of a single author, the two dominant China paradigms hinge onto a ubiquitous collective psyche and emotion that is often difficult to see, let alone to criticise from within.

Yet it is imperative that such self-criticism should occur, which entails problematising China watchers' own thought, vocabularies and taken-for-granted self-identity as disinterested rational observers. It requires us to pause and look into ourselves to examine, for example, why we constantly fear China, rather than taking that fear as given: 'We are wary of China because we are wary of China'. Self-watching demands an ironist awareness of the contingency, instability, and provinciality of mainstream China knowledge, its intertextual and emotional link to the fears and fantasies in the Western self-imagination, the political economy of its production, and the attendant normative, ethical and practical consequences both for dealing with China and for serving the power and special interests at home. Put it differently, it requires a deconstructive move of intellectual decolonisation of the latent (neo)colonial desire and mindset that, despite the formal end of colonialism decades ago, continues to actively operate in Orientalist knowledge and China watching, facilitated by its various scientific, theoretical, and pedagogical guises.

In this context, self-reflection cannot be confined to individual China watchers or even the China watching community. Never a purely personal pursuit or even a disciplinary matter, China knowledge is always inextricably linked with the general dynamism of Western knowledge, desire and power in global politics. Its self-reflection should thus extend to the shared collective self of the West, its assumed identity and associated foreign policy (China policy in particular). If China can be seen as a being-in-the-world, these issues are part and parcel of the world in which China finds itself and relates to others. But until now they have largely escaped the attention of China watchers. Maybe it is because these are primarily the business of scholars of Western/American culture, history and foreign relations, rather than that of China scholars. After all, there is a need for division of labour in social sciences. True, for various reasons it is unrealistic to expect China scholars to be at the same time experts on those 'non-China' issues. Nevertheless, since China watchers both rely on and contribute to their collective Western self-imagination in their understanding of China, it is crucial that they look at their collective Western self in the mirror. Take the negative image of China's brutal Soviet-style sports system for example. Every now and then, such an image will be reliably brought up to reinforce China's Otherness more generally. But if the ways American young talents are trained are put under the same spotlight, the difference between the US and China is no longer as vast as it appears.[14] In doing so, the previous China image is no longer as defensible as it seems. In brief, the broader point here is that the same China may take on quite different meanings when we are willing to subject ourselves to similar scrutiny. We may better appreciate why China looks the way it does when we are more self-conscious of the various lenses, paradigms, and fore-meanings through which we do China watching. Conversely, we cannot fully comprehend why the Chinese behave in a certain way until we pay attention to what we have done (to them), past and present. Such self-knowledge on the part of the West is essential to a better grasp of China. Without the former, China knowledge is incomplete and suspect.

Yet, to many, self-reflection is at best a luxurious distraction. At worst it amounts to navel-gazing and could turn into 'a prolix and self-indulgent discourse that is divorced from the real world'.[15] Such concern is hardly justified, however. The imagined Western self is integral to the real world, and critical self-reflection also helps reconnect China watching to the 'real' world of power relations to which it always belongs. By making one better aware of this connection, it helps open up space for emancipatory knowledge. As Mannheim notes:

> The criterion of such self-illumination is that not only the object but we ourselves fall squarely within our field of vision. We become visible to ourselves, not just vaguely as a knowing subject as such but in a certain role hitherto hidden from us, in a situation hitherto impenetrable to us, and with motivations of which we have not hitherto been aware. In such a moment the inner connection between our role, our motivations, and our type and manner of experiencing the world suddenly draws upon us. Hence the paradox underlying these experiences, namely the opportunity for relative emancipation from social determination, increases proportionately with insight into this determination.[16]

Still, there may be a lingering fear that excessive reflectivity could undo much of the hard-won China knowledge. But again to quote Mannheim, 'the extension of our knowledge of the world is closely related to increasing personal self-knowledge and self-control of the knowing personality'.[17] Even when that does expose our lack of knowledge about China, all is not lost. Such revelation is not a sign of ignorance, but an essential building block in the edifice of China knowledge. Confucius told us that 'To say that you know when you do know and say that you do not know when you do not know— that is [the way to acquire] knowledge'.[18] Thus, the knowing subject can emancipate itself from its delusion about its own being;[19] the real meaning of ignorance is that one claims to know when one does not or cannot know.

CHINA KNOWLEDGE AND DIALOGUE

There is no other way of knowing China than through representation, hence the need for critical reflection on representation. But once we have come to realise that Western representation is mired in the delusional fears and fantasies of its own autobiographical imagination, where to from here?

This is where Chinese discourses may come into play. Thus far, China watching has had a lot to say about what China does, but very little about what China says or thinks. In an enterprise that purports to understand China, it is odd that Chinese voices are rarely heard, let alone seriously engaged. As noted in the main chapters, the 'China's rise' literature overflows with monologue statements about what 'we' think China thinks. Both paradigms routinely ground their reading of China and Chinese subjectivities on Western subjectivity and self-experience, thereby reducing the former to merely a (desirable or not) shadow of the latter. In the 'China threat' discourse, the subjectivity of a rising China is seen as essentially a replica of the timeless realist subjectivity of (Western/European) great powers, a kind of subjectivity that China seems to have no agency to change or shake off.

However, to state the obvious, China is always constructed by Chinese as well as Western discourses. The former, however closely linked to the latter, are not their carbon copy. Consequently, they must be taken seriously and understood as far as possible in their 'own' terms and contexts. After all, how can we claim to have adequately understood China without taking into account its meanings given by the Chinese? Sure, strictly speaking, we cannot engage with such Chinese meanings entirely in their 'own' terms, as our understanding is inevitably constrained by our fore-understanding and intertextual surroundings. Still, that aspiration can be partially approximated through dialogue with the Chinese and engagement with Chinese discourses and ideas.[20] In doing so, we may better appreciate, for example, that China's rise not only has quite different meanings for the Chinese than for Western observers, but it may also mean different things to different people inside China. Essentially contested in nature, the trajectory and meaning of China's rise will be shaped to a large degree by the interaction of those 'indigenous' representations as well as by Western representational practices. Indeed, once the multiplicity of Chinese subjectivity is acknowledged, the statecentric term 'China's rise' itself may be called into question, for if used as an abstract frame of analysis it obscures more than it reveals, especially when it comes to the complexities of Chinese domestic political economy and global interconnectedness. In any event, the ethnocentric representations of a 'threat' (to us) and an 'opportunity' (for us), despite their empirical validity to some degree, are vastly inadequate as *the* knowledge about a changing China. Not only is the 'rise of China' caricature unable to paint a fuller picture of China in international relations, but even its rise—often driven by various Chinese local concerns, problems, hopes, and priorities—does not seem to be, in the first instance, about either deliberately challenging other countries or making itself an opportunity for them.

Certainly, we should be under no illusion that cross-cultural dialogue and engagement is easy or straightforward. First, mainstream China watching resembles the dominating and colonising subject's gaze at the colonised: it is 'an objectifying gaze, one that refuses mutual gazing, mutual subject-to-subject recognition'.[21] To engage in equal dialogue with Chinese subjectivity would imply precisely mutual gazing, which could threaten to dethrone the Western self as *the* privileged knowing subject and destabilise its assumed universality and ontological and epistemological security. For much of modern history, the West in general and the US in particular have not been seriously relativised in this way.[22] For the most part, like a spying eye, they want to see but do not want to be seen.

Second, formidable language barriers pose a challenge to effective dialogue, especially as many China experts today come from Strategic Studies or IR backgrounds rather than China studies.[23] It may be true that outsiders, unencumbered by the baggage of the Chinese language and culture, are in a better position to offer an unbiased, objective view of China.[24] But this claim can only be taken so far. Objectivity, as we have seen, is an illusion; after all, 'outsiders' do not observe China from nowhere. In area studies, although clearly we do not have to be Chinese or 'go native' to understand China, we could hardly deny the advantage of knowing its language and culture.[25] Without 'direct' access to Chinese discourses, one simply has no idea what one has been missing out on.

That said, native language fluency per se is not enough. Knowing another language may enable one to explore and appreciate the cultural, historical and subjective complexities of a society, or it may merely open a new channel for data collection.[26] There is of course nothing wrong with the latter, but this instrumentalist approach often has limited value for our understanding of 'Chinese' subjectivities. Indeed, it could easily be co-opted into existing paradigms (as exemplified by Johnston's *Cultural Realism*), or even give rise to what we might call the 'Rudd Paradox'. A fluent Mandarin speaker, the former Australian Prime Minister claimed the privileged ability to read the Chinese mind. Yet as far as engaging China is concerned he was arguably the least successful Australian leader in recent memory. Fairfax journalist John Garnaut notes that Rudd got China wrong partly because he had forgotten his own advice on avoiding distorting paradigms through which Australia had long looked at Asia and particularly China.[27]

Further, it is common but misleading to take a few samples of Chinese views and reify them as authentically Chinese. Like their Western counterparts, Chinese discourses are an extremely complex constellation, which is similarly interwoven with desires, interpretations and fore-meanings as well as linked to identity politics and power relations.[28] They require critical reflection just as Western discourses do. Therefore, we must be careful not to take them at face value or quickly declare our discovery of the 'real China' in them. In fact, it is difficult, if possible at all, to know what is 'Chinese' and what is not, for the Chinese themselves often debate on what Chineseness means; as a being-in-the world, too often what seems to be 'Chinese' turns out to be not so uniquely Chinese.[29] The upshot is that there is perhaps no such thing as an essential, authentic Chinese subjectivity, be it 'harmony', 'hierarchy', 'national humiliation', 'despotism', 'cruelty', or 'inscrutability'. Chinese subjectivities are capable of actively (re)interpreting and construct-ing their world, but at the same time they are always susceptible to an ongo-ing construction by that world. They cannot be substituted with Western subjectivities, nor can they be taken as self-contained homogeneous things.

Despite these challenges and pitfalls, it is still possible and all the more imperative that we enter into dialogue with Chinese subjectivities and dis-courses, even as we can never pinpoint precisely what 'Chinese' means in this context. This is because consciously or not some measure of 'dialogue' in global politics is always already under way, given the mutual responsive-ness of social relations and the 'double hermeneutic' nature of social under-standing. Even as we do not talk with the Chinese, the Chinese will watch and study how they are being watched and studied by us; they are then able to 'talk back'. What they are talking about is then a type of China knowledge we cannot afford to ignore. Their discourses are a constitutive part of our object of study that is China. The existence of Chinese discourses renders incomplete any China knowledge gained merely through 'objective' observa-tion. Ultimately China knowledge is not about discovering 'the real', 'the essential' or 'the universal' in a detached fashion, but about understanding 'the relational', 'the intersubjective' and 'the contextual' through dialogue.

I stress this point because in the end China knowledge is a kind of social, moral knowledge, which has no fixed external reality to fall back on. 'Moral knowledge', as Gadamer notes, 'can never be knowable in advance like knowledge that can be taught'.[30] Our knowledge of China (and for that matter, any country) is located *in*, rather than outside or prior to, our continuous engagement and dialogue with it. This is perhaps why newborns never seem to worry about their innate 'ignorance' of the world, nor had any of them demanded, even if they could, certain knowledge of that world before they are born into it. Similarly, none of us would wait for a complete set of fact-sheets about people before we greet and befriend them. Invoking these analogies is not to trivialise international relations or cross-cultural under-standing. Quite the contrary, the added complexity of global politics means that obtaining some a priori knowledge of other countries and cultures becomes all the more problematic. Knowing others always entails first engaging with them in practice and coming to terms with difference and uncertainty along the way. Such engagement, to be effective, requires 'doing things together' and treating 'the other-as-subject, equal to the *I* but different from it'.[31] Difference and uncertainty is not the nemesis of moral knowledge; it is the very condition and possibility of its meaningful construction.

As well as between China observers and their 'Chinese objects', dialogue should take place within the broader China watching community, including practitioners, where IR-oriented observers could benefit from insights of those who study various 'domestic' issues of China and vice versa. In any case, the dichotomies of 'domestic/international' and 'scholars/practitioners' are often artificial and unhelpful. Also, a healthy field of China watching should transcend the divisions of social sciences by engaging with a diversity of more self-conscious academic fields such as critical security studies, critical terrorism studies, feminist IR, postcolonial studies, psychoanalysis, ethnography, literary theory, cultural studies, reflective political science as well as interpretive and phronetic social science more generally.[32] Not that over there we are promised coherent analytical models readily applicable to China; rather, they could help us begin to reflect upon our own knowledge practice and its social implications.

In this sense, dialogue and critical self-reflection go hand in hand. The latter can best be done not in solitude, but in dialogue with difference/other as an equally self-conscious subject. James K. Boyce notes the 'anomaly' that some area studies, despite their Cold War pedigree, are able to develop 'a substantial body of scholarship not only independent but often deeply critical of U.S. foreign policy'. To him, this has to do with dialogue afforded by their ability to understand the languages of their objects of study.[33] Of course, by the same token, dialogue requires mutual critical reflectivity, without which it could become superficial, ceremonial and ultimately unproductive.

With both self-reflection and dialogue, the two China paradigms, entrenched and seductively repeatable as they are, are not beyond change. Their discursive hegemony in China studies, along with their practical impact on Sino-Western relations, has been constituted in history and through discourse, and thus can be (if only partially) deconstructed and reconstructed accordingly. 'We are as we are because we got that way', said Kenneth Boulding.[34] Without underestimating the structural, institutional, professional and subconscious obstacles to fundamental change in China watching, it is still possible as well as necessary to remake China knowledge and re-imagine our self-identity and our relations with the Chinese 'Other' in a less hegemonic and less dichotomised manner. The stakes have never been higher. In its present form the dominant China knowledge clearly has some volatile (both self-fulfilling and self-defeating) implications for international practice, and continued delay on this critical endeavour could further complicate those implications. For instance, it could perpetuate and reproduce the sterile clichés of China as a threat and/or an opportunity. Indeed, such hackneyed discourses not only figure prominently in the Australian Government's latest attempt to boost its China literacy, but also increasingly come to shape and underpin the debates and policies on China in a growing number of non-Western countries.[35] Moreover, there is evidence that some in China, too, have begun nurturing their own dreams, fears and fantasies as well as developing a similar positivist fad for hegemonic, dichotomised knowledge about other countries and cultures amidst China's growing interest in international studies.[36] Over time, a powerful 'intimate enemy' of the West could well emerge within China, which is capable of skilfully playing the West's own discursive and political games, albeit with some Chinese characteristics. One important (though not the only) way of preventing this from happening is for the West to overhaul its own unreflective way of watching China.

The rise of China is a concern not only for China scholars, but also for the IR scholarly community. What this book has said about Western representations of China's rise may be pertinent also to the broader IR field. Similar to the 'China's rise' literature, much of mainstream IR literature on various other 'Others'—be they 'terrorists', 'illegal migrants', 'rogue states', 'authoritarian regimes', 'the developing world', 'Islam' or even the world's 'largest democracy' India—has exhibited similar desires of fear and/or fantasy. Many celebrated analytical frameworks such as the 'clash of civilizations', the 'End of History', 'a world without the West', 'the Beijing Consensus', 'soft power/smart power', 'power transition', 'hegemonic stability' and 'democratic peace', once stripped of their scholarly pretensions, seem to betray similar structures of feeling. In this sense, the knowledge/desire/power framework employed in this book could have a wider disciplinary resonance in critically examining other subsets of IR knowledge, especially their association with desire and power. A hitherto neglected dimension in IR, desire and emotion has slowly begun to be taken seriously, but thus far its complicity both in the production of IR knowledge and in the service of power on the part of the subject of study (i.e., IR scholars) remains little understood. For this reason, the IR discipline as a whole could do well with some critical reflection of its own. Of course, some will be concerned that this could incite renewed 'theological debates between academic religions' and divert 'our professional and intellectual energies' away from 'studying things that matter'.[37] Yet, for all the inroads made by critical IR scholarship in the past quarter of a century, overall the discipline has not, contrary to claims by some, 'spent far too much time theorizing about theorizing instead of theorizing and researching international relations'.[38] In any case, as argued throughout the book, that differentiation is a false dichotomy. While those two types of research may look a world apart in some quarters of the IR community, doing the former *is* ultimately doing the latter and vice versa.

Also, despite its name, the IR discipline is far from *inter*-national in nature. To shake off its notoriety as an American/Western social science, IR ought to enter into more dialogue with 'the rest of the world', which for the most part has remained its 'objects', rather than equal dialogical subjects.[39] 'China's rise' has helped to bring into sharp relief the perceived challenge from those 'objects', but this challenge is not just a strategic or economic one—it is also theoretical in nature. It is a challenge for which we are all responsible. A critical study of Western knowledge on China's rise may help contribute to an ongoing collective effort to address the enduring IR problem of knowing and interacting with peoples and things different or 'non-Western'.[40]

Bradley Klein reminds us of 'a danger in any critical enterprise of its bearers announcing their particular truth as the latest and greatest newly dominant paradigm'.[41] Well aware of such a danger, this book has not sought to solicit the attention of other scholars on the basis of its discovery of truth about China. It is conscious that its grip on its subject—Western representations of China's rise—is tenuous and contingent, because that subject *qua* subject is by definition dynamic and not amenable to essentialist treatments. Furthermore, in shedding light on the ethical and practical implications of Western knowledge of China, the book is also not value-free or politically neutral (such things do not exist in social research). As briefly acknowledged at the end of Chapter 1, my study is a social text intertextually bound up with other social texts and the intellectual limits and social and political biases that go with them. This brief self-reflection, inadequate as it is, nevertheless indicates its centrality to my practice of knowing. Also, effective reflection needs to take place amidst continued dialogue and engagement with other scholars and observers. If this book looks incomplete, as it no doubt is, that is partly because it cannot be complete in its own right or in the absence of ongoing encounters with its readers and critics.

No doubt, many will likely remain unswayed in their 'business-as-usual' quest for empirically verifiable truth about China's rise. My point is that we can still study China and its international relations as we should and must, but a continued unreflective pursuit of truth claims is likely to limit, rather than broaden, our understanding of this global 'actor'. What we need, instead, is a new, more reflective form of social knowledge. The book has not and cannot provide any fully-fledged alternative knowledge template for China watchers to work with, nor has it prescribed a list of future research programmes. It has, however, made a case for a paradigm shift, which means among other things freeing ourselves from the modern positivist aspiration to grand theory or transcendental scientific paradigm itself.[42] Before we become immersed even deeper in the rising tide of the largely unselfconscious 'China's rise' literature and its various emotively charged paradigms, it is now time to start the dialogue on how to make that shift happen.

Notes

PREFACE

1. Global Language Monitor, 'Rise of China Still Tops all Stories', 5 May 2011, http://www. languagemonitor.com/top-news/bin-ladens-death-one-of-top-news-stories-of-21th-century/
2. A. T. Steele, *The American People and China*, New York: McGraw-Hill, 1966, p. 173.

CHAPTER 1 INTRODUCTION

1. Homi K. Bhabha, *The Location of Culture*, London: Routledge, 1994, p. 33.
2. Edward W. Said, *Orientalism: Western Conceptions of the Orient* (new edn), London: Penguin Books, 1995, p. 272.
3. E. H. Carr, *What Is History?* (2nd edn), Harmondsworth: Penguin Books, 1987, p. 22.
4. David Shambaugh, 'Studies of China's Foreign and Security Policies in the United States', in Robert Ash, David Shambaugh and Seiichiro Takagi (eds), *China Watching: Perspectives from Europe, Japan, and the United States*, London: Routledge, 2007, p. 213.
5. Gregory J. Moore, 'David C. Kang, *China Rising: Peace, Power, and Order in East Asia*' (Book Review), *East West Connections*, 9 (1), 2009, p. 146.
6. An incomplete but representative list of such works published in English in the past two decades may include David Shambaugh (ed.), *American Studies of Contemporary China*, Armonk, NY: M. E. Sharpe, 1993; Thomas W. Robinson and David Shambaugh (eds), *Chinese Foreign Policy: Theory and Practice*, Oxford: Clarendon Press, 1994; Lucien Bianco et al., *The Development of Contemporary China Studies*, Tokyo: Centre for East Asian Cultural Studies for UNESCO, The Toyo Bunko, 1994; Bruce Dickson (ed.), *Trends in China Watching: Observing the PRC at Fifty* (Sigur Center Asia Papers, No. 7), Washington DC: George Washington University, 1999; Alastair Iain Johnston and Robert S. Ross (eds), *New Directions in the Study of China's Foreign Policy*, Stanford, CA: Stanford University Press, 2006; Robert Ash, David Shambaugh and Seiichiro Takagi (eds), *China Watching: Perspectives from Europe, Japan, and the United States*, London: Routledge, 2007; as well as some book chapters and journal articles on this subject including David Shambaugh, 'PLA Studies Today: A Maturing Field', in James C. Mulvenon and Richard H. Yang (eds), *The People's Liberation Army in the Information Age*, Santa Monica, CA: RAND Corporation, 1999, pp. 7–21; Andrew G. Walder, 'The Transformation of Contemporary China Studies, 1977–2002', in David L. Szanton (ed.), *The Politics of Knowledge: Area Studies and the Disciplines*, Berkeley, CA: University of California Press, 2004, pp. 314–40; and David Shambaugh, 'Reflections on the American Study of Contemporary China', *Far Eastern Affairs*, 37 (4), 2009, pp. 151–8.
7. Robert S. Ross and Alastair Iain Johnston, 'Introduction', in Alastair Iain Johnston and Robert S. Ross (eds), *New Directions in the Study of China's Foreign Policy*, Stanford, CA: Stanford University Press, 2006, p. 1; and David Shambaugh, 'Introduction', in Thomas W. Robinson and David Shambaugh (eds), *Chinese Foreign Policy: Theory and Practice*, Oxford: Clarendon Press, 1994, p. 1.
8. Jason Kindopp, 'Trends in China Watching: Observing the PRC at 50: Conference Summary', in Bruce Dickson (ed.), *Trends in China Watching: Observing the PRC at Fifty*

(Sigur Center Asia Papers, No. 7), Washington DC: George Washington University, 1999, p. 1.

9. Ross and Johnston, 'Introduction', p. 1.
10. Robert Ash, David Shambaugh and Seiichiro Takagi, 'Introduction', in Robert Ash, David Shambaugh and Seiichiro Takagi (eds), *China Watching: Perspectives from Europe, Japan, and the United States*, London: Routledge, 2007, p. 1.
11. See Terry Eagleton, *Literary Theory: An Introduction* (2nd edn), Oxford: Blackwell, 1996, p. 117.
12. G. John Ikenberry and Michael Mastanduno, 'Introduction: International Relations Theory and the Search for Regional Stability', in G. John Ikenberry and Michael Mastanduno (eds), *International Relations Theory and the Asia-Pacific*, New York: Columbia University Press, 2003, p. 1.
13. Shambaugh, 'Introduction', p. 1.
14. Richard Baum, *China Watcher: Confessions of a Peking Tom*, Seattle, WA: University of Washington Press, 2010, pp. xi–xii.
15. George E. Marcus and Michael M. J. Fisher, *Anthropology as Cultural Critique: An Experimental Moment in the Human Sciences* (2nd edn), Chicago, IL: University of Chicago Press, 1999, pp. 111–12.
16. Ido Oren, *Our Enemies and US: America's Rivalries and the Making of Political Science*, Ithaca, NY: Cornell University Press, 2003, p. 172.
17. John Locke, *An Essay Concerning Human Understanding* (ed. Peter H. Nidditch), Oxford: Clarendon Press, 1975/1700, p. 43.
18. See Morgan Brigg and Roland Bleiker, 'Autoethnographic International Relations: Exploring the Self as a Source of Knowledge', *Review of International Studies*, 36 (3), 2010, pp. 779–98; Leon Anderson, 'Analytic Autoethnography', *Journal of Contemporary Ethnography*, 35 (4), 2006, pp. 373–95; Deborah E. Reed-Danahay (ed.), *Auto/Ethnography: Rewriting the Self and the Social*, Oxford: Berg, 1997; and Arthur P. Bochner and Carolyn Ellis (eds), *Ethnographically Speaking: Autoethnography, Literature, and Aesthetics*, Walnut Creek, CA: AltaMira Press, 2002.
19. Ezra F. Vogel, 'Contemporary China Studies in North America: Marginals in a Superpower', in Lucien Bianco et al., *The Development of Contemporary China Studies*, Tokyo: Centre for East Asian Cultural Studies for UNESCO, The Toyo Bunko, 1994, p. 187.
20. Jim George, *Discourses of Global Politics: A Critical (Re)Introduction to International Relations*, Boulder, CO: Lynne Rienner, 1994, p. 49.
21. Jürgen Habermas, *Knowledge and Human Interests* (2nd edn, trans. Jeremy J. Shapiro), London: Heinemann, 1978, p. 67.
22. David Martin Jones, *The Image of China in Western Social and Political Thought*, Basingstoke: Palgrave, 2001, pp. 9–10.
23. For an excellent review and critique of the reluctance to put the self at the centre of scientific inquiry in the field of IR, see Brigg and Bleiker, 'Autoethnographic International Relations'.
24. Jamie Morgan, 'Distinguishing Truth, Knowledge, and Belief: A Philosophical Contribution to the Problem of Images of China', *Modern China*, 30 (3), 2004, pp. 399–400; Chih-yu Shih, 'Connecting Knowledge of China Studies: Exploring an Ethical Relationship among Knowledge of Different Nature', in I Yuan (ed.), *Rethinking New International Order in East Asia: U.S., China, and Taiwan* (Institute of International Relations English Series No. 52), Taipei: National Chengchi University, 2005, pp. 111–46.
25. Jonathan Culler, *Literary Theory: A Very Short Introduction*, Oxford: Oxford University Press, 1997, p. 35.
26. Quoted in Gayatri Chakravorty Spivak, 'Can the Subaltern Speak?' in Cary Nelson and Lawrence Grossberg (eds), *Marxism and the Interpretation of Culture*, Urbana, IL: University of Illinois Press, 1988, p. 286.
27. Habermas, *Knowledge and Human Interests*, p. 242.

28. Aihwa Ong, 'Anthropological Concepts for the Study of Nationalism', in Pal Nyiri and Joana Breidenbach (eds), *China Inside Out: Contemporary Chinese Nationalism and Transnationalism*, Budapest: Central European University Press, 2005, p. 18. Ong's remark is made in the sense that culture, including Chinese culture, is not seamless, holistic or unchangeable, and thus cannot be studied in isolation or in its own right.
29. Martin Heidegger, *Being and Time* (trans. John Macquarrie and Edward Robinson), Oxford: Blackwell, 1967. For a brief, lucid explanation of Heidegger's 'being-in-the-world' concept, see Eagleton, *Literary Theory*, pp. 53–7.
30. R. G. Collingwood, *The Idea of History*, Oxford: Oxford University Press, 1946, p. 317.
31. Marcus and Fisher, *Anthropology as Cultural Critique*, p. 112.
32. An obviously incomplete list of the literature includes, for example, Steele, *The American People and China*; John G. Stoessinger, 'China and America: The Burden of Past Misperceptions', in John C. Farrell and Asa P. Smith (eds), *Image and Reality in World Politics*, New York: Columbia University Press, 1967, pp. 72–91; Raymond Dawson, *The Chinese Chameleon: An Analysis of European Perceptions of Chinese Civilization*, New York: Oxford University Press, 1967; John K. Fairbank, *China Perceived: Images & Policies in Chinese-American Relations*, London: André Deutsch, 1976; Warren I. Cohen, 'American Perceptions of China', in Michel Oksenberg and Robert B. Oxnam (eds), *Dragon and Eagle: United States-China Relations: Past and Future*, New York: Basic Books, 1978, pp. 54–86; Harold Isaacs, *Scratches on Our Minds: American Images of China and India*, Armonk, NY: M. E. Sharpe, 1980; Harry Harding, 'From China with Disdain: New Trends in the Study of China', *Asian Survey*, 22 (10), 1982, pp. 934–58; Paul A. Cohen, *Discovering History in China: American Historical Writing on the Recent Chinese Past*, New York: Columbia University Press, 1984; Steven W. Mosher, *China Misperceived: American Illusions and Chinese Reality*, New York: Basic Books, 1990; Jonathan Goldstein, Jerry Israel and Hilary Conroy (eds), *America Views China: American Images of China Then and Now*, London: Associated University Presses, 1991; Richard Madsen, *China and the American Dream: A Moral Inquiry*, Berkeley, CA: University of California Press, 1995; T. Christopher Jespersen, *American Images of China: 1931–1949*, Stanford, CA: Stanford University Press, 1996; Lachlan Strahan, *Australia's China: Changing Perceptions from the 1930s to the 1990s*, Cambridge: Cambridge University Press, 1996; Hongshan Li and Zhaohui Hong, *Image, Perception, and the Making of U.S.-China Relations*, Lanham, MD: University Press of America, 1998; Jonathan D. Spence, *The Chan's Great Continent: China in Western Minds*, New York: W. W. Norton, 1998; Colin Mackerras, *Western Images of China* (2nd edn), Oxford: Oxford University Press, 1999; Rupert Hodder, *In China's Image: Chinese Self-Perception in Western Thought*, London: Macmillan, 2000; Colin Mackerras, *Sinophiles and Sinophobes: Western Views of China*, New York: Oxford University Press, 2000; Jianwei Wang, *Limited Adversaries: Post-Cold War Sino-American Mutual Images*, Oxford: Oxford University Press, 2000; Thierry Dodin and Heinz Räther (eds), *Imagining Tibet: Perceptions, Projections, and Fantasies*, Boston, MA: Wisdom Publications, 2001; Thomas Laszlo Dorogi, *Tainted Perceptions: Liberal-Democracy and American Popular Images of China*, Lanham, MD: University Press of America, 2001; Jones, *The Image of China in Western Social and Political Thought*; Andrew A. Latham, 'China in the Contemporary American Geopolitical Imagination', *Asian Affairs: An American Review* 28 (3), 2001, pp. 138–45; Robert W. Snyder (ed.), *Covering China*, Piscataway, NJ: Transaction Publishers, 2001; Herbert Yee and Ian Storey (eds), *The China Threat: Perceptions, Myths and Reality*, London: RoutledgeCurzon, 2002; Alexander Liss, 'Images of China in the American Print Media: A Survey from 2000 to 2002', *Journal of Contemporary China*, 12 (35), 2002, pp. 299–318; Jingdong Liang, *How U.S. Correspondents Discover, Uncover, and Cover China: China Watching Transformed*, Lewiston, NY: Edwin Mellen, 2003; Carola McGiffert (ed.), *China in the American Political Imagination*, Washington, DC: The CSIS Press, 2003; Chengxin Pan, 'The "China Threat" in American Self-Imagination: The Discursive Construction of Other as Power Politics', *Alternatives*, 29 (3), 2004, pp. 305–31; Timothy Kendall, *Ways of Seeing China: From Yellow Peril to Shangrila*, Fremantle: Curtin University Books, 2005; Karen J. Leong, *The China Mystique: Pearl S. Buck, Anna May Wong, Mayling Soong, and*

the Transformation of American Orientalism, Berkeley, CA: University of California Press, 2005; Zhou Ning, *Tianchao yaoyuan: Xifang de Zhongguo xingxiang yanjiu* (China in the World: Studies of Western Images of China), Beijing: Peking University Press, 2006; Steven W. Hook and Xiaoyu Pu, 'Framing Sino-American Relations under Stress: A Reexamination of News Coverage of the 2001 Spy Plane Crisis', *Asian Affairs: An American Review*, 33 (3), 2006, pp. 167–83; James Mann, *The China Fantasy: How Our Leaders Explain Away Chinese Repression*, New York: Viking, 2007; Qing Cao et al., 'A Special Section: Reporting China in the British Media' (Special Issue), *China Media Research*, 3 (1), 2007, pp. 1–72; Eric Hayot, Haun Saussy and Steven G. Yao (eds), *Sinographies: Writing China*, Minneapolis, MN: University of Minnesota Press, 2008; David Martínez-Robles, 'The Western Representation of Modern China: Orientalism, Culturalism and Historiographical Criticism, *Digithum*, No. 10, 2008, pp. 7–16; Emma Mawdsley, 'Fu Manchu versus Dr Livingstone in the Dark Continent? Representing China, Africa and the West in British Broadsheet Newspapers', *Political Geography*, 27 (5), 2008, pp. 509–29; David Scott, *China and the International System, 1840–1949: Power, Presence, and Perceptions in a Century of Humiliation*, Albany, NY: State University of New York Press, 2008; Adrian Chan, *Orientalism in Sinology*, Palo Alto, CA: Academic Press, 2009; Benjamin I. Page and Tao Xie, *Living with the Dragon: How the American Public Views the Rise of China*, New York: Columbia University Press, 2010; Colin Sparks, 'Coverage of China in the UK National Press', *Chinese Journal of Communication*, 3 (3), 2010, pp. 347–65; Li Zhang, 'The Rise of China: Media Perception and Implications for International Politics', *Journal of Contemporary China*, 19 (64), 2010, pp. 233–54; Oliver Turner, 'Sino-US Relations Then and Now: Discourse, Images, Policy', *Political Perspectives*, 5 (3), 2011, pp. 27–45; and Qing Cao, 'Modernity and Media Portrayals of China', *Journal of Asian Pacific Communication*, 22 (1), 2012, pp. 1–21.

33. For example, Said, *Orientalism*; Tani E. Barlow (ed.), *Formations of Colonial Modernity in East Asia*, Durham, NC: Duke University Press, 1997; David Walker, *Anxious Nation: Australia and the Rise of Asia 1850–1939*, St Lucia: University of Queensland Press, 1999; Paul Hollander, *Political Pilgrims: Western Intellectuals in Search of the Good Society* (4th edn), New Brunswick, NJ: Transaction Publishers, 1998; Christina Klein, *Cold War Orientalism: Asia in the Middlebrow Imagination, 1945–1961*, Berkeley, CA: University of California Press, 2003; and Sheridan Prasso, *The Asian Mystique: Dragon Ladies, Geisha Girls, and Our Fantasies of the Exotic Orient*, New York: PublicAffairs, 2006.

34. See, for example, Cohen, *Discovering History in China*; Paul A. Cohen, *China Unbound: Evolving Perspectives on the Chinese Past*, London: RoutledgeCurzon, 2003; Bob Hodge and Kam Louie, *The Politics of Chinese Language and Culture: The Art of Reading Dragons*, London: Routledge, 1998; Alastair Pennycook, *English and the Discourse of Colonialism*, London: Routledge, 1998; Chan, *Orientalism in Sinology*; Mackerras, *Western Images of China*; Morgan, 'Distinguishing Truth, Knowledge, and Belief'; Suman Gupta, 'Writing China', *Wasafiri*, 23 (3), 2008, pp. 1–4; and Daniel Vukovich, 'China in Theory: The Orientalist Production of Knowledge in the Global Economy', *Cultural Critique*, No. 76, 2010, pp. 148–72.

35. As an exception, Shih briefly calls for China watchers 'to reconsider the relationships between the researcher and the researched' and 'recognize and stress China watchers' participation, albeit unintentionally or unwillingly, in the making of China and the China threat'. Chih-yu Shih, *Navigating Sovereignty: World Politics Lost in China*, Basingstoke: Palgrave, 2004, pp. xi–xii; see also Latham, 'China in the Contemporary American Geopolitical Imagination'; and Pan, 'The "China Threat" in American Self-Imagination'.

36. Leong Yew, *The Disjunctive Empire of International Relations*, Aldershot: Ashgate, 2003, p. 5.

37. Said, *Orientalism*, p. 326.

38. Stanley Hoffman, 'An American Social Science: International Relations', *Dædalus*, 106 (3), 1977, pp. 41–60; Ole Wæver, 'The Sociology of a Not So International Discipline: American and European Developments in International Relations', *International Organization*, 52 (4), 1998, pp. 687–727; Peter Monaghan, 'Does International-Relations Scholarship Reflect a Bias toward the U.S.?' *The Chronicle of Higher Education*, 46 (5), 1999, pp. A20–A22; Michael E. Latham, *Modernization as Ideology: American Social*

Science and "Nation Building" in the Kennedy Era, Chapel Hill, NC: The University of North Carolina Press, 2000; Oren, *Our Enemies and US*; and Amitav Acharya and Barry Buzan, 'Why Is There No Non-Western International Relations Theory? An Introduction', *International Relations of the Asia-Pacific*, 7 (3), 2007, pp. 287–312.

39. Michael J. Shapiro, *The Politics of Representation: Writing Practices in Biography, Photography, and Policy Analysis*, Madison, WS: University of Wisconsin Press, 1988; Roxanne Lynn Doty, *Imperial Encounters: The Politics of Representation in North-South Relations*, Minneapolis, MN: University of Minnesota Press, 1996; Iver B. Neumann, *Uses of the Other: "The East" in European Identity Formation*, Minneapolis, MN: University of Minnesota Press, 1999; Michael Pickering, *Stereotyping: The Politics of Representation*, Basingstoke: Palgrave, 2001; and L. H. M. Ling, *Postcolonial International Relations: Conquest and Desire between Asia and the West*, Basingstoke: Palgrave, 2002.

40. Said, *Orientalism*, p. 17. This Middle Eastern focus is even more apparent in his two subsequent books, which, together with *Orientalism*, form a trilogy on Western representation of the Orient. See Edward W. Said, *The Question of Palestine*, New York: Vintage Books, 1979; and Edward W. Said, *Covering Islam: How the Media and the Experts Determine How We See the Rest of the World*, New York: Pantheon Books, 1981. Similarly, in investigating 'European fantasies of the East', Alain Grosrichard's *The Sultan's Court* is concerned mainly with European accounts of the Ottoman Empire. Alain Grosrichard, *The Sultan's Court: European Fantasies of the East* (trans. Liz Heron), London: Verso, 1998.

41. Xiaomei Chen, *Occidentalism: A Theory of Counter-Discourse in Post-Mao China*, New York: Oxford University Press, 1995; Edward D. Graham, 'The "Imaginative Geography" of China', in Warren I. Cohen (ed.), *Reflections on Orientalism: Edward Said*, East Lansing, MI: Asian Studies Center, Michigan State University, 1983, pp. 31–43.

42. See for example, Gerald Segal, 'Does China Matter?' *Foreign Affairs*, 78 (5), 1999, pp. 24–36; David C. Kang, *China Rising: Peace, Power, and Order in East Asia*, New York: Columbia University Press, 2007; Steve Chan, *China, the U.S., and the Power-Transition Theory: A Critique*, London: Routledge, 2008; and Salvatore Babones, 'The Middle Kingdom: The Hype and the Reality of China's Rise', *Foreign Affairs*, 90 (5), 2011, pp. 79–88.

43. Brantly Womack, 'Introduction', in Brantly Womack (ed.), *China's Rise in Historical Perspective*, Lanham, MD: Rowman & Littlefield, 2010, p. 3.

44. Eric Hayot, Haun Saussy and Steven G. Yao, 'Introduction', in Eric Hayot, Haun Saussy and Steven G. Yao (eds), *Sinographies: Writing China*, Minneapolis, MN: University of Minnesota Press, 2008, p. xi (emphasis added).

45. Michel Foucault, *Power/Knowledge: Selected Interviews and Other Writings 1972–1977* (ed. Colin Gordon, trans. Colin Gordon, Leo Marshall, John Mepham, Kate Soper), New York: Pantheon Books, 1980; Hayden White, *Metahistory: The Historical Imagination in Nineteenth-Century Europe*, Baltimore, MD: Johns Hopkins University Press, 1973, p. ix; Said, *Orientalism*, p. 2.

46. Thomas Kuhn, *The Structure of Scientific Revolutions* (2nd enl. edn), Chicago, IL: University of Chicago Press, 1970.

47. Robert J. C. Young, *Colonial Desire: Hybridity in Theory, Culture, and Race*, London: Routledge, 1995, p. 166.

48. Jonathan Culler, *On Deconstruction: Theory and Criticism after Structuralism*, Ithaca, NY: Cornell University Press, 1982, pp. 85–6; Richard K. Ashley, 'Untying the Sovereign State: A Double Reading of the Anarchy Problematique', *Millennium: Journal of International Studies*, 17 (2), 1988, pp. 251–2; and Jens Bartelson, *A Genealogy of Sovereignty*, Cambridge: Cambridge University Press, 1995, p. 19.

49. Ernesto Laclau and Chantal Mouffe, *Hegemony and Socialist Strategy: Towards a Radical Democratic Politics* (2nd edn), London: Verso, 2001, p. 110.

50. Maja Zehfuss, *Constructivism in International Relations: The Politics of Reality*, Cambridge: Cambridge University Press, 2002, p. 196.

51. David Campbell, *Writing Security: United States Foreign Policy and the Politics of Identity* (rev. edn), Minneapolis, MN: University of Minnesota Press, 1998, p. 6.

52. Henry David Thoreau, quoted in Clifford Geertz, *The Interpretation of Cultures*, New York: Basic Books, 1973, p. 16.
53. Quoted in Ernest Cassirer, *Language and Myth* (trans. Susanne K. Langer), New York: Dover Publications, 1946, p. 9.
54. Edward W. Said, *The World, the Text, and the Critic*, Cambridge, MA: Harvard University Press, 1983, pp. 39–40.
55. Hans-Georg Gadamer, *Truth and Method* (trans. Joel Weinsheimer and Donald G. Marshall, 2nd rev. edn), London: Continuum, 2004, p. 335.
56. Eagleton, *Literary Theory*, p. 61; and Pennycook, *English and the Discourse of Colonialism*, p. 5.
57. Hans-Georg Gadamer, 'The Problem of Historical Consciousness', in Paul Rabinow and William M. Sullivan (eds), *Interpretive Social Science: A Second Look*, Berkeley, CA: University of California Press, 1987, p. 87.
58. Carr, *What Is History?*, pp. 24–5.
59. Said, *The World, the Text, and the Critic*, pp. 39–40.
60. Spence, *The Chan's Great Continent*, p. 241.
61. Baum, *China Watcher*, p. 236.
62. Richard Madsen, 'The Academic China Specialists', in David Shambaugh (ed.), *American Studies of Contemporary China*, Washington D.C.: Woodrow Wilson Center Press, 1993, pp. 164–5.
63. Richard White, 'Australian Journalists, Travel Writing and China: James Hingston, the "Vagabond" and G. E. Morrison', *Journal of Australian Studies*, 32 (2), 2008, p. 238.
64. China Digital Times, 'CDT Bookshelf: Interview with James Mann', 26 February 2007, http://chinadigitaltimes.net/2007/02/cdt-bookshelf-interview-with-james-mann/
65. Ibid.
66. Gupta, 'Writing China', p. 3.
67. Strahan, *Australia's China*, p. 5 (emphasis added).
68. David Hume, quoted in C. Fred Alford, *The Self in Social Theory: A Psychoanalytic Account of Its Construction in Plato, Hobbes, Locke, Rawls, and Rousseau*, New Haven, CT: Yale University Press, 1991, p.17.
69. Hans G. Furth, *Knowledge As Desire: An Essay on Freud and Piaget*, New York: Columbia University Press, 1987, p. 172.
70. Michel Foucault, *The History of Sexuality* (Volume 1: An Introduction, trans. Robert Hurley), London: Penguin Books, 1978, p. 72. Michel Foucault, *The Order of Things: An Archaeology of the Human Sciences*, London: Tavistock Publications, 1970, p. 209. Roland Barthes goes as far as saying that 'there is no other primary *significatum* in literary work than a certain desire: to write is a mode of Eros'. Roland Barthes, *Critical Essays*, Chicago, IL: Northwestern University Press, 1972, p. xvi.
71. Steele, *The American People and China*, p. 1.
72. Michel de Certeau, 'Walking in the City', in Simon During (ed.), *The Cultural Studies Reader*, London: Routledge, 1993, p. 152.
73. Richard J. Bernstein, *Beyond Objectivism and Relativism: Science, Hermeneutics, and Praxis*, Oxford: Basil Blackwell, 1983, p. 18.
74. John Dewey, *The Quest for Certainty: A Study of the Relation of Knowledge and Action*, New York: Minton, Balch & Company, 1929, p. 33 (emphasis in original).
75. Anthony Giddens, *The Consequences of Modernity*, Cambridge: Polity Press, 1990, p. 94.
76. Young, *Colonial Desire*, p. 115.
77. Ibid., p. 96.
78. Bhabha, *The Location of Culture*, p. 107.
79. Ibid., pp. 95, 102.
80. Said, *Orientalism*, p. 116. Interestingly, while noting the presence of the Orient as 'sexual promise (and threat), untiring sensuality, unlimited desire, deep generative energies' in Orientalist knowledge, Said himself did not probe deeply into the link between knowledge and desire, admitting that it is not his main analytical objective. Said, *Orientalism*, p. 188.
81. For example, David Bachman notes that 'An often unstated element of concern about China's rise is apparently racism. This may take other names: Huntington's "civilizations";

those who deliberately magnify a "China threat" such as California Congressman Dana Rohrabacher, Senator Jesse Helms, the Cox Commission; or a view in the corridors of power in Washington, D.C. that sees very few Asian-Americans in said corridors—"Yale, male, and pale"—that carries over into the world outside the United States.... Asians—nonwhites—coming to a leading position in the international system is deeply troubling to many (whites), who in true orientalist fashion project their hopes and fears onto China's rise in ways that have been much less common with the rise of other powers, especially those ruled by whites'. David Bachman, 'China's Democratization: What Difference Would It Make for U.S.-China Relations?' in Edward Friedman and Barrett McCormick (eds), *What If China Doesn't Democratize? Implications for War and Peace*, Armonk, NY: M. E. Sharpe, 2000, p. 212. James L. Hevia goes so far as to say that 'China knowledge was produced in ways identical to those found in other colonial settings, and it functioned in some cases through similar institutional structures'. James L. Hevia, *English Lessons: The Pedagogy of Imperialism in Nineteenth-Century China*, Durham, NC: Duke University Press, 2003, p. 348.

82. Foucault, *The History of Sexuality*, p. 81.
83. Michel Foucault, *Discipline and Punish: The Birth of the Prison*, New York: Vantage Books, 1977, p. 27; Foucault, *Power/Knowledge*.
84. Said, *The World, the Text, and the Critic*, p. 4.
85. George, *Discourses of Global Politics*, p. 30 (emphasis in original).
86. Nicholas Onuf, 'Constructivism: A User's Manual', in Vendulka Kubálková, Nicholas Onuf and Paul Kowert (eds), *International Relations in a Constructed World*, Armonk, NY: M. E. Sharpe, 1998, p. 59.
87. This expression was made by Karl Rove, George W. Bush's Senior Adviser. See Bob Woodward, *Plan of Attack*, New York: Simon & Schuster, 2004, p. 91.
88. Fredric Jameson, *The Political Unconscious: Narrative as a Socially Symbolic Act*, London: Methuen, 1981, p. 18.
89. For a detailed discussion of this concept and its Confucian rendition, see Chengxin Pan, '*Shu* and the Chinese Quest for Harmony: A Confucian Approach to Mediating across Difference', in Morgan Brigg and Roland Bleiker (eds), *Mediating across Difference: Oceanic and Asian Approaches to Conflict Resolution*, Honolulu, HI: University of Hawai'i Press, 2011, pp. 221–47.
90. Anthony Giddens, *The Constitution of Society*, Berkeley, CA: University of California Press, 1986, pp. 284, 374.
91. *Phronesis* is developed by Aristotle in *The Nicomachean Ethics* as a concept about a particular kind of knowledge (prudence or practical knowledge) as opposed to *episteme* (scientific knowledge) and *techne* (technical know-how). For discussion on moral knowledge and phronesis in social sciences, see, for example, Gadamer, *Truth and Method*; Bent Flyvbjerg, *Making Social Science Matter: Why Social Inquiry Fails and How It Can Succeed Again*, Cambridge: Cambridge University Press, 2001; and Sanford F. Schram and Brian Caterino (eds), *Making Political Science Matter: Debating Knowledge, Research, and Method*, New York: New York University Press, 2006.
92. Jameson, *The Political Unconscious*, p. 9.

CHAPTER 2 THREAT AND OPPORTUNITY

1. MacGregor Knox, 'Thinking War – History Lite?' *The Journal of Strategic Studies*, 34 (4), 2011, p. 498.
2. Bruce Gilley, *China's Democratic Future: How It Will Happen and Where It Will Lead*, New York: Columbia University Press, 2004, p. 243.
3. Claude Smadja, 'Dealing with Globalization', in Laurence J. Brahm (ed.), *China's Century: The Awakening of the Next Economic Powerhouse*, Singapore: John Wiley & Sons (Asia), 2001, p. 25.
4. Some illustrative works of the exceptions may include, for example, Timothy B. Weston and Lionel M. Jensen (eds), *China beyond the Headlines*, Lanham, MD: Rowman &

Littlefield, 2000; Shaun Breslin, 'Power and Production: Rethinking China's Global Economic Role', *Review of International Studies*, 31 (4), 2005, pp. 735–53; Jeffrey N. Wasserstrom, *China's Brave New World: And Other Tales for Global Times*, Bloomington: Indiana University Press, 2007; Randall Peerenboom, *China Modernizes: Threat to the West or Model for the Rest?* Oxford: Oxford University Press, 2007; Barry Sautman and Yan Hairong, 'The Forest for the Trees: Trade, Investment and the China-in-Africa Discourse', *Pacific Affairs*, 81 (1), 2008, pp. 9–29; Shaun Breslin and Ian Taylor, 'Explaining the Rise of "Human Rights" in Analyses of Sino-African Relations', *Review of African Political Economy*, 35 (115), 2008, pp. 59–71; Shogo Suzuki, 'Chinese Soft Power, Insecurity Studies, Myopia and Fantasy', *Third World Quarterly*, 30 (4), 2009, pp. 779–93; Shaun Breslin, 'China's Emerging Global Role: Dissatisfied Responsible Great Power', *Politics*, 30 (S1), 2010, pp. 52–62; Emilian Kavalski (ed.), *China and the Global Politics of Regionalization*, Farnham: Ashgate, 2009; and Michael Barr, *Who's Afraid of China? The Challenge of China's Soft Power*, London: Zed Books, 2011.

5. Liss, 'Images of China in the American Print Media', p. 300.
6. The term 'bifocal quality' is borrowed from Bruce Cumings, who employs it to describe the pessimistic-cum-optimistic nature of the American gaze on post-Cold War international relations. See Bruce Cumings, *Parallax Visions: Making Sense of American-East Asian Relations*, Durham, NC: Duke University Press, 1999, p. 220.
7. Kuhn, *The Structure of Scientific Revolutions*, p. viii.
8. Sanford F. Schram, 'Return to Politics: Perestroika, Phronesis, and Post-Paradigmatic Political Science', in Sanford F. Schram and Brian Caterino (eds), *Making Political Science Matter*, New York: New York University Press, 2006, p. 29.
9. Paul Rabinow and William M. Sullivan, 'The Interpretive Turn: A Second Look', in Paul Rabinow and William M. Sullivan (eds), *Interpretive Social Science: A Second Look*, Berkeley, CA: University of California Press, 1987, p. 5.
10. For a brief account of the dominance of paradigmatic analysis in IR research and teaching, see Rudra Sil and Peter J. Katzenstein (eds), *Beyond Paradigms: Analytic Eclecticism in the Study of World Politics*, Basingstoke: Palgrave, 2010, p. 24.
11. George Ritzer, *Sociological Theory* (4th edn), New York: McGraw-Hill, 1996, p. 637.
12. Kuhn, *The Structure of Scientific Revolutions*, p. 24.
13. Ibid., p. 61.
14. Quoted in Richard J. Bernstein, *The Restructuring of Social and Political Theory*, London: Methuen, 1976, p. 89.
15. Richard Madsen calls this paradigm a master narrative of China as 'revolutionary redeemer', see Madsen, *China and the American Dream*, pp. 52–7. For a critical analysis of this representational mode in relation to China, see, for example, Hollander, *Political Pilgrims*.
16. Quoted in Mahmood Elahi, 'America, A Chinese Protectorate?' *The Daily Star*, 27 August 2007, http://www.thedailystar.net/newDesign/news-details.php?nid=1435
17. 'Made in China Has Become a Warning Label', *Vancouver Sun*, 13 September 2007, p. C3; Warren I. Cohen, 'American Perceptions of China, 1789–1911', in Carola McGiffert (ed.), *China in the American Political Imagination*, Washington, DC: The CSIS Press, 2003, p. 29.
18. Jim Lobe, 'Two Countries, One Survey', *Asia Times Online*, 12 December 2007, http://www. atimes.com/atimes/China/IL12Ad01.html
19. 'Poll: Iran, Iraq, China Top US Enemies', Associated Press, 1 April 2008; and Geoff Dyer and Ben Hall, 'China Seen as Biggest Threat to Stability', *Financial Times* (Asia), 15 April 2008, p. 2.
20. The body of literature is too large to be listed here. Some illustrative examples include: Denny Roy, 'Hegemon on the Horizon? China's Threat to East Asian Security', *International Security*, 19 (1), 1994, pp. 149–68; Samuel P. Huntington, *The Clash of Civilizations and the Remaking of World Order*, London: Touchstone Books, 1996; Richard Bernstein and Ross H. Munro, *The Coming Conflict with China*, New York: Alfred A. Knopf, 1997; Edward Friedman, 'The Challenge of a Rising China: Another Germany?' in

Robert J. Lieber (ed.), *Eagle Adrift: American Foreign Policy at the End of the Century*, New York: Longman, 1997, pp. 215–45; Paul Wolfowitz, 'Bridging Centuries—Fin de siècle All Over Again', *National Interest*, No. 47, 1997, pp. 3–8; Ross H. Munro, 'China: The Challenge of a Rising Power', in Robert Kagan and William Kristol (eds), *Present Dangers: Crisis and Opportunity in American Foreign and Defense Policy*, San Francisco, CA: Encounter Books, 2000, pp. 47–73; John J. Mearsheimer, *The Tragedy of Great Power Politics*, New York: W. W. Norton & Company, 2001; Constantine C. Menges, *China: The Gathering Threat*, Nashville, TN: Thomas Nelson, 2005; Jed Babbin and Edward Timperlake, *Showdown: Why China Wants War with the United States*, Washington, DC: Regnery Publishing, 2006; and Peter Navarro, *The Coming China Wars: Where They Will Be Fought and How They Can Be Won*, Upper Saddle River, NJ: FT Press, 2007.

21. Patricia Cohen, 'Pentagon to Consult Academics on Security', *New York Times*, 18 June 2008, p. 1.

22. Douglas Lemke and Ronald L. Tammen, 'Power Transition Theory and the Rise of China', *International Interactions*, 29 (4), 2003, pp. 269–71; Ronald L. Tammen and Jacek Kugler, 'Power Transition and China-US Conflicts', *Chinese Journal of International Politics*, 1 (1), 2006, pp. 35–55; Robert D. Kaplan, 'The Geography of Chinese Power: How Far Can Beijing Reach on Land and at Sea?', *Foreign Affairs*, 89 (3), 2010, pp. 22–41; Arvind Subramanian, 'The Inevitable Superpower: Why China's Dominance Is a Sure Thing', *Foreign Affairs*, 90 (5), 2011, p. 66–78.

23. Kenneth N. Waltz, *Theory of International Politics*, Reading, MA: Addison-Wesley, 1979.

24. Bernstein and Munro, *The Coming Conflict with China*, pp. 70, 72.

25. US Department of Defense, *Quadrennial Defense Review Report*, Washington DC: U.S. Government Printing Office, 30 September 2001, p. 4; and US Department of Defense, *Quadrennial Defense Review Report*, Washington DC: U.S. Government Printing Office, 6 February 2006, p. 29.

26. International Security Advisory Board, *China's Strategic Modernization: Report from the ISAB Taskforce*, 2008, p. 1. http://www.fas.org/nuke/guide/china/ISAB2008.pdf

27. See Thomas J. Christensen, 'Posing Problems without Catching Up: China's Rise and Challenges for U.S. Security Policy', *International Security*, 25 (4), 2001, pp. 5–40; Ehsan Ahrari, 'China's Preoccupation with Asymmetric War: Lessons Learned from the Hezbollah-Israeli War', *Small Wars Journal*, October 2009, pp. 1–7; Andrew F. Krepinevich, *Why AirSea Battle?* Washington DC: Center for Strategic and Budgetary Assessments, 2010; and James Dobbins, David C. Gompert, David A. Shlapak and Andrew Scobell, *Conflict with China: Prospects, Consequences, and Strategies for Deterrence*, Santa Monica, CA: RAND Corporation, 2011.

28. Lester R. Brown, *Who Will Feed China? Wake-up Call for a Small Planet*, New York, NY: W. W. Norton, 1995.

29. See, for example, Nicholas D. Kristof, 'The Rise of China', *Foreign Affairs*, 72 (5), 1993, pp. 63–5; Andrew Yeh, 'Toxic Chinese Mercury Pollution Travelling to US', *Financial Times*, 12 April 2006, p. 8; Vaclav Smil, *China's Environmental Crisis*, Armonk, NY: M. E. Sharpe, 1993; Mark Hertsgaard, 'Our Real China Problem', *Atlantic Monthly*, 280 (5), 1997, pp. 96–114; and Brook Larmer and Alexandra A. Seno, 'A Reckless Harvest: China Is Protecting Its Own Trees, But Has Begun Instead to Devour Asia's Forests', *Newsweek* (international ed.), 27 January 2003, pp. 20–22.

30. Pete Engardio (ed.), *Chindia: How China and India Are Revolutionizing Global Business*, New York: McGraw-Hill, 2007, p. 59.

31. Eduardo Porter, 'Looking for a Villain, and Finding One in China', *New York Times*, 18 April 2004, Section 4, p. 3.

32. Glenn Thrush and Manu Raju, 'Barack Obama Pressed on China Showdown', Politico, 6 April 2010, http://www.politico.com/news/stories/0410/35458.html

33. The continued fear of 'Yellow Peril' in the West has been noted by Jagdish Bhagwati, 'Why China Is a Paper Tiger: The Emergence of the People's Republic Should Spell Opportunity – Not Doom – for Asian Economies', *Newsweek*, 18 February 2002, p. 23.

34. Navarro, *The Coming China Wars*, p. vii.

35. Paul Krugman, 'The Chinese Challenge', *New York Times*, 27 June 2005, p. 15; Tyler Marshall, 'Building a Bridge to China', *Los Angeles Times*, 18 July 2005, http://articles.latimes.com/2005/jul/18/world/fg-uschina18

36. International Monetary Fund, *World Economic Outlook April 2011: Tensions from the Two-Speed Recovery: Unemployment, Commodities, and Capital Flows*, Washington DC: International Monetary Fund, 2011.

37. Pew Research Center for the People & the Press, 'Strengthen Ties with China, But Get Tough on Trade', 12 January 2011, http://pewresearch.org/pubs/1855/china-poll-americans-want-closer-ties-but-tougher-trade-policy

38. Mearsheimer, *The Tragedy of Great Power Politics*, pp. 4, 56, 401.

39. Stefan Halper, 'Wrongly Mistaking China', *The American Spectator*, 40 (1), 2007, p. 20.

40. 'US Rights Report Critical of Arab Allies, Iran, China, Zimbabwe', *Voice of America*, 8 March 2006, http://www.voanews.com/english/archive/2006-03/2006-03-08-voa64.cfm

41. Bruce Russett, *Grasping the Democratic Peace: Principles for a Post-Cold War World*, Princeton, NJ: Princeton University Press, 1993, p. 11.

42. Roy, 'Hegemon on the Horizon?' p. 157.

43. Bernstein and Munro, *The Coming Conflict with China*, p. 18.

44. Huntington, *The Clash of Civilizations and the Remaking of World Order*, p. 224.

45. Frank Dikötter, 'Culture, "Race" and Nation: The Formation of National Identity in Twentieth Century China', *Journal of International Affairs*, 49 (2), 1996, pp. 590–605; and Edward Friedman, *National Identity and Democratic Projects in Socialist China*, Armonk, NY: M. E. Sharpe, 1995. Not all studies of Chinese nationalism subscribe to this view, of course. See Yongnian Zheng, *Discovering Chinese Nationalism in China: Modernization, Identity, and International Relations*, Cambridge: Cambridge University Press, 1999; and Peter Hays Gries, *China's New Nationalism: Pride, Politics, and Diplomacy*, Berkeley, CA: University of California Press, 2004.

46. For instance, U.S. Congressman Christopher Smith argues that 'China is playing an increasingly influential role on the continent of Africa and there is concern that the Chinese intend to aid and abet African dictators, gain a stranglehold on precious African natural resources, and undo much of the progress that has been made on democracy and governance in the last 15 years in African nations'. Quoted in Peerenboom, *China Modernizes*, p. 274. See also 'The Dragon in Africa' (Letter to the Editor), *The Daily Telegraph* (UK), 26 April 2006, p. 17; Joshua Kurlantzick, *Charm Offensive: How China's Soft Power Is Transforming the World*, New Haven, CT: Yale University Press, 2007; and Congressional Research Service, *China's Foreign Policy and "Soft Power" in South America, Asia, and Africa: A Study Prepared for the Committee on Foreign Relations, United States Senate*, Washington, DC: U.S. Government Printing Office, 2008, p. 130.

47. Mann, *The China Fantasy*, pp. 24, 105; see also Stefan Halper, *The Beijing Consensus: How China's Authoritarian Model Will Dominate the Twenty-First Century*, New York: Basic Books, 2010.

48. Robert Kagan, *The Return of History and the End of Dreams*, New York: Alfred A. Knopf, 2008, p. 4.

49. Huntington, *The Clash of Civilizations and the Remaking of World Order*, p. 228.

50. Samuel P. Huntington, *The Third Wave: Democratization in the Late Twentieth Century*, Norman, OK: University of Oklahoma Press, 1991, p. 307.

51. Huntington, *The Clash of Civilizations and the Remaking of World Order*, p. 94.

52. Martin Jacques, *When China Rules the World: The End of the Western World and the Birth of a New Global Order*, New York: The Penguin Press, 2009, p. 235.

53. Ibid., p. 15.

54. Alastair Iain Johnston, *Cultural Realism: Strategic Culture and Grand Strategy in Chinese History*, Princeton, NJ: Princeton University Press, 1995.

55. Robert Zoellick, 'Whither China? From Membership to Responsibility' (Remarks to the National Committee on U.S.-China Relations), *NBR Analysis*, 16 (4), 2005, pp. 5–14.

56. US Department of Defense, *Quadrennial Defense Review Report*, p. 60; see also US Department of Defense, *2010 Nuclear Posture Review*, Washington DC: Department of Defense, April 2010, p. 5.
57. Gilley, *China's Democratic Future*, p. ix.
58. Ibid., p. x.
59. John J. Hamre, 'Forward: Images Revisited', in Carola McGiffert (ed.), *China in the American Political Imagination*, Washington, DC: The CSIS Press, 2003, pp. x–xi.
60. Tzvetan Todorov, *The Conquest of America: The Question of the Other* (trans. Richard Howard), Norman, OK: University of Oklahoma Press, 1999, p. 11.
61. Foster Rhea Dulles, *China and America: The Story of Their Relations since 1784*, Princeton, NJ: Princeton University Press, 1946, p. 100.
62. Quoted in ibid., p. 25.
63. Carl Crow, *400 Million Customers*, London: Hamilton, 1937.
64. James McGregor, *One Billion Customers: Lessons from the Front Lines of Doing Business in China*, London: Nicholas Brealey, 2005.
65. Graeme Dobell, 'Treasury's China Star', *The Interpreter*, 12 May 2010, http://www.lowyinterpreter.org/post/2010/05/12/Treasury-China-star.aspx; and Glenda Korporaal, 'China Boom to Shore Up Coffers', *The Australian*, 14 May 2008, p. 3.
66. Julia Gillard, Speech to the AsiaLink and Asia Society Lunch, Melbourne, Australia, 28 September 2011, http://www.pm.gov.au/press-office/speech-asialink-and-asia-society-lunch-melbourne
67. Samuel Shen, 'Can't Beat That Return: China KFC's Big Fry', *The Age*, 7 May 2008, Business Day, p. 9.
68. George M. C. Fisher, 'Kodak and China: Seven Years of Kodak Moments', in Laurence J. Brahm (ed.), *China's Century: The Awakening of the Next Economic Powerhouse*, Singapore: John Wiley & Sons (Asia), 2001, p. 128.
69. Quoted in Joe Studwell, *The China Dream: The Quest for the Last Great Untapped Market on Earth*, New York: Grove Press, 2005, pp. 107–8.
70. Ted C. Fishman, *China Inc.: How the Rise of the Next Superpower Challenges America and the World*, New York: Scribner, 2006, pp. 142–3.
71. Quoted in Studwell, *The China Dream*, p. 108.
72. Fishman, *China Inc.*, p. 17.
73. Will Hutton, *Writing on the Wall: Why We Must Embrace China as a Partner or Face It as an Enemy*, New York: Free Press, 2006, p. 17; Engardio, *Chindia*, p. 14.
74. Engardio, *Chindia*, p. 40; and Fishman, *China Inc.*, p. 147.
75. Oded Shenkar, *The Chinese Century: The Rising Chinese Economy and Its Impact on the Global Economy, the Balance of Power, and Your Job*, Upper Saddle River, NJ: Wharton School Publishing, 2006, p. 20; Peter Cai, 'Our Bill to China: $5100 Per Family', *The Age*, 3 April 2012, p. 3.
76. C. Fred Bergsten, Bates Gill, Nicholas R. Lardy and Derek Mitchell, *China: The Balance Sheet: What the World Needs to Know Now about the Emerging Superpower*, New York: PublicAffairs, 2006, p. 116.
77. Samuel P. Huntington, *Political Order in Changing Societies*, New Haven, CT: Yale University Press, 1968, p. 32; Michael Mandelbaum, *The Ideas That Conquered the World: Peace, Democracy, and Free Markets in the Twenty-First Century*, New York: PublicAffairs, 2003, pp. 268–71.
78. Henry S. Rowen, 'The Short March: China's Road to Democracy', *The National Interest*, No. 45, 1996, p. 68. See also Julia Chang Bloch, 'Commercial Diplomacy', in Ezra F. Vogel (ed.), *Living with China: U.S./China Relations in the Twenty-First Century*, New York: W. W. Norton, 1997, p. 194; and George Gilboy and Eric Heginbotham, 'China's Coming Transformation', *Foreign Affairs*, 80 (4), 2001, pp. 26–39.
79. Merle Goldman, *Sowing the Seeds of Democracy in China: Political Reform in the Deng Xiaoping Era*, Cambridge, MA: Harvard University Press, 1994.
80. Minxin Pei, 'Creeping Democratization in China', *Journal of Democracy*, 6 (4), 1995, pp. 65–79; and Minxin Pei, 'China's Evolution Toward Soft Authoritarianism', in Edward

Friedman and Barrett McCormick (eds), *What If China Doesn't Democratize?* Armonk, NY: M. E. Sharpe, 2000, p. 75.

81. Quoted in Andrew J. Nathan, *China's Crisis: Dilemmas of Reform and Prospects for Democracy*, New York: Columbia University Press, 1990, p. 71.
82. Donald S. Zagoria, 'China's Quiet Revolution', *Foreign Affairs*, 62 (4), 1984, p. 880.
83. See, for example, Zbigniew Brzezinski, *The Grand Failure: The Birth and Death of Communism in the Twentieth Century*, New York: Charles Scribner's Sons, 1989, pp. 174, 250; and Nancy Bernkopf Tucker, 'America First', in Carola McGiffert (ed.), *China in the American Political Imagination*, Washington, DC: The CSIS Press, 2003, p. 20.
84. U.S President Ronald Reagan, 'Remarks at a Luncheon With Business Leaders in Fairbanks, Alaska', University of Alaska, 1 May 1984, http://www.reagan.utexas.edu/archives/speeches/1984/50184d.htm
85. Bill Clinton, *My Life*, New York: Alfred A. Knopf, 2004, p. 794.
86. Charles Wolf Jr., 'China's Capitalists Join the Party', *New York Times*, 13 August 2001, p. A17.
87. Francis Fukuyama, *The End of History and the Last Man*, New York: Free Press, 1992, p. 33.
88. Hutton, *The Writing on the Wall*, pp. 16–17.
89. 'US Urges Chinese Political Reform', BBC News, 16 November 2005, http://news.bbc.co.uk/2/hi/americas/4440860.stm
90. Jacob Heilbrunn, 'Team W.', *The New Republic*, 27 September 1999, p. 24. See also Brzezinski, *The Grand Failure*, p. 250; and Fukuyama, *The End of History and the Last Man*, pp. 33–4.
91. Fukuyama, *The End of History and the Last Man*, p. 34.
92. Robert L. Suettinger, *Beyond Tiananmen: The Politics of U.S.-China Relations, 1989–2000*, Washington DC: Brookings Institution Press, 2003, pp. 95–6.
93. George Bush and Brent Scowcroft, *A World Transformed*, New York: Alfred A. Knopf, 1998, p. 158.
94. Andrew J. Nathan (with contributions by Tianjian Shi and Helena V.S. Ho), *China's Transition*, New York: Columbia University Press, 1997, pp. 75–6. See also Andrew J. Nathan and Tianjian Shi, 'Cultural Requisites for Democracy in China', *Daedalus*, 122 (2), 1993, pp. 95–123.
95. Nathan, *China's Transition*, p. 13.
96. Barrett L. McCormick, 'Democracy or Dictatorship?: A Response to Gordon White', *Australian Journal of Chinese Affairs*, No. 31, 1994, p. 109.
97. Larry Diamond, 'Forward', in Suisheng Zhao (ed.), *China and Democracy: The Prospect for a Democratic China*, New York: Routledge, 2000, p. xiv.
98. Nicholas D. Kristof, 'Earthquake and Hope', *New York Times,* 22 May 2008, p. 31.
99. Zoellick, 'Whither China: from membership to responsibility?'
100. David Lake, 'American Hegemony and the Future of East-West Relations', *International Studies Perspective*, 7 (1), 2006, p. 24.
101. Bloch, 'Commercial Diplomacy', pp. 195–6; Ezra F. Vogel, 'Introduction: How Can the United States and China Pursue Common Interests and Manage Differences?' in Ezra F. Vogel, (ed.), *Living with China: U.S./China Relations in the Twenty-First Century*, New York: W. W. Norton, 1997, pp. 30–31. See also Samuel R. Berger, 'Don't Antagonize China', *Washington Post*, 8 July 2001, p. B7.
102. Henry S. Rowen, 'Off-Center on the Middle Kingdom', *The National Interest*, No. 48, 1997, p. 104.
103. Susan Shirk, *China: Fragile Power*, Oxford: Oxford University Press, 2007, p. 10.
104. Thomas L. Friedman, *The World Is Flat: The Globalized World in the Twenty-First Century*, London: Penguin Books, 2006, p. 524.
105. Diamond, 'Forward', pp. ix–x.
106. Gilley, *China's Democratic Future*, p. 227.
107. Ann Kent, 'China's Participation in International Organizations', in Yongjin Zhang and Greg Austin (eds), *Power and Responsibility in Chinese Foreign Policy*, Canberra: Asia

Pacific Press, 2001, p. 132; and David M. Lampton, 'A Growing China in a Shrinking World: Beijing and the Global Order', in Ezra F. Vogel (ed.), *Living with China: U.S./China Relations in the Twenty-First Century*, New York: W. W. Norton, 1997, pp. 120–40.

108. Harry Harding, *China's Second Revolution: Reform After Mao*, Sydney: Allen & Unwin, 1987, p. 243.

109. See, for example, Harold K. Jacobson and Michel Oksenberg, *China's Participation in the IMF, the World Bank, and GATT*, Ann Arbor, MI: University of Michigan Press, 1990; William R. Feeney, 'China's Relations with Multilateral Economic Institutions', in the Joint Economic Committee, Congress of the United States (ed.), *China's Economic Dilemmas in the 1990s: The Problems of Reforms, Modernization, and Interdependence*, Armonk, NY: M. E. Sharpe, 1992, pp. 795–816; Robinson and Shambaugh (eds), *Chinese Foreign Policy: Theory and Practice*; Yoichi Funabashi, Michel Oksenberg and Heinrich Weiss, *An Emerging China in a World of Interdependence*, New York: The Trilateral Commission, 1994; Ezra F. Vogel (ed.), *Living with China: U.S./China Relations in the Twenty-First Century*, New York: W. W. Norton, 1997; David S. G. Goodman and Gerald Segal (eds), *China Rising: Nationalism and Interdependence*, London: Routledge, 1997; Ann Kent, 'China, International Organizations and Regimes: The ILO as a Case Study in Organizational Learning', *Pacific Affairs*, 70 (4), 1997/1998, pp. 517–32; Elizabeth Economy and Michel Oksenberg (eds), *China Joins the World: Progress and Prospects*, New York: Council on Foreign Relations Press, 1999; Alastair Iain Johnston and Paul Evans, 'China's Engagement with Multilateral Security Institutions', in Alastair Iain Johnston and Robert S. Ross (eds), *Engaging China: The Management of an Emerging Power*, London: Routledge, 1999, p. 235; Ann Kent, *China, the United Nations, and Human Rights: The Limits of Compliance*, Philadelphia, PA: University of Pennsylvania Press, 1999; Rosemary Foot, *Rights beyond Borders: The Global Community and the Struggle over Human Rights in China*, Oxford: Oxford University Press, 2000; David M. Lampton, *Same Bed, Different Dreams: Managing U.S.-China Relations, 1989–2000*, Berkeley, CA: University of California Press, 2001, Chapter 4; Ann Kent, 'China's Participation in International Organizations'; Gary Klintworth, 'China and Arms Control: A Learning Process', in Yongjin Zhang and Greg Austin (eds), *Power and Responsibility in Chinese Foreign Policy*, Canberra: Asia Pacific Press, 2001, pp. 219–49; Nicholas R. Lardy, *Integrating China into the Global Economy*, Washington, DC: Brookings Institution Press, 2002; and Stuart Harris, 'Globalisation and China's Diplomacy: Structure and Process', Department of International Relations Working Paper No. 2002/9, Canberra: Australian National University, December 2002, pp. 1–24.

110. Michel Oksenberg and Elizabeth Economy, 'Introduction: China Joins the World', in Elizabeth Economy and Michel Oksenberg (eds), *China Joins the World: Progress and Prospects*, New York: Council on Foreign Relations Press, 1999, pp. 29, 5.

111. Robert A. Kapp, 'The Matter of Business', in Carola McGiffert (ed.), *China in the American Political Imagination*, Washington, DC: The CSIS Press, 2003, p. 89.

112. Quoted in Mann, *The China Fantasy*, p. 84.

113. Quoted in ibid., pp. 26–7.

114. Thomas W. Robinson, '[In][ter]dependence in China's Post-Cold War Foreign Relations', in Samuel S. Kim (ed.), *China and the World: Chinese Foreign Policy Facing the New Millennium*, Boulder, CO: Westview, 1998, pp. 202–3, 193.

115. Alastair Iain Johnston, *Social States: China in International Institutions, 1980–2000*, Princeton, NJ: Princeton University Press, 2008, p. 197; Alastair Iain Johnston, 'Socialization in International Institutions: The ASEAN Way and International Relations Theory', in G. John Ikenberry and Michael Mastanduno (eds), *International Relations Theory and the Asia-Pacific*, New York: Columbia University Press, 2003, pp. 130–31.

116. Alastair Iain Johnston, 'Chinese Middle Class Attitudes towards International Affairs: Nascent Liberalization?' *The China Quarterly*, 179 (1), 2004, pp. 603–28.

117. Kuhn, *The Structure of Scientific Revolutions*, p. 150.

118. Bernstein, *Beyond Objectivism and Relativism*, p. 85.

119. William A. Callahan, *Contingent States: Greater China and Transnational Relations*, Minneapolis, MN: University of Minnesota Press, 2004, Chapter 1, and p. 25. See also Kapp, 'The Matter of Business'.
120. Fishman, *China Inc.*, p. 257.
121. William Kristol and Robert Kagan, 'Introduction: National Interest and Global Responsibility', in Robert Kagan and William Kristol (eds), *Present Dangers: Crisis and Opportunity in American Foreign and Defense Policy*, San Francisco, CA: Encounter Books, 2000, p. 20.
122. In the book *China: The Balance Sheet*, the authors made it clear that China represents 'both an opportunity and threat to the United States in economic and security terms'. Bergsten et al., *China: The Balance Sheet*, p. 155; See also Douglas H. Paal, 'China and the East Asian Security Environment: Complementarity and Competition', in Ezra F. Vogel (ed.), *Living with China: U.S./China Relations in the Twenty-First Century*, New York: W. W. Norton, 1997, p. 99; and Lampton, *Same Bed, Different Dreams*, pp. 160–62.
123. Nicholas Lardy, for one, once asked the question of 'The Economic Rise of China: Threat or Opportunity?' *Federal Reserve Bank of Cleveland Economic Commentary*, 1 August 2003; Vincent Cable and Peter Ferdinand, 'China As an Economic Giant: Threat or Opportunity?', *International Affairs*, 70 (2), 1994, pp. 243–61; Barbara Hackman Franklin, 'China Today: Evil Empire or Unprecedented Opportunity?' *Heritage Lecture*, no. 589, 20 May 1997, http://www.heritage.org/Research/AsiaandthePacific/HL589.cfm; Ted Galen Carpenter and James A. Dorn (eds), *China's Future: Constructive Partner or Emerging Threat?* Washington, D.C.: Cato Institute, 2000; and Herbert S. Yee (ed.), *China's Rise – Threat or Opportunity?* London: Routledge, 2011.
124. Harding, 'From China, with Disdain', pp. 944–5, 952.
125. Isaacs, *Scratches on Our Minds*, p. 64.
126. Ian Bremmer, 'The Panda Hedgers', *New York Times*, 5 October 2005.

CHAPTER 3 OF FEARS AND FANTASIES

1. James Der Derian, 'The Value of Security: Hobbes, Marx, Nietzsche, and Baudrillard', in Ronnie D. Lipschutz (ed.), *On Security*, New York: Columbia University Press, 1995, p. 34.
2. Madsen, *China and the American Dream*, p. 117.
3. Hugh White, 'Power Shift: Australia's Future between Washington and Beijing', *Quarterly Essay*, No. 39, 2010, p. 33. The neoconservative commentator John Tkacik Jr. wrote approvingly that '"hedging" has become the watchword in China relations in Washington. It's about time'. Quoted in Kang, *China Rising*, p. 190. Naazneen Barma et al. argue that hedging has now become 'a Washington, DC mantra, with bipartisan support'. Naazneen Barma, Ely Ratner and Steven Weber, 'A World Without the West', *The National Interest*, No. 90, 2007, p. 23.
4. Johannes Fabian, *Time and the Other: How Anthropology Makes Its Object* (2nd edn), New York: Columbia University Press, 2002, pp. 89, 91.
5. Geertz, *The Interpretation of Cultures*, p. 346. See also Said, *Covering Islam*, p. 132; James Clifford, *The Predicament of Culture*, Cambridge, MA: Harvard University Press, 1988, p. 229; Ashis Nandy, *The Intimate Enemy: Loss and Recovery of Self under Colonialism*. New Delhi: Oxford University Press, 1983, p. 80.
6. Dominique Moïse, *The Geopolitics of Emotion: How Cultures of Fear, Humiliation and Hope are Reshaping the World*, London: Bodley Head, 2009, p. 92.
7. Isaacs, *Scratches on Our Minds*, p. 381.
8. Wasserstrom, *China's Brave New World*, p. xxiii.
9. See, for example, David Gress, *From Plato to NATO: The Idea of the West and Its Opponents*, New York: The Free Press, 1998; Jacinta O'Hagan, *Conceptions of the West in International Relations Thought: From Oswald Spengler to Edward Said*, Basingstoke: Macmillan, 2002.
10. Charles William Maynes, 'Contending Schools', *National Interest*, No. 63, 2001, p. 50.

11. Gregory Clark, *In Fear of China*, Melbourne: Lansdowne Press, 1967, p. xi.
12. Kristol and Kagan, 'Introduction', p. 4.
13. Charles Krauthammer, 'Universal Dominion', in Owen Harries (ed.), *America's Purpose: New Visions of U.S. Foreign Policy*, San Francisco, CA: ICS Press, 1991, pp. 5–13.
14. For a critical study of the construction of the China threat in the American self-imagination, see Pan, 'The "China Threat" in American Self-Imagination'.
15. Huntington, *The Clash of Civilizations and the Remaking of World Order*, p. 237.
16. Alex Vines, 'Mesmerised by Chinese String of Pearls Theory', *The World Today*, 68 (2), 2012, pp. 33–4.
17. Robert Kagan, *Of Paradise and Power: America and Europe in the New World Order*, New York: Vintage Books, 2004, pp. 3, 33.
18. Tucker, 'America First', p. 20.
19. Yu Bin, *East Asia: Geopolitique into the Twenty-first Century—A Chinese View*, Stanford, CA: Asia Pacific Research Center, Stanford University, June 1997, p. 9.
20. John Mearsheimer, 'The False Promise of International Institutions', *International Security*, 19 (3), 1994/95, p. 10.
21. C. B. Macpherson, 'Introduction', in Thomas Hobbes, *Leviathan* (ed. C. B. Macpherson), Harmondsworth: Penguin Books, 1968, pp. 38–9.
22. Before George W. Bush's election as President, Wolfowitz testified before a U.S. Senate Committee Hearing on Transfer of Satellite Technology to China that 'China is the process of becoming—albeit still quite slowly—probably the major strategic competitor and potential threat to the United States and its allies in the first half of the next century'. Paul Wolfowitz, 'Transfer of Missile Technology to China', *Congressional Testimony by Federal Document Clearing House*, 17 September 1998.
23. Wolfowitz, 'Bridging Centuries—Fin de Siècle All Over Again', p. 7 (emphasis added).
24. Richard K. Betts and Thomas J. Christensen, 'China: Getting the Questions Right', *The National Interest*, No. 62, 2000/2001, p. 23. For the Germany analogy, see Arthur Waldron, 'Statement of Dr Arthur Waldron', House Armed Services Committee, 21 June 2000, http://armedservices.house.gov/testimony/106thcongress/00-06-21waldron.html; Friedman, 'The Challenge of a Rising China: Another Germany?'; and Wolfowitz, 'Bridging Centuries—Fin de Siècle All Over Again'.
25. Aaron L. Friedberg, 'Will Europe's Past Be Asia's Future?' *Survival*, 42 (3), 2000, pp. 147–59.
26. Robert Kagan, 'Ambition and Anxiety: America's Competition with China', in Gary J. Schmitt (ed.), *The Rise of China: Essays on the Future Competition*, New York: Encounter Books, 2009, p. 2.
27. Mearsheimer, *The Tragedy of Great Power Politics*, p. 401.
28. The construction of threat through Western/American self-experience is not confined to the 'China threat' paradigm, but is also evident in the identification of terrorist threats. In a 1996 testimony on terrorism, CIA Director John Deutch insisted that international terrorists could easily mount attacks on the information infrastructure, use nuclear suitcase bombs, spread radiation and bacteria in public space, and poison urban water supplies. However, rarely, if ever, had those frightening scenarios actually taken place in the United States, and so the puzzle was: on what ground did Deutch come to know the existence of these threats? Explaining this anomaly, Lipschutz suggests that underlying these threat arguments is 'a not-so-subtle implication in Deutch's statement that the United States—perhaps through the National Security Agency—is itself capable of conducting information attacks, and has practised them. This, in turn, suggests self-induced fears generated by projecting U.S. national capabilities onto imagined others'. In other words, the 'terrorist threats' identified by Deutch are in large part a reflection of America's self-capacity and his fear that others might also acquire and use that capacity. See Ronnie D. Lipschutz, *After Authority: War, Peace, and Global Politics in the 21st Century*, New York: State University of New York Press, 2000, p. 47.
29. Mel Gurtov, *Global Politics in the Human Interest* (5th edn), Boulder, CO: Lynne Rienner, 2007, p. 241.

30. David Walker suggests that 'The invasion story was always there to say at least as much about "us" as about "them"'. Walker, *Anxious Nation*, p. 101. See also Catriona Ross, 'Prolonged Symptoms of Cultural Anxiety: The Persistence of Narratives of Asian Invasion within Multicultural Australia', *Journal of the Association for the Study of Australian Literature*, No. 5, 2006, p. 90.
31. See Neumann, *Uses of the Other*.
32. Michael Hardt and Antonio Negri, *Empire*, Cambridge, MA: Harvard University Press, 2000, pp. 127–8.
33. James Oliver Robertson, *American Myth, American Reality*, New York: Hill & Wang, 1980, p. 124.
34. Campbell, *Writing Security*, p. 168.
35. Ibid., p. 13.
36. Lionel M. Jensen and Timothy B. Weston (eds), *China's Transformations: Stories Behind the Headlines*, Lanham, MD: Rowman & Littlefield, 2007, p. xxxiii.
37. Lipschutz, *After Authority*, p. 45.
38. John J. Mearsheimer, 'Why We Will Soon Miss the Cold War', *Atlantic Monthly*, 266 (2), 1990, pp. 35–50.
39. Samuel P. Huntington, *Who Are We? America's Great Debate*, London: Free Press, 2004, p. xviii.
40. Samuel P. Huntington, 'The Erosion of American National Interests', *Foreign Affairs*, 76 (5), 1997, pp. 29–30.
41. Robert W. Tucker and David C. Hendrickson, *The Imperial Temptation: The New World Order and America's Purpose*, New York: Council on Foreign Relations Press, 1992, pp. 2–3; Owen Harries, 'The Collapse of "the West"', *Foreign Affairs*, 72 (4), 1993, p. 42.
42. Kristol and Kagan, 'Introduction', p. 4.
43. Quoted in Charles E. Nathanson, 'The Social Construction of the Soviet Threat: A Study in the Politics of Representation', *Alternatives*, 13 (4), 1988, p. 443.
44. Noam Chomsky, *The Chomsky Reader* (ed. James Peck), New York: Pantheon Books, 1987, p. 65 (emphasis added).
45. See, for example, Robert D. Kaplan, 'The Coming Anarchy', *Atlantic Monthly*, 273 (2), 1994, pp. 44–76; John Mearsheimer, 'Back to the Future: Instability in Europe After the Cold War', *International Security*, 15 (1), 1991, pp. 5–56; and Thomas H. Henriksen, 'The Coming Great Powers Competition', *World Affairs*, 158 (2), 1995, pp. 63–9; Charles Krauthammer, 'Do We Really Need a New Enemy?' *Time*, 23 March 1992, p. 76. 'Bush Needs the Bad Guys', *Guardian Weekly*, March 15–21, 2001, p. 14. On the relationship between the construction of 'Other' and America's drive for building national missile defence system, see Tan See Seng, 'What Fear Hath Wrought: Missile Hysteria and the Writing of "America"', Institute of Defence and Strategic Studies Working Paper No. 28, Singapore: Nanyang Technological University, 2002, pp. 1–28.
46. Quoted in Siobhán McEvoy-Levy, *American Exceptionalism and US Foreign Policy: Public Diplomacy at the End of the Cold War*, New York: Palgrave, 2001, p. 80.
47. This story is recounted in Chapter 3 of Fred Kaplan's book, *Daydream Believers: How a Few Grand Ideas Wrecked American Power*, Hoboken, NJ: John Wiley & Sons, 2008.
48. Bruce Cumings, 'The World Shakes China', *The National Interest*, No. 43, 1996, p. 39.
49. Compared to the shadowy Al Qaeda, Iraq seemed to offer more certainty and familiarity (as a target). And the decision over going to war in Iraq might have a lot to do with that feeling of certainty. As summarised by a Democratic Consultant: 'We can't invade al Qaeda. We can't occupy it. We can't even find it. Okay. Fine. But we do know where Baghdad is. We've got a map. We can find it on a map. And they've got oil and an evil guy. So let's go there'. Quoted in James Moore and Wayne Slater, *Bush's Brain: How Karl Rove Made George W. Bush Presidential*, New Jersey, NJ: John Wiley & Sons, 2003, p. 301.
50. Steve Chan, 'Relating to China: Problematic Approaches and Feasible Emphases', *World Affairs*, 161 (4), 1999, p. 179.
51. G. John Ikenberry and Anne-Marie Slaughter, *Forging A World of Liberty Under Law: U.S. National Security in the 21st Century Final Report of the Princeton Project on National*

Security (The Princeton Project Papers), Princeton, NJ: The Woodrow Wilson School of Public and International Affairs, Princeton University, 2006.

52. Christensen, 'Posing Problems without Catching Up', p. 5.
53. Gerald Segal, 'Understanding East Asian International Relations', *Review of International Studies*, 23 (4), 1997, p. 504.
54. Fairbank, *China Perceived*, p. 85.
55. Bernstein and Munro, *The Coming Conflict with China*, p. 53.
56. Ibid., pp. 4, 11.
57. Ibid., p. 8. For an alternative account of China's goals, see Jia Qingguo, 'Economic Development, Political Stability, and International Respect', *Journal of International Affairs*, 49 (2), 1996, pp. 572–89.
58. Huntington, *The Clash of Civilizations and the Remaking of World Order*, pp. 106, 68–72.
59. Ibid., pp. 43, 125.
60. Johnston, *Cultural Realism*, p. xi.
61. For a systematic deconstruction of this book, see Anthony A. Loh, 'Deconstructing *Cultural Realism*', in Wang Gungwu and Zheng Yongnian (eds), *China and the New International Order*, London: Routledge, 2008, pp. 281–92.
62. Johnston, *Cultural Realism,* p. 247.
63. Ibid., p. 30.
64. Ibid.
65. Ibid., p. 253.
66. Ibid., p. 216n1.
67. Warren I. Cohen, 'China's Strategic Culture', *Atlantic Monthly*, 279 (3), 1997, p. 105.
68. Ibid., p. 103.
69. Betts and Christensen, 'China: Getting the Questions Right', pp. 19, 22 (emphases added).
70. Ibid., pp. 18, 28.
71. John J. Mearsheimer, 'The Future of the American Pacifier', *Foreign Affairs*, 80 (5), 2001, p. 60.
72. Yongjin Zhang, 'China's Security Problematique: Critical Reflections', in Yongjin Zhang and Greg Austin (eds), *Power and Responsibility in Chinese Foreign Policy*, Canberra: Asia Pacific Press, 2001, p. 255.
73. Another example is from John Derbyshire, who is proud that he got his education as a China-watcher from the old China hands of Hong Kong. As he writes, 'In fact, one of the more depressing things about China, if you are a person with a deep interest in the country and its history, is how little the Chinese themselves know. Any foreigner who makes an effort to do so can easily become better informed about recent Chinese history than the Chinese are'. John Derbyshire, 'China: A Reality Check', *National Review*, 17 September 2001, p. 42.
74. Lucian W.Pye, 'China: Erratic State, Frustrated Society', *Foreign Affairs*, 69 (4), 1990, p. 56.
75. Friedman, *National Identity and Democratic Prospects in Socialist China*, pp. ix–x.
76. Mann, *The China Fantasy*, p. 82.
77. Quoted in James Peck, *Washington's China: The National Security World, the Cold War, and the Origins of Globalism*, Amherst, MA: University of Massachusetts Press, 2006, p. 71.
78. Bhagwati, 'Why China Is a Paper Tiger', p. 23.
79. Quoted in Chomsky, *The Chomsky Reader*, p. 79.
80. Ethan Gutmann, *Losing the New China: A Story of American Commerce, Desire, and Betrayal*, San Francisco, CA: Encounter Books, 2004, p. 145 (emphasis in original).
81. James Farrows, 'China Makes, the World Takes', *Atlantic Monthly*, 300 (1), 2007, p. 58.
82. Kapp, 'The Matter of Business', p. 89.
83. Zoellick, 'Whither China? From Membership to Responsibility?'
84. In the context of anthropology, Johannes Fabian defines the 'denial of coevalness' as '*a persistent and systematic tendency to place the referent(s) of anthropology in a Time other*

than the present of the producer of anthropological discourse'. Fabian, *Time and the Other*, p. 31 (emphasis in original).

85. Oksenberg and Economy, 'Introduction: China Joins the World', p. 5.
86. Rosemary Foot, 'China and the Idea of a Responsible State', in Yongjin Zhang and Greg Austin (eds), *Power and Responsibility in Chinese Foreign Policy*, Canberra: Asia Pacific Press, 2001, p. 42.
87. Patrick E. Tyler, *A Great Wall: Six Presidents and China: An Investigative History*, New York: Century Foundation Book, 2000, p. 422; Johnston, *Social States*, p. xxiv.
88. Nathan and Shi, 'Cultural Requisites for Democracy in China', p. 116.
89. Todorov, *The Conquest of America*, p. 165.
90. Michael Mandelbaum, 'Westernizing Russia and China', *Foreign Affairs*, 76 (3), 1997, p. 93.
91. Rob Gifford, *China Road: A Journey into the Future of a Rising Power*, New York: Random House, 2007, p. 295.
92. Jonathan Goldstein, 'Cantonese Artefacts, Chinoiserie, and Early American Idealization of China', in Jonathan Goldstein, Jerry Israel and Hilary Conroy (eds), *America Views China: American Images of China Then and Now*, Bethlehem, PA: Lehigh University Press, 1991, p. 51.
93. Quoted in J. Rogers Hollingsworth, *Nation and State Building in America: Comparative Historical Perspectives*, Boston, MA: Little, Brown, 1971, p. 2.
94. Warren I. Cohen, *America's Response to China: A History of Sino-American Relations* (4th edn), New York: Columbia University Press, 2000, p. 179.
95. Quoted in Jonathan D. Spence, *To Change China: Western Advisers in China 1620–1960*, London: Penguin Books, 1980, p. 130.
96. Harry Harding, *A Fragile Relationship: The United States and China since 1972*, Washington, DC: Brookings Institution, 1992, pp. 240–41.
97. Jonathan Unger, 'Recent Trends in Modern China Studies in the English-language World: An Editor's Perspective', in Lucien Bianco et al., *The Development of Contemporary China Studies*, Tokyo: Centre for East Asian Cultural Studies for UNESCO, 1994, p. 183.
98. Quoted in Doug Guthrie, *China and Globalization: The Social, Economic and Political Transformation* (2nd edn), London: Routledge, 2008, p. 286.
99. Roland Barthes, *Mythologies* (trans. Annette Lavers), St Albans: Paladin, 1973, p. 152.
100. Johnston, *Social States*, p. xxiii. See also Johnston and Evans, 'China's Engagement with Multilateral Security Institutions', pp. 255, 257.
101. William A. Callahan, 'Future Imperfect: The European Union's Encounter with China (and the United States)', *Journal of Strategic Studies*, 30 (4), 2007, pp. 779, 784.
102. The European Commission, 'The Sectoral Dialogues between the EU and China – an Overview', Policy Dialogues Support Facility, n.d., http://www.eu-chinapdsf.org/english/Column.asp?ColumnId=5
103. Klein, *Cold War Orientalism*, p. 38.
104. Quoted in ibid., p. 38.
105. Ibid., pp. 38–9, 41–2.
106. Madsen, *China and the American Dream*, p. 80.
107. Ibid., p. 87.
108. Quoted in ibid., p. 80.
109. Richard Rorty, *Contingency, Irony, and Solidarity*, Cambridge: Cambridge University Press, 1989, p. 86.
110. Quoted in Stephen Duncombe, *Dream: Re-imagining Progressive Politics in an Age of Fantasy*, New York: The New Press, 2007, p. 36.
111. Michel Oksenberg, 'Taiwan, Tibet, and Hong Kong in Sino-American Relations', in Ezra F. Vogel, (ed.), *Living with China: U.S./China Relations in the Twenty-First Century*, New York: W. W. Norton, 1997, p. 59.
112. Tang Tsou, *America's Failure in China*, Berkeley, CA: University of California Press, 1963, p. 5.

113. Michael H. Hunt, 'Chinese Foreign Relations in Historical Perspective', in Harry Harding (ed.), *China's Foreign Relations in the 1980s*, New Haven, CT: Yale University Press, 1984, pp. 40–41.
114. Gilley, *China's Democratic Future*, p. xvi.
115. Ling, *Postcolonial International Relations*, p. 119.

CHAPTER 4 THE POLITICAL ECONOMY OF FEAR

1. Hayden White, *The Content of the Form: Narrative Discourse and Historical Representation*. Baltimore, MD: Johns Hopkins University Press, 1987, p. ix.
2. Quoted in Steven Erlanger, 'Searching for an Enemy and Finding China', *New York Times*, 6 April 1997, p. 4.
3. Michael J. Shapiro, *Reading the Postmodern Polity: Political Theory as Textual Practice*, Minneapolis, MN: University of Minnesota Press, 1992, pp. 123, 127.
4. Barry Buzan writes that 'the subjective feeling of safety or confidence has no necessary connections with actually being safe or right'. Barry Buzan, *People, States and Fear: An Agenda for International Security Studies in the Post-Cold War Era* (2nd edn), Hemel Hempstead: Harvester Wheatsheaf, 1991, p. 36.
5. David L. Altheide, *Creating Fear: News and the Construction of Crisis*, New York: Aldine de Gruyter, 2002, pp. 41–2.
6. Shapiro, *Reading the Postmodern Polity*, p. 125.
7. Moïse, *The Geopolitics of Emotion*, p. 92.
8. Niccolò Machiavelli, *The Prince* (trans. George Bull), London: Penguin Books, 1995, p. 52.
9. Robert Higgs, 'Fear: The Foundation of Every Government's Power', *Independent Review*, 10 (3), 2006, pp. 447–66.
10. Quoted in Kenneth N. Waltz, *Man, the State, and War*, New York: Columbia University Press, 1959, p. 81.
11. Adam Smith, quoted in Higgs, 'Fear', p. 461.
12. David W. Chen, 'China Emerges as a Scapegoat in Campaign Ads', *New York Times*, 9 October 2010, p. 1.
13. James Mann, *About Face: A History of America's Curious Relationship with China, from Nixon to Clinton*, New York: Vintage Books, 2000, pp. 260–64.
14. Ibid., p. 266.
15. Ibid., p. 242. For discussion on the partisan influence on U.S. China policy, see Robert Sutter, 'The U.S. Congress: Personal, Partisan, Political', in Ramon H. Myers, Michel C. Oksenberg, and David Shambaugh (eds), *Making China Policy: Lessons from the Bush and Clinton Administrations*, Lanham, MD: Roman & Littlefield, 2001, pp. 79–111.
16. Hillary Clinton Foreign Policy Speech (audio file), 25 February 2008, http://www.prx.org/pieces/24241
17. Lisa Lerer, 'Clinton Adviser Quits Over China Rhetoric', Politico, 19 April 2008, http://www.politico.com/news/stories/0408/9719.html
18. Associated French Press, 'Clinton, Obama Fire New Economic Jabs at China', 14 April 2008, http://www.channelnewsasia.com/stories/afp_world/view/341518/1/.html
19. Kent Wong and Elaine Bernard, 'Rethinking the China Campaign', *New Labor Forum*, No. 7, 2000, http://www.hrichina.org/crf/article/4805
20. Keith Bradsher, 'Senators' China Trip Highlights Their Differences on Currency', *New York Times*, 26 March 2006; Jonathan Weisman, 'In Washington, Chevron Works to Scuttle Chinese Bid', *Washington Post*, 16 July 2005, p. D1.
21. Agencies/FT, 'US Lawmakers Meddle in CNOOC's Unocal Bid', *China Daily*, 6 July 2005. http://www.chinadaily.com.cn/english/doc/2005-07/06/content_457677.htm
22. Tomas Kellner, 'Open for Business', *Forbes*, 6 September 2004. http://www.forbes.com/forbes/2004/0906/106_print.html
23. Joe Klein, 'Think Twice about a Pullout', *Time*, 20 November 2005, http://www.time.com/time/columnist/klein/article/0,9565,1132784,00.html

24. Ibid.
25. Robert Scheer, 'Indefensible Spending', *Los Angeles Times*, 1 June 2008.
26. Chalmers Johnson, *Nemesis: The Last Days of the American Republic*, Melbourne: Scribe Publications, 2006, pp. 273, 138.
27. Quoted in Alex Roland, 'The Military-Industrial Complex: Lobby and Trope', in Andrew J. Bacevich (ed.), *The Long War: A New History of U.S. National Security Policy Since World War II*, New York: Columbia University Press, 2007, p. 339.
28. Quoted in ibid., p. 337.
29. See William D. Hartung and Michelle Ciarrocca, *The Ties that Bind: Arms Industry Influence in the Bush Administration and Beyond* (Special Report), New York: World Policy Institute, October 2004, p. 6; Ismael Hossein-Zadeh, *The Political Economy of U.S. Militarism*, New York: Palgrave Macmillan, 2006, p. 17.
30. Chalmers Johnson, *The Sorrow of Empire: Militarism, Secrecy, and the End of the Republic*, New York: Metropolitan Books, 2004, pp. 62–3.
31. Hossein-Zadeh, *The Political Economy of U.S. Militarism*, p. 17.
32. See ibid., p. 13.
33. Quoted in Helen Caldicott, *The New Nuclear Danger: George W. Bush's Military-Industrial Complex*, New York: The New Press, 2002, p. xix.
34. Martin Feldstein, 'The Underfunded Pentagon', *Foreign Affairs*, 86 (2), 2007, p. 134.
35. C. Wright Mills, *The Power Elite* (new edn), Oxford: Oxford University Press, 2000, p. 275.
36. Quoted in Ted Galen Carpenter, *A Search for Enemies: America's Alliances after the Cold War*, Washington, DC: Cato Institute, 1992, p. 140.
37. Between August 1990, when Iraq invaded Kuwait, and October 1993, Saudi Arabia ordered almost $31 billion US military equipment and services. Dan Smith, 'Arms Sales to Saudi Arabia and Taiwan Video Transcript', The Center for Defense Information, 28 November 1993, http://www.cdi.org/adm/711/
38. Scheer, 'Indefensible Spending'; Valdas Anelauskas, *Discovering America As It Is*, Atlanta, GA: Clarity Press, 1999, p. 413.
39. Mark Thompson, 'Gates Down on the F-22', *Time*, 7 February 2008, http://www.time.com/time/nation/article/0,8599,1710944,00.html
40. Caldicott, *The New Nuclear Danger*, p. xii.
41. Alec Klein, 'The Army's $200 Billion Makeover', *Washington Post*, 7 December 2007, p. A01.
42. Chalmers Johnson, 'The Military-Industrial Man: How Local Politics Works in America—or a "Duke" in Every District', 14 September 2004, http://www.tomdispatch.com/post/1818/chalmers_johnson_on_electing_the_pentagon_s_man
43. Quoted in Hossein-Zadeh, *The Political Economy of U.S. Militarism*, p. 15.
44. US Department of Defense, *Quadrennial Defense Review Report*, 2006, p. 29.
45. 'Disaster Planning', *Journal of Electronic Defense*, 28 (12), 2005, p. 17.
46. Thompson, 'Gates Down on the F-22'.
47. Bettina H. Chavanne, 'General Says USAF Will Procure 380 F-22s, Despite OSD', *Aerospace Daily & Defense Report*, 225 (31), 2008, p. 3.
48. Ted McKenna, 'US DoD Ponders China Threat', *Journal of Electronic Defense*, 28 (9), 2005, p. 33.
49. Fred Kaplan, 'The China Syndrome: Why the Pentagon Keeps Overestimating Beijing's Military Strength', 26 May 2006, http://www.slate.com/id/2141966/
50. Klein, 'Think Twice about a Pullout'.
51. Andrew J. Bacevich, *The New American Militarism: How Americans Are Seduced by War*, Oxford: Oxford University Press, 2005, p. 34.
52. The term 'embedded experts' is borrowed from Jonny Burnett and Dave Whyte, 'Embedded Expertise and the New Terrorism', *Journal for Crime, Conflict and the Media*, 1 (4), 2005, pp. 1–18.

53. Inderjeet Parmar, 'Catalysing Events, Think Tanks and American Foreign Policy Shifts: A Comparative Analysis of the Impacts of Pearl Harbor 1941 and September 11 2001', *Government and Opposition*, 40 (1), 2005, p. 12.

54. William Hartung, *How Much Are You Making on the War, Daddy? A Quick and Dirty Guide to War Profiteering in the George W. Bush Administration*, New York: Nation Books, 2003, p. 58.

55. J. Michael Waller, 'Blue Team Takes on Red China', *Insight Magazine*, 17 (21), 2001, p. 24; see also Robert G. Kaiser and Steven Mufson, '"Blue Team" Draws a Hard Line on Beijing: Action on Hill Reflects Informal Group's Clout', *Washington Post*, 22 February 2000, p. A1.

56. The Weekly Standard, *The Weekly Standard Media Kit*, January 2010, http://www.weeklystandard.com/advertising/mediakit.pdf

57. Hartung, *How Much Are You Making on the War, Daddy?*, p. 113.

58. William D. Hartung and Michelle Ciarrocca, 'Reviving Star Wars', *The Baltimore Sun*, 21 January 2001, http://articles.baltimoresun.com/2001-01-21/topic/0101200170_1_nmd-national-missile-defense-system/2

59. Oren, *Our Enemies and US*, p. 187n48.

60. See Chalmers Johnson, 'The CIA and Me', *Bulletin of Concerned Asian Scholars*, 29 (1), 1997, pp. 34–7.

61. Nicholas Turse, 'The Military-Academic Complex', TomDispatch, 29 April 2004, http://www.countercurrents.org/us-turse290404.htm

62. Hartung, *How Much Are You Making on the War, Daddy?*, p. 101; and Caldicott, *The New Nuclear Danger*, p. 27.

63. Kurt Campbell, 'China Watchers Fighting a Turf War of Their Own', *New York Times*, 20 May 2000, p. B13.

64. Christopher Simpson, 'Universities, Empire, and the Production of Knowledge: An Introduction', in Christopher Simpson (ed.), *Universities and Empire: Money and Politics in the Social Sciences During the Cold War*, New York: The New Press, 1998, p. xviii; and Lawrence Soley, 'The New Corporate Yen for Scholarship', in Christopher Simpson (ed.), *Universities and Empire: Money and Politics in the Social Sciences During the Cold War*, New York: The New Press, 1998, p. 232; and Cumings, *Parallax Visions*, Chapter 7.

65. See Cohen, 'Pentagon to Consult Academics on Security', p. 1.

66. US Department of Defense, 'The Minerva Initiative', http://minerva.dtic.mil/

67. On Project Camelot, see Mark Solovey, 'Project Camelot and the 1960s Epistemological Revolution: Rethinking the Politics-Patronage-Social Science Nexus', *Social Studies of Science*, 31 (2), 2001, pp. 171–206. For a Chinese view on the Minerva Initiative, see Yu Tiejun and Qi Haotian, 'Meiguo Guofangbu "Miniewa" Jihua shuping' (Notes on the US Defense Department's 'Minerva' Initiative), *Zhanlue zongheng* (Strategic Survey) (Center for International & Strategic Studies, Peking University), 2011–12, pp. 1–21.

68. Soley, 'The New Corporate Yen for Scholarship', p. 235.

69. Walter Pincus, 'Taiwan Paid State Nominee for Papers on U.N. Reentry; Bolton's Objectivity on China Is Questioned', *Washington Post*, 9 April 2001, p. A17.

70. See Richard J. Newman and Kevin Whitelaw, 'China: How Big a Threat? Inside the Bitter Fight Over Assessing China's Intentions', *U.S. News and World Report*, 23 July 2001, http://www.fas.org/sgp/news/2001/07/usn072301.html

71. Monaghan, 'Does International-Relations Scholarship Reflect a Bias Toward the U.S.?', p. A21.

72. See Foucault, *Power/Knowledge*, pp. 96, 102.

73. Cumings, *Parallax Visions*, p. 174.

CHAPTER 5 A SELF-FULFILLING PROPHECY

1. Alexander Wendt, *Social Theory of International Politics*, Cambridge: Cambridge University Press, 1999, p. 263.

2.   Gries, *China's New Nationalism*, p. 135.
3.   Charles Frazier, *Cold Mountain*, New York: Vintage Books, 1997, p. 17.
4.   Richard N. Haass, *The Opportunity: America's Moment to Alter History's Course*, New York: PublicAffairs, 2005, p. 25.
5.   Quoted in Robert Jervis, *Perception and Misperception in International Relations*, Princeton, NJ: Princeton University Press, 1976, pp. 76–7.
6.   William I. Thomas and Dorothy S. Thomas, *The Child in America*, New York: Alfred A. Knopf, 1928, pp. 571–2.
7.   Thucydides, *History of the Peloponnesian War* (trans. Rex Warner), London: Penguin Books, 1972, p. 49.
8.   X (George Kennan), 'The Sources of Soviet Conduct', *Foreign Affairs*, 25 (4), 1947, p. 569.
9.   Thomas J. Christensen, 'Fostering Stability or Creating a Monster? The Rise of China and U.S. Policy Toward East Asia', *International Security*, 31 (1), 2006, p. 108.
10.   Quoted in Michael H. Hunt, *Ideology and U.S. Foreign Policy*, New Haven, CT: Yale University Press, 1987, p. xi.
11.   Joseph S. Nye, Jr., 'Scholars on the Sidelines', *Washington Post*, 13 April 2009; Bruce W. Jentleson and Ely Ratner, 'Bridging the Beltway-Ivory Tower Gap', *International Studies Review*, 13 (2), 2011, pp. 6–11; and Allan Gyngell and Michael Wesley, *Making Australian Foreign Policy* (2nd edn), Cambridge: Cambridge University Press, 2007, pp. 7–8.
12.   Bernard Schaffer, 'Policy Making', in Adam Kuper and Jessica Kuper (eds), *The Social Science Encyclopedia* (2nd edn), London: Routledge, 1996, p. 621.
13.   Frank Bruni, 'For Bush, a Mission and a Role in History', *New York Times*, 22 September 2001, p. A1. After addressing a Joint Session of Congress on 20 September 2001, Bush said that 'I have never felt more comfortable in my life'. Bob Woodward, *Bush at War*, New York: Simon & Schuster, 2002, p. 109.
14.   Bernstein and Munro, *The Coming Conflict with China*, p. 203.
15.   Mearsheimer, *The Tragedy of Great Power Politics*, p. 402.
16.   Charles Krauthammer, 'Why We Must Contain China', *Time*, 31 July 1995, p. 72.
17.   Peter Navarro, *The Coming China Wars*, p. 199.
18.   Ibid., pp. 201–3.
19.   Kagan and Kristol, 'Introduction', p. 20.
20.   Ibid., p. 20.
21.   Bacevich, *The New American Militarism*, p. 89.
22.   *The Weekly Standard Media Kit*.
23.   Dan Blumenthal, Aaron Friedberg, Randall Schriver and Ashley J. Tellis, 'Bush Should Keep His Word on Taiwan', *Wall Street Journal*, 19 July 2008, p. A9.
24.   Neil King Jr., 'Secret Weapon: Inside Pentagon, a Scholar Shapes Views of China', *Wall Street Journal*, 8 September 2005, p. A1.
25.   US Department of Defense, *Quadrennial Defense Review Report*, 2006, p. 29.
26.   Soyoung Ho, 'Panda Slugger', *Washington Monthly*, 38 (7), 2006, p. 27.
27.   Michael Green, 'US Turns Its Gaze to the Pacific', *The World Today*, 68 (2), 2012, p. 32.
28.   Nicholas Phan, 'U.S.-Japan Security Alliance under the Democratic Party of Japan (DPJ)', in the Edwin O. Reischauer Center for East Asian Studies, (ed.), *The United States and Japan in Global Context: 2011*, Washington DC: The Johns Hopkins University Paul H. Nitze School of Advanced International Studies, 2011, p. 17.
29.   Robert S. Ross, 'Assessing the China Threat', *National Interest*, No. 81, 2005, pp. 81–7.
30.   See Richard Halloran, 'Guam to Become the "Pivot Point" for the US' Pacific Forces', *Taipei Times*, 14 March 2006; and Simon Tisdall, 'Japan Emerges as America's Deputy Sheriff in the Pacific', *The Guardian*, 19 April 2005, p. 13; Johnson, *Nemesis*, p. 202.
31.   Daniel Twining, 'America's Grand Design in Asia', *The Washington Quarterly*, 30 (3), 2007, p. 85; and John Gershman, 'Asia', in John Feffer (ed.), *Power Trip: U.S. Unilateralism and Global Strategy After September 11*, New York: Seven Stories Press, 2003, p. 162.

32. Quoted in Michael T. Klare, 'Revving Up the China Threat', *The Nation*, 24 October 2005, p. 32.
33. Margaret Talev, Tom Lasseter and Kevin G. Hall, 'China Looms as Obama Tries to Strengthen Ties with Asian Democracies', *Pittsburgh Post-Gazette*, 14 November 2010, p. A-3.
34. Hugh White, 'Mr President, We Beg to Differ over the Future of Asia', *The Age*, 16 November 2011, p. 21.
35. Purnendra Jain, 'A "Little NATO" against China', *Asia Times Online*, 18 March 2006, http://www.atimes.com/atimes/China/HC18Ad01.html.
36. Quoted in Simon Tisdall, 'US Tries to Spin a Web Strong Enough to Contain China', *The Guardian*, 10 August 2005, p. 12.
37. Paul Richter, 'In Deal with India, Bush Has Eye on China', *Los Angeles Times*, 4 March 2006; Twining, 'America's Grand Design in Asia', pp. 82–3 and p. 92n19.
38. Berger, 'Don't Antagonize China', p. B7.
39. Richard C. Bush and Michael E. O'Hanlon, *A War Like No Other: The Truth about China's Challenge to America*, Hoboken, NJ: John Wiley & Sons, 2007, p. 27.
40. Jean A. Garrison, *Making China Policy: From Nixon to G. W. Bush*, Boulder, CO: Lynne Rienner, 2005, p. 179.
41. William M. Arkin, 'America's New China War Plan', *Washington Post*, 24 May 2006. http://blog.washingtonpost.com/earlywarning/2006/05/americas_new_china_war_plan.html
42. Ibid.
43. See A. Tom Grunfeld, '"God We Had Fun": CIA in China and Sino-American Relations', *Critical Asian Studies*, 35 (1), 2003, pp. 125–6.
44. Robert D. Kaplan, 'How We Would Fight China', *Atlantic Monthly*, 295 (5), 2005, pp. 58–9.
45. Bill Gertz, 'Pentagon "Hedge" Strategy Targets China', *Washington Times*, 17 March 2006, p. A06.
46. Keir A. Lieber and Daryl G. Press, 'Superiority Complex', *Atlantic Monthly*, 300 (1), 2007, p. 88.
47. See Michael R. Gordon, 'To Build Trust, U.S. Navy Holds a Drill with China', *New York Times*, 23 September 2006, p. A5.
48. Marshall, 'Building a Bridge to China'.
49. Martin Crutsinger, 'U.S. Hardens Stance on Trade with China', Associated Press, 14 February 2006; and Jon Cronin, 'Fears of Growing US Trade Rift with China', BBC News, 17 February 2006, http://news.bbc.co.uk/1/hi/business/4719826.stm.
50. Frank Hornig and Wieland Wagner, 'Dueling Titans: China, the US and Battle to Lead a Globalized World', *Spiegel Online*, 3 February 2006, http://www.spiegel.de/international/spiegel/0,1518,398844,00.html
51. Foster Klug, 'Gates Says US Ready for Any China "Threat"', Associated Press Newswires, 28 January 2009; Kenneth Lieberthal, 'The American Pivot to Asia', Foreign Policy Online, 21 December 2011, http://www.foreignpolicy.com/articles/2011/12/21/the_american_pivot_to_asia
52. Walter Russell Mead, 'Softly, Softly: Beijing Turns Other Cheek – For Now', *The American Interest*, 19 November 2011, http://blogs.the-american-interest.com/wrm/2011/11/19/softly-softly-beijing-turns-other-cheek-for-now/
53. Similar 'realities' in India, for example, have generated rather different perceptions on the part of the US. See Priya Chacko, 'Interpreting the "Rise of India": India-US Relations, Power Transition and Ontological Security', paper presented at the ISA Asia-Pacific Regional Section Inaugural Conference, Brisbane, 29–30 September 2011.
54. Judith Goldstein and Robert O. Keohane, 'Ideas and Foreign Policy: An Analytical Framework', in Judith Goldstein and Robert O. Keohane (eds), *Ideas and Foreign Policy: Beliefs, Institutions, and Political Change*, Ithaca, NY: Cornell University Press, 1993, p. 12.
55. Munro, 'China: The Challenge of a Rising Power', pp. 48–9.
56. International Security Advisory Board, *China's Strategic Modernization*, p. 6.

57. Robert Kagan and William Kristol, 'A National Humiliation', *Weekly Standard*, 16–23 April 2001, p. 14.
58. Lampton, *Same Bed, Different Dreams*, p. 49.
59. Marshall, 'Building a Bridge to China'.
60. Otto Klineberg, *The Human Dimension in International Relations*, New York: Holt, Rinehart and Winston, 1964, p. 151.
61. See Krepinevich, *Why AirSea Battle?*
62. Wang Jisi and Wang Yong, 'A Chinese Account: The Interaction of Policies', in Ramon H. Myers, Michel C. Oksenberg and David Shambaugh (eds), *Making China Policy: Lessons from the Bush and Clinton Administrations*, Lanham, MD: Roman & Littlefield, 2001, p. 277.
63. See Cohen, *America's Response to China*.
64. Johnston, *Cultural Realism*; Fairbank, *China Perceived*, pp. 136–7; James Townsend, 'Chinese Nationalism', *The Australian Journal of Chinese Affairs*, No. 27, 1992, p. 113; and John Fitzgerald, 'The Nationless State: The Search for a Nation in Modern Chinese Nationalism', in Jonathan Unger (ed.), *Chinese Nationalism*, Armonk, NY: M. E. Sharpe, 1996, p. 61.
65. Joseph Fewsmith and Stanley Rosen, 'The Domestic Context of Chinese Foreign Policy: Does "Public Opinion" Matter?' in David M. Lampton (ed.), *The Making of Chinese Foreign and Security Policy in the Era of Reform, 1978–2000*, Stanford, CA: Stanford University Press, 2001, p. 186.
66. Suisheng Zhao, '"We are Patriots First and Democrats Second": The Rise of Chinese Nationalism in the 1990s', in Edward Friedman and Barrett McCormick (eds), *What If China Doesn't Democratize?* Armonk, New York: M. E. Sharpe, 2000, pp. 24–5.
67. See Zheng, *Discovering Chinese Nationalism in China*, p. 90.
68. Kenneth Lieberthal, *Governing China: From Revolution Through Reform* (2nd edn), New York: W. W. Norton, 2003, p. 222.
69. Quoted in Suisheng Zhao, 'The Olympics and Chinese Nationalism', *China Security*, 4 (3), 2008, p. 48.
70. Suisheng Zhao, 'Chinese Foreign Policy: Pragmatism and Strategic Behavior', in Suisheng Zhao (ed.), *Chinese Foreign Policy: Pragmatism and Strategic Behaviour*, Armonk, NY: M. E. Sharpe, 2004, p. 7.
71. See Shih, *Navigating Sovereignty*, pp. 128–9; Thomas A. Metzger and Ramon H. Myers. 'Chinese Nationalism and American Policy', *Orbis*, 42 (1), 1998, p. 35; Fei-ling Wang, 'Self-Image and Strategic Intentions: National Confidence and Political Insecurity', in Yong Deng and Fei-ling Wang (eds), *In the Eyes of the Dragon: China Views the World*, Lanham, MD: Rowman & Littlefield, 1999, p. 35; Christopher Hughes, 'Globalisation and Nationalism: Squaring the Circle in Chinese International Relations Theory', *Millennium: Journal of International Studies*, 26 (1), 1997, p. 123; Zhao, 'The Olympics and Chinese Nationalism', p. 54.
72. David Zweig, *Internationalizing China: Domestic Interests and Global Linkages*, Ithaca, NY: Cornell University Press, 2002.
73. Zheng, *Discovering Chinese Nationalism in China*, p. 50.
74. Su Xiaokang and Wang Luxiang, *Deathsong of the River: A Reader's Guide to the Chinese TV Series Heshang* (trans. and (eds), Richard W. Bodman and Pin P. Wan), Ithaca: Cornell East Asia Series, 1991. Sometimes the title of this TV series is also translated as *River Elegy*.
75. See Madsen, *China and the American Dream*, p. 196; Merle Goldman, Perry Link and Su Wei, 'China's Intellectuals in the Deng Era: Loss of Identity with the State', in Lowell Dittmer and Samuel S. Kim (eds), *China's Quest for National Identity*, Ithaca, NY: Cornell University Press, 1993, p. 145.
76. Wang Xiaodong, 'Zhongguo de minzuzhuyi he Zhongguo de weilai' (Chinese Nationalism and China's Future), in Fang Ning, Wang Xiaodong, Song Qiang, et al., *Quanqiuhua yinying xia de Zhongguo zhilu* (China's Road under the Shadow of Globalisation), Beijing: Zhongguo shehuikexue chubanshe, 1999, pp. 82–6.

77. Song Qiang et al., *Zhongguo keyi shuo bu: Lengzhan hou shidai de zhengzhi yu qinggan jueze* (China Can Say No: Political and Sentimental Choices During the Post-Cold War Era), Beijing: Zhonghua Gongshang Lianhe Chubanshe, 1996. Indeed, this book quickly sparked a new genre of 'say no' literature in China. See, for example, Zhang Zangzang et al., *Zhongguo haishi keyi shuo bu: Guoji guanxi bianshu yu women de xianshi yingdui* (China Still Can Say No: International Relations Factors and Our Realistic Response), Beijing: Zhonghua Gongshang Lianhe Chubanshe, 1996; Peng Qian et al., *Zhongguo weishenme shuo bu?* (Why Does China Say No?), Beijing: Xinshijie Chubanshe, 1996; Xi Laiwang, *Ershiyi shiji Zhongguo zhanlue da cehua: Waijiao moulue* (China's Grand Strategy into the Twenty-first Century: Strategic Calculus of China's Diplomacy), Beijing: Hongqi Chubanshe, 1996; Chen Feng et al., *Zhong Mei jiaoliang da xiezhen* (True Stories of Sino-America Contention), Beijing: Zhongguo Renshi Chubanshe, 1996; Guo Jishan, *Zouxiang zuguo tongyi de zuji* (Steps Toward the Reunification of the Motherland), Beijing: Hongqi Chubanshe, 1996; and Li Xiguang, Liu Kang, et al., *Yaomohua Zhongguo de beihou* (Behind the Demonisation of China), Beijing: Zhongguo shehui kexue chubanshe, 1996.

78. Aihwa Ong, *Flexible Citizenship: The Cultural Logics of Transnationality*, Durham, NC: Duke University Press, 1999, p. 197.

79. In July-August 1993, The *Yinhe*, a Chinese vessel, suspected by the U.S. to be carrying chemical weapon materials to Iran, was pursued by U.S. warships and aircraft and eventually was forced to accept U.S. inspection of its cargo in Saudi Arabia. While no such chemicals aboard the ship were found, the U.S. refused to apologise for its action. See Tyler, *A Great Wall*, pp. 396–400.

80. See William A. Callahan, 'Report on Conferences: Nationalism & International Relations in China', Centre for Contemporary China Studies, Durham University, 2002. www.dur.ac.uk/resources/china.studies/shanghaireportonthe%20conference.doc

81. Song Qiang et al., *Zhongguo keyi shuo bu*, p. 2 (Preface).

82. Song Qiang, 'Cang tian dang si, huang tian dang li' (The Blue Sky Must Die, and the Yellow Sky Must Stand Up), in Song Qiang et al., *Zhongguo keyi shuo bu: Lengzhan hou shidai de zhengzhi yu qinggan jueze* (China Can Say No: Political and Sentimental Choices During the Post-Cold War Era), Beijing: Zhonghua Gongshang Lianhe Chubanshe, 1996, pp. 1–51.

83. Li Xiguang et al., *Yaomohua Zhongguo de beihou*, p. 2.

84. Elisabeth Rosenthal, 'China Students Are Caught Up by Nationalism', *New York Times*, 12 May 1999, p. A1.

85. Simon Shen, *Redefining Nationalism in Modern China*, Basingstoke: Palgrave, 2007, p. 59.

86. During an online chat with netizens through *Qiangguo luntan* in June 2008, Chinese President Hu Jintao stressed that this online forum was one of his favourite websites. *Qiangguo luntan*, 'Hu Jintao Zongshuji tong wangyou zaixian jiaoliu' (General Secretary Hu Jintao's Online Chats with Netizens), 20 June 2008, http://www.people.com.cn/GB/32306/33093/125024/index.html

87. Quoted in Zhao, 'The Olympics and Chinese Nationalism', p. 52.

88. Fan Shiming, 'Aihen jiaorong' zhong de fan Mei zhuyi' (Anti-Americanism in a 'Love-Hate' Complex), *Guoji zhengzhi yanjiu* (International Politics Quarterly), No. 2, 2005, p. 57.

89. Zheng, *Discovering Chinese Nationalism in China*, p. 156.

90. Thomas Christensen, 'Chinese Realpolitik', *Foreign Affairs*, 75 (5), 1996, p. 37.

91. Zhang Wenmu, 'Quanqiuhua jincheng zhong de Zhongguo guojia liyi' (China's National Interests in the Process of Globalisation), *Zhanlue yu guanli* (Strategy and Management), No. 1, 2002, p. 58.

92. Zhu Feng, 'Guojiguanxi lilun zai Zhongguo de fazhan: Wenti yu sikao' (The Development of International Relations Theory in China: Problems and Reflection), *Shijie jingji yu zhengzhi* (World Economics and International Politics), No. 3, 2003, p. 25.

93. Zhang Ruizhuang, 'Zhongguo ying xuanze shenmeyang de waijiao zhexue?' (What Kind of Foreign Policy Thinking Should China Choose?), *Zhanlue yu guanli* (Strategy and

Management), no. 1, 1999, p. 61; Zhang Ruizhuang, '"Chenzhuo yingdui" yu "zifeiwugong"' ('Meet Challenges with Calm' and 'Voluntarily Relinquish One's Own Prowess'), *Shijie jingji yu zhengzhi* (World Economics and International Politics), no. 1, 2002, p. 72.

94. Yan Xuetong, *Zhongguo guojia liyi fenxi* (An Analysis of China's National Interests), Tianjin: Tianjin renmin chubanshe, 1996, p. 311. See also Wang Xiaodong, '99 duanxiang' (Reflections on the Year 1999), in Fang Ning, Wang Xiaodong, Song Qiang, et al., *Quanqiuhua yinying xia de Zhongguo zhilu* (China's Road under the Shadow of Globalisation), Beijing: Zhongguo shehuikexue chubanshe, 1999, p. 44.

95. Michael H. Hunt, 'CCP Foreign Policy: "Normalizing" the Field', in Michael H. Hunt and Niu Jun (eds), *Toward a History of Chinese Communist Foreign Relations, 1920s–1960s: Personalities and Interpretive Approaches*, Washington, DC: Woodrow Wilson Center Asia Program, n.d., p. 173.

96. Mark Leonard, *What Does China Think?* New York: PublicAffairs, 2008, pp. 90–91.

97. Daniel A. Bell, 'Introduction', in Yan Xuetong et al., *Ancient Chinese Thought, Modern Chinese Power*, Princeton, NJ: Princeton University Press, 2011, pp. 1–2.

98. Shen, *Redefining Nationalism in Modern China*, p. 89.

99. Wang Yizhou, *Quanqiu zhengzhi he Zhongguo waijiao: Tanxue xin de shijiao yu jieshi* (Global Politics and China's Foreign Policy: In Search of New Perspectives and Interpretations), Beijing: Shijie zhishi chubanshe, 2003, p. 10; and Wang Yizhou, *Dangdai guoji zhengzhi xilun* (An Analysis of Contemporary International Politics), Shanghai: Shanghai renmin chubanshe, 1995, p. 13.

100. The 'impact-response' approach, championed by John K. Fairbank, was widely used in the study of Chinese history and its international relations during the twentieth century. For a critique of this approach, see Cohen, *Discovering History in China*.

101. Ssu-yu Teng and John K. Fairbank et al., *China's Response to the West: A Documentary Survey 1839–1923*, Cambridge, MA: Harvard University Press, 1954, pp. 26, 28.

102. Andrew J. Nathan and Bruce Gilley, *China's New Rulers: The Secret Files*, New York: New York Review of Books, 2002, p. 207.

103. Ibid., pp. 207–8.

104. Gries, *China's New Nationalism*, p. 138.

105. Hutton, *The Writing on the Wall*, p. 235; see also Morton Abramowitz and Stephen Bosworth, 'America Confronts the Asian Century', *Current History*, 105 (690), 2006, p. 150.

106. John Pomfret, 'U.S Now a "Threat" in China's Eyes', *Washington Post*, 15 November 2000, p. A1.

107. Clinton, *My Life*, p. 855.

108. Edward Friedman, 'Reflecting Mirrors across the Taiwan Straits: American Perspectives on a China threat', in Herbert Yee and Ian Storey (eds), *The China Threat: Perceptions, Myths and Reality*, London: RoutledgeCurzon, 2002, p. 76; Lampton, *Same Bed, Different Dreams*, p. 251–2.

109. Owen Harries, 'A Year of Debating China', *The National Interest*, No. 58, 1999/2000, p. 145.

110. Shen, *Redefining Nationalism in Modern China*, p. 60.

111. Klare, 'Revving up the China Threat', p. 29.

112. Glenn C. Buchan, David Matonick, Calvin Shipbaugh and Richard Mesic, *Future Roles of U.S. Nuclear Forces: Implications for U.S. Strategy*, Santa Monica, CA: RAND, 2003, p. 92.

113. Shen Dingli, 'US-S. Korean Maritime War Games Needlessly Provocative', *Global Times*, 14 July 2010, http://opinion.globaltimes.cn/commentary/2010-07/551234.html

114. Al Pessin, 'US, South Korean Navies Will Exercise in Yellow Sea Despite Chinese Objections', Voice of America, 14 July 2010, http://www.voanews.com/english/news/US-South-Korean-Navies-Will-Exercise-in-Yellow-Sea-Despite-Chinese-Objections-98453279.html

115. Mann, *About Face*, p. 266.

116. Wang Jisi, 'China's Search for Stability with America', *Foreign Affairs*, 84 (5), 2005, pp. 39–48; Jia Qingguo, 'Learning to Live with the Hegemon: Evolution of China's Policy toward the US since the End of the Cold War', *Journal of Contemporary China*, 14 (44), 2005, pp. 395–407; and Zhu Feng, 'China's Rise Will Be Peaceful: How Unipolarity Matters', in Robert S. Ross and Zhu Feng (eds), *China's Ascent: Power, Security, and the Future of International Politics*, Ithaca, NY: Cornell University Press, 2008, pp. 34–54.

117. Robert Axelrod, *The Evolution of Cooperation* (rev. edn), New York: Basic Books, 2006, pp. 120–21.

118. See Andrew Small, *Preventing the Next Cold War: A View from Beijing*, London: Foreign Policy Centre, 2005, pp. 37–46.

119. *China's National Defense in 2008*, Beijing: China State Council Information Office, 20 January 2009, p. 6.

120. Ashton B. Carter and Jennifer C. Bulkeley, 'America's Strategic Response to China's Military Modernization', *Harvard Asia Pacific Review*, 1 (9), 2007, p. 50; see also Brad Roberts, Robert A. Manning and Ronald N. Montaperto, 'China: The Forgotten Nuclear Power', *Foreign Affairs*, 79 (4), 2000, pp. 53–4.

121. Lampton, *Same Bed, Different Dreams*, p. 73.

122. Owen Harries, 'How Not to Handle China', *National Review*, 149 (9), 1997, p. 36 (emphasis in original).

123. Chalmers Johnson, 'Containing China: U.S. and Japan Drift Toward Disaster', *Japan Quarterly*, 43 (4), 1996, p. 12.

124. Ching Cheong, 'US Plans Huge Show of Force in Pacific', *Straits Times*, 30 June 2004.

125. Kenneth B. Sherman, 'Flashpoint Taiwan Straits', *Journal of Electronic Defense*, 27 (11), 2004, p. 57.

126. Peter Hays Gries, 'Nationalism and Chinese Foreign Policy', in Yong Deng and Fei-ling Wang (eds), *China Rising: Power and Motivation in Chinese Foreign Policy*, Lanham, MD: Rowman & Littlefield, 2005, p. 104.

127. Shen, *Redefining Nationalism in Modern China*, p. 78.

128. See Gries, 'Nationalism and Chinese Foreign Policy', p. 112.

129. Peter Lee, 'The New Face of U.S.-China Relations: "Strategic Reassurance" or Old-Fashioned Rollback?' *The Asia-Pacific Journal: Japan Focus*, 19 July 2010.

130. 'US Has to Pay for Provoking China' (editorial), *Global Times*, 6 July 2010.

131. Michael Sainsbury, 'Our Hard Line Turns Out to Be Prescient', *The Australian*, 8 January 2011, p. 10.

132. Roberts, Manning and Montaperto, 'China: The Forgotten Nuclear Power', p. 59.

133. Carter and Bulkeley, 'America's Strategic Response to China's Military Modernization', p. 52; Steven Lee Myers, 'Study Said to Find U.S. Missile Shield Might Incite China', *New York Times*, 10 August 2000, p. 1.

134. Mike Moore, 'A New Cold War?' *SAIS Review*, 16 (1), 2006, p. 183. See also Johnson, *Nemesis*, p. 215.

135. Victor Mallet, 'The Geopolitical Genius of China's Satellite Kill', *Financial Times*, 25 January 2007, p. 11. See also Noam Chomsky, *Imperial Ambitions: Conversations with Noam Chomsky on the Post-9/11 World* (Interviews with David Barsamian), New York: Metropolitan Books, 2005, p. 86.

136. David M. Lampton, *The Three Faces of Chinese Power: Might, Money, and Minds*, Berkeley, CA: University of California Press, 2008, p. 113.

137. See Michael Hunt, *Crisis in U.S. Foreign Policy: An International History Reader*, New Haven, CT: Yale University Press, 1996, pp. 170–71; Lampton, *Same Bed, Different Dreams*, p. 356.

138. Jervis, *Perception and Misperception in International Relations*, p. 74.

139. See Kenneth Lieberthal and Wang Jisi, *Assessing U.S.-China Strategic Distrust* (John L. Thornton China Center Monograph Series, No. 4), Washington DC: Brookings Institution, 2012.

CHAPTER 6 FALSE PROMISES (AND PREMISES)

1. Spence, *To Change China*, p. 278.
2. John Bryan Starr, *Understanding China*, London: Profile Books, 1997, p. 304.
3. Robert A. Kapp's Testimony, in *United States-China Trade Relations: Hearing before the Subcommittee on Trade, Committee on Ways and Means, US House of Representatives, One Hundred Third Congress, Second Session*, Washington, DC: US Government Printing Office, 24 February 1994, p. 194.
4. Clinton, *My Life*, p. 598.
5. Quoted in Paul A. Papayoanou and Scott L. Kastner, 'Sleeping with the (Potential) Enemy: Assessing the U.S. Policy of Engagement with China', *Security Studies*, 9 (1), 1999, p. 157.
6. Quoted in Mann, *The China Fantasy*, p. 2.
7. Quoted in ibid., p. 3.
8. Johnston and Evans, 'China's Engagement with Multilateral Security Institutions', p. 235.
9. See Kent, *China, The United Nations and Human Rights*. According to Michael Yahuda, 'China may be said to have become a status quo power in the sense of the way that is understood by the "English School". China has internalized the norms of inter-state regional order'. Michael Yahuda, 'China's Multilateralism and Regional Order', in Guoguang Wu and Helen Lansdowne (eds), *China Turns to Multilateralism: Foreign Policy and Regional Security*, London: Routledge, 2008, p. 88; Johnston and Evans, 'China's Engagement with Multilateral Security Institutions', pp. 239–44.
10. Chengxin Pan, '"Peaceful Rise" and China's New International Contract: The State in Change in Transnational Society', in Linda Chelan Li (ed.), *The Chinese State in Transition: Processes and Contests in Local China*, London: Routledge, 2009, pp. 127–44.
11. Barrett L. McCormick, 'Conclusion: Points of Agreement and Disagreement and a Few Thoughts on U.S.-Chinese Relations', in Edward Friedman and Barrett McCormick (eds), *What If China Doesn't Democratize?* Armonk, New York: M. E. Sharpe, 2000, p. 332.
12. Kent, *China, the United Nations, and Human Rights*, p. 2; Guy Sorman, *The Empire of Lies: The Truth About China in the Twenty-First Century* (trans. Asha Puri), New York: Encounter Books, 2008, p. xix; and Mann, *The China Fantasy*, p. 24.
13. John Peterson, 'José Manuel Barroso = Political Scientist: John Peterson Interviews the European Commission President', *EU-Consent* (Constructing Europe Network), 17 July 2007, pp. 4–5, http://www.eu-consent.net/library/BARROSO-transcript.pdf
14. Kagan, *Of Paradise and Power*, p. 3.
15. See Katinka Barysch with Charles Grant and Mark Leonard, *Embracing the Dragon: The EU's Partnership with China*, London: Centre for European Reform, 2005, p. 52.
16. Robert S. Ross, 'Engagement in US China Policy', in Alastair Iain Johnston and Robert S. Ross, (eds), *Engaging China: The Management of an Emerging Power*, London: Routledge, 1999, p. 201; and Charles A. Kupchan, *The End of the American Era*, New York: Vantage Books, 2002, p. 275–6.
17. Alastair Iain Johnston and Robert S. Ross, 'Conclusion', in Alastair Iain Johnston and Robert S. Ross, (eds), *Engaging China: The Management of an Emerging Power*, London: Routledge, 1999, p. 278.
18. John Owen notes that 'If the United States is an imperial power, the world may never have known such a benevolent empire'. John M. Owen, 'Transnational Liberalism and U.S. Primacy', *International Security*, 26 (3), 2002, p. 151; Adrian Hyde-Price, 'A "Tragic Actor"? A Realist Perspective on "Ethical Power Europe"', *International Affairs*, 84 (1), 2008, p. 29.
19. Clinton, *My Life*, p. 598.
20. Kristol and Kagan, 'Introduction', p. 20.
21. Johnston and Evans, 'China's Engagement with Multilateral Security Institutions'; Kent, *China, The United Nations and Human Rights*, p. 7; and Johnston, *Social States*.
22. Quoted in Duncombe, *Dream*, p. 2. For a critique of ontological privileging of 'our' rules and 'our' society as a 'manifested' reality, see Ronen Palan, 'A World of Their Making: An

Evaluation of the Constructivist Critique of International Relations', *Review of International Studies*, 26 (4), 2000, pp. 575–98.

23. Emmanuel Levinas, *Time and the Other* (trans. Richard A. Cohen), Pittsburgh: Duquesne University Press, 1987, p. 83.

24. David S. G. Goodman, 'How Open Is Chinese Society?', in David S. G. Goodman and Gerald Segal (eds), *China Rising: Nationalism and Interdependence*, London: Routledge, 1997, pp. 27–52.

25. See Nick Knight, *Imagining Globalisation in China: Debates on Ideology, Politics and Culture*, Cheltenham: Edward Elgar, 2008, pp. 70–72, 201.

26. Qian Qichen, 'U.S. Strategy to Be Blamed', *China Daily*, 1 November 2004.

27. Kagan, *The Return of History and the End of Dreams*, p. 9.

28. Liu Fei, 'Intergovernmentalism and China-EU Relations', in David Kerr and Liu Fei (eds), *The International Politics of EU-China Relations*, Oxford: Oxford University Press, 2007, p. 119; and Barysch et al., *Embracing the Dragon*, p. 8.

29. Kalypso Nicolaïdis and Robert Howse, '"This Is My EUtopia...": Narrative as Power', *Journal of Common Market Studies*, 40 (4), 2002, pp. 771, 781 (emphasis added).

30. Peter J. Katzenstein and Robert O. Keohane, 'Conclusion: Anti-Americanism and the Polyvalence of America', in Peter J. Katzenstein and Robert O. Keohane (eds), *Anti-Americanisms in World Politics*, Ithaca, NY: Cornell University Press, 2007, p. 306.

31. Huntington, *The Third Wave*, pp. 29–30.

32. Bacevich, *The New American Militarism*, p. 1.

33. See Huntington, *Who Are We?* p. 147.

34. Gress, *From Plato to NATO*, p. 3.

35. See Moïsi, *The Geopolitics of Emotion*, Chapter 4.

36. Gress, *From Plato to NATO*, p. 16.

37. Said, *Orientalism*; Neumann, *Uses of the Other*.

38. Harries, 'The Collapse of "the West"', p. 42.

39. Madsen, *China and the American Dream*, p. 218.

40. Hongying Wang, 'Multilateralism in Chinese Foreign Policy: The Limits of Socialization', in Weixing Hu, Gerald Chan and Daojiong Zha (eds), *China's International Relations in the 21st Century: Dynamics of Paradigm Shifts*, Lanham, MD: University Press of America, 2000, p. 82.

41. Friedman, *National Identity and Democratic Prospects in Socialist China*, p. 4.

42. Foot, *Rights Beyond Borders*, p. 13.

43. Gutmann, *Losing the New China*, p. 156.

44. Quoted in George Monbiot, 'The Most Potent Weapon Wielded by the Empires of Murdoch and China', *The Guardian*, 22 April 2008, p. 29.

45. Yunxiang Yan, 'McDonald's in Beijing: The Localization of Americana', in James L. Watson (ed.), *Golden Arches East: McDonald's in East Asia* (2nd edn), Stanford, CA: Stanford University Press, 2006, pp. 57, 75.

46. McGregor, *One Billion Customers*, p. 291.

47. Spence, *To Change China*, p. 176.

48. Madsen, *China and the American Dream*, p. 210.

49. Bhabha, *The Location of Culture*, p. 160. For a study of hybridity in the context of colonial discourse, see Young, *Colonial Desire*.

50. Madsen, *China and the American Dream*, pp. xiv–xv.

51. Leonard, *What Does China Think?* p. 77. Human Rights Watch, *Race to the Bottom: Corporate Complicity in Chinese Internet Censorship*, New York: Human Rights Watch, 2006, http://www.hrw.org/reports/2006/china0806/; Some argue that this is Chinese authoritarianism, American-style. John W. Whitehead, 'Chinese Totalitarianism, American-Style', *Huffington Post*, 31 July 2008.

52. Gutmann, *Losing the New China*, p. 138.

53. Francis Bacon, quoted in Michael Yahuda, 'The Sino-European Encounter: Historical Influences on Contemporary Relations', in David Shambaugh, Eberhard Sandschneider and

Zhou Hong (eds), *China-Europe Relations: Perceptions, Policies and Prospects*, London: Routledge, 2008, pp. 13–14.

54. James Mann, 'Our China Illusions', *The American Prospect*, 30 November 2002, p. 25.
55. Jeremy Paltiel, 'Peaceful Rise? Soft Power? Human Rights in China's New Multilateralism', in Guoguang Wu and Helen Lansdowne (eds), *China Turns to Multilateralism: Foreign Policy and Regional Security*, London: Routledge, 2008, p. 201.
56. Ibid., pp. 201–2.
57. John Fox and François Godement, *A Power Audit of EU-China Relations*, London: European Council on Foreign Relations, 2009, p. 1.
58. Margaret M. Pearson, 'The Major Multilateral Economic Institutions Engage China', in Alastair Iain Johnston and Robert S. Ross (eds), *Engaging China: The Management of an Emerging Power*, London: Routledge, 1999, p. 227.
59. Andrew Nathan calls China 'a taker and not a shaper' of emerging international norms and institutions concerning human rights. Quoted in Kent, *China, the United Nations, and Human Rights*, p. 3.
60. Quoted in Paltiel, 'Peaceful Rise? Soft Power?' p. 200.
61. Wang Gungwu, *Anglo-Chinese Encounters since 1800: War, Trade, Science and Governance*, Cambridge: Cambridge University Press, 2003, p. 9. See also Spence, *To Change China*.
62. Spence, *To Change China*, pp. 289–90.
63. David Shambaugh, 'Learning from Abroad to Reinvent Itself: External Influence on Internal CCP Reforms', in Cheng Li (ed.), *China's Changing Political Landscape: Prospects for Democracy*, Washington DC: Brookings Institution Press, 2008, pp. 283–301.
64. Christopher Marsh, 'Learning from Your Comrade's Mistakes: The Impact of the Soviet Past on China's Future', *Communist and Post-Communist Studies*, 36 (3), 2003, pp. 259–72.
65. Friedman, *National Identity and Democratic Prospects in Socialist China*, p. 5.
66. Quoted in Rey Chow, 'King Kong in Hong Kong: Watching the "Handover" from the U.S.A.', in Xudong Zhang (ed.), *Whither China? Intellectual Politics in Contemporary China*, Durham, NC: Duke University Press, 2001, p. 214 (Chow's emphasis).
67. John K. Fairbank, *China: The People's Middle Kingdom and the U.S.A.*, Cambridge, MA: Belknap Press, 1967, p. 97.
68. Quoted in Chomsky, *The Chomsky Reader*, p. 81.
69. Fairbank, *China Perceived*, pp. 90, 86.
70. Terrill E. Lautz, 'Hopes and Fears of 60 Years: American Images of China, 1911–1972', in Carola McGiffert (ed.), *China in the American Political Imagination*, Washington, DC: The CSIS Press, 2003, p. 32; and Phillip Knightley, *The First Casualty: The War Correspondent as Hero, Propagandist and Myth-Maker from the Crimea to Iraq*, London: André Deutsch, 2003, p. 295.
71. Michael H. Hunt, *The Making of a Special Relationship: The United States and China to 1914*, New York: Columbia University Press, 1983, p. x.
72. Dulles, *China and America*, p. 255.
73. David Aikman, *Jesus in Beijing: How Christianity Is Transforming China and Changing the Global Balance of Power*, Washington, DC: Regnery Publishing, 2003, p. 37.
74. Hunt, *The Making of a Special Relationship*, p. 3; Isaacs, *Scratches on Our Minds*, p. 135.
75. Feng Guifen (Feng Kuei-fen), 'On the Manufacture of Foreign Weapons', in Ssu-yu Teng and John K. Fairbank et al., *China's Response to the West: A Documentary Survey 1839–1923*, Cambridge, MA: Harvard University Press, 1954, p. 53.
76. Hunt, *The Making of a Special Relationship*, p. 304.
77. Quoted in Lampton, *The Three Faces of Chinese Power*, p. 91.
78. Quoted in ibid., p. 78.
79. Hunt, *The Making of a Special Relationship*, p. 38.
80. Gutmann, *Losing the New China*, pp. 138–9.
81. David Lampton, 'The China Fantasy, Fantasy', *The China Quarterly*, No. 191, 2007, p. 746.

82. Toshihiro Nakayama, 'Politics of U.S. Policy Toward China: Analysis of Domestic Factors', Center for Northeast Asian Policy Studies, Brookings Institution, 2006, p. 13. http://www.brookings.edu/~/media/Files/rc/papers/2006/09china_nakayama/nakayama2006.pdf

83. Studwell, *The China Dream*, p. 111.

84. Nakayama, 'Politics of U.S. Policy Toward China', p. 13; Suettinger, *Beyond Tiananmen*, pp. 190–92; Robert Dreyfuss, 'The New China Lobby', *The American Prospect*, No. 30, 1997, p. 35.

85. Sutter, 'The U.S. Congress', p. 87.

86. Johnston and Ross, 'Conclusion', pp. 286, 288–9.

87. Johnston and Evans, 'China's Engagement with Multilateral Security Institutions', p. 245.

88. Pearson, 'The Major Multilateral Economic Institutions Engage China', p. 212.

89. Jack S. Levy, 'Learning and Foreign Policy: Sweeping a Conceptual Minefield', *International Organization*, 48 (2), 1994, pp. 279–312; Alastair Iain Johnston, 'Learning Versus Adaptation: Explaining Change in Chinese Arms Control Policy in the 1980s and 1990s', *The China Journal*, No. 35, 1996, pp. 27–62.

90. See the debate between David Lampton and James Mann. David M. Lampton and James Mann, 'What's Your China Fantasy', Foreign Policy Online, 15 May 2007, http://www.foreignpolicy.com/articles/2007/05/14/whats_your_china_fantasy

91. Clinton, *My Life*, p. 768.

92. Lampton, *The Three Faces of Chinese Power*, p. 260.

93. Charles Taylor, *Philosophy and the Human Sciences*, Cambridge: Cambridge University Press, 1985, p. 39. For a study of the linkage between the shared meaning of Westphalian sovereignty and cross-strait conflict, see Chengxin Pan, 'Westphalia and the Taiwan Conundrum: A Case against the Exclusionist Construction of Sovereignty and Identity', *Journal of Chinese Political Science*, 15 (4), 2010, pp. 371–89.

94. Quoted in Cao, 'Modernity and Media Portrayals of China', p. 17.

95. Slavoj Žižek, *Tarrying with the Negative: Kant, Hegel, and the Critique of Ideology*, Durham, NC: Duke University Press, 1993, p. 121.

96. J. Hillis Miller, quoted in Ronald J. Heckelman, '"The Swelling Act": The Psychoanalytic Geography of Fantasy', in George E. Slusser and Eric S. Rabkin (eds), *Mindscapes: The Geographies of Imagined Worlds*, Carbondale: Southern Illinois University Press, 1989, p. 40.

97. See, for example, Human Rights Watch, *World Report 2007*, New York: Human Rights Watch, 2007, p. 258; Peerenboom, *China Modernizes*, p. 174; and Maureen Fan, 'China's Rights Record Criticized', *Washington Post*, 12 January 2007, p. A10.

98. Kagan, *The Return of History and the End of Dreams*, p. 62.

99. Raymond Williams, *Keywords: A Vocabulary of Culture and Society*, London: Flemingo, 1983, p. 94. The 'godfather' of neoconservatism Irving Kristol made a similar point. See Irving Kristol, 'The Neoconservative Persuasion: What It Was, and What It Is', in Irwin Stelzer (ed.), *The Neocon Reader*, New York: Grove Press, 2004, p. 34.

100. See Hollander, *Political Pilgrims*, p. 37.

101. Cao, 'Modernity and Media Portrayals of China', p. 6.

102. Foot, 'Chinese Power and the Idea of a Responsible State', p. 38.

103. Shih, *Navigating Sovereignty*, p. 167.

104. Huntington, *The Clash of Civilizations and the Remaking of World Order*, p. 94.

105. Harry Harding, 'Breaking the Impasse over Human Rights', in Ezra F. Vogel (ed.), *Living with China: U.S./China Relations in the Twenty-First Century*, New York: W. W. Norton & Company, 1997, p. 176.

106. Hutton, *The Writing on the Wall*, p. 302.

107. Quoted in Chris Brown, 'Cultural Diversity and International Political Theory: From the Requirement to "Mutual Respect"?' *Review of International Studies*, 26 (2), 2000, p. 202; Anthony Bevins, 'Mission Possible', *The Independent*, 13 May 1997, p. 13.

108. Hutton, *The Writing on the Wall*, p. 302.

109. Peerenboom, *China Modernizes*, p. 10 and Chapter 5: 'Of Rights and Wrongs: Why China Is Subject to a Double Standard on Rights'.
110. Cohen, *America's Response to China*, p. 225.
111. Gerald Segal, 'Tying China in (and down)', in Gerald Segal and Richard H. Yang (eds), *Chinese Economic Reform: The Impact on Security*, London: Routledge, 1996. See also, Gerald Segal, 'Tying China into the International System', *Survival*, 37 (2), 1995, pp. 60–73.
112. Haass, *The Opportunity*, p. 23.
113. Robert S. Ross, 'Why Our Hardliners Are Wrong', *The National Interest*, No. 49, 1997, p. 51 (emphasis added); Barber B. Conable, Jr. and David M. Lampton, 'China: The Coming Power', *Foreign Affairs*, 71 (5), 1992/1993, p. 147; and Chas W. Freeman, Jr. 'Sino-American Relations: Back to Basics', *Foreign Policy*, No. 104, 1996, p. 10.
114. Bill Clinton, 'In Clinton's Words: "An Outstretched Hand"', *New York Times*, 20 September 2000, p. A16 (emphasis added). By 1998, the term 'Most Favored Nation' (MFN) was changed to 'normal trade relations' so as to avoid the misleading connotation that China was receiving favourable treatment in its trade with the United States.
115. Peerenboom, *China Modernizes*, pp. 278–9. On the 'control' dimension of the term 'responsibility', see also Philip Stephens, 'The Financial Crisis Marks out a New Geopolitical Order', *Financial Times*, 10 October 2008, p. 9; and Christopher Layne, 'China's Challenge to US Hegemony', *Current History*, 107 (705), 2008, p. 15.
116. Ronald Steel, quoted in James L. Watson, 'Introduction: Transnationalism, Localization, and Fast Foods in East Asia', in James L. Watson (ed.), *Golden Arches East: McDonald's in East Asia* (2nd edn), Stanford, CA: Stanford University Press, 2006, p. 5.
117. Kagan, *The Return of History and the End of Dreams*, p. 50.
118. Gary Dorrien, *Imperial Designs: Neoconservatism and the New Pax Americana*, New York: Routledge, 2004, p. 225.
119. Johnston, *Social States*, p. 26.
120. Bhabha, *The Location of Culture*, p. 123.
121. Nandy, *The Intimate Enemy*; Fitzgerald, 'The Nationless State', p. 60.
122. Henry Kissinger, *Diplomacy*, New York: Simon & Schuster, 1994, p. 42.
123. Fairbank, *China Perceived*, pp.79–80.

CHAPTER 7 THE INTERNATIONAL POLITICS OF DISILLUSIONMENT

1. Kagan, *The Return of History and the End of Dreams*, p. 4.
2. Duncombe, *Dream*, p. 26.
3. Madsen, *China and the American Dream*, p. 82.
4. Roland Bleiker and Emma Hutchison, 'Fear No More: Emotions and World Politics', *Review of International Studies*, 34 (1), 2008, pp. 115–35.
5. Robert Gehrke, 'Huntsman Looks for Rebound in U.S.-China Relations', 7 May 2010, http://www.sltrib.com/sltrib/home/49545828-73/huntsman-china-relationship-think.html. csp
6. Sewell Chan, 'Geithner to Signal Tougher Stance on China Currency', *New York Times*, 15 September 2010.
7. Sam Sedaei, 'Obama's Push-Back Against China Is Bitter Medicine', *Huffington Post*, 15 February 2010, http://www.huffingtonpost.com/sam-sedaei/american-push-back-agains_b_462971.html; Jeremy Page, Patrick Barta and Jay Solomon, 'U.S., ASEAN to Push Back Against China', *Wall Street Journal Asia*, 23 September 2010, p. 1; and Lee, 'The New Face of U.S.-China Relations'.
8. John Lee, 'Obama Switching Sides Over China', The Weekly Standard Blog, 30 July 2010.
9. Thomas L. Friedman, 'Containment-Lite', *New York Times*, 10 November 2010, p. 35.

10. James B. Steinberg, 'China's Arrival: The Long March to Global Power', Keynote Address at the Center for a New American Security, 24 September 2009, http://www.cnas.org/files/multimedia/documents/Deputy%20Secretary%20James%20Steinberg's%20September%2024,%202009%20Keynote%20Address%20Transcript.pdf

11. See for example, David Shambaugh, 'China and Europe: The Emerging Axis', *Current History*, 103 (674), 2004, pp. 243–48, and 'The New Strategic Triangle: U.S. and European Reactions to China's Rise', *The Washington Quarterly*, 28 (3), 2005, pp. 7–25.

12. David Shambaugh, 'China Eyes Europe in the World: Real Convergence or Cognitive Dissonance?' in David Shambaugh, Eberhard Sandschneider and Zhou Hong (eds), *China-Europe Relations: Perceptions, Policies and Prospects*, London: Routledge, 2008, pp. 127–47.

13. Fox and Godement, *A Power Audit of EU-China Relations*, p. 13.

14. Kevin Rudd, 'A Conversation with China's Youth on the Future', Speech at Peking University, Beijing, 9 April 2008, http://www.theaustralian.com.au/news/kevin-rudds-speech-at-beijing-uni/story-e6frg6n6-1111116015758; Australian Department of Defence, *Defending Australia in the Asia Pacific Century: Force 2030*, Commonwealth of Australia, 2009, p. 34; and Cameron Stewart and Patrick Walters, 'Spy Chiefs Cross Swords over China – PM Backs Defence Hawks', *The Australian*, 11 April 2009, p. 1.

15. Paul Maley, 'Wikileaks Cable Exposes Then PM as "A Brutal Realist on China": Rudd's Plan to Contain Beijing', *The Australian*, 6 December 2010, p. 1. For an analysis of Australia's recent debate on China's rise, see Chengxin Pan, 'Getting Excited about China', in David Walker and Agnieszka Sobocinska (eds), *Australia's Asia: From Yellow Peril to Asian Century*, Crawley, WA: UWA Publishing, 2012, pp. 245–66.

16. Evan S. Medeiros, 'Strategic Hedging and the Future of Asia-Pacific Stability', *The Washington Quarterly*, 29 (1), 2005/2006, p. 148.

17. Kagan, 'Ambition and Anxiety', p. 2. See also Peter Beinart, 'Think Again Ronald Reagan', *Foreign Policy*, No. 180, July/August 2010, p. 33; and Alan Dupont, 'U.S. Enlists China's Worried Neighbours', *The Australian*, 3 August 2010, p. 10.

18. Michael Sheridan, 'China's Hawks Demand Cold War on the US', *The Sunday Times*, 7 February 2010, p. 30.

19. Wang Jisi, 'Zhong-Mei jiegouxing maodun shangsheng, zhanglue jiaoliang nanyi bimian' (Sino-U.S. Structural Contradictions on the Rise, Strategic Competition Difficult to Avoid), *International and Strategic Studies Report* (Beijing: Center for International and Strategic Studies, Peking University), No. 47, 23 July 2010, pp. 1–4.

20. Friedman, 'Containment-Lite'.

21. Liu Feitao, 'US Making Waves in South China Sea', *Global Times*, 8 November 2010. http://opinion.globaltimes.cn/commentary/2010-11/590145.htm; Shi Jianxun, 'Aoyun shenghuo yu Aolinpike jingshen burong xiedu (The Sacred Olympic Flame and Olympic Spirit Brook No Blasphemy), *Wenhuibao* (Wenhui Daily), 10 April 2008, p. 5; and Shao Feng, 'Aoyun huoju chuandi tuxian hexie shijie waijiao de zhongyaoxing' (Olympic Torch Relay Highlights the Importance for Harmonious World Diplomacy), *Zhongguo Shehuikexueyuan Yuanbao* (Journal of the Chinese Academy of Social Sciences), 29 April 2008, p. 3.

22. Robert Dreyfuss, 'China in the Driver's Seat', *The Nation*, 2 September 2010, p. 17.

23. Mann, *The China Fantasy*, p. 109.

24. Ying Ma, 'China's Stubborn Anti-Democracy', *Policy Review*, No. 141, 2007, p. 3.

25. Daniel Blumenthal, 'Is the West Turning on China?' Foreign Policy Online, 18 March 2010, http://shadow.foreignpolicy.com/posts/2010/03/18/is_the_west_turning_on_china

26. Gutmann, *Losing the New China*, p. 113–14.

27. See, for example, Robert Kagan, 'The Illusion of "Managing" China', *Washington Post*, 15 May 2005, p. B07.

28. David Shambaugh, 'Coping with a Conflicted China', *The Washington Quarterly*, 34 (1), 2011, p. 24.

29. Will Inboden, 'The Reality of the "China Fantasy"', Foreign Policy Online, 16 June 2010, http://shadow.foreignpolicy.com/posts/2010/06/16/the_reality_of_the_china_fantasy

30. Guy Dinmore and Geoff Dyer, 'Immelt Hits Out at China and Obama', *Financial Times* (FT.Com), 1 July 2010.
31. Wu Jianmin, 'Ou Mei Ri yi Hua, sange "diyici" qiansuoweijian' (Suspicions of China among Europe, the U.S., and Japan: Three Unprecedented 'First' Phenomena), 10 January 2011, http://mgb.chinareviewnews.com/doc/1015/6/5/2/101565260.html?coluid=93& kindid=2788&docid=101565260
32. Sorman, *The Empire of Lies*, p. 228.
33. Jonathan Holslag, 'The European Union and China: The Great Disillusion', *European Foreign Affairs Review*, 11 (4), 2006, p. 578.
34. Alan Dupont, 'Many Shared Interests but Few Shared Values with China', *The Australian*, 12 April 2010, p. 14.
35. Halper, 'Wrongly Mistaking China'; Robert J. Samuelson, 'The Danger behind China's "Me First" Worldview', *Washington Post*, 15 February 2010, http://www.washingtonpost. com/wp-dyn/content/article/2010/02/14/AR2010021402892.html
36. Spence, *To Change China*, p. 292.
37. Richard Stengel, 'The Chinese Challenge', *Time*, 22 January 2007, p. 6. See also Fareed Zakaria, *The Post-American World*, New York: W. W. Norton, 2008.
38. White, 'Power Shift', p. 2.
39. Jacques, *When China Rules the World*, p. 3. Hugh White expresses a similar view. See White, 'Power Shift', p. 6.
40. Barma, Ratner and Weber, 'A World Without the West', pp. 23–30.
41. Joshua Cooper Ramo, *The Beijing Consensus*, London: Foreign Policy Centre, 2004.
42. U.S. National Intelligence Council, *Global Trends 2025: A Transformed World*, Washington, DC: U.S. Government Printing Office, 2008, p. 3.
43. Sewell Chan, Sheryl Gay Stolberg and David E. Sanger, 'Obama's Economic View Is Rejected on World Stage', *New York Times*, 12 November 2010, p. 1.
44. Gutmann, *Losing the New China*, pp. xiii–xiv.
45. See, for example, Naazneen Barma and Ely Ratner, 'China's Illiberal Challenge', *Democracy: A Journal of Ideas*, 1 (2), 2006, pp. 56–68; Halper, *The Beijing Consensus*.
46. Alain Gresh, 'Understanding the Beijing Consensus', *Le Monde*, November 2008.
47. Edward Friedman, 'China: A Threat to or Threatened by Democracy?' *Dissent*, 56 (1), 2009, p. 12.
48. David Henry Hwang, quoted in Ling, *Postcolonial International Relations*, p. 138. See also Prasso, *The Asian Mystique*, pp. 11–12.
49. Holslag, 'The European Union and China', p. 573.
50. Mann, *The China Fantasy*, pp. 59–61.
51. Gary Schmitt, 'Kowtowing to China', *Weekly Standard*, 1 December 2009.
52. Callahan, 'Future Imperfect', p. 789; 'Spotlight on Asia.view: Welcome to Oz?', *The Economist*, 28 June 2008, p. 27; 'Rudd Must not Succumb to Turnbull's China Taunt' (editorial), *The Age*, 1 April 2009, p. 18.
53. Gutmann, *Losing the New China*, p. 15.
54. Leonard, *What Does China Think?* p. 77. See also Whitehead, 'Chinese Totalitarianism, American-Style'.
55. Philippe Naughton, 'Google and Yahoo Face Their Congressional Critics', *The Sunday Times*, 15 February 2006, http://www.timesonline.co.uk/tol/news/world/asia/article731031. ece
56. Mann, *The China Fantasy*, p. 22.
57. Ibid., p. 26.
58. Ibid., p. 104.
59. Aaron L. Friedberg, 'Are We Ready for China?' *Commentary*, 124 (3), 2007, p. 41.
60. Barma, Ratner and Weber, 'A World Without the West', p. 30.
61. White, 'Power Shift', p. 38.
62. Barack Obama, 'Remarks by the President to the United Nations General Assembly', United Nations Headquarters, New York, 23 September 2009; Steinberg, 'China's Arrival'.

63. Yan Xuetong, 'The Instability of China-US Relations', *The Chinese Journal of International Politics*, 3 (3), 2010, pp. 278–80.
64. Willy Lam, 'Reassurance or Appeasement?' *Far Eastern Economic Review*, 172 (9), 2009, p. 13.
65. Robert Kagan, 'Obama's Year One: *Contra*', *World Affairs*, 172 (3), 2010, p. 16.
66. Gary J. Schmitt, 'Our One-China Cowardice', *Wall Street Journal*, 15 January 2008, p. A12.
67. Ellen Bork, 'Obama's Rights Retreat', *Wall Street Journal Asia*, 27 May 2010, p. 13; Ellen Bork, 'Obama's Timidity on Tibet', *Wall Street Journal Asia*, 20 August 2010, p. 11.
68. Dan Blumenthal, 'China in Obama's World', *Far East Economic Review*, 172 (10), 2009, p. 43.
69. Garrison, *Making China Policy*, pp. 150, 153; Robert A. Manning and James Przystup, 'Clinton's Inscrutable China Policy', *National Review*, 49 (23), 1997, p. 22.
70. Zalmay Khalilzad, 'Sweet and Sour: Recipe for a New China Policy', *Rand Review*, 23 (3), 1999/2000, pp. 6–11.
71. Henry Nau, 'Why We Fight over Foreign Policy', *Policy Review*, No. 142, 2007, pp. 25–42.
72. Kagan, *The Return of History and the End of Dreams*, p. 57.
73. Mann, *The China Fantasy*, p. 27.
74. Quoted in Mackerras, *Western Images of China*, 1999, p. 175.
75. Blumenthal, 'China in Obama's World', p. 42. Paula J. Dobriansky, 'The Realist Case for Tibetan Autonomy', *Wall Street Journal*, 7 January 2010, p. A15; Beinart, 'Think Again Ronald Reagan', p. 33; and Ellen Bork, 'The White House Chickens Out', *Weekly Standard*, 15 (5), 2009, p. 13.
76. Manning and Przystup, 'Clinton's Inscrutable China Policy', p. 22.
77. Joel Brinkley, 'In New Tone, Rice Voices Frustration with China', *New York Times*, 20 August 2005, p. 1.
78. Tania Branigan, 'China Must Tackle Human Rights, Mandelson Says', *The Guardian*, 8 September 2009, http://www.guardian.co.uk/world/2009/sep/08/mandelson-china-eu-arms-embargo
79. Stanley Crossick, 'Whither EU-China Relations?' 22 October 2007, http://crossick.blogactiv.eu/2007/10/22/whither-eu-china-relations-2/
80. Commission of the European Communities, *EU-China: Closer Partners, Growing Responsibilities*, COM(2006) 631 final, Brussels, 24 October 2006, p. 7.
81. See Chengxin Pan, 'Problematizing "Constructive Engagement" in EU China Policy', in C. Roland Vogt (ed.), *Europe and China: Strategic Partners or Rivals?*, Hong Kong: Hong Kong University Press, 2012, pp. 37–57.
82. Blumenthal, 'China in Obama's World', p. 41.
83. See for example, David E. Bell, 'Disappointment in Decision Making under Uncertainty', *Operations Research*, 33 (1), 1985, pp. 1–27.
84. Akira Iriye, *Across the Pacific: An Inner History of American-East Asian Relations*, New York: Harcourt, Brace & World, Inc., 1967, p. 19.
85. Dulles, *China and America*, p. 136.
86. See Hollander, *Political Pilgrims*.
87. Inboden, 'The Reality of the "China Fantasy"'.
88. See Xu Guoqi, *Olympic Dreams: China and Sports 1895–2008*, Cambridge, MA: Harvard University Press, 2008, p. 248; James Lilley, *China Hands: Nine Decades of Adventure, Espionage, and Diplomacy in Asia*, New York: PublicAffairs, 2004, p. 378.
89. Jay Nordlinger, 'The Road to Beijing', *National Review*, 60 (10), 2008, p. 43.
90. Jonathan Alter, 'Boycott Opening Ceremonies', *Newsweek*, 12 April 2008, p. 36.
91. Amnesty International, 'The Olympics Countdown—Crackdown on Activists Threatens Olympics Legacy', 1 April 2008, p. 1 (emphasis in original), http://www.amnesty.eu/static/documents/2008/OlympicsCountdown0408_170502008.pdf
92. Amnesty International, 'The Olympics Countdown—Broken Promises', 29 July 2008, http://www.amnesty.org/en/library/info/ASA17/089/2008/en

93. 'Beijing's Bad Faith Olympics' (editorial), *New York Times*, 23 August 2008, p. 18.
94. Fu Ying, 'Western Media Has "Demonised" China', *The Telegraph*, 13 April 2008.
95. Dick Thornburgh, 'Bearing Witness to Chinese Persecution', Real Clear World, 18 December 2009, http://www.realclearworld.com/articles/2009/12/18/liu_xiaobo_bearing_witness_to_chinas_persecuted.html
96. Dinmore and Dyer, 'Immelt Hits Out at China and Obama'; Shai Oster, Norihiko Shirouzu and Paul Glader, 'China Squeezes Foreigners for Share of Global Riches', Wall Street Journal Online, 28 December 2010.
97. Fisher, 'Kodak and China', p. 134.
98. Sherrod Brown, *Myths of Free Trade: Why American Trade Policy Has Failed*, New York: The New Press, 2004, p. 127.
99. Heckelman, '"The Swelling Act"', p. 47.
100. Slavoj Žižek argues that one of the ways fantasy keeps our desire intact as desire is by finding a scapegoat for our lack of enjoyment. See Jodi Dean, *Democracy and Other Neoliberal Fantasies*, Durham, NC: Duke University Press, 2009, p. 58.
101. See Madsen, *China and the American Dream*, p. 11.
102. Tani E. Barlow, 'Colonialism's Career in Postwar China Studies', in Tani E. Barlow (ed.), *Formations of Colonial Modernity in East Asia*, Durham, NC: Duke University Press, 1997, p. 384.
103. Lucian W. Pye, *The Spirit of Chinese Politics*, Cambridge, MA: Harvard University Press, 1992, p. 233.
104. Gilley, *China's Democratic Future*, p. x.
105. Jeane Kirkpatrick, 'Neoconservatism as a Response to the Counter-Culture', in Irwin Stelzer (ed.), *The Neocon Reader*, New York: Grove Press, 2004, p. 235.
106. Mann, *The China Fantasy*, pp. 112, 110, 72.
107. Jean A. Garrison, 'The Domestic Political Game behind the Engagement Strategy', in Suisheng Zhao (ed.), *China-U.S. Relations Transformed: Perspectives and Strategic Interactions*, London: Routledge, 2008, p. 154.
108. See Cao, 'Modernity and Media Portrayals of China', pp. 7–10.
109. Alain Peyrefitte, *The Collision of Two Civilisations: The British Expedition to China 1792–4* (trans. Jon Rothschild), London: Harvill, 1992, pp. 463, 466, 488.
110. Steele, *The American People and China*, Chapter 4.
111. Hunt, *The Making of a Special Relationship*, pp. 172–3.
112. Isaacs, *Scratches on Our Minds*, p. xxiv.
113. Hunt, 'Chinese Foreign Relations in Historical Perspective', p. 41.
114. Isaacs, *Scratches on Our Minds*, p. xxvii. See also Peck, *Washington's China*, pp. 2–3, 5–6.

CHAPTER 8 TOWARDS REFLECTION AND DIALOGUE

1. Collingwood, *The Idea of History*, p. 205.
2. Quoted in Kissinger, *Diplomacy*, p. 835.
3. Robert Ash, David Shambaugh and Seiichiro Takagi, 'International China Watching in the Twenty-first Century: Coping with a Changing Profession', in Robert Ash, David Shambaugh and Seiichiro Takagi (eds), *China Watching: Perspectives from Europe, Japan and the United States*, London: Routledge, 2007, p. 245. See also Samuel S. Kim, 'New Directions and Old Puzzles in Chinese Foreign Policy', in Samuel S. Kim (ed.), *China and the World: New Directions in Chinese Foreign Relations*, Boulder, CO: Westview Presss, 1989, p. 4.
4. Gutmann, *Losing the New China*, back cover.
5. Karl Mannheim, *Ideology and Utopia: An Introduction to the Sociology of Knowledge* (trans. Louis Wirth and Edward Shils), New York: Harvest/HBJ, 1936, p. 6.
6. See Oren, *Our Enemies and US*, pp. 164–5.
7. Judith Butler, *Gender Trouble: Feminism and the Subversion of Identity*, New York: Routledge, 1999, p. 5.

8. Quoted in Culler, *On Deconstruction*, p. 156.
9. Jonathan D. Pollack, quoted in Wang Jisi, 'International Relations Theory and the Study of Chinese Foreign Policy: A Chinese Perspective', in Thomas W. Robinson and David Shambaugh (eds), *Chinese Foreign Policy: Theory and Practice*, Oxford: Clarendon Press, 1994, p. 500.
10. Collingwood, *The Idea of History*, p. 1.
11. Rorty, *Contingency, Irony, and Solidarity*, pp. 73–4.
12. Isaacs, *Scratches on Our Minds*, p. 381.
13. Baum, *China Watcher*, p. xii.
14. See Susan Brownell, Beijing's Games: What the Olympics Mean to China, Lanham, MD: Rowman & Littlefield, 2008, pp. 156–60.
15. Stephen M. Walt, 'The Renaissance of Security Studies', *International Studies Quarterly*, 35 (2), 1991, p. 223. Walt made this comment in the context of the perceived devastating impact postmodern approaches on security studies.
16. Mannheim, *Ideology and Utopia*, pp. 47–8.
17. Ibid., p. 48.
18. Confucius, *The Analects*, 2:17, in *A Source Book in Chinese Philosophy* (trans. and comp. by Wing-Tsit Chan), Princeton, NJ: Princeton University Press, 1963, p. 24.
19. Habermas, *Knowledge and Human Interests*, p. 378.
20. There have been some worthy attempts at such dialogue and engagement. See, for example, Zheng, *Discovering Chinese Nationalism in China*; Zheng Yongnian (ed.), *China and International Relations: The Chinese View and the Contribution of Wang Gungwu*, London: Routledge, 2010; Callahan, *Contingent States*; Leonard, *What Does China Think?*; and Yan Xuetong et al., *Ancient Chinese Thought, Modern Chinese Power*, Princeton, NJ: Princeton University Press, 2011.
21. Ann Kaplan, quoted in Yew, *The Disjunctive Empire of International Relations*, p. 38.
22. Ella Shohat and Robert Stam, *Unthinking Eurocentrism: Multiculturalism and the Media*, London: Routledge, 1994, p. 359.
23. Campbell, 'China Watchers Fighting a Turf War of Their Own', p. B13. It should be noted that the language barriers between the West and China are not a one-way affair.
24. See, for example, Simon Leys, 'Introduction', in *The Analects of Confucius* (trans. Simon Leys), New York: W. W. Norton & Company, 1997, p. xvii.
25. John W. Garver, 'Forward', in Yong Deng and Fei-ling Wang (eds), *In the Eyes of the Dragon: China Views the World*, Lanham, MD: Rowman & Littlefield, 1999, pp. viii–ix.
26. See Thomas J. Christensen, Alastair Iain Johnston and Robert S. Ross, 'Conclusions and Future Directions', in Alastair Iain Johnston and Robert S. Ross (eds), *New Directions in the Study of China's Foreign Policy*, Stanford, CA: Stanford University Press, 2006, pp. 394–404.
27. John Garnaut, 'The El Dorado Factor: How We Got China So Wrong', *The Age*, 13 July 2009, p. 1.
28. See William A. Callahan, *China: The Pessoptimist Nation*, Oxford: Oxford University Press, 2009.
29. See Tu Wei-ming (ed.), *The Living Tree: The Changing Meaning of Being Chinese Today*, Stanford, CA: Stanford University Press, 1994; and Chengxin Pan, 'What Is Chinese About Chinese Businesses? Locating the "Rise of China" in Global Production Networks', *Journal of Contemporary China*, 18 (58), 2009, pp. 7–25.
30. Gadamer, *Truth and Method*, p. 318.
31. Emilian Kavalski, '"Do as I do": The Global Politics of China's Regionalization', in Emilian Kavalski (ed.), *China and the Global Politics of Regionalization*, Farnham, UK: Ashgate, 2009, p. 5; Todorov, *The Conquest of America*, p. 247.
32. For example, Keith Krause and Michael C. Williams (eds), *Critical Security Studies: Concepts and Cases*, Minneapolis, MN: University of Minnesota Press, 1997; Ken Booth (ed.), *Critical Security Studies and World Politics*, Boulder, CO: Lynne Rienner, 2005; Marie Breen Smyth, Jeroen Gunning and Richard Jackson (eds), *Critical Terrorism Studies: A New Research Agenda*, London: Routledge, 2009; Brooke A. Ackerly, Maria

Stern and Jacqui True (eds), *Feminist Methodologies for International Relations*, Cambridge: Cambridge University Press, 2006; Naeem Inayatullah and David L. Blaney, *International Relations and the Problem of Difference*, New York: Routledge, 2004; Naeem Inayatullah (ed.), *Autobiographical International Relations: I, IR*, London: Routledge, 2010; Oren, *Our Enemies and US; Schram and Caterino (eds), Making Political Science Matter; Flyvbjerg, Making Social Science Matter*; Paul Rabinow and William M. Sullivan (eds), *Interpretive Social Science: A Second Look*, Berkeley, CA: University of California Press, 1987; Matthew Eagleton-Pierce, 'Advancing a Reflexive International Relations', *Millennium: Journal of International Studies*, 39 (3), 2011, pp. 805–23; and Chris Brown, 'The "Practice Turn", *Phronesis* and Classical Realism: Towards a Phronetic International Political Theory?', *Millennium: Journal of International Studies*, 40 (3), 2012, pp. 439–56.

33. James K. Boyce, 'Area Studies and the National Security State', *Bulletin of Concerned Asian Scholars*, 29 (1), 1997, pp. 27–8.

34. Quoted in Ken Booth, 'Security and Self: Reflections of a Fallen Realist', in Keith Krause and Michael C. Williams (eds), *Critical Security Studies: Concepts and Cases*, Minneapolis, MN: University of Minnesota Press, 1997, p. 101.

35. Gillard, 'Speech to the AsiaLink and Asia Society Lunch'. See also, Yee (ed.), *China's Rise – Threat or Opportunity?*; and Ramgopal Agarwala, *The Rise of China: Threat or Opportunity?*, New Delhi: Bookwell Books, 2002. In 1998, after India tested its nuclear weapons, Prime Minister Vajpayee wrote a letter to President Bill Clinton that blamed the test on the threat from China. See Shirk, *China: Fragile Superpower*, pp. 115–16.

36. See, for example, Song Xiaojun, Wang Xiaodong, Huang Jisu, Song Qiang and Liu Yang, *Zhongguo bu gaoxing: Da shidai, da mubiao ji Zhongguo de neiyouwaihuan* (Unhappy China: New Epoch, Grand Vision and Challenges for China), Taipei: INK Literary Monthly Publishing, 2009; and Liu Mingfu, *Zhongguo meng: Hou Meiguo shidai de daguo siwei yu zhanlue dingwei* (The Chinese Dream: Great Power Thinking and Strategic Orientation in the Post-American Era), Beijing: Zhongguo youyi chuban gongsi, 2010.

37. David A. Lake, 'Why "isms" Are Evil: Theory, Epistemology, and Academic Sects as Impediments to Understanding and Progress', *International Studies Quarterly*, 55 (2), 2011, pp. 465, 471.

38. Charles W. Kegley Jr., 'Bridge-Building in the Study of International Relations: How "Kuhn" We Do Better?', in Donald J. Puchala (ed.), *Visions of International Relations: Assessing an Academic Field*, Columbia, SC: University of South Carolina Press, 2002, p. 78. See also Lake, 'Why "isms" Are Evil', p. 471.

39. There are always exceptions. More intellectual efforts than before now take 'non-Western' subjectivities and cultures seriously by consciously involving both Western and non-Western participants to facilitate dialogue. See, for example, Stephen Chan, Peter Mandaville and Roland Bleiker (eds), *The Zen of International Relations: IR Theory from East to West*, London: Palgrave, 2001; Richard Rosecrance and Gu Guoliang (eds), *Power and Restraint: A Shared Vision for the U.S.-China Relationship*, New York: PublicAffairs, 2009; Morgan Brigg and Roland Bleiker (eds), *Mediating across Difference: Oceanic and Asian Approaches to Conflict Resolution*, Honolulu, HI: University of Hawai'i Press, 2011. Meanwhile, a growing number of non-Western and Chinese scholars have made increasingly significant contributions to the fields of IR and China's IR in particular.

40. See Todorov, *The Conquest of America*; Inayatullah and Blaney, *International Relations and the Problem of Difference*.

41. Bradley S. Klein, 'Conclusion: Every Month Is "Security Awareness Month"', in Keith Krause and Michael C. Williams (eds), *Critical Security Studies: Concepts and Cases*, Minneapolis, MN: University of Minnesota Press, 1997, p. 363.

42. For a similar argument on 'post-paradigmatic political science', see Schram, 'Return to Politics'.

Bibliography

Abramowitz, Morton and Stephen Bosworth (2006), 'America Confronts the Asian Century', *Current History*, **105** (690), 147–52.

Acharya, Amitav and Barry Buzan (2007), 'Why Is There No Non-Western International Relations Theory? An Introduction', *International Relations of the Asia-Pacific*, **7** (3), 287–312.

Ackerly, Brooke A., Maria Stern and Jacqui True (eds) (2006), *Feminist Methodologies for International Relations*, Cambridge: Cambridge University Press.

Agarwala, Ramgopal (2002), *The Rise of China: Threat or Opportunity?*, New Delhi: Bookwell Books.

Age, The (2009), 'Rudd Must not Succumb to Turnbull's China Taunt' (editorial), 1 April, p. 18.

Agencies/FT (2005), 'US Lawmakers Meddle in CNOOC's Unocal Bid', *China Daily*, 6 July, http://www.chinadaily.com.cn/english/doc/2005-07/06/content_457677.htm

Ahrari, Ehsan (2009), 'China's Preoccupation with Asymmetric War: Lessons Learned from the Hezbollah-Israeli War', *Small Wars Journal*, October, 1–7, http://smallwarsjournal.com/blog/journal/docs-temp/307-ahrari.pdf

Aikman, David (2003), *Jesus in Beijing: How Christianity Is Transforming China and Changing the Global Balance of Power*, Washington, DC: Regnery Publishing.

Alford, C. Fred (1991), *The Self in Social Theory: A Psychoanalytic Account of Its Construction in Plato, Hobbes, Locke, Rawls, and Rousseau*, New Haven, CT: Yale University Press.

Alter, Jonathan (2008), 'Boycott Opening Ceremonies', *Newsweek*, 12 April, p. 36.

Altheide, David L. (2002), *Creating Fear: News and the Construction of Crisis*, New York: Aldine de Gruyter.

Amnesty International (2008), 'The Olympics Countdown—Crackdown on Activists Threatens Olympics Legacy', 1 April, http://www.amnesty.eu/static/documents/2008/OlympicsCountdown0408_170502008.pdf

Amnesty International (2008), 'The Olympics Countdown—Broken Promises', 29 July, http://www.amnesty.org/en/library/info/ASA17/089/2008/en

Anderson, Leon (2006), 'Analytic Autoethnography', *Journal of Contemporary Ethnography*, **35** (4), 373–95.

Anelauskas, Valdas (1999), *Discovering America As It Is*, Atlanta, GA: Clarity Press.

Arkin, William M. (2006), 'America's New China War Plan', *Washington Post*, 24 May, http://blog.washingtonpost.com/earlywarning/2006/05/americas_new_china_war_plan.html

Ash, Robert, David Shambaugh and Seiichiro Takagi (2007), 'Introduction', in Robert Ash, David Shambaugh and Seiichiro Takagi (eds), *China Watching: Perspectives from Europe, Japan, and the United States*, London: Routledge, pp. 1–15.

Ash, Robert, David Shambaugh and Seiichiro Takagi (2007), 'International China Watching in the Twenty-first Century: Coping with a Changing Profession', in Robert Ash, David Shambaugh and Seiichiro Takagi (eds), *China Watching:*

Perspectives from Europe, Japan and the United States, London: Routledge, pp. 243–8.

Ash, Robert, David Shambaugh and Seiichiro Takagi (eds) (2007), *China Watching: Perspectives from Europe, Japan, and the United States*, London: Routledge.

Ashley, Richard K. (1988), 'Untying the Sovereign State: A Double Reading of the Anarchy Problematique', *Millennium: Journal of International Studies*, **17** (2), 227–62.

Associated French Press (2008), 'Clinton, Obama Fire New Economic Jabs at China', 14 April, http://www.channelnewsasia.com/stories/afp_world/view/341518/1/.html

Associated Press (2008), 'Poll: Iran, Iraq, China Top US Enemies', 1 April.

Australian Department of Defence (2009), *Defending Australia in the Asia Pacific Century: Force 2030*, Commonwealth of Australia.

Axelrod, Robert (2006), *The Evolution of Cooperation* (rev. edn), New York: Basic Books.

Babbin, Jed and Edward Timperlake (2006), *Showdown: Why China Wants War with the United States*, Washington, DC: Regnery Publishing.

Babones, Salvatore (2011), 'The Middle Kingdom: The Hype and the Reality of China's Rise', *Foreign Affairs*, **90** (5), 79–88.

Bacevich, Andrew J. (2005), *The New American Militarism: How Americans Are Seduced by War*, Oxford: Oxford University Press.

Bachman, David (2000), 'China's Democratization: What Difference Would It Make for U.S.-China Relations?' in Edward Friedman and Barrett McCormick (eds), *What If China Doesn't Democratize? Implications for War and Peace*, Armonk, NY: M. E. Sharpe, pp. 195–223.

Barlow, Tani E. (1997), 'Colonialism's Career in Postwar China Studies', in Tani E. Barlow (ed.), *Formations of Colonial Modernity in East Asia*, Durham, NC: Duke University Press, pp. 373–411.

Barlow, Tani E. (ed.) (1997), *Formations of Colonial Modernity in East Asia*, Durham, NC: Duke University Press.

Barma, Naazneen and Ely Ratner (2006), 'China's Illiberal Challenge', *Democracy: A Journal of Ideas*, **1** (2), 56–68.

Barma, Naazneen, Ely Ratner and Steven Weber (2007), 'A World Without the West', *The National Interest*, No. 90, pp. 23–30.

Barr, Michael (2011), *Who's Afraid of China? The Challenge of China's Soft Power*, London: Zed Books.

Bartelson, Jens (1995), *A Genealogy of Sovereignty*, Cambridge: Cambridge University Press.

Barthes, Roland (1972), *Critical Essays*, Chicago, IL: Northwestern University Press.

Barthes, Roland (1973), *Mythologies* (trans. Annette Lavers), St Albans: Paladin.

Barysch, Katinka (with Charles Grant and Mark Leonard) (2005), *Embracing the Dragon: The EU's Partnership with China*, London: Centre for European Reform.

Baum, Richard (2010), *China Watcher: Confessions of a Peking Tom*, Seattle, WA: University of Washington Press.

BBC News (2005), 'US Urges Chinese Political Reform', 16 November, http://news.bbc.co.uk/2/hi/americas/4440860.stm

Beinart, Peter (2010), 'Think Again Ronald Reagan', *Foreign Policy*, No. 180, July/August, pp. 28–33.

Bell, Daniel A. (2011), 'Introduction', in Yan Xuetong et al., *Ancient Chinese Thought, Modern Chinese Power*, Princeton, NJ: Princeton University Press, pp. 1–18.

Bell, David E. (1985), 'Disappointment in Decision Making under Uncertainty', *Operations Research*, **33** (1), 1–27.

Berger, Samuel R. (2001), 'Don't Antagonize China', *Washington Post*, 8 July, p. B7.

Bergsten, C. Fred, Bates Gill, Nicholas R. Lardy and Derek Mitchell (2006), *China: The Balance Sheet: What the World Needs to Know Now about the Emerging Superpower*, New York: PublicAffairs.

Bernstein, Richard and Ross H. Munro (1997), *The Coming Conflict with China*, New York: Alfred A. Knopf.

Bernstein, Richard J. (1976), *The Restructuring of Social and Political Theory*, London: Methuen.

Bernstein, Richard J. (1983), *Beyond Objectivism and Relativism: Science, Hermeneutics, and Praxis*, Oxford: Basil Blackwell.

Betts, Richard K. and Thomas J. Christensen (2000/2001), 'China: Getting the Questions Right', *The National Interest*, No. 62, pp. 17–29.

Bevins, Anthony (1997), 'Mission Possible', *The Independent*, 13 May, p. 13.

Bhabha, Homi K. (1994), *The Location of Culture*, London: Routledge.

Bhagwati, Jagdish (2002), 'Why China Is a Paper Tiger: The Emergence of the People's Republic Should Spell Opportunity – Not Doom – for Asian Economies', *Newsweek*, 18 February, p. 23.

Bianco, Lucien et al. (1994), *The Development of Contemporary China Studies*, Tokyo: Centre for East Asian Cultural Studies for UNESCO, The Toyo Bunko.

Bleiker, Roland and Emma Hutchison (2008), 'Fear No More: Emotions and World Politics', *Review of International Studies*, **34** (1), 115–35.

Bloch, Julia Chang (1997), 'Commercial Diplomacy', in Ezra F. Vogel (ed.), *Living with China: U.S./China Relations in the Twenty-First Century*, New York: W. W. Norton, pp. 185–216.

Blumenthal, Dan (2009), 'China in Obama's World', *Far East Economic Review*, **172** (10), 40–43.

Blumenthal, Dan, Aaron Friedberg, Randall Schriver and Ashley J. Tellis (2008), 'Bush Should Keep His Word on Taiwan', *Wall Street Journal*, 19 July, p. A9.

Blumenthal, Daniel (2010), 'Is the West Turning on China?' Foreign Policy Online, 18 March, http://shadow.foreignpolicy.com/posts/2010/03/18/is_the_west_turning_on_china

Bochner, Arthur P. and Carolyn Ellis (eds) (2002), *Ethnographically Speaking: Autoethnography, Literature, and Aesthetics*, Walnut Creek, CA: AltaMira Press.

Booth, Ken (1997), 'Security and Self: Reflections of a Fallen Realist', in Keith Krause and Michael C. Williams (eds), *Critical Security Studies: Concepts and Cases*, Minneapolis, MN: University of Minnesota Press, pp. 83–119.

Booth, Ken (ed.) (2005), *Critical Security Studies and World Politics*, Boulder, CO: Lynne Rienner.

Bork, Ellen (2009), 'The White House Chickens Out', *Weekly Standard*, **15** (5), 13.

Bork, Ellen (2010), 'Obama's Rights Retreat', *Wall Street Journal Asia*, 27 May, p. 13.

Bork, Ellen (2010), 'Obama's Timidity on Tibet', *Wall Street Journal Asia*, 20 August, p. 11.

Boyce, James K. (1997), 'Area Studies and the National Security State', *Bulletin of Concerned Asian Scholars*, **29** (1), 27–9.

Bradsher, Keith (2006), 'Senators' China Trip Highlights Their Differences on Currency', *New York Times*, 26 March, http://www.nytimes.com/2006/03/26/politics/26cnd-yuan.html

Branigan, Tania (2009), 'China Must Tackle Human Rights, Mandelson Says', *The Guardian*, 8 September, http://www.guardian.co.uk/world/2009/sep/08/mandelson -china-eu-arms-embargo

Bremmer, Ian (2005), 'The Panda Hedgers', *New York Times*, 5 October, http://www.nytimes.com/2005/10/04/opinion/04iht-edbremmer.html

Breslin, Shaun (2005), 'Power and Production: Rethinking China's Global Economic Role', *Review of International Studies*, **31** (4), 735–53.

Breslin, Shaun (2010), 'China's Emerging Global Role: Dissatisfied Responsible Great Power', *Politics*, **30** (S1), 52–62.

Breslin, Shaun and Ian Taylor (2008), 'Explaining the Rise of "Human Rights" in Analyses of Sino-African Relations', *Review of African Political Economy*, **35** (115), 59–71.

Brigg, Morgan and Roland Bleiker (2010), 'Autoethnographic International Relations: Exploring the Self as a Source of Knowledge', *Review of International Studies*, **36** (3), 779–98.

Brigg, Morgan and Roland Bleiker (eds) (2011), *Mediating across Difference: Oceanic and Asian Approaches to Conflict Resolution*, Honolulu, HI: University of Hawai'i Press.

Brinkley, Joel (2005), 'In New Tone, Rice Voices Frustration with China', *New York Times*, 20 August, p. 1.

Brown, Chris (2000), 'Cultural Diversity and International Political Theory: From the *Requirement* to "Mutual Respect"?' *Review of International Studies*, **26** (2), 199–213.

Brown, Chris (2012), 'The "Practice Turn", *Phronesis* and Classical Realism: Towards a Phronetic International Political Theory?', *Millennium: Journal of International Studies*, **40** (3), 439–56.

Brown, Lester R. (1995), *Who Will Feed China? Wake-up Call for a Small Planet*, New York: W. W. Norton.

Brown, Sherrod (2004), *Myths of Free Trade: Why American Trade Policy Has Failed*, New York: The New Press.

Bruni, Frank (2001), 'For Bush, a Mission and a Role in History', *New York Times*, 22 September, p. A1.

Brzezinski, Zbigniew (1989), *The Grand Failure: The Birth and Death of Communism in the Twentieth Century*, New York: Charles Scribner's Sons.

Buchan, Glenn C., David Matonick, Calvin Shipbaugh and Richard Mesic (2003), *Future Roles of U.S. Nuclear Forces: Implications for U.S. Strategy*, Santa Monica, CA: RAND.

Burnett, Jonny and Dave Whyte (2005), 'Embedded Expertise and the New Terrorism', *Journal for Crime, Conflict and the Media*, **1** (4), 1–18.

Bush, George and Brent Scowcroft (1998), *A World Transformed*, New York: Alfred A. Knopf.

Bush, Richard C. and Michael E. O'Hanlon (2007), *A War Like No Other: The Truth about China's Challenge to America*, Hoboken, NJ: John Wiley & Sons.

Butler, Judith (1999), *Gender Trouble: Feminism and the Subversion of Identity*, New York: Routledge.

Buzan, Barry (1991), *People, States and Fear: An Agenda for International Security Studies in the Post-Cold War Era* (2nd edn), Hemel Hempstead: Harvester Wheatsheaf.

Cable, Vincent and Peter Ferdinand (1994), 'China As an Economic Giant: Threat or Opportunity?', *International Affairs*, **70** (2), 243–61.

Cai, Peter (2012), 'Our Bill to China: $5100 Per Family', *The Age*, 3 April, p. 3.

Caldicott, Helen (2002), *The New Nuclear Danger: George W. Bush's Military-Industrial Complex*, New York: The New Press.

Callahan, William A. (2002), 'Report on Conferences: Nationalism & International Relations in China', Centre for Contemporary China Studies, Durham University, www.dur.ac.uk/resources/china.studies/shanghaireportonthe%20conference.doc

Callahan, William A. (2004), *Contingent States: Greater China and Transnational Relations*, Minneapolis, MN: University of Minnesota Press.

Callahan, William A. (2007), 'Future Imperfect: The European Union's Encounter with China (and the United States)', *Journal of Strategic Studies*, **30** (4), 777–807.

Callahan, William A. (2009), *China: The Pessoptimist Nation*, Oxford: Oxford University Press.

Campbell, David (1998), *Writing Security: United States Foreign Policy and the Politics of Identity* (rev. edn), Minneapolis, MN: University of Minnesota Press.

Campbell, Kurt (2000), 'China Watchers Fighting a Turf War of Their Own', *New York Times*, 20 May, p. B13.

Cao, Qing (2012), 'Modernity and Media Portrayals of China', *Journal of Asian Pacific Communication*, **22** (1), 1–21.

Cao, Qing et al. (2007), 'A Special Section: Reporting China in the British Media' (Special Issue), *China Media Research*, **3** (1), 1–72.

Carpenter, Ted Galen (1992), *A Search for Enemies: America's Alliances after the Cold War*, Washington, DC: Cato Institute.

Carpenter, Ted Galen and James A. Dorn (eds) (2000), *China's Future: Constructive Partner or Emerging Threat?*, Washington, D.C.: Cato Institute.

Carr, E. H. (1987), *What Is History?* (2nd edn), Harmondsworth: Penguin Books.

Carter, Ashton B. and Jennifer C. Bulkeley (2007), 'America's Strategic Response to China's Military Modernization', *Harvard Asia Pacific Review*, **1** (9), 50–52.

Cassirer, Ernest (1946), *Language and Myth* (trans. Susanne K. Langer), New York: Dover Publications.

Certeau, Michel de (1993), 'Walking in the City', in Simon During (ed.), *The Cultural Studies Reader*, London: Routledge.

Chacko, Priya (2011), 'Interpreting the "Rise of India": India-US Relations, Power Transition and Ontological Security', paper presented at the ISA Asia-Pacific Regional Section Inaugural Conference, Brisbane, 29–30 September, pp. 1–31.

Chan, Adrian (2009), *Orientalism in Sinology*, Palo Alto, CA: Academic Press.

Chan, Sewell (2010), 'Geithner to Signal Tougher Stance on China Currency', *New York Times*, 15 September, http://www.nytimes.com/2010/09/16/business/global/16yuan.html

Chan, Sewell, Sheryl Gay Stolberg and David E. Sanger (2010), 'Obama's Economic View Is Rejected on World Stage', *New York Times*, 12 November, p. 1.

Chan, Stephen, Peter Mandaville and Roland Bleiker (eds) (2001), *The Zen of International Relations: IR Theory from East to West*, London: Palgrave.

Chan, Steve (1999), 'Relating to China: Problematic Approaches and Feasible Emphases', *World Affairs*, **161** (4), 179–85.

Chan, Steve (2008), *China, the U.S., and the Power-Transition Theory: A Critique*, London: Routledge.

Chan, Wing-Tsit (trans.) (1963), *A Source Book in Chinese Philosophy*, Princeton, NJ: Princeton University Press.

Chavanne, Bettina H. (2008), 'General Says USAF Will Procure 380 F-22s, Despite OSD', *Aerospace Daily & Defense Report*, **225** (31), 3.

Chen Feng et al. (1996), *Zhong mei jiaoliang da xiezhen* (True Stories of Sino-America Contention), Beijing: Zhongguo Renshi Chubanshe.

Chen, David W. (2010), 'China Emerges as a Scapegoat in Campaign Ads', *New York Times*, 9 October, p. 1.

Chen, Xiaomei (1995), *Occidentalism: A Theory of Counter-Discourse in Post-Mao China*, New York: Oxford University Press.

China Digital Times (2007), 'CDT Bookshelf: Interview with James Mann', 26 February, http://chinadigitaltimes.net/2007/02/cdt-bookshelf-interview-with-james-mann/

China State Council Information Office (2009), *China's National Defense in 2008*, Beijing: China State Council Information Office, 20 January.

Ching Cheong (2004), 'US Plans Huge Show of Force in Pacific', *Straits Times*, 30 June.

Chomsky, Noam (1987), *The Chomsky Reader* (ed. James Peck), New York: Pantheon Books.

Chomsky, Noam (2005), *Imperial Ambitions: Conversations with Noam Chomsky on the Post-9/11 World* (Interviews with David Barsamian), New York: Metropolitan Books.

Chow, Rey (2001), 'King Kong in Hong Kong: Watching the "Handover" from the U.S.A.', in Xudong Zhang (ed.), *Whither China? Intellectual Politics in Contemporary China*, Durham, NC: Duke University Press, pp. 211–27.

Christensen, Thomas J. (1996), 'Chinese Realpolitik', *Foreign Affairs*, **75** (5), 37–52.

Christensen, Thomas J. (2001), 'Posing Problems without Catching Up: China's Rise and Challenges for U.S. Security Policy', *International Security*, **25** (4), 5–40.

Christensen, Thomas J. (2006), 'Fostering Stability or Creating a Monster? The Rise of China and U.S. Policy Toward East Asia', *International Security*, **31** (1), 81–126.

Christensen, Thomas J., Alastair Iain Johnston and Robert S. Ross (2006), 'Conclusions and Future Directions', in Alastair Iain Johnston and Robert S. Ross (eds), *New Directions in the Study of China's Foreign Policy*, Stanford, CA: Stanford University Press, pp. 394–404.

Clark, Gregory (1967), *In Fear of China*, Melbourne: Lansdowne Press.

Clifford, James (1988), *The Predicament of Culture*, Cambridge, MA: Harvard University Press.

Clinton, Bill (2000), 'In Clinton's Words: "An Outstretched Hand"', *New York Times*, 20 September, p. A16.

Clinton, Bill (2004), *My Life*, New York: Alfred A. Knopf.

Clinton, Hillary (2008), Foreign Policy Speech (audio file), 25 February, http://www.prx.org/pieces/24241

Cohen, Patricia (2008), 'Pentagon to Consult Academics on Security', *New York Times*, 18 June, p. 1.

Cohen, Paul A. (1984), *Discovering History in China: American Historical Writing on the Recent Chinese Past*, New York: Columbia University Press.

Cohen, Paul A. (2003), *China Unbound: Evolving Perspectives on the Chinese Past*, London: RoutledgeCurzon.

Cohen, Warren I. (1978), 'American Perceptions of China', in Michel Oksenberg and Robert B. Oxnam (eds), *Dragon and Eagle: United States-China Relations: Past and Future*, New York: Basic Books, pp. 54–86.

Cohen, Warren I. (1997), 'China's Strategic Culture', *Atlantic Monthly*, **279** (3), 103–5.

Cohen, Warren I. (2000), *America's Response to China: A History of Sino-American Relations* (4th edn), New York: Columbia University Press.

Cohen, Warren I. (2003), 'American Perceptions of China, 1789–1911', in Carola McGiffert (ed.), *China in the American Political Imagination*, Washington, DC: The CSIS Press, pp. 25–30.

Collingwood, R. G. (1946), *The Idea of History*, Oxford: Oxford University Press.

Commission of the European Communities (2006), *EU-China: Closer Partners, Growing Responsibilities*, COM(2006) 631 final, Brussels, 24 October.

Conable, Barber B., Jr. and David M. Lampton (1992/1993), 'China: The Coming Power', *Foreign Affairs*, **71** (5), 133–49.

Congressional Research Service (2008), *China's Foreign Policy and "Soft Power" in South America, Asia, and Africa: A Study Prepared for the Committee on Foreign Relations, United States Senate*, Washington, DC: U.S. Government Printing Office.

Cronin, Jon (2006), 'Fears of Growing US Trade Rift with China', BBC News, 17 February, http://news.bbc.co.uk/1/hi/business/4719826.stm.

Crossick, Stanley (2007), 'Whither EU-China Relations?' 22 October, http://crossick. blogactiv.eu/2007/10/22/whither-eu-china-relations-2/

Crow, Carl (1937), *400 Million Customers*, London: Hamilton.

Crutsinger, Martin (2006), 'U.S. Hardens Stance on Trade with China', Associated Press, 14 February.

Culler, Jonathan (1982), *On Deconstruction: Theory and Criticism after Structuralism*, Ithaca, NY: Cornell University Press.

Culler, Jonathan (1997), *Literary Theory: A Very Short Introduction*, Oxford: Oxford University Press.

Cumings, Bruce (1996), 'The World Shakes China', *The National Interest*, No. 43, pp. 28–41.

Cumings, Bruce (1999), *Parallax Visions: Making Sense of American-East Asian Relations*, Durham, NC: Duke University Press.

Daily Telegraph (UK) (2006), 'The Dragon in Africa' (Letter to the Editor), 26 April.

Dawson, Raymond (1967), *The Chinese Chameleon: An Analysis of European Perceptions of Chinese Civilization*, New York: Oxford University Press.

Dean, Jodi (2009), *Democracy and Other Neoliberal Fantasies*, Durham, NC: Duke University Press.

Der Derian, James (1995), 'The Value of Security: Hobbes, Marx, Nietzsche, and Baudrillard', in Ronnie D. Lipschutz (ed.), *On Security*, New York: Columbia University Press, pp. 24–45.

Derbyshire, John (2001), 'China: A Reality Check', *National Review*, 17 September, pp. 38–43.

Dewey, John (1929), *The Quest for Certainty: A Study of the Relation of Knowledge and Action*, New York: Minton, Balch & Company.

Diamond, Larry (2000), 'Forward', in Suisheng Zhao (ed.), *China and Democracy: The Prospect for a Democratic China*, New York: Routledge, pp. ix–xv.

Dickson, Bruce (ed.) (1999), *Trends in China Watching: Observing the PRC at Fifty* (Sigur Center Asia Papers, No. 7), Washington DC: George Washington University.

Dikötter, Frank (1996), 'Culture, "Race" and Nation: The Formation of National Identity in Twentieth Century China', *Journal of International Affairs*, **49** (2), 590–605.

Dinmore, Guy and Geoff Dyer (2010), 'Immelt Hits Out at China and Obama', *Financial Times* (FT.Com), 1 July, http://www.ft.com/intl/cms/s/0/ed654fac-8518-11df-adfa-00144feabdc0.html

Dobbins, James, David C. Gompert, David A. Shlapak and Andrew Scobell (2011), *Conflict with China: Prospects, Consequences, and Strategies for Deterrence*, Santa Monica, CA: RAND Corporation.

Dobell, Graeme (2010), 'Treasury's China Star', *The Interpreter*, 12 May, http://www.lowyinterpreter.org/post/2010/05/12/Treasury-China-star.aspx

Dobriansky, Paula J. (2010), 'The Realist Case for Tibetan Autonomy', *Wall Street Journal*, 7 January, p. A15.

Dodin, Thierry and Heinz Räther (eds) (2001), *Imagining Tibet: Perceptions, Projections, and Fantasies*, Boston, MA: Wisdom Publications.

Dorogi, Thomas Laszlo (2001), *Tainted Perceptions: Liberal-Democracy and American Popular Images of China*, Lanham, MD: University Press of America.

Dorrien, Gary (2004), *Imperial Designs: Neoconservatism and the New Pax Americana*, New York: Routledge.

Doty, Roxanne Lynn (1996), *Imperial Encounters: The Politics of Representation in North-South Relations*, Minneapolis, MN: University of Minnesota Press.

Dreyfuss, Robert (1997), 'The New China Lobby', *The American Prospect*, No. 30, pp. 30–37.

Dreyfuss, Robert (2010), 'China in the Driver's Seat', *The Nation*, 20 September, pp. 11–18.

Dulles, Foster Rhea (1946), *China and America: The Story of Their Relations since 1784*, Princeton, NJ: Princeton University Press.

Duncombe, Stephen (2007), *Dream: Re-imagining Progressive Politics in an Age of Fantasy*, New York: The New Press.

Dupont, Alan (2010), 'Many Shared Interests but Few Shared Values with China', *The Australian*, 12 April, p. 14.

Dupont, Alan (2010), 'U.S. Enlists China's Worried Neighbours', *The Australian*, 3 August, p. 10.

Dyer, Geoff and Ben Hall (2008), 'China Seen as Biggest Threat to Stability', *Financial Times* (Asia), 15 April, p. 2.

Eagleton, Terry (1996), *Literary Theory: An Introduction* (2nd edn), Oxford: Blackwell.

Eagleton-Pierce, Matthew (2011), 'Advancing a Reflexive International Relations', *Millennium: Journal of International Studies*, **39** (3), 805–23.

Economist (2008), 'Spotlight on Asia.view: Welcome to Oz?', 28 June, p. 27.

Economy, Elizabeth and Michel Oksenberg (eds) (1999), *China Joins the World: Progress and Prospects*, New York: Council on Foreign Relations Press.

Elahi, Mahmood (2007), 'America, A Chinese Protectorate?' *The Daily Star*, 27 August, http://www.thedailystar.net/newDesign/news-details.php?nid= 1435

Engardio, Pete (ed.) (2007), *Chindia: How China and India Are Revolutionizing Global Business*, New York: McGraw-Hill.

Erlanger, Steven (1997), 'Searching for an Enemy and Finding China', *New York Times*, 6 April, p. 4.

European Commission (n.d.), 'The Sectoral Dialogues between the EU and China – an Overview', Policy Dialogues Support Facility, http://www.eu-chinapdsf.org/english/Column.asp?ColumnId=5

Fabian, Johannes (2002), *Time and the Other: How Anthropology Makes Its Object* (2nd edn), New York: Columbia University Press.

Fairbank, John K. (1967), *China: The People's Middle Kingdom and the U.S.A.*, Cambridge, MA: Belknap Press.

Fairbank, John K. (1976), *China Perceived: Images & Policies in Chinese-American Relations*, London: André Deutsch.

Fallows, James (2007), 'China Makes, the World Takes', *Atlantic Monthly*, **300** (1), 48–72.

Fan Shiming (2005), '"Aihen jiaorong" zhong de fan Mei zhuyi' (Anti-Americanism in a 'Love-Hate' Complex), *Guoji zhengzhi yanjiu* (International Politics Quarterly), No. 2, pp. 52–8.

Fan, Maureen (2007), 'China's Rights Record Criticized', *Washington Post*, 12 January, p. A10.

Fang Ning, Wang Xiaodong, Song Qiang, et al. (1999), *Quanqiuhua yinying xia de Zhongguo zhilu* (China's Road under the Shadow of Globalisation), Beijing: Zhongguo shehuikexue chubanshe.

Feeney, William R. (1992), 'China's Relations with Multilateral Economic Institutions', in the Joint Economic Committee, Congress of the United States (ed.), *China's Economic Dilemmas in the 1990s: The Problems of Reforms, Modernization, and Interdependence*, Armonk, NY: M. E. Sharpe, pp. 795–816.

Feldstein, Martin (2007), 'The Underfunded Pentagon', *Foreign Affairs*, **86** (2), 134–40.

Feng Guifen (Feng Kuei-fen) (1954), 'On the Manufacture of Foreign Weapons', in Ssu-yu Teng and John K. Fairbank et al., *China's Response to the West: A Documentary Survey 1839–1923*, Cambridge, MA: Harvard University Press, pp. 52–4.

Fewsmith, Joseph and Stanley Rosen (2001), 'The Domestic Context of Chinese Foreign Policy: Does "Public Opinion" Matter?' in David M. Lampton (ed.), *The Making of Chinese Foreign and Security Policy in the Era of Reform, 1978–2000*, Stanford, CA: Stanford University Press, pp. 151–87.

Fisher, George M. C. (2001), 'Kodak and China: Seven Years of Kodak Moments', in Laurence J. Brahm (ed.), *China's Century: The Awakening of the Next Economic Powerhouse*, Singapore: John Wiley & Sons (Asia), pp. 127–35.

Fishman, Ted C. (2006), *China Inc.: How the Rise of the Next Superpower Challenges America and the World*, New York: Scribner.

Fitzgerald, John (1996), 'The Nationless State: The Search for a Nation in Modern Chinese Nationalism', in Jonathan Unger (ed.), *Chinese Nationalism*, Armonk, NY: M. E. Sharpe, pp. 56–85.

Flyvbjerg, Bent (2001), *Making Social Science Matter: Why Social Inquiry Fails and How It Can Succeed Again*, Cambridge: Cambridge University Press.

Foot, Rosemary (2000), *Rights beyond Borders: The Global Community and the Struggle over Human Rights in China*, Oxford: Oxford University Press.

Foot, Rosemary (2001), 'China and the Idea of a Responsible State', in Yongjin Zhang and Greg Austin (eds), *Power and Responsibility in Chinese Foreign Policy*, Canberra: Asia Pacific Press, pp. 21–47.

Foucault, Michel (1970), *The Order of Things: An Archaeology of the Human Sciences*, London: Tavistock Publications.

Foucault, Michel (1977), *Discipline and Punish: The Birth of the Prison*, New York: Vantage Books.

Foucault, Michel (1978), *The History of Sexuality* (Volume 1: An Introduction, trans. Robert Hurley), London: Penguin Books.

Foucault, Michel (1980), *Power/Knowledge: Selected Interviews and Other Writings 1972–1977* (ed. Colin Gordon, trans. Colin Gordon, Leo Marshall, John Mepham, Kate Soper), New York: Pantheon Books.

Fox, John and François Godement (2009), *A Power Audit of EU-China Relations*, London: European Council on Foreign Relations.

Franklin, Barbara Hackman (1997), 'China Today: Evil Empire or Unprecedented Opportunity?' *Heritage Lecture*, no. 589, 20 May, http://www.heritage.org /Research/AsiaandthePacific/HL589.cfm

Frazier, Charles (1997), *Cold Mountain*, New York: Vintage Books.

Freeman, Chas W., Jr. (1996), 'Sino-American Relations: Back to Basics', *Foreign Policy*, No. 104, pp. 3–17.

Friedberg, Aaron L. (2000), 'Will Europe's Past Be Asia's Future?' *Survival*, **42** (3), 147–59.

Friedberg, Aaron L. (2007), 'Are We Ready for China?' *Commentary*, **124** (3), 39–43.

Friedman, Edward (1995), *National Identity and Democratic Projects in Socialist China*, Armonk, NY: M. E. Sharpe.

Friedman, Edward (1997), 'The Challenge of a Rising China: Another Germany?' in Robert J. Lieber (ed.), *Eagle Adrift: American Foreign Policy at the End of the Century*, New York: Longman, pp. 215–45.

Friedman, Edward (2002), 'Reflecting Mirrors across the Taiwan Straits: American Perspectives on a China threat', in Herbert Yee and Ian Storey (eds), *The China Threat: Perceptions, Myths and Reality*, London: RoutledgeCurzon, pp. 65–85.

Friedman, Edward (2009), 'China: A Threat to or Threatened by Democracy?' *Dissent*, **56** (1), 7–12.

Friedman, Thomas L. (2006), *The World Is Flat: The Globalized World in the Twenty-First Century*, London: Penguin Books.

Friedman, Thomas L. (2010), 'Containment-Lite', *New York Times*, 10 November, p. 35.

Fu Ying (2008), 'Western Media Has "Demonised" China', *The Telegraph*, 13 April, http://www.telegraph.co.uk/comment/personal-view/3557186/Chinese-ambassador-Fu-Ying-Western-media-has-demonised-China.html

Fukuyama, Francis (1992), *The End of History and the Last Man*, New York: Free Press.

Funabashi, Yoichi, Michel Oksenberg and Heinrich Weiss (1994), *An Emerging China in a World of Interdependence*, New York: The Trilateral Commission.

Furth, Hans G. (1987), *Knowledge As Desire: An Essay on Freud and Piaget*, New York: Columbia University Press.

Gadamer, Hans-Georg (1987), 'The Problem of Historical Consciousness', in Paul Rabinow and William M. Sullivan (eds), *Interpretive Social Science: A Second Look*, Berkeley, CA: University of California Press, pp. 82–140.

Gadamer, Hans-Georg (2004), *Truth and Method* (trans. Joel Weinsheimer and Donald G. Marshall, 2nd rev. edn), London: Continuum.

Garnaut, John (2009), 'The El Dorado Factor: How We Got China So Wrong', *The Age*, 13 July, p. 1.

Garrison, Jean A. (2005), *Making China Policy: From Nixon to G. W. Bush*, Boulder, CO: Lynne Rienner.

Garrison, Jean A. (2008), 'The Domestic Political Game behind the Engagement Strategy', in Suisheng Zhao (ed.), *China–U.S. Relations Transformed: Perspectives and Strategic Interactions*, London: Routledge, pp. 141–58.

Garver, John W. (1999), 'Forward', in Yong Deng and Fei-ling Wang (eds), *In the Eyes of the Dragon: China Views the World*, Lanham, MD: Rowman & Littlefield, pp. viii–ix.

Geertz, Clifford (1973), *The Interpretation of Cultures*, New York: Basic Books.

Gehrke, Robert (2010), 'Huntsman Looks for Rebound in U.S.-China Relations', 7 May, http://www.sltrib.com/sltrib/home/49545828-73/huntsman-china-relationship -think.html.csp

George, Jim (1994), *Discourses of Global Politics: A Critical (Re)Introduction to International Relations*, Boulder, CO: Lynne Rienner.

Gershman, John (2003), 'Asia', in John Feffer (ed.), *Power Trip: U.S. Unilateralism and Global Strategy After September 11*, New York: Seven Stories Press, pp. 161–72.

Gertz, Bill (2006), 'Pentagon "Hedge" Strategy Targets China', *Washington Times*, 17 March, p. A06.

Giddens, Anthony (1986), *The Constitution of Society*, Berkeley, CA: University of California Press.

Giddens, Anthony (1990), *The Consequences of Modernity*, Cambridge: Polity Press.

Gifford, Rob (2007), *China Road: A Journey into the Future of a Rising Power*, New York: Random House.

Gilboy, George and Eric Heginbotham (2001), 'China's Coming Transformation', *Foreign Affairs*, **80** (4), 26–39.

Gillard, Julia (2011), Speech to the AsiaLink and Asia Society Lunch, Melbourne, 28 September, http://www.pm.gov.au/press-office/speech-asialink-and-asia-society-lunch-melbourne

Gilley, Bruce (2004), *China's Democratic Future: How It Will Happen and Where It Will Lead*, New York: Columbia University Press.

Global Language Monitor, 'Rise of China Still Tops all Stories', 5 May 2011, http://www.languagemonitor.com/top-news/bin-ladens-death-one-of-top-news-stories-of-21th-century/

Global Times (2010), 'US Has to Pay for Provoking China' (editorial), 6 July, http://www.globaltimes.cn/opinion/editorial/2010-07/548629.html

Goldman, Merle (1994), *Sowing the Seeds of Democracy in China: Political Reform in the Deng Xiaoping Era*, Cambridge, MA: Harvard University Press.

Goldman, Merle, Perry Link and Su Wei (1993), 'China's Intellectuals in the Deng Era: Loss of Identity with the State', in Lowell Dittmer and Samuel S. Kim (eds), *China's Quest for National Identity*, Ithaca, NY: Cornell University Press, pp. 125–53.

Goldstein, Jonathan (1991), 'Cantonese Artefacts, Chinoiserie, and Early American Idealization of China', in Jonathan Goldstein, Jerry Israel and Hilary Conroy (eds), *America Views China: American Images of China Then and Now*, Bethlehem, PA: Lehigh University Press, pp. 43–55.

Goldstein, Jonathan, Jerry Israel and Hilary Conroy (eds) (1991), *America Views China: American Images of China Then and Now*, London: Associated University Presses.

Goldstein, Judith and Robert O. Keohane (1993), 'Ideas and Foreign Policy: An Analytical Framework', in Judith Goldstein and Robert O. Keohane (eds), *Ideas and Foreign Policy: Beliefs, Institutions, and Political Change*, Ithaca, NY: Cornell University Press, pp. 3–30.

Goodman, David S. G. (1997), 'How Open Is Chinese Society?', in David S. G. Goodman and Gerald Segal (eds), *China Rising: Nationalism and Interdependence*, London: Routledge, pp. 27–52.

Goodman, David S. G. and Gerald Segal (eds) (1997), *China Rising: Nationalism and Interdependence*, London: Routledge.

Gordon, Michael R. (2006), 'To Build Trust, U.S. Navy Holds a Drill with China', *New York Times*, 23 September, p. A5.

Graham, Edward D. (1983), 'The "Imaginative Geography" of China', in Warren I. Cohen (ed.), *Reflections on Orientalism: Edward Said*, East Lansing, MI: Asian Studies Center, Michigan State University, pp. 31–43.

Green, Michael (2012), 'US Turns Its Gaze to the Pacific', *The World Today*, **68** (2), 30–33.
Gresh, Alain (2008), 'Understanding the Beijing Consensus', *Le Monde*, November, http://mondediplo.com/2008/11/03beijingconsensus
Gress, David (1998), *From Plato to NATO: The Idea of the West and Its Opponents*, New York: The Free Press.
Gries, Peter Hays (2004), *China's New Nationalism: Pride, Politics, and Diplomacy*, Berkeley, CA: University of California Press.
Gries, Peter Hays (2005), 'Nationalism and Chinese Foreign Policy', in Yong Deng and Fei-ling Wang (eds), *China Rising: Power and Motivation in Chinese Foreign Policy*, Lanham, MD: Rowman & Littlefield, pp. 103–20.
Grosrichard, Alain (1998), *The Sultan's Court: European Fantasies of the East* (trans. Liz Heron), London: Verso.
Grunfeld, A. Tom (2003), '"God We Had Fun": CIA in China and Sino-American Relations', *Critical Asian Studies*, **35** (1), 113–38.
Guardian Weekly (2001), 'Bush Needs the Bad Guys', 15–21 March, p. 14.
Guo Jishan (1996), *Zouxiang zuguo tongyi de zuji* (Steps Toward the Reunification of the Motherland), Beijing: Hongqi Chubanshe.
Gupta, Suman (2008), 'Writing China', *Wasafiri*, **23** (3), 1–4.
Gurtov, Mel (2007), *Global Politics in the Human Interest* (5th edn), Boulder, CO: Lynne Rienner.
Guthrie, Doug (2008), *China and Globalization: The Social, Economic and Political Transformation* (2nd edn), London: Routledge.
Gutmann, Ethan (2004), *Losing the New China: A Story of American Commerce, Desire, and Betrayal*, San Francisco, CA: Encounter Books.
Gyngell, Allan and Michael Wesley (2007), *Making Australian Foreign Policy* (2nd edn), Cambridge: Cambridge University Press.
Haass, Richard N. (2005), *The Opportunity: America's Moment to Alter History's Course*, New York: PublicAffairs.
Habermas, Jürgen (1978), *Knowledge and Human Interests* (2nd edn, trans. Jeremy J. Shapiro), London: Heinemann.
Halloran, Richard (2006), 'Guam to Become the "Pivot Point" for the US' Pacific Forces', *Taipei Times*, 14 March, http://www.taipeitimes.com/news/editorials/archives/2006/03/14/2003297313
Halper, Stefan (2007), 'Wrongly Mistaking China', *The American Spectator*, **40** (1), 14–20.
Halper, Stefan (2010), *The Beijing Consensus: How China's Authoritarian Model Will Dominate the Twenty-First Century*, New York: Basic Books.
Hamre, John J. (2003), 'Forward: Images Revisited', in Carola McGiffert (ed.), *China in the American Political Imagination*, Washington, DC: The CSIS Press, pp. ix–xi.
Harding, Harry (1982), 'From China with Disdain: New Trends in the Study of China', *Asian Survey*, **22** (10), 934–58.
Harding, Harry (1987), *China's Second Revolution: Reform After Mao*, Sydney: Allen & Unwin.
Harding, Harry (1992), *A Fragile Relationship: The United States and China since 1972*, Washington, DC: Brookings Institution.
Harding, Harry (1997), 'Breaking the Impasse over Human Rights', in Ezra F. Vogel (ed.), *Living with China: U.S./China Relations in the Twenty-First Century*, New York: W. W. Norton & Company, pp. 165–84.
Hardt, Michael and Antonio Negri (2000), *Empire*, Cambridge, MA: Harvard University Press.

Harries, Owen (1993), 'The Collapse of "the West"', *Foreign Affairs*, **72** (4), 41–53.
Harries, Owen (1997), 'How Not to Handle China', *National Review*, **149** (9), 35–8.
Harries, Owen (1999/2000), 'A Year of Debating China', *The National Interest*, No. 58, pp. 141–7.
Harris, Stuart (2002), 'Globalisation and China's Diplomacy: Structure and Process', Department of International Relations Working Paper No. 2002/9, Canberra: Australian National University, December, pp. 1–24.
Hartung, William D. (2003), *How Much Are You Making on the War, Daddy? A Quick and Dirty Guide to War Profiteering in the George W. Bush Administration*, New York: Nation Books.
Hartung, William D. and Michelle Ciarrocca (2001), 'Reviving Star Wars', *The Baltimore Sun*, 21 January, http://articles.baltimoresun.com/2001-01-21/topic/0101200170_1_nmd-national-missile-defense-system/2
Hartung, William D. and Michelle Ciarrocca (2004), *The Ties that Bind: Arms Industry Influence in the Bush Administration and Beyond* (Special Report), New York: World Policy Institute, October.
Hayot, Eric, Haun Saussy and Steven G. Yao (2008), 'Introduction', in Eric Hayot, Haun Saussy and Steven G. Yao (eds), *Sinographies: Writing China*, Minneapolis, MN: University of Minnesota Press, pp. vii–xxi.
Hayot, Eric, Haun Saussy and Steven G. Yao (eds) (2008), *Sinographies: Writing China*, Minneapolis, MN: University of Minnesota Press.
Heckelman, Ronald J. (1989), '"The Swelling Act": The Psychoanalytic Geography of Fantasy', in George E. Slusser and Eric S. Rabkin (eds), *Mindscapes: The Geographies of Imagined Worlds*, Carbondale: Southern Illinois University Press, pp. 34–59.
Heidegger, Martin (1967), *Being and Time* (trans. John Macquarrie and Edward Robinson), Oxford: Blackwell.
Heilbrunn, Jacob (1999), 'Team W.', *The New Republic*, 27 September, pp. 22–5.
Henriksen, Thomas H. (1995), 'The Coming Great Powers Competition', *World Affairs*, **158** (2), 63–9.
Hertsgaard, Mark (1997), 'Our Real China Problem', *Atlantic Monthly*, **280** (5), 96–114.
Hevia, James L. (2003), *English Lessons: The Pedagogy of Imperialism in Nineteenth-Century China*, Durham, NC: Duke University Press.
Higgs, Robert (2006), 'Fear: The Foundation of Every Government's Power', *Independent Review*, **10** (3), 447–66.
Ho, Soyoung (2006), 'Panda Slugger', *Washington Monthly*, **38** (7), 26–31.
Hodder, Rupert (2000), *In China's Image: Chinese Self-Perception in Western Thought*, London: Macmillan.
Hodge, Bob and Kam Louie (1998), *The Politics of Chinese Language and Culture: The Art of Reading Dragons*, London: Routledge.
Hoffman, Stanley (1977), 'An American Social Science: International Relations', *Dædalus*, **106** (3), 41–60.
Hollander, Paul (1998), *Political Pilgrims: Western Intellectuals in Search of the Good Society* (4th edn), New Brunswick, NJ: Transaction Publishers.
Hollingsworth, J. Rogers (1971), *Nation and State Building in America: Comparative Historical Perspectives*, Boston, MA: Little, Brown.
Holslag, Jonathan (2006), 'The European Union and China: The Great Disillusion', *European Foreign Affairs Review*, **11** (4), 555–81.

Hook, Steven W. and Xiaoyu Pu (2006), 'Framing Sino-American Relations under Stress: A Reexamination of News Coverage of the 2001 Spy Plane Crisis', *Asian Affairs: An American Review*, **33** (3), 167–83.

Hornig, Frank and Wieland Wagner (2006), 'Dueling Titans: China, the US and Battle to Lead a Globalized World', *Spiegel Online*, 3 February, http://www.spiegel.de/international/spiegel/0,1518,398844,00.html

Hossein-Zadeh, Ismael (2006), *The Political Economy of U.S. Militarism*, New York: Palgrave Macmillan.

Hughes, Christopher (1997), 'Globalisation and Nationalism: Squaring the Circle in Chinese International Relations Theory', *Millennium: Journal of International Studies*, **26** (1), 103–24.

Human Rights Watch (2006), *Race to the Bottom: Corporate Complicity in Chinese Internet Censorship*, New York: Human Rights Watch, http://www.hrw.org/reports/2006/china0806/

Human Rights Watch (2007), *World Report 2007*, New York: Human Rights Watch.

Hunt, Michael H. (1983), *The Making of a Special Relationship: The United States and China to 1914*, New York: Columbia University Press.

Hunt, Michael H. (1984), 'Chinese Foreign Relations in Historical Perspective', in Harry Harding (ed.), *China's Foreign Relations in the 1980s*, New Haven, CT: Yale University Press, pp. 1–42.

Hunt, Michael H. (1987), *Ideology and U.S. Foreign Policy*, New Haven, CT: Yale University Press.

Hunt, Michael H. (1996), *Crisis in U.S. Foreign Policy: An International History Reader*, New Haven, CT: Yale University Press.

Hunt, Michael H. (n.d.), 'CCP Foreign Policy: "Normalizing" the Field', in Michael H. Hunt and Niu Jun (eds), *Toward a History of Chinese Communist Foreign Relations, 1920s–1960s: Personalities and Interpretive Approaches*, Washington, DC: Woodrow Wilson Center Asia Program, pp. 163–91.

Huntington, Samuel P. (1968), *Political Order in Changing Societies*, New Haven, CT: Yale University Press.

Huntington, Samuel P. (1991), *The Third Wave: Democratization in the Late Twentieth Century*, Norman, OK: University of Oklahoma Press.

Huntington, Samuel P. (1996), *The Clash of Civilizations and the Remaking of World Order*, London: Touchstone Books.

Huntington, Samuel P. (1997), 'The Erosion of American National Interests', *Foreign Affairs*, **76** (5), 28–49.

Huntington, Samuel P. (2004), *Who Are We? America's Great Debate*, London: Free Press.

Hutton, Will (2006), *Writing on the Wall: Why We Must Embrace China as a Partner or Face It as an Enemy*, New York: Free Press.

Hyde-Price, Adrian (2008), 'A "Tragic Actor"? A Realist Perspective on "Ethical Power Europe"', *International Affairs*, **84** (1), 29–44.

Ikenberry, G. John and Anne-Marie Slaughter (2006), *Forging A World of Liberty Under Law: U.S. National Security in the 21st Century Final Report of the Princeton Project on National Security* (The Princeton Project Papers), Princeton, NJ: The Woodrow Wilson School of Public and International Affairs, Princeton University.

Ikenberry, G. John and Michael Mastanduno (2003), 'Introduction: International Relations Theory and the Search for Regional Stability', in G. John Ikenberry and Michael Mastanduno (eds), *International Relations Theory and the Asia-Pacific*, New York: Columbia University Press.

Inayatullah, Naeem (ed.) (2010), *Autobiographical International Relations: I, IR*, London: Routledge.

Inayatullah, Naeem and David L. Blaney (2004), *International Relations and the Problem of Difference*, New York: Routledge.

Inboden, Will (2010), 'The Reality of the "China Fantasy"', Foreign Policy Online, 16 June, http://shadow.foreignpolicy.com/posts/2010/06/16/the_reality_of_the_china_fantasy

International Monetary Fund (2011), *World Economic Outlook April 2011: Tensions from the Two-Speed Recovery: Unemployment, Commodities, and Capital Flows*, Washington DC: International Monetary Fund.

International Security Advisory Board (2008), *China's Strategic Modernization: Report from the ISAB Taskforce*, http://www.fas.org/nuke/guide/china/ISAB2008.pdf

Iriye, Akira (1967), *Across the Pacific: An Inner History of American-East Asian Relations*, New York: Harcourt, Brace & World, Inc.

Isaacs, Harold (1980), *Scratches on Our Minds: American Images of China and India*, Armonk, NY: M. E. Sharpe.

Jacobson, Harold K. and Michel Oksenberg (1990), *China's Participation in the IMF, the World Bank, and GATT*, Ann Arbor, MI: University of Michigan Press.

Jacques, Martin (2009), *When China Rules the World: The End of the Western World and the Birth of a New Global Order*, New York: The Penguin Press.

Jain, Purnendra (2006), 'A "Little NATO" against China', Asia Times Online, 18 March, http://www.atimes.com/atimes/China/HC18Ad01.html

Jameson, Fredric (1981), *The Political Unconscious: Narrative as a Socially Symbolic Act*, London: Methuen.

Jensen, Lionel M. and Timothy B. Weston (eds) (2007), *China's Transformations: Stories Behind the Headlines*, Lanham, MD: Rowman & Littlefield.

Jentleson, Bruce W. and Ely Ratner (2011), 'Bridging the Beltway-Ivory Tower Gap', *International Studies Review*, **13** (2), 6–11.

Jervis, Robert (1976), *Perception and Misperception in International Relations*, Princeton, NJ: Princeton University Press.

Jespersen, T. Christopher (1996), *American Images of China: 1931–1949*, Stanford, CA: Stanford University Press.

Jia Qingguo (1996), 'Economic Development, Political Stability, and International Respect', *Journal of International Affairs*, **49** (2), 572–89.

Jia Qingguo (2005), 'Learning to Live with the Hegemon: Evolution of China's Policy toward the US since the End of the Cold War', *Journal of Contemporary China*, **14** (44), 395–407.

Johnson, Chalmers (1996), 'Containing China: U.S. and Japan Drift Toward Disaster', *Japan Quarterly*, **43** (4), 10–18.

Johnson, Chalmers (1997), 'The CIA and Me', *Bulletin of Concerned Asian Scholars*, **29** (1), 34–7.

Johnson, Chalmers (2004), 'The Military-Industrial Man: How Local Politics Works in America—or a "Duke" in Every District', 14 September, http://www.tomdispatch.com/post/1818/chalmers_johnson_on_electing_the_pentagon_s_man

Johnson, Chalmers (2004), *The Sorrow of Empire: Militarism, Secrecy, and the End of the Republic*, New York: Metropolitan Books.

Johnson, Chalmers (2006), *Nemesis: The Last Days of the American Republic*, Melbourne: Scribe Publications.

Johnston, Alastair Iain (1995), *Cultural Realism: Strategic Culture and Grand Strategy in Chinese History*. Princeton, NJ: Princeton University Press.

Johnston, Alastair Iain (1996), 'Learning Versus Adaptation: Explaining Change in Chinese Arms Control Policy in the 1980s and 1990s', *The China Journal*, No. 35, pp. 27–62.

Johnston, Alastair Iain (2003), 'Socialization in International Institutions: The ASEAN Way and International Relations Theory', in G. John Ikenberry and Michael Mastanduno (eds), *International Relations Theory and the Asia-Pacific*, New York: Columbia University Press, pp. 107–62.

Johnston, Alastair Iain (2004), 'Chinese Middle Class Attitudes towards International Affairs: Nascent Liberalization?' *The China Quarterly*, **179** (1), 603–28.

Johnston, Alastair Iain (2008), *Social States: China in International Institutions, 1980–2000*, Princeton, NJ: Princeton University Press.

Johnston, Alastair Iain and Paul Evans (1999), 'China's Engagement with Multilateral Security Institutions', in Alastair Iain Johnston and Robert S. Ross (eds), *Engaging China: The Management of an Emerging Power*, London: Routledge, pp. 235–72.

Johnston, Alastair Iain and Robert S. Ross (1999), 'Conclusion', in Alastair Iain Johnston and Robert S. Ross, (eds), *Engaging China: The Management of an Emerging Power*, London: Routledge, pp. 273–95.

Johnston, Alastair Iain and Robert S. Ross (eds) (2006), *New Directions in the Study of China's Foreign Policy*, Stanford, CA: Stanford University Press.

Jones, David Martin (2001), *The Image of China in Western Social and Political Thought*, Basingstoke: Palgrave.

Journal of Electronic Defense (2005), 'Disaster Planning', **28** (12), 17.

Kagan, Robert (2004), *Of Paradise and Power: America and Europe in the New World Order*, New York: Vintage Books.

Kagan, Robert (2005), 'The Illusion of "Managing" China', *Washington Post,* 15 May, p. B07.

Kagan, Robert (2008), *The Return of History and the End of Dreams*, New York: Alfred A. Knopf.

Kagan, Robert (2009), 'Ambition and Anxiety: America's Competition with China', in Gary J. Schmitt (ed.), *The Rise of China: Essays on the Future Competition*, New York: Encounter Books, pp. 1–23.

Kagan, Robert (2010), 'Obama's Year One: *Contra*', *World Affairs*, **172** (3), 12–18.

Kagan, Robert and William Kristol (2001), 'A National Humiliation', *Weekly Standard*, 16–23 April, pp. 11–16.

Kaiser, Robert G. and Steven Mufson (2000), '"Blue Team" Draws a Hard Line on Beijing: Action on Hill Reflects Informal Group's Clout', *Washington Post,* 22 February, p. A1.

Kang, David C. (2007), *China Rising: Peace, Power, and Order in East Asia*, New York: Columbia University Press.

Kaplan, Fred (2006), 'The China Syndrome: Why the Pentagon Keeps Overestimating Beijing's Military Strength', 26 May, http://www.slate.com/id/2141966/

Kaplan, Fred (2008), *Daydream Believers: How a Few Grand Ideas Wrecked American Power*, Hoboken, NJ: John Wiley & Sons.

Kaplan, Robert D. (1994), 'The Coming Anarchy', *Atlantic Monthly*, **273** (2), 44–76.

Kaplan, Robert D. (2005), 'How We Would Fight China', *Atlantic Monthly*, **295** (5), 49–64.

Kaplan, Robert D. (2010), 'The Geography of Chinese Power: How Far Can Beijing Reach on Land and at Sea?', *Foreign Affairs*, **89** (3), 22–41.

Kapp, Robert A. (1994), 'Testimony', in *United States-China Trade Relations: Hearing before the Subcommittee on Trade, Committee on Ways and Means, US*

House of Representatives, One Hundred Third Congress, Second Session, Washington, DC: US Government Printing Office, 24 February, pp. 192–4.

Kapp, Robert A. (2003), 'The Matter of Business', in Carola McGiffert (ed.), *China in the American Political Imagination*, Washington, DC: The CSIS Press, pp. 82–92.

Katzenstein, Peter J. and Robert O. Keohane (2007), 'Conclusion: Anti-Americanism and the Polyvalence of America', in Peter J. Katzenstein and Robert O. Keohane (eds), *Anti-Americanisms in World Politics*, Ithaca, NY: Cornell University Press, pp. 306–16.

Kavalski, Emilian (2009), '"Do as I do": The Global Politics of China's Regionalization', in Emilian Kavalski (ed.), *China and the Global Politics of Regionalization*, Farnham, UK: Ashgate, pp. 1–16.

Kavalski, Emilian (ed.) (2009), *China and the Global Politics of Regionalization*, Farnham: Ashgate.

Kegley, Charles W., Jr. (2002), 'Bridge-Building in the Study of International Relations: How "Kuhn" We Do Better?', in Donald J. Puchala (ed.), *Visions of International Relations: Assessing an Academic Field*, Columbia, SC: University of South Carolina Press, pp. 62–80.

Kellner, Tomas (2004), 'Open for Business', *Forbes*, 6 September, http://www.forbes.com/forbes/2004/0906/106_print.html

Kendall, Timothy (2005), *Ways of Seeing China: From Yellow Peril to Shangrila*, Fremantle: Curtin University Books.

Kent, Ann (1997/1998), 'China, International Organizations and Regimes: The ILO as a Case Study in Organizational Learning', *Pacific Affairs*, **70** (4), 517–32.

Kent, Ann (1999), *China, the United Nations, and Human Rights: The Limits of Compliance*, Philadelphia, PA: University of Pennsylvania Press.

Kent, Ann (2001), 'China's Participation in International Organizations', in Yongjin Zhang and Greg Austin (eds), *Power and Responsibility in Chinese Foreign Policy*, Canberra: Asia Pacific Press, pp. 132–66.

Khalilzad, Zalmay (1999/2000), 'Sweet and Sour: Recipe for a New China Policy', *Rand Review*, **23** (3), 6–11.

Kim, Samuel S. (1989), 'New Directions and Old Puzzles in Chinese Foreign Policy', in Samuel S. Kim (ed.), *China and the World: New Directions in Chinese Foreign Relations*, Boulder, CO: Westview Presss, pp. 3–30.

Kindopp, Jason (1999), 'Trends in China Watching: Observing the PRC at 50: Conference Summary', in Bruce Dickson (ed.), *Trends in China Watching: Observing the PRC at Fifty* (Sigur Center Asia Papers, No. 7), Washington DC: George Washington University, pp. 1–12.

King, Neil, Jr. (2005), 'Secret Weapon: Inside Pentagon, a Scholar Shapes Views of China', *Wall Street Journal*, 8 September, p. A1.

Kirkpatrick, Jeane (2004), 'Neoconservatism as a Response to the Counter-Culture', in Irwin Stelzer (ed.), *The Neocon Reader*, New York: Grove Press, pp. 235–40.

Kissinger, Henry (1994), *Diplomacy*, New York: Simon & Schuster.

Klare, Michael T. (2005), 'Revving Up the China Threat', *The Nation*, 24 October, pp. 28–32.

Klein, Alec (2007), 'The Army's $200 Billion Makeover', *Washington Post*, 7 December, p. A01.

Klein, Bradley S. (1997), 'Conclusion: Every Month Is "Security Awareness Month"', in Keith Krause and Michael C. Williams (eds), *Critical Security Studies: Concepts and Cases*, Minneapolis, MN: University of Minnesota Press, pp. 359–68.

Klein, Christina (2003), *Cold War Orientalism: Asia in the Middlebrow Imagination, 1945–1961*, Berkeley, CA: University of California Press.

Klein, Joe (2005), 'Think Twice about a Pullout', *Time*, 20 November, http://www.time.com/time/columnist/klein/article/0,9565,1132784,00.html

Klineberg, Otto (1964), *The Human Dimension in International Relations*, New York: Holt, Rinehart and Winston.

Klintworth, Gary (2001), 'China and Arms Control: A Learning Process', in Yongjin Zhang and Greg Austin (eds), *Power and Responsibility in Chinese Foreign Policy*, Canberra: Asia Pacific Press, pp. 219–49.

Klug, Foster (2009), 'Gates Says US Ready for Any China "Threat"', Associated Press Newswires, 28 January.

Knight, Nick (2008), *Imagining Globalisation in China: Debates on Ideology, Politics and Culture*, Cheltenham: Edward Elgar.

Knightley, Phillip (2003), *The First Casualty: The War Correspondent as Hero, Propagandist and Myth-Maker from the Crimea to Iraq*, London: André Deutsch.

Knox, MacGregor (2011), 'Thinking War – History Lite?' *The Journal of Strategic Studies*, **34** (4), 489–500.

Korporaal, Glenda (2008), 'China Boom to Shore Up Coffers', *The Australian*, 14 May, p. 3.

Krause, Keith and Michael C. Williams (eds) (1997), *Critical Security Studies: Concepts and Cases*, Minneapolis, MN: University of Minnesota Press.

Krauthammer, Charles (1991), 'Universal Dominion', in Owen Harries (ed.), *America's Purpose: New Visions of U.S. Foreign Policy*, San Francisco, CA: ICS Press, pp. 5–13.

Krauthammer, Charles (1992), 'Do We Really Need a New Enemy?' *Time*, 23 March, p. 76.

Krauthammer, Charles (1995), 'Why We Must Contain China', *Time*, July 31, p. 72.

Krepinevich, Andrew F. (2010), *Why AirSea Battle?* Washington DC: Center for Strategic and Budgetary Assessments.

Kristof, Nicholas D. (1993), 'The Rise of China', *Foreign Affairs*, **72** (5), 63–5.

Kristof, Nicholas D. (2008), 'Earthquake and Hope', *New York Times,* 22 May, p. 31.

Kristol, Irving (2004), 'The Neoconservative Persuasion: What It Was, and What It Is', in Irwin Stelzer (ed.), *The Neocon Reader*, New York: Grove Press, pp. 33–7.

Kristol, William and Robert Kagan (2000), 'Introduction: National Interest and Global Responsibility', in Robert Kagan and William Kristol (eds), *Present Dangers: Crisis and Opportunity in American Foreign and Defense Policy*, San Francisco, CA: Encounter Books, pp. 3–24.

Krugman, Paul (2005), 'The Chinese Challenge', *New York Times*, 27 June, p. 15.

Kuhn, Thomas (1970), *The Structure of Scientific Revolutions* (2nd enl. edn), Chicago, IL: University of Chicago Press.

Kupchan, Charles A. (2002), *The End of the American Era*, New York: Vantage Books.

Kurlantzick, Joshua (2007), *Charm Offensive: How China's Soft Power Is Transforming the World*, New Haven, CT: Yale University Press.

Laclau, Ernesto and Chantal Mouffe (2001), *Hegemony and Socialist Strategy: Towards a Radical Democratic Politics* (2nd edn), London: Verso.

Lake, David A. (2006), 'American Hegemony and the Future of East-West Relations', *International Studies Perspective*, **7** (1), 23–30.

Lake, David A. (2011), 'Why "isms" Are Evil: Theory, Epistemology, and Academic Sects as Impediments to Understanding and Progress', *International Studies Quarterly*, **55** (2), 465–80.

Lam, Willy (2009), 'Reassurance or Appeasement?' *Far Eastern Economic Review*, **172** (9), 12–15.

Lampton, David M. (1997), 'A Growing China in a Shrinking World: Beijing and the Global Order', in Ezra F. Vogel (ed.), *Living with China: U.S./China Relations in the Twenty-First Century*, New York: W. W. Norton, pp. 120–40.

Lampton, David M. (2001), *Same Bed, Different Dreams: Managing U.S.-China Relations, 1989–2000*, Berkeley, CA: University of California Press.

Lampton, David M. (2007), '*The China Fantasy*, Fantasy', *The China Quarterly*, No. 191, pp. 745–9.

Lampton, David M. (2008), *The Three Faces of Chinese Power: Might, Money, and Minds*, Berkeley, CA: University of California Press.

Lampton, David M. and James Mann (2007), 'What's Your China Fantasy', Foreign Policy Online, 15 May, http://www.foreignpolicy.com/articles/2007/05/14/whats_your_china_fantasy

Lardy, Nicholas R. (2002), *Integrating China into the Global Economy*, Washington, DC: Brookings Institution Press.

Lardy, Nicholas R. (2003), 'The Economic Rise of China: Threat or Opportunity?' *Federal Reserve Bank of Cleveland Economic Commentary*, 1 August, http://www.clevelandfed.org/research/commentary/2003/0801.pdf

Larmer, Brook and Alexandra A. Seno (2003), 'A Reckless Harvest: China Is Protecting Its Own Trees, But Has Begun Instead to Devour Asia's Forests', *Newsweek* (international edn), 27 January, pp. 20–22.

Latham, Andrew A. (2001), 'China in the Contemporary American Geopolitical Imagination', *Asian Affairs: An American Review* **28** (3), 138–45.

Latham, Michael E. (2000), *Modernization as Ideology: American Social Science and "Nation Building" in the Kennedy Era*, Chapel Hill, NC: The University of North Carolina Press.

Lautz, Terrill E. (2003), 'Hopes and Fears of 60 Years: American Images of China, 1911–1972', in Carola McGiffert (ed.), *China in the American Political Imagination*, Washington, DC: The CSIS Press, pp. 31–7.

Layne, Christopher (2008), 'China's Challenge to US Hegemony', *Current History*, **107** (705), 13–18.

Lee, John (2010), 'Obama Switching Sides Over China', The Weekly Standard Blog, 30 July, http://www.weeklystandard.com/blogs/obama-switching-sides-over-china

Lee, Peter (2010), 'The New Face of U.S.-China Relations: "Strategic Reassurance" or Old-Fashioned Rollback?' *The Asia-Pacific Journal: Japan Focus*, 19 July, http://www.japanfocus.org/-Peter-Lee/3385

Lemke, Douglas and Ronald L. Tammen (2003), 'Power Transition Theory and the Rise of China', *International Interactions*, **29** (4), 269–71.

Leonard, Mark (2008), *What Does China Think?* New York: PublicAffairs.

Leong, Karen J. (2005), *The China Mystique: Pearl S. Buck, Anna May Wong, Mayling Soong, and the Transformation of American Orientalism*, Berkeley, CA: University of California Press.

Lerer, Lisa (2008), 'Clinton Adviser Quits Over China Rhetoric', Politico, 19 April, http://www.politico.com/news/stories/0408/9719.html

Levinas, Emmanuel (1987), *Time and the Other* (trans. Richard A. Cohen), Pittsburgh: Duquesne University Press.

Levy, Jack S. (1994), 'Learning and Foreign Policy: Sweeping a Conceptual Minefield', *International Organization*, **48** (2), 279–312.

Leys, Simon (1997), 'Introduction', in *The Analects of Confucius* (trans. Simon Leys), New York: W. W. Norton & Company, pp. xv–xxxii.

Li, Hongshan and Zhaohui Hong (1998), *Image, Perception, and the Making of U.S.-China Relations*, Lanham, MD: University Press of America.

Li Xiguang, Liu Kang, et al. (1996), *Yaomohua Zhongguo de beihou* (Behind the Demonization of China), Beijing: Zhongguo shehui kexue chubanshe.

Liang, Jingdong (2003), *How U.S. Correspondents Discover, Uncover, and Cover China: China Watching Transformed*, Lewiston, NY: Edwin Mellen.

Lieber, Keir A. and Daryl G. Press (2007), 'Superiority Complex', *Atlantic Monthly*, **300** (1), 86–92.

Lieberthal, Kenneth (2003), *Governing China: From Revolution Through Reform* (2nd edn), New York: W. W. Norton.

Lieberthal, Kenneth (2011), 'The American Pivot to Asia', Foreign Policy Online, 21 December, http://www.foreignpolicy.com/articles/2011/12/21/the_american_pivot _to _asia

Lieberthal, Kenneth and Wang Jisi (2012), *Assessing U.S.-China Strategic Distrust* (John L. Thornton China Center Monograph Series, No. 4), Washington DC: Brookings Institution.

Lilley, James (2004), *China Hands: Nine Decades of Adventure, Espionage, and Diplomacy in Asia*, New York: PublicAffairs.

Ling, L. H. M. (2002), *Postcolonial International Relations: Conquest and Desire between Asia and the West*, Basingstoke: Palgrave.

Lipschutz, Ronnie D. (2000), *After Authority: War, Peace, and Global Politics in the 21st Century*, New York: State University of New York Press.

Liss, Alexander (2002), 'Images of China in the American Print Media: A Survey from 2000 to 2002', *Journal of Contemporary China*, **12** (35), 299–318.

Liu Fei (2007), 'Intergovernmentalism and China-EU Relations', in David Kerr and Liu Fei (eds), *The International Politics of EU-China Relations*, Oxford: Oxford University Press, pp. 118–28.

Liu Feitao (2010), 'US Making Waves in South China Sea', *Global Times*, 8 November, http://opinion.globaltimes.cn/commentary/2010-11/590145.htm

Liu Mingfu (2010), *Zhongguo meng: Hou Meiguo shidai de daguo siwei yu zhanlue dingwei* (The Chinese Dream: Great Power Thinking and Strategic Orientation in the Post-American Era), Beijing: Zhongguo youyi chuban gongsi.

Lobe, Jim (2007), 'Two Countries, One Survey', Asia Times Online, 12 December, http://www.atimes.com/atimes/China/IL12Ad01.html

Locke, John (1700/1975), *An Essay Concerning Human Understanding* (ed. Peter H. Nidditch), Oxford: Clarendon Press.

Loh, Anthony A. (2008), 'Deconstructing *Cultural Realism*', in Wang Gungwu and Zheng Yongnian (eds), *China and the New International Order*, London: Routledge, pp. 281–92.

Ma, Ying (2007), 'China's Stubborn Anti-Democracy', *Policy Review*, No. 141, pp. 3–16.

Machiavelli, Niccolò (1995), *The Prince* (trans. George Bull), London: Penguin Books.

Mackerras, Colin (1999), *Western Images of China* (2nd edn), Oxford: Oxford University Press.

Mackerras, Colin (2000), *Sinophiles and Sinophobes: Western Views of China*, New York: Oxford University Press.

Macpherson, C. B. (1968), 'Introduction', in Thomas Hobbes, *Leviathan* (ed. C. B. Macpherson), Harmondsworth: Penguin Books, pp. 38–63.

Madsen, Richard (1993), 'The Academic China Specialists', in David Shambaugh (ed.), *American Studies of Contemporary China*, Washington D.C.: Woodrow Wilson Center Press, pp. 163–75.

Madsen, Richard (1995), *China and the American Dream: A Moral Inquiry*, Berkeley, CA: University of California Press.

Maley, Paul (2010), 'Wikileaks Cable Exposes Then PM as "A Brutal Realist on China": Rudd's Plan to Contain Beijing', *The Australian*, 6 December, p. 1.

Mallet, Victor (2007), 'The Geopolitical Genius of China's Satellite Kill', *Financial Times*, 25 January, p. 11.

Mandelbaum, Michael (1997), 'Westernizing Russia and China', *Foreign Affairs*, **76** (3), 80–95.

Mandelbaum, Michael (2003), *The Ideas That Conquered the World: Peace, Democracy, and Free Markets in the Twenty-First Century*, New York: PublicAffairs.

Mann, James (2000), *About Face: A History of America's Curious Relationship with China, from Nixon to Clinton*, New York: Vintage Books.

Mann, James (2002), 'Our China Illusions', *The American Prospect*, 30 November, pp. 22–7.

Mann, James (2007), *The China Fantasy: How Our Leaders Explain Away Chinese Repression*, New York: Viking.

Mannheim, Karl (1936), *Ideology and Utopia: An Introduction to the Sociology of Knowledge* (trans. Louis Wirth and Edward Shils), New York: Harvest/HBJ.

Manning, Robert A. and James Przystup (1997), 'Clinton's Inscrutable China Policy', *National Review*, **49** (23), 22–4.

Marcus, George E. and Michael M. J. Fisher (1999), *Anthropology as Cultural Critique: An Experimental Moment in the Human Sciences* (2nd edn), Chicago, IL: University of Chicago Press.

Marsh, Christopher (2003), 'Learning from Your Comrade's Mistakes: The Impact of the Soviet Past on China's Future', *Communist and Post-Communist Studies*, **36** (3), 259–72.

Marshall, Tyler (2005), 'Building a Bridge to China', *Los Angeles Times*, 18 July, http://articles.latimes.com/2005/jul/18/world/fg-uschina18

Martínez-Robles, David (2008), 'The Western Representation of Modern China: Orientalism, Culturalism and Historiographical Criticism', *Digithum*, No. 10, pp. 7–16.

Mawdsley, Emma (2008), 'Fu Manchu versus Dr Livingstone in the Dark Continent? Representing China, Africa and the West in British Broadsheet Newspapers', *Political Geography*, **27** (5), 509–29.

Maynes, Charles William (2001), 'Contending Schools', *The National Interest*, No. 63, pp. 49–58.

McCormick, Barrett L. (1994), 'Democracy or Dictatorship?: A Response to Gordon White', *Australian Journal of Chinese Affairs*, No. 31, pp. 95–110.

McCormick, Barrett L. (2000), 'Conclusion: Points of Agreement and Disagreement and a Few Thoughts on U.S.-Chinese Relations', in Edward Friedman and Barrett McCormick (eds), *What If China Doesn't Democratize?* Armonk, New York: M. E. Sharpe, pp. 329–41.

McEvoy-Levy, Siobhán (2001), *American Exceptionalism and US Foreign Policy: Public Diplomacy at the End of the Cold War*, New York: Palgrave.

McGiffert, Carola (ed.) (2003), *China in the American Political Imagination*, Washington, DC: The CSIS Press.

McGregor, James (2005), *One Billion Customers: Lessons from the Front Lines of Doing Business in China*, London: Nicholas Brealey.

McKenna, Ted (2005), 'US DoD Ponders China Threat', *Journal of Electronic Defense*, **28** (9), 32–3.

Mead, Walter Russell (2011), 'Softly, Softly: Beijing Turns Other Cheek – For Now', *The American Interest*, 19 November, http://blogs.the-american-interest.com/wrm/2011/11/19/softly-softly-beijing-turns-other-cheek-for-now/

Mearsheimer, John J. (1990), 'Why We Will Soon Miss the Cold War', *Atlantic Monthly*, **266** (2), 35–50.

Mearsheimer, John J. (1991), 'Back to the Future: Instability in Europe After the Cold War', *International Security*, **15** (1), 5–56.

Mearsheimer, John J. (1994/1995), 'The False Promise of International Institutions', *International Security*, **19** (3), 5–49.

Mearsheimer, John J. (2001), 'The Future of the American Pacifier', *Foreign Affairs*, **80** (5), 46–61.

Mearsheimer, John J. (2001), *The Tragedy of Great Power Politics*, New York: W. W. Norton & Company.

Medeiros, Evan S. (2005/2006), 'Strategic Hedging and the Future of Asia-Pacific Stability', *The Washington Quarterly*, **29** (1), 145–67.

Menges, Constantine C. (2005), *China: The Gathering Threat*, Nashville, TN: Thomas Nelson.

Metzger, Thomas A. and Ramon H. Myers (1998), 'Chinese Nationalism and American Policy', *Orbis*, **42** (1), 21–36.

Mills, C. Wright (2000), *The Power Elite* (new edn), Oxford: Oxford University Press.

Moïse, Dominique (2009), *The Geopolitics of Emotion: How Cultures of Fear, Humiliation and Hope are Reshaping the World*, London: Bodley Head.

Monaghan, Peter (1999), 'Does International-Relations Scholarship Reflect a Bias toward the U.S.?' *The Chronicle of Higher Education*, **46** (5), A20–A22.

Monbiot, George (2008), 'The Most Potent Weapon Wielded by the Empires of Murdoch and China', *The Guardian*, 22 April, p. 29.

Moore, Gregory J. (2009), 'David C. Kang, *China Rising: Peace, Power, and Order in East Asia*' (Book Review), *East West Connections*, **9** (1), 146–8.

Moore, James and Wayne Slater (2003), *Bush's Brain: How Karl Rove Made George W. Bush Presidential*, New Jersey, NJ: John Wiley & Sons.

Moore, Mike (2006), 'A New Cold War?' *SAIS Review*, **16** (1), 175–88.

Morgan, Jamie (2004), 'Distinguishing Truth, Knowledge, and Belief: A Philosophical Contribution to the Problem of Images of China', *Modern China*, **30** (3), 398–427.

Mosher, Steven W. (1990), *China Misperceived: American Illusions and Chinese Reality*, New York: Basic Books.

Munro, Ross H. (2000), 'China: The Challenge of a Rising Power', in Robert Kagan and William Kristol (eds), *Present Dangers: Crisis and Opportunity in American Foreign and Defense Policy*, San Francisco, CA: Encounter Books, pp. 47–73.

Myers, Steven Lee (2000), 'Study Said to Find U.S. Missile Shield Might Incite China', *New York Times*, 10 August, p. 1.

Nakayama, Toshihiro (2006), 'Politics of U.S. Policy Toward China: Analysis of Domestic Factors', Center for Northeast Asian Policy Studies, Brookings Institution, http://www.brookings.edu/~/media/Files/rc/papers/2006/09china_nakayama/nakayama2006.pdf

Nandy, Ashis (1983), *The Intimate Enemy: Loss and Recovery of Self under Colonialism*. New Delhi: Oxford University Press.

Nathan, Andrew J. (1990), *China's Crisis: Dilemmas of Reform and Prospects for Democracy*, New York: Columbia University Press.

Nathan, Andrew J. (with Tianjian Shi and Helena V.S. Ho) (1997), *China's Transition*, New York: Columbia University Press.

Nathan, Andrew J. and Bruce Gilley (2002), *China's New Rulers: The Secret Files*, New York: New York Review of Books.

Nathan, Andrew J. and Tianjian Shi (1993), 'Cultural Requisites for Democracy in China', *Daedalus*, **122** (2), 95–123.

Nathanson, Charles E. (1988), 'The Social Construction of the Soviet Threat: A Study in the Politics of Representation', *Alternatives*, **13** (4), 443–83.

Nau, Henry (2007), 'Why We Fight over Foreign Policy', *Policy Review*, No. 142, pp. 25–42.

Naughton, Philippe (2006), 'Google and Yahoo Face Their Congressional Critics', *The Sunday Times*, 15 February, http://www.timesonline.co.uk/tol/news/world/asia/article731031.ece

Navarro, Peter (2007), *The Coming China Wars: Where They Will Be Fought and How They Can Be Won*, Upper Saddle River, NJ: FT Press.

Neumann, Iver B. (1999), *Uses of the Other: "The East" in European Identity Formation*, Minneapolis, MN: University of Minnesota Press.

New York Times (2008), 'Beijing's Bad Faith Olympics' (editorial), 23 August, p. 18.

Newman, Richard J. and Kevin Whitelaw (2001), 'China: How Big a Threat? Inside the Bitter Fight Over Assessing China's Intentions', *U.S. News and World Report*, 23 July, http://www.fas.org/sgp/news/2001/07/usn072301.html

Nicolaïdis, Kalypso and Robert Howse (2002), '"This Is My EUtopia...": Narrative as Power', *Journal of Common Market Studies*, **40** (4), 767–92.

Nordlinger, Jay (2008), 'The Road to Beijing', *National Review*, **60** (10), 39–43.

Nye, Joseph S., Jr. (2009), 'Scholars on the Sidelines', *Washington Post*, 13 April, http://www.washingtonpost.com/wp-dyn/content/article/2009/04/12/AR2009041202260.html

O'Hagan, Jacinta (2002), *Conceptions of the West in International Relations Thought: From Oswald Spengler to Edward Said*, Basingstoke: Macmillan.

Obama, Barack (2009), 'Remarks by the President to the United Nations General Assembly', United Nations Headquarters, New York, 23 September, http://www.whitehouse.gov/the_press_office/remarks-by-the-president-to-the-united-nations-general-assembly

Oksenberg, Michel (1997), 'Taiwan, Tibet, and Hong Kong in Sino-American Relations', in Ezra F. Vogel (ed.), *Living with China: U.S./China Relations in the Twenty-First Century*, New York: W. W. Norton, pp. 53–96.

Oksenberg, Michel and Elizabeth Economy (1999), 'Introduction: China Joins the World', in Elizabeth Economy and Michel Oksenberg (eds), *China Joins the World: Progress and Prospects*, New York: Council on Foreign Relations Press, pp. 1–41.

Ong, Aihwa (1999), *Flexible Citizenship: The Cultural Logics of Transnationality*, Durham, NC: Duke University Press.

Ong, Aihwa (2005), 'Anthropological Concepts for the Study of Nationalism', in Pal Nyiri and Joana Breidenbach (eds), *China Inside Out: Contemporary Chinese Nationalism and Transnationalism*, Budapest: Central European University Press, pp. 1–34.

Onuf, Nicholas (1998), 'Constructivism: A User's Manual', in Vendulka Kubálková, Nicholas Onuf and Paul Kowert (eds), *International Relations in a Constructed World*, Armonk, NY: M. E. Sharpe, pp. 58–78.

Oren, Ido (2003), *Our Enemies and US: America's Rivalries and the Making of Political Science*, Ithaca, NY: Cornell University Press.

Oster, Shai, Norihiko Shirouzu and Paul Glader (2010), 'China Squeezes Foreigners for Share of Global Riches', Wall Street Journal Online, 28 December, http://online.wsj.com/article/SB10001424052970203731004576045684068308042 .html

Owen, John M. (2002), 'Transnational Liberalism and U.S. Primacy', *International Security*, **26** (3), 117–52.

Paal, Douglas H. (1997), 'China and the East Asian Security Environment: Complementarity and Competition', in Ezra F. Vogel (ed.), *Living with China: U.S./China Relations in the Twenty-First Century*, New York: W. W. Norton, pp. 97–119.

Page, Benjamin I. and Tao Xie (2010), *Living with the Dragon: How the American Public Views the Rise of China*, New York: Columbia University Press.

Page, Jeremy, Patrick Barta and Jay Solomon (2010), 'U.S., ASEAN to Push Back Against China', *Wall Street Journal Asia*, 23 September, p. 1.

Palan, Ronen (2000), 'A World of Their Making: An Evaluation of the Constructivist Critique of International Relations', *Review of International Studies*, **26** (4), 575– 98.

Paltiel, Jeremy (2008), 'Peaceful Rise? Soft Power? Human Rights in China's New Multilateralism', in Guoguang Wu and Helen Lansdowne (eds), *China Turns to Multilateralism: Foreign Policy and Regional Security*, London: Routledge, pp. 198–221.

Pan, Chengxin (2004), 'The "China Threat" in American Self-Imagination: The Discursive Construction of Other as Power Politics', *Alternatives*, **29** (3), 305–31.

Pan, Chengxin (2009), '"Peaceful Rise" and China's New International Contract: The State in Change in Transnational Society', in Linda Chelan Li (ed.), *The Chinese State in Transition: Processes and Contests in Local China*, London: Routledge, pp. 127–44.

Pan, Chengxin (2009), 'What Is Chinese About Chinese Businesses? Locating the "Rise of China" in Global Production Networks', *Journal of Contemporary China* **18** (58), 7–25.

Pan, Chengxin (2010), 'Westphalia and the Taiwan Conundrum: A Case against the Exclusionist Construction of Sovereignty and Identity', *Journal of Chinese Political Science*, **15** (4), 371–89.

Pan, Chengxin (2011), '*Shu* and the Chinese Quest for Harmony: A Confucian Approach to Mediating across Difference', in Morgan Brigg and Roland Bleiker (eds), *Mediating across Difference: Oceanic and Asian Approaches to Conflict Resolution*, Honolulu, HI: University of Hawai'i Press, pp. 221–47.

Pan, Chengxin (2012), 'Problematizing "Constructive Engagement" in EU China Policy', in C. Roland Vogt (ed.), *Europe and China: Strategic Partners or Rivals?*, Hong Kong: Hong Kong University Press, pp. 37–57.

Pan, Chengxin (2012), 'Getting Excited about China', in David Walker and Agnieszka Sobocinska (eds), *Australia's Asia: From Yellow Peril to Asian Century*, Crawley, WA: UWA Publishing, pp. 245–66.

Papayoanou, Paul A. and Scott L. Kastner (1999), 'Sleeping with the (Potential) Enemy: Assessing the U.S. Policy of Engagement with China', *Security Studies*, **9** (1), 157–87.

Parmar, Inderjeet (2005), 'Catalysing Events, Think Tanks and American Foreign Policy Shifts: A Comparative Analysis of the Impacts of Pearl Harbor 1941 and September 11 2001', *Government and Opposition*, **40** (1), 1–25.

Pearson, Margaret M. (1999), 'The Major Multilateral Economic Institutions Engage China', in Alastair Iain Johnston and Robert S. Ross (eds), *Engaging China: The Management of an Emerging Power*, London: Routledge, pp. 207–34.

Peck, James (2006), *Washington's China: The National Security World, the Cold War, and the Origins of Globalism*, Amherst, MA: University of Massachusetts Press.

Peerenboom, Randall (2007), *China Modernizes: Threat to the West or Model for the Rest?* Oxford: Oxford University Press.

Pei, Minxin (1995), 'Creeping Democratization in China', *Journal of Democracy*, **6** (4), 65–79.

Pei, Minxin (2000), 'China's Evolution Toward Soft Authoritarianism', in Edward Friedman and Barrett McCormick (eds), *What If China Doesn't Democratize?* Armonk, NY: M. E. Sharpe, pp. 74–98.

Peng Qian et al. (1996), *Zhongguo weishenme shuo bu?* (Why Does China Say No?), Beijing: Xinshijie Chubanshe.

Pennycook, Alastair (1998), *English and the Discourse of Colonialism*, London: Routledge.

Pessin, Al (2010), 'US, South Korean Navies Will Exercise in Yellow Sea Despite Chinese Objections', Voice of America, 14 July, http://www.voanews.com/english /news/US-South-Korean-Navies-Will-Exercise-in-Yellow-Sea-Despite-Chinese-Objections-98453279.html

Peterson, John (2007), 'José Manuel Barroso = Political Scientist: John Peterson Interviews the European Commission President', *EU-Consent* (Constructing Europe Network), 17 July, pp. 4–5, http://www.eu-consent.net/library/BARROSO-transcript.pdf

Pew Research Center for the People & the Press (2011), 'Strengthen Ties with China, But Get Tough on Trade', 12 January, http://pewresearch.org/pubs/1855/china-poll-americans-want-closer-ties-but-tougher-trade-policy

Peyrefitte, Alain (1992), *The Collision of Two Civilisations: The British Expedition to China 1792–4* (trans. Jon Rothschild), London: Harvill.

Phan, Nicholas (2011), 'U.S.-Japan Security Alliance under the Democratic Party of Japan (DPJ)', in the Edwin O. Reischauer Center for East Asian Studies, (ed.), *The United States and Japan in Global Context: 2011*, Washington DC: The Johns Hopkins University Paul H. Nitze School of Advanced International Studies, pp. 1–19.

Pickering, Michael (2001), *Stereotyping: The Politics of Representation*, Basingstoke: Palgrave.

Pincus, Walter (2001), 'Taiwan Paid State Nominee for Papers on U.N. Reentry; Bolton's Objectivity on China Is Questioned', *Washington Post*, 9 April, p. A17.

Pomfret, John (2000), 'U.S Now a "Threat" in China's Eyes', *Washington Post*, 15 November, p. A1.

Porter, Eduardo (2004), 'Looking for a Villain, and Finding One in China', *New York Times*, 18 April, Section 4, p. 3.

Prasso, Sheridan (2006), *The Asian Mystique: Dragon Ladies, Geisha Girls, and Our Fantasies of the Exotic Orient*, New York: PublicAffairs.

Pye, Lucian W. (1990), 'China: Erratic State, Frustrated Society', *Foreign Affairs*, **69** (4), 56–74.

Pye, Lucian W. (1992), *The Spirit of Chinese Politics*, Cambridge, MA: Harvard University Press.

Qian Qichen (2004), 'US Strategy to Be Blamed', *China Daily*, 1 November.

Qiangguo luntan (2008), 'Hu Jintao Zongshuji tong wangyou zaixian jiaoliu' (General Secretary Hu Jintao's Online Chats with Netizens), 20 June, http://www.people.com.cn/GB/32306/33093/125024/index.html

Rabinow, Paul and William M. Sullivan (1987), 'The Interpretive Turn: A Second Look', in Paul Rabinow and William M. Sullivan (eds), *Interpretive Social Science: A Second Look*, Berkeley, CA: University of California Press, pp. 1–30.

Rabinow, Paul and William M. Sullivan (eds) (1987), *Interpretive Social Science: A Second Look*, Berkeley, CA: University of California Press.

Ramo, Joshua Cooper (2004), *The Beijing Consensus*, London: Foreign Policy Centre.

Reagan, Ronald (1984), 'Remarks at a Luncheon With Business Leaders in Fairbanks, Alaska', University of Alaska, 1 May, http://www.reagan.utexas.edu/archives/speeches/1984/50184d.htm

Reed-Danahay, Deborah E. (ed.) (1997), *Auto/Ethnography: Rewriting the Self and the Social*, Oxford: Berg.

Richter, Paul (2006), 'In Deal with India, Bush Has Eye on China', *Los Angeles Times*, 4 March, http://articles.latimes.com/2006/mar/04/world/fg-usindia4

Ritzer, George (1996), *Sociological Theory* (4th edn), New York: McGraw-Hill.

Roberts, Brad, Robert A. Manning and Ronald N. Montaperto (2000), 'China: The Forgotten Nuclear Power', *Foreign Affairs*, **79** (4), 53–63.

Robertson, James Oliver (1980), *American Myth, American Reality*, New York: Hill & Wang.

Robinson, Thomas W. (1998), '[In][ter]dependence in China's Post-Cold War Foreign Relations', in Samuel S. Kim (ed.), *China and the World: Chinese Foreign Policy Facing the New Millennium*, Boulder, CO: Westview, pp. 193–216.

Robinson, Thomas W. and David Shambaugh (eds) (1994), *Chinese Foreign Policy: Theory and Practice*, Oxford: Clarendon Press.

Roland, Alex (2007), 'The Military-Industrial Complex: Lobby and Trope', in Andrew J. Bacevich (ed.), *The Long War: A New History of U.S. National Security Policy Since World War II*, New York: Columbia University Press, pp. 335–70.

Rorty, Richard (1989), *Contingency, Irony, and Solidarity*, Cambridge: Cambridge University Press.

Rosecrance, Richard and Gu Guoliang (eds) (2009), *Power and Restraint: A Shared Vision for the U.S.-China Relationship*, New York: PublicAffairs.

Rosenthal, Elisabeth (1999), 'China Students Are Caught Up by Nationalism', *New York Times*, 12 May, p. A1.

Ross, Catriona (2006), 'Prolonged Symptoms of Cultural Anxiety: The Persistence of Narratives of Asian Invasion within Multicultural Australia', *Journal of the Association for the Study of Australian Literature*, No. 5, pp. 86–99.

Ross, Robert S. (1997), 'Why Our Hardliners Are Wrong', *The National Interest*, No. 49, pp. 42–51.

Ross, Robert S. (1999), 'Engagement in US China Policy', in Alastair Iain Johnston and Robert S. Ross, (eds), *Engaging China: The Management of an Emerging Power*, London: Routledge, pp. 176–206.

Ross, Robert S. (2005), 'Assessing the China Threat', *The National Interest*, No. 81, pp. 81–7.

Ross, Robert S. and Alastair Iain Johnston (2006), 'Introduction', in Alastair Iain Johnston and Robert S. Ross (eds), *New Directions in the Study of China's Foreign Policy*, Stanford, CA: Stanford University Press.

Rowen, Henry S. (1996), 'The Short March: China's Road to Democracy', *The National Interest*, No. 45, pp. 61–70.

Rowen, Henry S. (1997), 'Off-Center on the Middle Kingdom', *The National Interest*, No. 48, pp. 101–4.

Roy, Denny (1994), 'Hegemon on the Horizon? China's Threat to East Asian Security', *International Security*, **19** (1), 149–68.

Rudd, Kevin (2008), 'A Conversation with China's Youth on the Future', Speech at Peking University, Beijing, 9 April, http://www.theaustralian.com.au/news/kevin-rudds-speech-at-beijing-uni/story-e6frg6n6-1111116015758

Russett, Bruce (1993), *Grasping the Democratic Peace: Principles for a Post-Cold War World*, Princeton, NJ: Princeton University Press.

Said, Edward W. (1979), *The Question of Palestine*, New York: Vintage Books.

Said, Edward W. (1981), *Covering Islam: How the Media and the Experts Determine How We See the Rest of the World*, New York: Pantheon Books.

Said, Edward W. (1983), *The World, the Text, and the Critic*, Cambridge, MA: Harvard University Press.

Said, Edward W. (1995), *Orientalism: Western Conceptions of the Orient* (new edn), London: Penguin Books.

Sainsbury, Michael (2011), 'Our Hard Line Turns Out to Be Prescient', *The Australian*, 8 January, p. 10.

Samuelson, Robert J. (2010), 'The Danger behind China's "Me First" Worldview', *Washington Post*, 15 February, http://www.washingtonpost.com/wp-dyn/content/article/2010/02/14/AR2010021402892.html

Sautman, Barry and Yan Hairong (2008), 'The Forest for the Trees: Trade, Investment and the China-in-Africa Discourse', *Pacific Affairs*, **81** (1), 9–29.

Schaffer, Bernard (1996), 'Policy Making', in Adam Kuper and Jessica Kuper (eds), *The Social Science Encyclopedia* (2nd edn), London: Routledge, p. 621.

Scheer, Robert (2008), 'Indefensible Spending', *Los Angeles Times*, 1 June, http://www.latimes.com/news/opinion/commentary/la-op-scheer1-2008jun01,0,5177531. story

Schmitt, Gary J. (2008), 'Our One-China Cowardice', *Wall Street Journal*, 15 January, p. A12.

Schmitt, Gary J. (2009), 'Kowtowing to China', *Weekly Standard*, 1 December.

Schram, Sanford F. (2006), 'Return to Politics: Perestroika, Phronesis, and Post-Paradigmatic Political Science', in Sanford F. Schram and Brian Caterino (eds), *Making Political Science Matter: Debating Knowledge, Research, and Method*, New York: New York University Press, pp. 17–32.

Schram, Sanford F. and Brian Caterino (eds) (2006), *Making Political Science Matter: Debating Knowledge, Research, and Method*, New York: New York University Press.

Scott, David (2008), *China and the International System, 1840–1949: Power, Presence, and Perceptions in a Century of Humiliation*, Albany, NY: State University of New York Press.

Sedaei, Sam (2010), 'Obama's Push-Back Against China Is Bitter Medicine', *Huffington Post*, 15 February, http://www.huffingtonpost.com/sam-sedaei/american-push-back-agains_b_462971.html

Segal, Gerald (1995), 'Tying China into the International System', *Survival*, **37** (2), 60–73.

Segal, Gerald (1996), 'Tying China in (and down)', in Gerald Segal and Richard H. Yang (eds), *Chinese Economic Reform: The Impact on Security*, London: Routledge, pp. 191–206.

Segal, Gerald (1997), 'Understanding East Asian International Relations', *Review of International Studies*, **23** (4), 501–6.

Segal, Gerald (1999), 'Does China Matter?' *Foreign Affairs*, **78** (5), 24–36.
Shambaugh, David (1994), 'Introduction', in Thomas W. Robinson and David Shambaugh (eds), *Chinese Foreign Policy: Theory and Practice*, Oxford: Clarendon Press, pp. 1–10.
Shambaugh, David (1999), 'PLA Studies Today: A Maturing Field', in James C. Mulvenon and Richard H. Yang (eds), *The People's Liberation Army in the Information Age*, Santa Monica, CA: RAND Corporation, pp. 7–21.
Shambaugh, David (2004), 'China and Europe: The Emerging Axis', *Current History*, **103** (674), 243–48.
Shambaugh, David (2005), 'The New Strategic Triangle: U.S. and European Reactions to China's Rise', *The Washington Quarterly*, **28** (3), 7–25.
Shambaugh, David (2007), 'Studies of China's Foreign and Security Policies in the United States', in Robert Ash, David Shambaugh and Seiichiro Takagi (eds), *China Watching: Perspectives from Europe, Japan, and the United States*, London: Routledge, pp. 213–40.
Shambaugh, David (2008), 'China Eyes Europe in the World: Real Convergence or Cognitive Dissonance?' in David Shambaugh, Eberhard Sandschneider and Zhou Hong (eds), *China-Europe Relations: Perceptions, Policies and Prospects*, London: Routledge, pp. 127–47.
Shambaugh, David (2008), 'Learning from Abroad to Reinvent Itself: External Influence on Internal CCP Reforms', in Cheng Li (ed.), *China's Changing Political Landscape: Prospects for Democracy*, Washington DC: Brookings Institution Press, pp. 283–301.
Shambaugh, David (2009), 'Reflections on the American Study of Contemporary China', *Far Eastern Affairs*, **37** (4), 151–8.
Shambaugh, David (2011), 'Coping with a Conflicted China', *The Washington Quarterly*, **34** (1), 7–27.
Shambaugh, David (ed.) (1993), *American Studies of Contemporary China*, Armonk, NY: M. E. Sharpe.
Shao Feng (2008), 'Aoyun huoju chuandi tuxian hexie shijie waijiao de zhongyaoxing' (Olympic Torch Relay Highlights the Importance for Harmonious World Diplomacy), *Zhongguo Shehuikexueyuan Yuanbao* (Journal of the Chinese Academy of Social Sciences), 29 April, p. 3.
Shapiro, Michael J. (1988), *The Politics of Representation: Writing Practices in Biography, Photography, and Policy Analysis*, Madison, WS: University of Wisconsin Press.
Shapiro, Michael J. (1992), *Reading the Postmodern Polity: Political Theory as Textual Practice*, Minneapolis, MN: University of Minnesota Press.
Shen Dingli (2010), 'US-S. Korean Maritime War Games Needlessly Provocative', *Global Times*, 14 July, http://opinion.globaltimes.cn/commentary/2010-07/551234.html
Shen, Samuel (2008), 'Can't Beat That Return: China KFC's Big Fry', *The Age*, 7 May, Business Day, p. 9.
Shen, Simon (2007), *Redefining Nationalism in Modern China*, Basingstoke: Palgrave.
Shenkar, Oded (2006), *The Chinese Century: The Rising Chinese Economy and Its Impact on the Global Economy, the Balance of Power, and Your Job*, Upper Saddle River, NJ: Wharton School Publishing.
Sheridan, Michael (2010), 'China's Hawks Demand Cold War on the US', *The Sunday Times*, 7 February, p. 30.
Sherman, Kenneth B. (2004), 'Flashpoint Taiwan Straits', *Journal of Electronic Defense*, **27** (11), 51–9.

Shi Jianxun (2008), 'Aoyun shenghuo yu Aolinpike jingshen burong xiedu (The Sacred Olympic Flame and Olympic Spirit Brook No Blasphemy), *Wenhuibao* (Wenhui Daily), 10 April, p. 5.

Shih, Chih-yu (2004), *Navigating Sovereignty: World Politics Lost in China*, Basingstoke: Palgrave.

Shih, Chih-yu (2005), 'Connecting Knowledge of China Studies: Exploring an Ethical Relationship among Knowledge of Different Nature', in I Yuan (ed.), *Rethinking New International Order in East Asia: U.S., China, and Taiwan* (Institute of International Relations English Series No. 52), Taipei: National Chengchi University, pp. 111–46.

Shirk, Susan (2007), *China: Fragile Power*, Oxford: Oxford University Press.

Shohat, Ella and Robert Stam (1994), *Unthinking Eurocentrism: Multiculturalism and the Media*, London: Routledge.

Sil, Rudra and Peter J. Katzenstein (eds) (2010), *Beyond Paradigms: Analytic Eclecticism in the Study of World Politics*, Basingstoke: Palgrave.

Simpson, Christopher (1998), 'Universities, Empire, and the Production of Knowledge: An Introduction', in Christopher Simpson (ed.), *Universities and Empire: Money and Politics in the Social Sciences During the Cold War*, New York: The New Press, pp. xi–xxxiv.

Smadja, Claude (2001), 'Dealing with Globalization', in Laurence J. Brahm (ed.), *China's Century: The Awakening of the Next Economic Powerhouse*, Singapore: John Wiley & Sons (Asia), pp. 25–37.

Small, Andrew (2005), *Preventing the Next Cold War: A View from Beijing*, London: Foreign Policy Centre.

Smil, Vaclav (1993), *China's Environmental Crisis*, Armonk, NY: M. E. Sharpe.

Smith, Dan (1993), 'Arms Sales to Saudi Arabia and Taiwan Video Transcript', The Center for Defense Information, 28 November, http://www.cdi.org /adm/711/

Smyth, Marie Breen, Jeroen Gunning and Richard Jackson (eds) (2009), *Critical Terrorism Studies: A New Research Agenda*, London: Routledge.

Snyder, Robert W. (ed.) (2001), *Covering China*, Piscataway, NJ: Transaction Publishers.

Soley, Lawrence (1998), 'The New Corporate Yen for Scholarship', in Christopher Simpson (ed.), *Universities and Empire: Money and Politics in the Social Sciences During the Cold War*, New York: The New Press, pp. 229–49.

Solovey, Mark (2001), 'Project Camelot and the 1960s Epistemological Revolution: Rethinking the Politics-Patronage-Social Science Nexus', *Social Studies of Science*, **31** (2), 171–206.

Song Qiang (1996), 'Cang tian dang si, huang tian dang li' (The Blue Sky Must Die, and the Yellow Sky Must Stand Up), in Song Qiang et al., *Zhongguo keyi shuo bu: Lengzhan hou shidai de zhengzhi yu qinggan jueze* (China Can Say No: Political and Sentimental Choices During the Post-Cold War Era), Beijing: Zhonghua Gongshang Lianhe Chubanshe, pp. 1–51.

Song Qiang et al. (1996), *Zhongguo keyi shuo bu: Lengzhan hou shidai de zhengzhi yu qinggan jueze* (China Can Say No: Political and Sentimental Choices During the Post-Cold War Era), Beijing: Zhonghua Gongshang Lianhe Chubanshe.

Song Xiaojun, Wang Xiaodong, Huang Jisu, Song Qiang and Liu Yang (2009), *Zhongguo bu gaoxing: Da shidai, da mubiao ji Zhongguo de neiyouwaihuan* (Unhappy China: New Epoch, Grand Vision and Challenges for China), Taipei: INK Literary Monthly Publishing.

Sorman, Guy (2008), *The Empire of Lies: The Truth About China in the Twenty-First Century* (trans. Asha Puri), New York: Encounter Books.

Sparks, Colin (2010), 'Coverage of China in the UK National Press', *Chinese Journal of Communication*, **3** (3), 347–65.

Spence, Jonathan D. (1980), *To Change China: Western Advisers in China 1620–1960*, London: Penguin Books.

Spence, Jonathan D. (1998), *The Chan's Great Continent: China in Western Minds*, New York: W. W. Norton.

Spivak, Gayatri Chakravorty (1988), 'Can the Subaltern Speak?' in Cary Nelson and Lawrence Grossberg (eds), *Marxism and the Interpretation of Culture*, Urbana, IL: University of Illinois Press, pp. 271–313.

Starr, John Bryan (1997), *Understanding China*, London: Profile Books.

Steele, A. T. (1966), *The American People and China*, New York: McGraw-Hill.

Steinberg, James B. (2009), 'China's Arrival: The Long March to Global Power', Keynote Address at the Center for a New American Security, 24 September, http://www.cnas.org/files/multimedia/documents/Deputy%20Secretary%20James %20Steinberg's%20September%2024,%202009%20Keynote%20Address%20Tran script.pdf

Stengel, Richard (2007), 'The Chinese Challenge', *Time*, 22 January, p. 6.

Stephens, Philip (2008), 'The Financial Crisis Marks out a New Geopolitical Order', *Financial Times*, 10 October, p. 9.

Stewart, Cameron and Patrick Walters (2009), 'Spy Chiefs Cross Swords over China – PM Backs Defence Hawks', *The Australian*, 11 April, p. 1.

Stoessinger, John G. (1967), 'China and America: The Burden of Past Misperceptions', in John C. Farrell and Asa P. Smith (eds), *Image and Reality in World Politics*, New York: Columbia University Press, pp. 72–91.

Strahan, Lachlan (1996), *Australia's China: Changing Perceptions from the 1930s to the 1990s*, Cambridge: Cambridge University Press.

Studwell, Joe (2005), *The China Dream: The Quest for the Last Great Untapped Market on Earth*, New York: Grove Press.

Su Xiaokang and Wang Luxiang (1991), *Deathsong of the River: A Reader's Guide to the Chinese TV Series Heshang* (trans. and eds Richard W. Bodman and Pin P. Wan), Ithaca, NY: Cornell East Asia Series.

Subramanian, Arvind (2011), 'The Inevitable Superpower: Why China's Dominance Is a Sure Thing', *Foreign Affairs*, **90** (5), 66–78.

Suettinger, Robert L. (2003), *Beyond Tiananmen: The Politics of U.S.-China Relations*, 1989–2000, Washington DC: Brookings Institution Press.

Sutter, Robert (2001), 'The U.S. Congress: Personal, Partisan, Political', in Ramon H. Myers, Michel C. Oksenberg and David Shambaugh (eds), *Making China Policy: Lessons from the Bush and Clinton Administrations*, Lanham, MD: Roman & Littlefield, pp. 79–111.

Suzuki, Shogo (2009), 'Chinese Soft Power, Insecurity Studies, Myopia and Fantasy', *Third World Quarterly*, **30** (4), 779–93.

Talev, Margaret, Tom Lasseter and Kevin G. Hall (2010), 'China Looms as Obama Tries to Strengthen Ties with Asian Democracies', *Pittsburgh Post-Gazette*, 14 November, p. A-3.

Tammen, Ronald L. and Jacek Kugler (2006), 'Power Transition and China-US Conflicts', *Chinese Journal of International Politics*, **1** (1), 35–55.

Tan See Seng (2002), 'What Fear Hath Wrought: Missile Hysteria and the Writing of "America"', Institute of Defence and Strategic Studies Working Paper No. 28, Singapore: Nanyang Technological University, pp. 1–28.

Taylor, Charles (1985), *Philosophy and the Human Sciences*, Cambridge: Cambridge University Press.

Teng, Ssu-yu and John K. Fairbank et al. (1954), *China's Response to the West: A Documentary Survey 1839–1923*, Cambridge, MA: Harvard University Press.
Thomas, William I. and Dorothy S. Thomas (1928), *The Child in America*, New York: Alfred A. Knopf.
Thompson, Mark (2008), 'Gates Down on the F-22', *Time*, 7 February, http://www.time.com/time/nation/article/0,8599,1710944,00.html
Thornburgh, Dick (2009), 'Bearing Witness to Chinese Persecution', Real Clear World, 18 December, http://www.realclearworld.com/articles/2009/12/18/liu_xiaobo_bearing_witness_to_chinas_persecuted.html
Thrush, Glenn and Manu Raju (2010), 'Barack Obama Pressed on China Showdown', Politico, 6 April, http://www.politico.com/news/stories/0410/35458. html
Thucydides (1972), *History of the Peloponnesian War* (trans. Rex Warner), London: Penguin Books.
Tisdall, Simon (2005), 'Japan Emerges as America's Deputy Sheriff in the Pacific', *The Guardian*, 19 April, p. 13.
Tisdall, Simon (2005), 'US Tries to Spin a Web Strong Enough to Contain China', *The Guardian*, 10 August, p. 12.
Todorov, Tzvetan (1999), *The Conquest of America: The Question of the Other* (trans. Richard Howard), Norman, OK: University of Oklahoma Press.
Townsend, James (1992), 'Chinese Nationalism', *The Australian Journal of Chinese Affairs*, No. 27, pp. 97–130.
Tsou, Tang (1963), *America's Failure in China*, Berkeley, CA: University of California Press.
Tu Wei-ming (ed.) (1994), *The Living Tree: The Changing Meaning of Being Chinese Today*, Stanford, CA: Stanford University Press.
Tucker, Nancy Bernkopf (2003), 'America First', in Carola McGiffert (ed.), *China in the American Political Imagination*, Washington, DC: The CSIS Press, pp. 16–21.
Tucker, Robert W. and David C. Hendrickson (1992), *The Imperial Temptation: The New World Order and America's Purpose*, New York: Council on Foreign Relations Press.
Turner, Oliver (2011), 'Sino-US Relations Then and Now: Discourse, Images, Policy', *Political Perspectives*, **5** (3), 27–45.
Turse, Nicholas (2004), 'The Military-Academic Complex', TomDispatch, 29 April, http://www.countercurrents.org/us-turse290404.htm
Twining, Daniel (2007), 'America's Grand Design in Asia', *The Washington Quarterly*, **30** (3), 79–94.
Tyler, Patrick E. (2000), *A Great Wall: Six Presidents and China: An Investigative History*, New York: Century Foundation Book.
Unger, Jonathan (1994), 'Recent Trends in Modern China Studies in the English-language World: An Editor's Perspective', in Lucien Bianco et al., *The Development of Contemporary China Studies*, Tokyo: Centre for East Asian Cultural Studies for UNESCO, pp. 179–86.
US Department of Defense (2001), *Quadrennial Defense Review Report*, Washington DC: U.S. Government Printing Office, 30 September.
US Department of Defense (2006), *Quadrennial Defense Review Report*, Washington DC: U.S. Government Printing Office, 6 February.
US Department of Defense (2010), *2010 Nuclear Posture Review*, Washington DC: Department of Defense, April.
US Department of Defense (n.d.), 'The Minerva Initiative', http://minerva.dtic.mil/
US National Intelligence Council (2008), *Global Trends 2025: A Transformed World*, Washington, DC: U.S. Government Printing Office.

Vancouver Sun (2007), 'Made in China Has Become a Warning Label', 13 September, p. C3.

Vines, Alex (2012), 'Mesmerised by Chinese String of Pearls Theory', *The World Today*, **68** (2), 33–4.

Vogel, Ezra F. (1994), 'Contemporary China Studies in North America: Marginals in a Superpower', in Lucien Bianco et al., *The Development of Contemporary China Studies*, Tokyo: Centre for East Asian Cultural Studies for UNESCO, The Toyo Bunko, pp. 187–95.

Vogel, Ezra F. (1997), 'Introduction: How Can the United States and China Pursue Common Interests and Manage Differences?' in Ezra F. Vogel, (ed.), *Living with China: U.S./China Relations in the Twenty-First Century*, New York: W. W. Norton, pp. 17–52.

Vogel, Ezra F. (ed.) (1997), *Living with China: U.S./China Relations in the Twenty-First Century*, New York: W. W. Norton.

Voice of America (2006), 'US Rights Report Critical of Arab Allies, Iran, China, Zimbabwe', 8 March, http://www.voanews.com/english/archive/2006-03/2006-03-08-voa64.cfm

Vukovich, Daniel (2010), 'China in Theory: The Orientalist Production of Knowledge in the Global Economy', *Cultural Critique*, No. 76, pp. 148–72.

Wæver, Ole (1998), 'The Sociology of a Not So International Discipline: American and European Developments in International Relations', *International Organization*, **52** (4), 687–727.

Walder, Andrew G. (2004), 'The Transformation of Contemporary China Studies, 1977–2002', in David L. Szanton (ed.), *The Politics of Knowledge: Area Studies and the Disciplines*, Berkeley, CA: University of California Press, pp. 314–40.

Waldron, Arthur (2000), 'Statement of Dr Arthur Waldron', House Armed Services Committee, 21 June, http://armedservices.house.gov/testimony/106thcongress/00-06-21waldron.html

Walker, David (1999), *Anxious Nation: Australia and the Rise of Asia 1850–1939*, St Lucia: University of Queensland Press.

Waller, J. Michael (2001), 'Blue Team Takes on Red China', *Insight Magazine*, **17** (21), 24.

Walt, Stephen M. (1991), 'The Renaissance of Security Studies', *International Studies Quarterly*, **35** (2), 211–39.

Waltz, Kenneth N. (1959), *Man, the State, and War*, New York: Columbia University Press.

Waltz, Kenneth N. (1979), *Theory of International Politics*, Reading, MA: Addison-Wesley.

Wang, Fei-ling (1999), 'Self-Image and Strategic Intentions: National Confidence and Political Insecurity', in Yong Deng and Fei-ling Wang (eds), *In the Eyes of the Dragon: China Views the World*, Lanham, MD: Rowman & Littlefield, pp. 21–45.

Wang Gungwu (2003), *Anglo-Chinese Encounters since 1800: War, Trade, Science and Governance*, Cambridge: Cambridge University Press.

Wang, Hongying (2000), 'Multilateralism in Chinese Foreign Policy: The Limits of Socialization', in Weixing Hu, Gerald Chan and Daojiong Zha (eds), *China's International Relations in the 21st Century: Dynamics of Paradigm Shifts*, Lanham, MD: University Press of America, pp. 71–91.

Wang, Jianwei (2000), *Limited Adversaries: Post-Cold War Sino-American Mutual Images*, Oxford: Oxford University Press.

Wang Jisi (1994), 'International Relations Theory and the Study of Chinese Foreign Policy: A Chinese Perspective', in Thomas W. Robinson and David Shambaugh (eds), *Chinese Foreign Policy: Theory and Practice*, Oxford: Clarendon Press, pp. 481–505.

Wang Jisi (2005), 'China's Search for Stability with America', *Foreign Affairs*, **84** (5), 39–48.

Wang Jisi (2010), 'Zhong-Mei jiegouxing maodun shangsheng, zhanglue jiaoliang nanyi bimian' (Sino-U.S. Structural Contradictions on the Rise, Strategic Competition Difficult to Avoid), *International and Strategic Studies Report* (Beijing: Center for International and Strategic Studies, Peking University), No. 47, 23 July, pp. 1–4.

Wang Jisi and Wang Yong (2001), 'A Chinese Account: The Interaction of Policies', in Ramon H. Myers, Michel C. Oksenberg and David Shambaugh (eds), *Making China Policy: Lessons from the Bush and Clinton Administrations*, Lanham, MD: Roman & Littlefield, pp. 269–95.

Wang Xiaodong (1999), 'Zhongguo de minzuzhuyi he Zhongguo de weilai' (Chinese Nationalism and China's Future), in Fang Ning, Wang Xiaodong, Song Qiang, et al., *Quanqiuhua yinying xia de Zhongguo zhilu* (China's Road under the Shadow of Globalisation), Beijing: Zhongguo shehuikexue chubanshe, pp. 81–106.

Wang Xiaodong (1999), '99 duanxiang' (Reflections on the Year 1999), in Fang Ning, Wang Xiaodong, Song Qiang, et al., *Quanqiuhua yinying xia de Zhongguo zhilu* (China's Road under the Shadow of Globalisation), Beijing: Zhongguo shehuikexue chubanshe, pp. 42–57.

Wang Yizhou (1995), *Dangdai guoji zhengzhi xilun* (An Analysis of Contemporary International Politics), Shanghai: Shanghai renmin chubanshe.

Wang Yizhou (2003), *Quanqiu zhengzhi he Zhongguo waijiao: Tanxue xin de shijiao yu jieshi* (Global Politics and China's Foreign Policy: In Search of New Perspectives and Interpretations), Beijing: Shijie zhishi chubanshe.

Wasserstrom, Jeffrey N. (2007), *China's Brave New World: And Other Tales for Global Times*, Bloomington: Indiana University Press.

Watson, James L. (2006), 'Introduction: Transnationalism, Localization, and Fast Foods in East Asia', in James L. Watson (ed.), *Golden Arches East: McDonald's in East Asia* (2nd edn), Stanford, CA: Stanford University Press, pp. 1–38.

Weekly Standard (2010), *The Weekly Standard Media Kit*, January, http://www.weeklystandard.com/advertising/mediakit.pdf

Weisman, Jonathan (2005), 'In Washington, Chevron Works to Scuttle Chinese Bid', *Washington Post*, 16 July, p. D1.

Wendt, Alexander (1999), *Social Theory of International Politics*, Cambridge: Cambridge University Press.

Weston, Timothy B. and Lionel M. Jensen (eds) (2000), *China beyond the Headlines*, Lanham, MD: Rowman & Littlefield.

White, Hayden (1973), *Metahistory: The Historical Imagination in Nineteenth-Century Europe*, Baltimore, MD: Johns Hopkins University Press.

White, Hayden (1987), *The Content of the Form: Narrative Discourse and Historical Representation*, Baltimore, MD: Johns Hopkins University Press.

White, Hugh (2010), 'Power Shift: Australia's Future between Washington and Beijing', *Quarterly Essay*, No. 39, pp. 1–74.

White, Hugh (2011), 'Mr President, We Beg to Differ over the Future of Asia', *The Age*, 16 November, p. 21.

White, Richard (2008), 'Australian Journalists, Travel Writing and China: James Hingston, the "Vagabond" and G. E. Morrison', *Journal of Australian Studies*, **32** (2), 237–50.

Whitehead, John W. (2008), 'Chinese Totalitarianism, American-Style', *Huffington Post*, 31 July, http://www.huffingtonpost.com/john-w-whitehead/chinese-totalitarianism-a_b_116057.html

Williams, Raymond (1983), *Keywords: A Vocabulary of Culture and Society*, London: Flemingo.

Wolf, Charles, Jr. (2001), 'China's Capitalists Join the Party', *New York Times*, 13 August, p. A17.

Wolfowitz, Paul (1997), 'Bridging Centuries—Fin de Siècle All Over Again', *The National Interest*, No. 47, pp. 3–8.

Wolfowitz, Paul (1998), 'Transfer of Missile Technology to China', Testimony before the U.S Senate Committee on Commerce, Science and Transportation Hearing on Transfer of Satellite Technology to China, *Congressional Testimony by Federal Document Clearing House*, 17 September, retrieved from Factiva.

Womack, Brantly (2010), 'Introduction', in Brantly Womack (ed.), *China's Rise in Historical Perspective*, Lanham, MD: Rowman & Littlefield, pp. 1–15.

Wong, Kent and Elaine Bernard (2000), 'Rethinking the China Campaign', *New Labor Forum*, No. 7, http://www.hrichina.org/crf/article/4805

Woodward, Bob (2002), *Bush at War*, New York: Simon & Schuster.

Woodward, Bob (2004), *Plan of Attack*, New York: Simon & Schuster.

Wu Jianmin (2011), 'Ou Mei Ri yi Hua, sange "diyici" qiansuoweijian' (Suspicions of China among Europe, the U.S., and Japan: Three Unprecedented 'First' Phenomena), 10 January, http://mgb.chinareviewnews.com/doc/1015/6/5/2/101565260.html?coluid=93&kindid=2788&docid=101565260

X (George Kennan) (1947), 'The Sources of Soviet Conduct', *Foreign Affairs*, **25** (4), 566–82.

Xi Laiwang (1996), *Ershiyi shiji Zhongguo zhanlue da cehua: Waijiao moulue* (China's Grand Strategy into the Twenty-first Century: Strategic Calculus of China's Diplomacy), Beijing: Hongqi Chubanshe.

Xu Guoqi (2008), *Olympic Dreams: China and Sports 1895–2008*, Cambridge, MA: Harvard University Press.

Yahuda, Michael (2008), 'China's Multilateralism and Regional Order', in Guoguang Wu and Helen Lansdowne (eds), *China Turns to Multilateralism: Foreign Policy and Regional Security*, London: Routledge, pp. 75–89.

Yahuda, Michael (2008), 'The Sino-European Encounter: Historical Influences on Contemporary Relations', in David Shambaugh, Eberhard Sandschneider and Zhou Hong (eds), *China-Europe Relations: Perceptions, Policies and Prospects*, London: Routledge, pp. 13–32.

Yan Xuetong (1996), *Zhongguo guojia liyi fenxi* (An Analysis of China's National Interests), Tianjin: Tianjin renmin chubanshe.

Yan Xuetong (2010), 'The Instability of China-US Relations', *The Chinese Journal of International Politics*, **3** (3), 263–92.

Yan Xuetong et al. (2011), *Ancient Chinese Thought, Modern Chinese Power*, Princeton, NJ: Princeton University Press.

Yan, Yunxiang (2006), 'McDonald's in Beijing: The Localization of Americana', in James L. Watson (ed.), *Golden Arches East: McDonald's in East Asia* (2nd edn), Stanford, CA: Stanford University Press, pp. 39–76.

Yee, Herbert S. (ed.) (2011), *China's Rise – Threat or Opportunity?* London: Routledge.

Yee, Herbert and Ian Storey (eds) (2002), *The China Threat: Perceptions, Myths and Reality*, London: RoutledgeCurzon.

Yeh, Andrew (2006), 'Toxic Chinese Mercury Pollution Travelling to US', *Financial Times*, 12 April, p. 8.

Yew, Leong (2003), *The Disjunctive Empire of International Relations*, Aldershot: Ashgate.

Young, Robert J. C. (1995), *Colonial Desire: Hybridity in Theory, Culture, and Race*, London: Routledge.

Yu Bin (1997), *East Asia: Geopolitique into the Twenty-first Century—A Chinese View* (Discussion Paper), Stanford, CA: Asia Pacific Research Center, Stanford University, June.

Yu Tiejun and Qi Haotian, 'Meiguo Guofangbu "Miniewa" Jihua shuping' (Notes on the US Defense Department's 'Minerva' Initiative), *Zhanlue zongheng* (Strategic Survey) (Center for International & Strategic Studies, Peking University), 2011– 12, pp. 1–21.

Zagoria, Donald S. (1984), 'China's Quiet Revolution', *Foreign Affairs*, **62** (4), 879– 904.

Zakaria, Fareed (2008), *The Post-American World*, New York: W. W. Norton.

Zehfuss, Maja (2002), *Constructivism in International Relations: The Politics of Reality*, Cambridge: Cambridge University Press.

Zhang, Li (2010), 'The Rise of China: Media Perception and Implications for International Politics', *Journal of Contemporary China*, **19** (64), 233–54.

Zhang Ruizhuang (1999), 'Zhongguo ying xuanze shenmeyang de waijiao zhexue?' (What Kind of Foreign Policy Thinking Should China Choose?), *Zhanlue yu guanli* (Strategy and Management), No. 1, pp. 54–67.

Zhang Ruizhuang (2002), '"Chenzhuo yingdui" yu "zifeiwugong"' ('Meet Challenges with Calm' and 'Voluntarily Relinquish One's Own Prowess'), *Shijie jingji yu zhengzhi* (World Economics and International Politics), No. 1, pp. 68–72.

Zhang Wenmu (2002), 'Quanqiuhua jincheng zhong de Zhongguo guojia liyi' (China's National Interests in the Process of Globalisation), *Zhanlue yu guanli* (Strategy and Management), No. 1, pp. 52–64.

Zhang Zangzang et al. (1996), *Zhongguo haishi keyi shuo bu: Guoji guanxi bianshu yu women de xianshi yingdui* (China Still Can Say No: International Relations Factors and Our Realistic Response), Beijing: Zhonghua Gongshang Lianhe Chubanshe.

Zhang, Yongjin (2001), 'China's Security Problematique: Critical Reflections', in Yongjin Zhang and Greg Austin (eds), *Power and Responsibility in Chinese Foreign Policy*, Canberra: Asia Pacific Press, pp. 250–71.

Zhao, Suisheng (2000), '"We are Patriots First and Democrats Second": The Rise of Chinese Nationalism in the 1990s', in Edward Friedman and Barrett McCormick (eds), *What If China Doesn't Democratize?* Armonk, New York: M. E. Sharpe, pp. 21–48.

Zhao, Suisheng (2004), 'Chinese Foreign Policy: Pragmatism and Strategic Behavior', in Suisheng Zhao (ed.), *Chinese Foreign Policy: Pragmatism and Strategic Behaviour*, Armonk, NY: M. E. Sharpe, pp. 3–20.

Zhao, Suisheng (2008), 'The Olympics and Chinese Nationalism', *China Security*, **4** (3), 48–57.

Zheng, Yongnian (1999), *Discovering Chinese Nationalism in China: Modernization, Identity, and International Relations*, Cambridge: Cambridge University Press.

Zheng Yongnian (ed.) (2010), *China and International Relations: The Chinese View and the Contribution of Wang Gungwu*, London: Routledge.

Zhou Ning (2006), *Tianchao yaoyuan: Xifang de Zhongguo xingxiang yanjiu* (China in the World: Studies of Western Images of China), Beijing: Peking University Press.

Zhu Feng (2003), 'Guojiguanxi lilun zai Zhongguo de fazhan: Wenti yu sikao' (The Development of International Relations Theory in China: Problems and Reflection), *Shijie jingji yu zhengzhi* (World Economics and International Politics), No. 3, pp. 23–25.

Zhu Feng (2008), 'China's Rise Will Be Peaceful: How Unipolarity Matters', in Robert S. Ross and Zhu Feng (eds), *China's Ascent: Power, Security, and the Future of International Politics*, Ithaca, NY: Cornell University Press, pp. 34–54.

Žižek, Slavoj (1993), *Tarrying with the Negative: Kant, Hegel, and the Critique of Ideology*, Durham, NC: Duke University Press.

Zoellick, Robert (2005), 'Whither China? From Membership to Responsibility' (Remarks to the National Committee on U.S.-China Relations), *NBR Analysis*, **16** (4), 5–14.

Zweig, David (2002), *Internationalizing China: Domestic Interests and Global Linkages*, Ithaca, NY: Cornell University Press.

Index

Printed and bound by CPI Group (UK) Ltd, Croydon, CR0 4YY

16/04/2025

14658492-0004